Third World Resource Directory

Third World Resource Directory

Edited by
Thomas P. Fenton
and
Mary J. Heffron

ORBIS BOOKS
Maryknoll, New York 10545

The Catholic Foreign Mission Society of America (Maryknoll) recruits and trains people for overseas missionary service. Through Orbis Books Maryknoll aims to foster the international dialogue that is essential to mission. The books published, however, reflect the opinions of their authors and are not meant to represent the official position of the society.

Second Printing, May 1985

Graphics Credits

Africa Resource Center: pp. 16, 41, 221

Kamal Boullata (Palestine): pp. 126, 243

Community Press Features: pp. 88, 161

Disarmament Catalogue: pp. 182, 188

Enrique Chagoya: pp. 54, 67, 149, 167

Human Rights Internet: pp. 45, 90, 123

Liberation News Service: p. 196

The Link: pp. 135, 138

Praxis: p. 247

Solidaridad II: pp. 80, 169, 180, 201

Rini Templeton/Data Center Graphics Collection: pp. 4, 32, 39, 59, 109, 117, 146, 157, 176, 203, 213, 216, 219, 235

Library of Congress Cataloging in Publication Data

Main entry under title:

Third World resource directory.

 Bibliography: p.
 Includes index.
 1. Underdeveloped areas—Bibliography. 2. Underdeveloped areas—Audio-visual aids—Catalogs.
I. Heffron, Mary J. II. Fenton, Thomas, P.
Z7164.U5T46 1984 [HC59.7]   016.909'09724   83-6783
ISBN 0-88344-509-3 (pbk.)

For Michael Heffron Fenton,
that he and children everywhere
may wake before long to the dawn
of a more just and peaceful world

In memory of
Mary Elizabeth Fenton (1914–1981)

Contents

PART ONE: AREAS

PART TWO: ISSUES

PART THREE: INDEXES

Foreword

"But what can I do to help?" This question—one I've heard so often—was addressed recently to a couple of seminarians who had just described their visit to El Salvadoran refugee camps in Honduras. More often than not the response to this question involves a request for donations of material aid or even a call to go to the particular country to offer some skilled service.

In this case the seminarians returned from Honduras with a different answer— one they had heard from the refugees themselves: "Go back to your country and tell your people what you have learned. Tell them what the U.S. government is doing here. Ask them to change things in your country."

Like these refugees from El Salvador, many in the Third World have come to realize that one of the keys to changing oppressive social and economic structures in Third World countries is reorientation of the U.S. policies and institutions that undergird them.

Well-intentioned Americans may find this point of view surprising and shocking. Those who give this viewpoint the serious consideration it deserves will find no better place to begin than with the resources described in this directory.

The organizations listed here have been set up by people who have dedicated themselves to finding out how the powers-that-be in this country have increased the misery of the Third World. These are the groups that reveal the private interests behind the public policies, that counter disinformation campaigns and publicize the other side of the story, that try to cut through insularity, racism, sexism, and anticommunism in the search for the root causes of social and economic problems, and—finally—that identify the allies and opponents you will have as you work to bring about change.

What can you do to help? Study the resources that Mary and Tom have gathered and annotated and offer whatever help you can to the organizations who are working—on behalf of Third World peoples—to "change things" here in the United States.

•

Others will benefit from this directory. Researchers and organizers in the Third World, for instance. They have learned from experience that information critical to their struggle for social justice—information about the realities of power in their own countries—is often available only here in the United States.

The *Third World Resource Directory* catalogs the key sources of such information. It is a guide to organizations that systematically pore over reports of congressional hearings, carefully analyze corporate and government documents, meticulously monitor the press, and, in general, make it their business to gather, study, and disseminate this critical information.

As someone who has worked closely over the last two decades with a number of the groups listed here I want to acknowledge another contribution this directory makes. All too often the limited resources available to these organizations are consumed by the process of producing a given book, pamphlet, newsletter, or film. Little energy or money remains for adequately publicizing these resources. The *Third World Resource Directory* performs this promotional service in admirable fashion.

•

I view this directory as a guide to modern-day prophets who are attempting to speak truth to the illegitimate use of U.S. corporate and governmental power. Like the prophets of biblical times they tend to live on barebones budgets; they speak at times in tones that are not pleasant to the ear; and they are usually ridiculed and dismissed by those in power. But also like the prophets they rivet our attention on fundamental injustices that, if left uncorrected, will bring consequences that will be felt for generations to come.

Fred Goff
President, Data Center
Oakland, Calif.

Preface

This book is a guide to resources about the Third World and United States involvement in the affairs of Third World nations and peoples.

AUDIENCE

Our reasons for compiling this directory varied as we considered the needs of three audiences: (1) professional educators; (2) committed church and political activists; and (3) other concerned Americans.

1. Those involved in education for justice in the United States know how difficult it is to find a handy and comprehensive source of information on the Third World-related issues we've covered in this directory. Educators must go from organization to organization collecting materials from each. This method is successful only if the educator has time (rarely the case) and only if she or he is already familiar with the variety of organizations listed in this directory.

Our directory is intended to expedite the collection of resources by bringing them all to the educator in one convenient form. Further, we'd like to improve the quality of education for justice by providing educators with a rich variety of resources.

2. People who are already committed to action are probably familiar with the resources available on one or more of the subjects we have covered. We've sought to service these church and political activists by providing an up-to-date reference book for the areas and issues that are their specialities.

Beyond this, we have collected resources that can further expand their horizons and personal contacts by providing information on issues and regions that are not their principal areas of interest and by encouraging cross-fertilization and exchange of resources between political and church activists.

3. For other concerned Americans we've aimed to provide an introductory guide to U.S. relations with the Third World. We'd like this directory to aid those who have heard a moving presentation on some Third World-related theme or who have been troubled by what they read in the papers about U.S. political, economic, or military involvement overseas.

OUR PERSPECTIVE

Much of the work we've been doing over the past fifteen to twenty years has revolved around issues of justice and peace, especially regarding our own country and its relations with the Third World. Our training in Maryknoll and our later work in the Third World have given us a perspective on these issues that many would judge to be unconventional. Because this perspective has heavily influenced our choice of resources we feel it requires some explanation.

Just as architects, masons, and interior decorators each bring a different set of eyes to the examination of a building, so too do political scientists, missionaries, business executives, and military personnel each interpret Third World realities in the light of their specific fields of interest and expertise.

In our case we were trained in Maryknoll to bring a concern for "social justice" to our study of international affairs. The questions we raised had more to do with the morality of given situations than with the bottom line of corporate profits or the national security concerns of a particular presidential administration. The answers reached differed from person to person within Maryknoll, but at least our eyes were focused on the same concerns.

Following our initial training in Maryknoll we each began our fieldwork—Mary, with the Maryknoll Sisters in the southern Philippines, and Tom, with Maryknoll's justice and peace education programs in the United States. Later, as a married couple, we lived in Hong Kong and other parts of Asia for six years. This fieldwork concretized and intensified the concerns raised in our earlier academic training.

(We acknowledge that our training and experience is unique, but we want to emphasize that the perspective we now have is not inextricably wedded to our personal histories. Others—including you, the reader—may have come to similar conclusions through far different training and experience.)

MARY: On the day that astronaut Neil Armstrong set foot on the moon, two grieving parents were making their way down from the mountains above Sigaboy in the southern Philippines. They were carrying the emaciated body of their dead infant daughter to the parish church where I happened to be that July afternoon. As the American astronauts walked about on the moon I stood with the parents and some local catechists over the body of the infant. As we prayed and sang I couldn't help but wonder about the economic priorities we citizens of this earth had set for ourselves.

My study and experience in the intervening years has revealed to me the ways in which the world outside touched the lives of that family in the mountains of Mindanao. Wasteful military expenditures by the Marcos government, the refusal of highly educated Filipino doctors and nurses to work in the rural areas of their own country, exorbitant profit-taking by U.S. and other transnational corporations—these, among other factors, had their indirect effects upon the parents and their child in Sigaboy.

The problem, I've come to see, is not simply one of misplaced priorities or economic disparities. The much more complex problem is how and why the wealthy and powerful few—in the Philippines and in the United States—are permitted to run the economic, political, and military machinery of this world for their personal enrichment.

The years I spent living, working, and traveling in Asia impressed upon me the need for drastic—I'd say *radical*—changes in the political and economic rules of the game. As an American, I'm particularly concerned about the ways in which the public and private institutions of my own country bring their enormous power to bear on the formulation and execution of those rules.

TOM: In the fall of 1976 Mary and I set up a research and information center in Hong Kong to gather and analyze information on U.S. military, political, and economic involvement in Asia.

In early 1978 we clipped an article from the *Singapore Straits Times* about the building of a household iron manufacturing plant in Singapore by the General Electric corporation. The significance of this particular clipping came home to me years later when I was editing the Data Center's monthly *Plant Shutdowns Monitor*. In April 1981 I clipped a story on GE's plans to close a profit-making iron manufacturing plant in Ontario, California, and to shift production to the Singapore plant.

As I wrote in a series of articles in the *Maryknoll* magazine that year (see 9.64 below), GE's decision had a disastrous effect upon Ontario (the GE plant was the city's third largest source of jobs) and upon the one thousand GE workers who were to be dismissed. (Some of them were third generation employees at the plant.)

GE's shutdown in southern California and its earlier investment in Singapore are examples of the unregulated power that some individuals in the United States have to make decisions with catastrophic social impact purely for the economic gain of themselves and their shareholders. The United States and Canada are alone among the industrialized nations in allowing private citizens this much latitude.

The exercise of such power in the international arena often gives rise to a misplaced us-against-them attitude. Rather than focusing on those who own and control corporations as a source of the problem, working people in America are led to believe that it is their fellow workers in Singapore—or in other Third World countries—who are to blame for economic problems in the United States.

A union official cautioned the Ontario workers against this type of thinking: "Our quarrel is not with the workers in Singapore, Japan, Taiwan, or elsewhere. They are being exploited, too, to add to the profits of the huge corporations that go there to pay them pennies. Our quarrel is with the system that permits a company, after more than half a century of profitable operations out of the labor of its employees, to pick up and leave."

My own experience and study lead me to the same conclusion. The lines are not drawn between *us* here and *them* in the Third World, but between those who govern and control and those who are dominated. The governors and controllers sit in public offices and corporate boardrooms in Caracas, Pretoria, and Kuala Lampur, as well as in New York and Washington, D.C. Those who are dominated are unemployed miners in Anaconda, Montana, as well as sweatshop workers in Seoul, South Korea.

Our training and experience lead us to conclude that:

• reforms in the system are not enough; the crying need is for radical (that is, fundamental) changes;

• change will come about through struggles (though not necessarily violent ones) between the "powerful" and the "powerless";

• U.S. institutional power in the Third World often frustrates genuine development.

Our survey of hundreds of educational resources about the Third World has us concerned that most resources—and certainly the bulk of what we're exposed to in the media—ignore this "radical" analysis in favor of one that:

• stresses reforms;

• addresses all Americans as if they're rich and powerful and describes all in the Third World as if they're poor and powerless;

• judges all struggles for radical social change to be Soviet-inspired and, therefore, to be opposed.

The resources we have compiled in this directory are—by and large—partisan and biased in favor of the radical analysis we have advanced. Most illuminate the problems and prospects of Third World peoples from the point of view of the "powerless." Many are critical of the role that the American government and U.S.-based transnational corporations play in the Third World.

By compiling this particular collection of resources we are not advocating the wholesale substitution of one body of thought for another. We are simply concerned that equal time and thoughtful consideration be given to an analysis that we—and many others—have found to be true. For we believe that people literally suffer and die when the truths in this analysis are ignored. Our aim is to promote critical and responsible study of these—as well as all other—resources on the United States and the Third World.

While we take responsibility for this directory as a whole the responsibility for the style and content of each particular item rests with the originator of the book, article, audiovisual, or other resource.

DEFINITIONS

Our use of the term *Third World* is intentionally popular and unscientific. We mean the nations and peoples of the world that are struggling to rid themselves of years of economic and political domination and impoverishment.

The term embodies both a *geographical* and a *class* sense. We rightfully speak of foreign relations between our country and the entire country of Tanzania, for instance. At the same time, many of the resources in this directory reinforce the point that distinctions between classes of Americans and Tanzanians are valid and necessary.

The *Middle East* is another potentially confusing term. Many Asians reject the old London-based divisions of the world into Middle and Far East and refer to this region as West Asia. Then, too, there is the overlap between this region and the Arab nations of North Africa.

We've elected to retain the Middle East designation and take as our guide the territorial integrity of the African continent. Thus, resources on Egypt, Libya, and other Arab countries on the African continent will be found in the Africa chapter. Both the Africa and Middle East chapters should be checked, however, for resources on Africa north of the Sahara.

LIMITS

We've worked within these boundaries in collecting resources for this directory:

1. We've emphasized resources on *U.S. relations* with the Third World. We looked primarily for resources that would shed some light on the ways in which U.S. public and private organizations touch the lives of those in the Third World. We have also included resources that treat Third World issues with little if any relation to the United States. These are offered because they provide necessary background.

2. We've limited our sources—with but a few exceptions—to *U.S.-based* organizations. We made this choice reluctantly because we know of the many fine organizations in Canada, Europe, and in the Third World itself whose resources would make worthy additions to the list we've compiled.

The directories compiled periodically by Human Rights Internet (see 7.12 below) are excellent sources of information on non-U.S. organizations and their resources related to rather broadly defined issues of human rights.

3. We've selected only five issues: food, transnational corporations, women, militarism, and human rights. In future editions of this directory we intend to expand this list to include nuclear arms and energy; native peoples; labor; international trade and aid; and more. We welcome your suggestions in this area.

4. We've focused our attention, for the most part, on the problem areas that exist between the United States and the Third World. Furthermore, we've highlighted the political and economic difficulties facing the Third World and neglected, among other things, the cultural riches of Third World peoples. The dimensions missing in our directory should be searched for in other resources.

NEWSLETTER

We intend to begin publishing a quarterly newsletter in 1984 on the themes covered in the *Third World Resource Directory*. The newsletter will update information on the resources in this edition of the directory and will lay the groundwork for projected future editions by carrying notices and reviews of new organizations, books, periodicals, audiovisuals, and other resources.

The geographical categories will remain the same. The issues, however, will be expanded to cover other relevant subjects.

Write to us in care of the Data Center (464 19th Street, Oakland, CA 94612) for information on subscriptions to the newsletter or to notify us of resources that you'd like to see mentioned in the publication.

We welcome also your constructive criticisms of this edition of the *Third World Resource Directory* and your suggestions for improvements in future editions.

APPRECIATION

From our earlier training and years of service in Maryknoll to our married lives together in Asia and on both coasts of the United States we have been privileged to be part of communities of people—both secular and religious—whose vision is as expansive as their political commitment is profound. We thank these friends for their encouragement and support throughout this project.

We regret any oversights in the listing of organizations and other resources. We'd appreciate it if you'd call these to our attention.

We owe special thanks to the organizations who contributed the funds that made the *Third World Resource Directory* a reality. They are the Maryknoll Fathers and Brothers, the Women's Division of the United Methodist Church, the Sisters of St. Joseph of Carondelet, the Sisters of the Holy Child Jesus, and the Jubilee Fund.

Prefaces often end with tributes to the patience of the author's long-suffering spouse and children. In our case it's our six-year old's impatience that we have to acknowledge. Mike has lived with this directory for half his life. Frustrated with our preoccupation with this project Mike ruled one morning at breakfast that there would be no further discussion of "the directory" at mealtimes.

Thus we were prompted to end our search for the most recent book, the latest address, and the newest slideshow and to go with the directory as it is. We know—and Mike suspects—that his redirection of our conversations around the table is but a temporary one.

Introduction

This directory is divided into two major *parts*: Areas and Issues. Each of the five chapters within each part is divided into *sections*: Key Resources, Organizations, Printed Resources, Audiovisual Resources, and Other Resources. Divisions within the sections (books within the Printed Resources section, for example) we call *subsections*.

Abbreviations and indexes are at the back of the book. Each item in the directory has been assigned a number to facilitate use of the index and to aid in cross-referencing.

A "See also" list will be found at the end of most subsections. We have designed these cross-references to be specific to the type of resource. Thus, if you are interested in articles on Latin America, the first place to check is the Pamphlets and Articles subsection of the chapter on Latin America. At the end of this subsection you will find cross-references to Latin America-related articles in other chapters, such as the one on Food, Hunger, Agribusiness.

If you want a list of all the resources—be they audiovisuals or books—on a given area or issue, check the "See also" references at the end of each subsection in the relevant chapter.

The running heads at the top of each page will tell you which chapter you are in and which sections you'll find on that page.

KEY RESOURCES

Each chapter begins with a one-page listing of the resources that we have found to be the most informative and useful on the topic. If you are new to a particular issue or region we would recommend that you start with the organizations, books, and other resources described in this section.

ORGANIZATIONS

Each item in this section includes address, telephone number, and descriptors about the organization's identity and functions.

Names, addresses, and telephone numbers are also given in the Organization index. Included as well are cross-references to other places in the directory where the organization is mentioned.

The descriptive terms that we have assigned to each organization are grouped under these headings: religious and political affiliation (if any); focus (first geographical, then issues); activities; resources, periodicals; and special projects.

These descriptors are neither all-inclusive nor scientific. They are meant only to provide a quick overview of an organization's orientation, activities, and resources.

PRINTED RESOURCES

In this section of each chapter we include books, periodicals, and pamphlets and articles. Printed materials will also be found in the Other Resources section (see below).

The Organization index will give you the address and telephone number for organizations cited in connection with a book, magazine, or pamphlet.

Books

Book citations include author, title, publisher's information, number of pages, and price (in paperback unless otherwise noted). Each book is briefly annotated.

The Printed Resources section of the Third World chapter (1.105–1.109) opens with a list of book stores and services that may be able to provide you with copies of the books described in this directory. We encourage you to write to them for their mail-order catalogs.

See the Organization index for addresses and telephone numbers of book publishers.

Periodicals

Annotated descriptions of periodicals include name, address, frequency of publication, and subscription price.

Check through the Organization sections of each chapter for additional periodicals and refer to the Periodical index for a complete list of magazines, newsletters, action alerts, and other regular publications.

Some periocicals—*Monthly Review*, for example—never lose their timeliness. Articles selected from the back issues of such magazines are often still very appropriate for use in educational programs. The Data Center (see 1.35 below) has archives of over 400 political, labor, religious, and mainstream periodicals. If you want a back issue of a certain periodical contact the Center's Search Service to see if a photocopy is available.

Note the two periodical indexes described in 1.139 and 1.140.

Pamphlets and Articles

Our aim in this subsection is to point you to printed resource materials that are inexpensive, brief, and easily available, often at bulk rates. See the Organization index for the addresses of sources given in this subsection.

General articles on U.S. involvement in the Third World are not readily available, so the Third World chapter does not have a Pamphlets and Articles subsection.

AUDIOVISUAL RESOURCES

This section includes films, slideshows, and videotapes—all listed in alphabetical order.

The "audio" side—tapes and records—was slighted in this edition of the resource directory. We intend to strengthen this aspect of the audiovisual section in future editions.

It was impossible for us to preview most of the audiovisuals described in this directory. As a result we have had to rely on the reviews of others and on descriptive literature from the distributors. We caution you, then, to arrange for your own preview of a film or slideshow in order to determine its suitably for use in your particular setting.

The audiovisual section of the Third World chapter opens with a list of distributors and descriptions of guides and catalogs that we have found helpful.

For each audiovisual we have given title, date, length, source, rental/sale data, and other descriptive information. See the Organization index for addresses of audiovisual distributors.

OTHER RESOURCES

In this section you will find a mix of resources. Some, like simulation games, fall obviously into an "other" category. Others overlap with sections we already have, such as printed resources and organizations.

In the case of organizations, we have grouped church-related organizations into the Other Resources section in three chapters: the Middle East; Food, Hunger, Agribusiness; and Transnational Corporations. We did so because we felt there was no need to describe the activities of the individual church agencies and because we judged the impact of one listing of like-minded denominational programs to be stronger.

Though we have supplied church listings in these three areas only it can be assumed that national church offices have similar programs related to the other areas and issues included in this directory.

We had two reasons for overlapping printed materials into the Other Resources section: to keep uniform subsections in the Printed Resources sections (books; periodicals; pamphlets and articles); and to group—and highlight—similar types of printed resources, such as research guides, directories, and bibliographies.

It's wise, then, to check both sections for printed resource materials. To guarantee that nothing falls between the cracks we have overlapped the indexes of printed resources so that a bound book of audiovisual materials will be found in both the *Book* and *Audiovisual Bibliographies* indexes. Similarly, a curriculum resource that is in pamphlet form will be listed in both the *Pamphlets and Articles* and the *Curriculum Resources* indexes.

Our caution about audiovisual materials also applies to simulation games. We were able to play or to preview only a handful of these exercises. *Starpower* (1.227) we can recommend without any reservations. All the others you should preview yourself before bringing them into the classroom.

PART ONE

AREAS

Third World

Africa

Asia and Pacific

Latin America and Caribbean

Middle East

Chapter 1

Third World

KEY RESOURCES

Organizations

Certain organizations in this Third World chapter are structured in such a way that they embody what we aim to foster in this directory: a cross-organizational, inter-disciplinary approach to understanding U.S. relations with and effects on Third World nations.

Chief among these organizations are the **American Friends Service Committee, Clergy and Laity Concerned,** and the **Coalition for a New Foreign and Military Policy**. These three organizations have regional chapters that are open to the active participation of all; they all have a wealth of experience regarding U.S. foreign affairs; and they have abundant resources on a variety of political, economic, and military issues.

The services and resources of the **Data Center** are used by concerned people from all walks of life: journalists, consumer advocates, labor educators, clergy and religious workers, political activists, and academics. The Center is a "one-stop" storehouse for virtually anything you need to know about U.S. involvement in the Third World.

Printed Resources

Andre Gunder Frank's *Crisis: In the Third World* and Harry Magdoff's *Imperialism: From the Colonial Age to the Present* are remarkable for their clarity and straightforward presentation of complex and often sensitive political and economic issues.

Pierre Jalée's works are excellent introductions to the economics of U.S. relations with the developing nations, while books by the Kolkos and William Appleman Williams situate political and economic issues in the broader historical context.

Of all the periodicals described in this chapter we give our highest recommendation to these: *Dollars & Sense, Monthly Review, The Nation*, and *The Progressive*. These four are noteworthy for their skillful blend of popular style writing and consistently informed and acute political analysis.

Audiovisual Resources

Five Billion People and *The History Book* are two multi-unit audiovisuals that are well-suited to educational programs. The AFSC slideshow *Sharing Global Resources* is an excellent discussion-starter for small group use.

Other Resources

Three other resource guides serve as complements to this directory: Thomas Fenton, *Education for Justice* (Orbis), James McGinnis et al., *Educating for Peace and Justice: A Manual for Teachers* (The Institute for Peace and Justice); and Sandra Graff, *Global Education Resource Guide* (Global Education Associates).

ORGANIZATIONS

1.1   Alternative Press Syndicate, Box 1347, Ansonia Station, New York, NY 10023. Tel: 212-974-1990.

FOCUS: Third world general • international • Latin America. Human rights • political repression • international awareness • corporate responsibility • social justice • press freedom.

ACTIVITIES: Popular education • constituency education • research and writing • library services • press service • networking • media • documentation and information.

RESOURCES: Speakers • literature distribution • publications • library • reports.

PERIODICALS: **1.2** *Alternative Media.* Quarterly magazine. $7.50/year.

1.3   Alternatives, 1124 Main St., Box 1707, Forest Park, GA 30051. Tel: 404-361-5823.

FOCUS: Global. Military spending • world hunger • native peoples • other issues as they relate to the personal lifestyles of Americans.

ACTIVITIES: Popular education • constituency education • media • promotion of alternative celebrations campaigns with religious congregations.

RESOURCES: Bookstore • literature • study-action guides • audiovisuals • speakers • publications • curriculum guides • consultant services.

PERIODICALS: **1.4** *Alternatives: An Alternate Lifestyle Newsletter*. Quarterly. $6/year.

SPECIAL PROJECTS: National media campaigns around holidays such as Christmas and Thanksgiving • production of "alternative celebrations bulletins" for use in church services.

1.5 American Friends Service Committee, International Division, 1501 Cherry St., Philadelphia, PA 19102. Tel: 215-241-7147.

RELIGIOUS AFFILIATION: Religious Society of Friends (Quakers).

FOCUS: International • Asia and Pacific • Middle East • Africa • Latin America and Caribbean. Disarmament • United Nations • human rights • nuclear arms and energy • social justice • transnational corporations • refugees • relief assistance • political repression.

ACTIVITIES: Constituency education • congressional testimony • intern programs • foreign service (relief; development) • networking through regional offices • documentation and information • research and writing • workshops and seminars.

RESOURCES: Audiovisuals • publications • literature • reports • speakers • study-action guides. Catalog available: **1.6** *Educational Resources from The International Division*.

PERIODICALS: **1.7** *Quaker Service Bulletin*. 3 issues/year. Contribution. **1.8** *International Division Bulletin*. Quarterly. Constituency.

CALC. See Clergy and Laity Concerned.

1.9 Center for Development Policy, 418 Tenth St., SE, Washington, DC 20003. Tel: 202-547-6406.

FOCUS: Third World general. Political repression • militarism • nuclear arms and energy • foreign trade and aid • transnational corporations • corporate responsibility.

ACTIVITIES: Popular education • legislative action • research and writing • congressional testimony • intern programs • foreign service (development) • library services • press service • networking • media • policy-oriented research and writing.

RESOURCES: Speakers • audiovisuals • publications • research services • library • reports.

PERIODICALS: **1.10** *Country Notes*. Monthly. $2/year. **1.11** *Policy Impact Papers*. Monthly. $2/year.

1.12 Center for Ethics and Social Policy, 2465 Le Conte Ave., Berkeley, CA 94709. Tel: 415-841-9811; 848-1674.

FOCUS: International. Corporate policy • environmental ethics • world resources distribution • nuclear weapons • organizational ethics.

1.13 **Center for International Policy,** 120 Maryland Ave., NE, Washington, DC 20002. Tel: 202-544-4666.

FOCUS: Third World general. Human rights • political economy.

ACTIVITIES: Research and writing • congressional testimony • documentation and information • policy-oriented research and writing.

RESOURCES: Publications • reports.

PERIODICALS: **1.14** *International Policy Report*. Monthly. $9/year. **1.15** *Current Issues*. Occasional. 75 cents each. **1.16** *Indochina Issues*. Monthly. $9/year. All publications $18/year.

1.17 **Center for Investigative Reporting,** 54 Mint St., San Francisco, CA 94103. Tel: 415-543-1200.

FOCUS: Global • international. Human rights • political repression • disarmament • nuclear arms and energy • foreign trade and aid • export of hazardous products.

ACTIVITIES: Research and writing • intern programs • library services • media • documentation and information • workshops and seminars.

RESOURCES: Consultant services • research services • library.

PERIODICALS: **1.18** *In House*. Quarterly. Free.

1.19 **Center for Teaching International Relations,** University of Denver, Boulder, CO 80208. Tel: 303-753-3106.

FOCUS: Global • international. Human rights • foreign trade and aid • international awareness.

ACTIVITIES: Academic and professional education • intern programs • workshops and seminars.

RESOURCES: Speakers • publications • curriculum guides • consultant services. Catalog of publications available.

PERIODICALS: **1.20** *The Global Issue*. 5 issues/year. $5/year.

1.21 **Center of Concern,** 3700 13 St., NE, Washington, DC 20017. Tel: 202-635-2757.

FOCUS: Third World general • international. Church • labor • disarmament • political economy • social justice • transnational corporations • world hunger • trade and aid • women and development.

ACTIVITIES: Research and writing • popular education • workshops and seminars • constituency education • intern programs.

RESOURCES: Reports • speakers • consultant and research services • audiovisuals • publications.

PERIODICALS: **1.22** *Center Focus*. Bimonthly. Free.

1.23 **Christians for Socialism,** National Office, 3540 14 St., Detroit, MI 48208. Tel: 313-833-3987.

POLITICAL AFFILIATION: Socialist.

RELIGIOUS AFFILIATION: Ecumenical.

FOCUS: International. Socialist construction • political economy • socialism • national liberation struggles.

ACTIVITIES: Popular education • political action • research and writing • solidarity work • networking • documentation and information • workshops and seminars • labor and strike support.

RESOURCES: Audiovisuals • publications • study-action guides • reports.

.24 Church of the Brethren, World Ministries Commission, 1451 Dundee Ave., Elgin, IL 60120. Tel: 312-742-5100.

RELIGIOUS AFFILIATION: Protestant.

FOCUS: International • Middle East • Africa • Latin America. Militarism • disarmament • nuclear arms and energy • international awareness • national liberation struggles • corporate responsibility • social justice • economic justice.

ACTIVITIES: Constituency education • political action • legislative action • congressional testimony • foreign service • overseas project support • justice and peace ministries • workshops and seminars.

RESOURCES: Speakers • audiovisuals • literature • consultant services.

PERIODICALS: **1.25** *Messenger.* Monthly magazine. $10/year. Membership periodical.

SPECIAL PROJECTS: Brethren Volunteer Service.

.26 Church Women United, Rm. 812, 475 Riverside Dr., New York, NY 10115. Tel: 212-870-2347.

FOCUS: National and international affairs. Human rights • environment • social justice • disarmament • United Nations • racial justice.

ACTIVITIES: Church constituency education and action • worship • workshops and seminars.

RESOURCES: Literature • materials for religious celebrations. Resource list available from Church Women United, Box 37815, Cincinnati, OH 45237.

PERIODICALS: **1.27** *The Church Woman.* Bimonthly magazine. $6/year.

1.28 Church World Service, c/o NCC/DOM, 475 Riverside Dr., New York, NY 10115. Tel: 212-870-2061.

FOCUS: Global. Nuclear arms and energy • international assistance • relief awareness.

ACTIVITIES: Foreign service • popular education • constituency education • research and writing • congressional testimony • intern programs • networking • media • overseas project support • policy-oriented research and writing • fund raising.

RESOURCES: Speakers • audiovisuals • literature • publications.

Circus. See New York Circus.

1.29 Clergy and Laity Concerned (CALC), 198 Broadway, Rm. 302, New York, NY 10038. Tel: 212-964-6730.

FOCUS: International • Third World general • Latin America • South Africa • Namibia • Vietnam. Militarism • political repression • politics of food • human rights • disarmament • nuclear arms and energy • international awareness • national liberation struggles • corporate responsibility • social justice.

ACTIVITIES: Constituency education • political action • legislative action • solidarity work • networking through regional chapters • justice and peace ministries • workshops and seminars.

RESOURCES: Literature • audiovisuals • speakers • publications.

PERIODICALS: **1.30** *CALC Report.* 8 issues/year. With $20 annual membership.

SPECIAL PROJECTS: A nationwide speaking tour of leaders of the European Peace Movement, co-sponsored with the American Friends Service Committee.

1.31 **Coalition for a New Foreign and Military Policy,** 120 Maryland Ave., NE, Washington, DC 20002. Tel: 202-546-8400.

FOCUS: Third World general. Human rights • militarism • disarmament • U.S. foreign policy.

ACTIVITIES: Constituency education • political action • legislative action • congressional testimony • networking policy-oriented research and writing/ workshops and seminars.

RESOURCES: Speakers ("Foreign Policy Speakers Brochure" available) • literature • legislative guides.

PERIODICALS: **1.32** *Coalition Close-Up.* Monthly. With $10 annual membership in Coalition network. **1.33** *Action Guides* and *Action Alerts.* Occasional. With annual membership.

1.34 **Consortium on Peace Research, Education and Development (COPRED),** Center for Peaceful Change, Kent State University, Kent, OH 44242. Tel: 216-672-3143.

FOCUS: Global. Militarism • disarmament • peace education.

ACTIVITIES: Popular education • research and writing • networking.

RESOURCES: Publications • curriculum guides and materials • library.

1.35 **Data Center,** 464 19 St., Oakland, CA 94612. Tel: 415-835-4692.

FOCUS: National and international. Corporations • political and economic issues.

ACTIVITIES: Public interest research and information center • search service • corporate profiles • periodical clipping services.

RESOURCES: Library • research services • literature • publications.

PERIODICALS: **1.36** *Data Center Newsletter.* Quarterly. With $15 annual membership (individuals); $35 (supporting); $100 or more (sustaining); $125 (organizational).

1.37 **Democratic Socialists of America,** National Office, 853 Broadway, Suite 801, New York, NY 10003. Tel: 212-260-3270.

POLITICAL AFFILIATION: Merger of Democratic Socialists Organizing Committee (DSOC) and New American Movement (NAM).

FOCUS: International. Human rights • militarism • disarmament • foreign trade and aid • political economy • socialism • national liberation struggles • corporate responsibility.

ACTIVITIES: Popular education • constituency education • political action • legislative action • networking • policy-oriented research and writing • regional chapters.

RESOURCES: Speakers • publications.

PERIODICALS: **1.38** *Socialist Forum.* $10/year. **1.39** *Democratic Left.* 10 issues/year. $8/year.

.40 The 8th Day Center, 22 E. Van Buren, Chicago, IL 60605. Tel: 312-427-4351.

RELIGIOUS AFFILIATION: Roman Catholic.

FOCUS: Third World general • international • South Africa • Latin America. Food policy • militarism • social justice • nuclear arms and energy • disarmament • human rights • women's rights • corporate responsibility.

ACTIVITIES: Popular education • political action • networking • intern programs • legislative action • solidarity work • research and writing • media • justice and peace ministries • workshops and seminars.

RESOURCES: Literature • speakers • audiovisuals • publications • study-action guides • consultant services • library.

Publications and audiovisuals catalogs available.

PERIODICALS: **1.41** *8th Day Report.* Bimonthly. $5/year. **1.42** *LAS Bulletin.* Summary of legislative action related to the Center's issue areas. Monthly. Contribution. **1.43** *Issue Packets.* Occasional. Contribution.

SPECIAL PROJECTS: Food Justice Program; Interfaith Coalition for Justice to Immigrants.

44 Friends Committee on National Legislation, 245 Second St., NE, Washington, DC 20002. Tel: 202-547-6000.

RELIGIOUS AFFILIATION: Religious Society of Friends (Quakers).

FOCUS: Global • international. Middle East. Human rights • militarism • disarmament • nuclear arms and energy • foreign trade and aid • political economy • international awareness • social justice • civil liberties • dissent.

ACTIVITIES: Constituency education • political action • legislative action • research and writing • congressional testimony • intern programs • networking • documentation and information • justice and peace ministries • policy-oriented research and writing • workshops and seminars.

RESOURCES: Literature distribution • publications • study-action guides • reports.

PERIODICALS: **1.45** *FCNL Washington Newsletter.* 11 issues/year. $15/year.

46 Global Education Associates, 552 Park Ave., East Orange, NJ 07017. Tel: 201-675-1409.

FOCUS: Global. Arms race • alternative futures • food • world resources • women • global spirituality • racial justice • human rights • national security.

ACTIVITIES: Popular education • curriculum development • workshops and seminars • networking.

RESOURCES: Speakers • publications • study-action guides.

PERIODICALS: **1.47** *The Whole Earth Papers.* Occasional. $20/year. **1.48** *The Associates Newsletter.* Quarterly. $5/year.

49 Global Learning, 40 S. Fullerton Ave., Montclair, NJ 07042. Tel: 201-783-7616.

FOCUS: Global. World hunger • development • conflict resolution • multicultural education • environmental studies.

ACTIVITIES: Teacher training • workshops • curriculum development.

1.50 **Global Negotiations Information Project,** 777 UN Plaza, 11th Floor, New York, NY 10017. Tel: 212-682-3633.

FOCUS: International. United Nations-sponsored international negotiations • trade • energy • food • raw materials.

ACTIVITIES: Constituency education • research and analysis • consultant services.

PERIODICALS: **1.51** *Global Negotiation Action Notes.* Monthly.

1.52 **Global Perspectives in Education,** 218 E. 18 St., New York, NY 10003. Tel: 212-475-0850.

FOCUS: Global • international. Global trends • environmental studies • humanities and language arts • culture and area studies • international awareness.

ACTIVITIES: Teacher training • curriculum development • consultant services • networking • political action • legislative action • constituency education.

RESOURCES: Classroom materials • publications • consultant services. Publications catalog available.

PERIODICALS: **1.53** *Intercom.* 3 issues/year. $10/year. Apply for other rates. **1.54** *Global Perspectives.* 8 issues/year. Contribution. **1.55** *GPE Clearinghouse Memo.* Occasional.

1.56 **Greenpeace,** National Office, 2007 R St., NW, Washington, DC 20009. Tel: 202-462-1177.

FOCUS: Global. Militarism • disarmament • nuclear arms and energy • environment • international awareness.

ACTIVITIES: Popular education and action • legislative action • research and writing • networking through regional offices • documentation and information.

RESOURCES: Speakers • publications.

PERIODICALS: **1.57** *Greenpeace Examiner,* Box 6677, Portland, OR 97228. Quarterly magazine. Contribution.

1.58 **Institute for Peace and Justice,** 4144 Lindell St., #400, St. Louis, MO 63108. Tel: 314-533-4445.

FOCUS: Third World general • global. Social justice • global economic injustice • world hunger • racism • militarism • family life and justice and peace.

ACTIVITIES: Workshops and seminars • constituency education • research and writing • solidarity work • justice and peace ministries • leadership training • in-service teacher education.

RESOURCES: Publications • speakers • audiovisuals • curriculum guides • consultant services. Resources catalog available.

PERIODICALS: **1.59** *NPPJN Newsletter.* Quarterly. $10/year.

1.60 **Institute for Policy Studies,** 1901 Q St., NW, Washington, DC 20009. Tel: 202-234-9382.

FOCUS: National and international. Transnational corporations • human rights • military.

ACTIVITIES: Policy-oriented research and writing.

RESOURCES: Publications • speakers.

1.61 **Institute for World Order,** 777 UN Plaza, New York, NY 10017. Tel: 212-490-0010.

FOCUS: International. Peace • militarism • disarmament • nuclear arms and energy • foreign trade and aid • ecology • social justice • economic development.

ACTIVITIES: Popular education • research and writing • curriculum development • policy research • networking • workshops and seminars.

RESOURCES: Audiovisuals • publications • curriculum guides • teaching fellowship program. Catalog of publications available.

PERIODICALS: **1.62** *Alternatives: A Journal of World Policy.* Quarterly. $16/year. **1.63** *Transition.* 2 issues/year. $3/year. Bulk rates available. **1.64** *Macroscope.* Occasional. $3/year.

1.65 **Intercommunity Center for Justice and Peace,** 20 Washington Sq. N., New York, NY 10011. Tel: 212-475-6677.

FOCUS: Third World general • international. Africa • Latin America. Human rights • political repression • militarism • disarmament • nuclear arms and energy • foreign trade and aid • political economy • socialism • international awareness • national liberation struggles • corporate responsibility • social justice.

ACTIVITIES: Popular education • constituency education • political action • legislative action • research and writing • congressional testimony • solidarity work • intern programs • library services • networking • media • justice and peace ministries • workshops and seminars.

RESOURCES: Speakers • audiovisuals • literature • curriculum guides • consultant services • library.

1.66 **Jesuit Social Ministry,** 1717 Massachusetts Ave., NW, Rm. 402, Washington DC 20036. Tel: 202-462-7008.

FOCUS: Third World general. Native American rights • nuclear disarmament • corporate responsibility.

ACTIVITIES: Service to Jesuits in social ministry • constituency education • networking • documentation and information • justice and peace ministries.

PERIODICALS: **1.67** *Promotio Justitiae.* Internal journal.

1.68 **Laos,** 4920 Piney Branch Rd., NW, Washington, DC 20011. Tel: 202-723-8273.

FOCUS: International. Militarism • nuclear energy • distribution of global resources • human rights.

ACTIVITIES: Voluntary service in the United States and Latin America • workshops.

1.69 **Maryknoll Fathers and Brothers,** Justice and Peace Office, Maryknoll, NY 10545. Tel: 914-941-7590.

FOCUS: International. Church • social justice • human rights • development.

ACTIVITIES: Church constituency education • networking • overseas service.

RESOURCES: Audiovisuals • speakers • publications (through Orbis Books).

PERIODICALS: **1.70** *News Notes.* Monthly. Contribution.

1.71 **Maryknoll Sisters,** Desk of Social Concern, Maryknoll, NY 10545. Tel: 914-941-7575.

FOCUS: International. Church • social justice • human rights • development.

ACTIVITIES: Church constituency education • networking • overseas service.

RESOURCES: Seminars • speakers • audiovisuals.

1.72 **Methodist Federation for Social Action,** Shalom House, 76 Clinton Ave., Staten Island, NY 10301. Tel: 212-273-4941.

FOCUS: Third World general. Human rights • political repression • militarism • disarmament • nuclear arms and energy • political economy • socialism • international awareness • national liberation struggles • corporate responsibility • social justice • liberation theology • relation of faith and action.

ACTIVITIES: Constituency education • political action • research and writing • solidarity work • intern programs • networking • justice and peace ministries • workshops and seminars.

RESOURCES: Speakers • publications • study-action guides • consultant services.

PERIODICALS: **1.73** *Social Questions Bulletin*. Bimonthly. $6/year.

SPECIAL PROJECTS: Emergency Peace Project, emphasizing the economic roots of U.S. militarism.

1.74 **Mid-America Program for Global Perspectives in Education,** Social Studies Development Center, Indiana University, 513 N. Park Ave., Bloomington, IN 47401. Tel: 812-335-0455.

FOCUS: Global. Foreign trade and aid • international awareness.

ACTIVITIES: Research and writing • networking • workshops and seminars.

RESOURCES: Publications • consultant services • reports.

PERIODICALS: **1.75** *Global Studies Bibliography*. Annual. $2/year.

1.76 **Movement for a New Society,** 4722 Baltimore Ave., Philadelphia, PA 19143. Tel: 215-724-1464.

FOCUS: National and international. Social justice • nuclear arms and energy • environment • militarism • racial, sexual, and class oppression • non-violent social change.

ACTIVITIES: Non-violent training and action • networking • analysis and study • communications • outreach • celebrations.

RESOURCES: Audiovisuals • publications.

PERIODICALS: **1.77** *The Grapevine*. Monthly newsletter. With membership in MNS of $17/year.

1.78 **National Federation of Priests' Councils,** Ministry for Justice and Peace, 1307 S. Wabash Ave., Chicago, IL 60605. Tel: 312-427-0115.

RELIGIOUS AFFILIATION: Roman Catholic (priests).

FOCUS: Third World general • global • Latin America. Human rights • militarism • political economy • corporate responsibility • social justice.

ACTIVITIES: Constituency education • legislative action • networking • justice and peace ministries • workshops and seminars.

RESOURCES: Publications • consultant services.

PERIODICALS: **1.79** *NFPC News Notes.* 8 issues/year. $10/year.

1.80 NETWORK, 806 Rhode Island Ave., NE, Washington, DC 20018. Tel: 202-526-4070.

RELIGIOUS AFFILIATION: Roman Catholic.

FOCUS: International. Church • militarism • foreign trade and aid • nuclear arms and energy • corporate responsibility • political ministry • theology of social justice.

ACTIVITIES: Constituency education • lobbying • seminars and workshops • legislative action • research and writing • intern programs • political ministry • political action.

RESOURCES: Publications • speakers.

PERIODICALS: **1.81** *NETWORK Newsletter.* Bimonthly. With $18 annual membership. **1.82** *Action Alerts.* Periodic. With membership.

SPECIAL PROJECTS: Election workshops.

1.83 New Directions Educational Fund, 2000 P St., NW, Suite 515, Washington, DC 20036. Tel: 202-833-3140.

FOCUS: Third World general • international. Human rights • disarmament • nuclear arms and energy • political economy • international awareness.

ACTIVITIES: Popular education • research and writing • press service • networking • media • workshops and seminars.

RESOURCES: Speakers.

1.84 New York Circus, Box 37, Times Square Station, New York, NY 10108. Tel: 212-663-8112.

FOCUS: International • Latin America. Social justice • international awareness • church • Christian ministry • human rights • political repression • militarism • foreign trade and aid • political economy • socialism • national liberation struggles • corporate responsibility • theology of liberation.

ACTIVITIES: Popular education • political action • research and writing • solidarity work • intern programs • library services • networking • overseas project support • documentation and information • justice and peace ministries • policy-oriented research and writing • workshops and seminars.

RESOURCES: Speakers • literature • publications • study-action guides • curriculum-guides • consultant services • library • reports • Bible studies.

PERIODICALS: **1.85** *Lucha/Struggle.* Bimonthly. $10/year individual; $20/year-institutional.

SPECIAL PROJECTS: Immigrants Rights Project. Nicaragua Project. Chilean Health Care Project.

1.86 Office for World Justice and Peace, Archdiocese of New York, 1011 First Ave., New York, NY 10022. Tel: 212-371-1000, ext. 2565.

RELIGIOUS AFFILIATION: Roman Catholic.

FOCUS: Third World general • global. Human rights • militarism • nuclear arms and energy • foreign trade and aid • international awareness • social justice.

ACTIVITIES: Legislative action • research and writing • documentation and information • workshops and seminars.

RESOURCES: Publications • consultant services • reports.

PERIODICALS: **1.87** *Agenda,* 9 issues/year. Free to members of the Archdiocese.

1.88 **Oxfam-America,** 115 Broadway, Boston, MA 02116. Tel: 617-482-1211.

FOCUS: Third World general. Asia and Pacific • Africa • Latin America. Women • development • food • hunger.

ACTIVITIES: Popular education • constituency education • political action • legislative action • research and writing • congressional testimony • intern programs • foreign service • networking • media • overseas project support • documentation and information • policy-oriented research and writing • workshops and seminars • press tours and study tours to Third World countries.

RESOURCES: Speakers • audiovisuals • publications • study-action and curriculum guides.

PERIODICALS: **1.89** *Impact Audit.* 3 issues/year. $5/year.

1.90 **Packard-Manse Media Project,** Box 450, Stoughton, MA 02072. Tel: 617-344-3259.

FOCUS: Third World general • international. Latin America. Political repression • militarism • disarmament • nuclear arms and energy • political economy • international awareness • national liberation struggles • corporate responsibility • social justice • militarization of U.S. economy.

ACTIVITIES: Popular education • constituency education • networking • audiovisuals.

RESOURCES: Audiovisuals.

1.91 **Presbyterian Church in the USA,** General Assembly Mission Board, 341 Ponce de Leon Ave., NE, Atlanta, GA 30365. Tel: 404-873-1531.

FOCUS: Asia and Pacific • Middle East • Africa • Latin America. Human rights • international awareness • corporate responsibility • social and economic justice • peacemaking • community development.

ACTIVITIES: Constituency education • intern programs • foreign service • overseas project support • justice and peace ministries • workshops and seminars.

RESOURCES: Speakers • audiovisuals (Ecu-Film) • literature • bookstore • curriculum guides.

PERIODICALS: **1.92** *Response-Ability.* Quarterly. Constituency journal.

1.93 **Project for Global Education,** 777 UN Plaza, New York, NY 10017. Tel: 212-490-0010.

ORGANIZATIONAL AFFILIATION: A project of the Institute for World Order.

FOCUS: Global. Education on: human rights • political repression • militarism • disarmament • nuclear arms and energy • foreign trade and aid • political economy • socialism • international awareness • national liberation struggles • corporate responsibility • social justice • ecology • environmental deterioration.

ACTIVITIES: Academic education • networking • workshops and seminars.

RESOURCES: Speakers • audiovisuals • publications • study-action guides • curriculum guides • consultant services.

PERIODICALS: **1.94** *Project for Global Education/COPRED Chronicle Newsletter.* Monthly. Free.

SPECIAL PROJECTS: **1.95** Preparation of book, *Peace and World Order Studies: A Program Guide,* 4th ed., forthcoming 1984.

1.96   **Union for Radical Political Economics,** 41 Union Sq. W., Rm. 901, New York, NY 10003. Tel: 212-691-5722.

FOCUS: Third World general • international. Political repression • militarism • disarmament • nuclear arms and energy • foreign trade and aid • political economy • socialism • corporate responsibility • social justice.

ACTIVITIES: Popular education • constituency education • research and writing • library services • networking • media • documentation and information • workshops and seminars.

RESOURCES: Speakers • literature • publications • study-action guides • curriculum guides • consultant services • research services.

PERIODICALS: **1.97** *Review of Radical Political Economy.* Quarterly. $25/year. **1.98** *URPE Newsletter.* Bimonthly. $6/year. Apply for URPE membership fees and for other subscription rates.

SPECIAL PROJECTS: Women's Work Project. Economic Education Project.

1.99   **United Church Board for World Ministries,** 475 Riverside Dr., 16th Floor, New York, NY 10115. Tel: 212-870-2711.

FOCUS: International. Church • social justice • development • corporate responsibility • human rights.

ACTIVITIES: Overseas missionary service • justice and peace ministries • disaster relief • hunger action • constituency education.

PERIODICALS: **1.100** *Whole Earth* newsletter. 3 issues/year. Contribution.

.101   **United Methodist Church,** Board of Global Ministries, 475 Riverside Dr., New York, NY 10115. Tel: 212-678-6161.

FOCUS: International. Church • social justice • development • human rights • militarism • transnational corporations • women.

ACTIVITIES: Overseas missionary service • constituency education • intern programs • overseas project support • justice and peace ministries • workshops and seminars.

RESOURCES: Speakers • audiovisuals • publications • reports.

PERIODICALS: **1.102** *New World Outlook.* Monthly. $4/year.

.103   **United Methodist Seminars on National and International Affairs,** 777 UN Plaza, New York, NY 10017. Tel: 212-682-3633 and 100 Maryland Ave., NE, Washington, DC 20002. Tel: 202-488-5611.

ORGANIZATIONAL AFFILIATION: Sponsored by the Board of Church and Society and the Women's Division, Board of Global Ministries, United Methodist Church.

FOCUS: Third World general • international. Human rights • militarism • disarmament • foreign trade and aid • political economy • socialism • national liberation struggles • power and powerlessness • corporate responsibility.

ACTIVITIES: Educational programming for interdenominational and interreligious groups • regional outreach.

RESOURCES: Speakers • audiovisuals • literature • consultant services • curriculum guides.

1.104 **U.S. Catholic Conference,** Office of International Justice and Peace, 1312 Massachusetts Ave., NW, Washington, DC 20005. Tel: 202-659-6812.

RELIGIOUS AFFILIATION: Roman Catholic.

FOCUS: International. Human rights • militarism • disarmament • foreign trade and aid • social justice • corporate responsibility.

ACTIVITIES: Constituency education • congressional testimony • justice and peace ministries • research and writing.

RESOURCES: Speakers • publications. Publications list available.

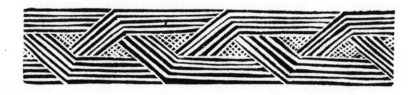

PRINTED RESOURCES

Distributors

Ordering recent catalogs from the publishers listed throughout this directory is one obvious way of keeping up-to-date on literature related to U.S. involvement in the Third World.

Another way is to make use of book distributors who offer both catalogs (with publications from a variety of publishers) and mail order services. Four such distributors are:

1.105 **Food for Thought Books,** 325 Main St., Amherst, MA 01002. Tel: 413-253-5432. Catalog price: 25 cents.

1.106 **Guild Books & Periodicals,** 2456 N. Lincoln Ave., Chicago, IL 60614. Tel: 312-525-3667. Catalog price: $1.

1.107 **Modern Times Bookstore,** 968 Valencia St., San Francisco, CA 94110. Tel: 415-282-9246. Catalog price: $1.

1.108 **Social Studies School Service,** 10,000 Culver Blvd., Box 802, Culver City, CA 90230. Tel: 213-839-2436. **1.109** Catalog: *Global Education.* Free.

Books

.110   Corson-Finnerty, Adam D. *World Citizen: Action for Global Justice.* Mary-
        knoll, N.Y.: Orbis Books, 1982. 178pp. $6.95
        World Citizen is divided into two sections: a narrative introduction to issues of
        global justice and peace and sixty pages of selected resources.
        The first section covers issues such as colonialism, militarism, the environ-
        ment, and the United Nations. The second section is an annotated list of organi-
        zations and books that are related to themes of global citizenship.
.111   Falk, Richard, et.al., eds. *Toward a Just World Order.* Boulder, Colo.: West-
        view Press, 1982. 652pp. $16.50
        The first of three volumes of the "Studies on a Just World Order" series in-
        cludes contributions by Steve Biko, Paulo Freire, Eqbal Ahmad, Immanuel Wal-
        lerstein, Norman Cousins, and others. A world order perspective is developed by
        examining the writings of victims of oppression and of those who speak for such
        victims. The nature of global change, as well as its possibility, are explored in
        areas such as militarism and war, poverty, economic underdevelopment, denial
        of human rights, and ecological decay.
.112   Farhang, Mansour. *U.S. Imperialism: The Spanish American War to the Ira-
        nian Revolution.* Boston: South End Press, 1981. 250pp. $7
        Mansour Farhang, former Iranian ambassador to the United Nations, presents
        in this work a historical analysis of U.S. international relations with particular
        emphasis on U.S. relations with Third World countries. Farhang includes a criti-
        cal assessment of liberal and Marxist theories of U.S. motives and involvements
        abroad. He then posits alternative multi-dimensional approaches that pay atten-
        tion not only to economics, but also to politics, culture, and racial issues.
.113   Frank, Andre Gunder. *Crisis: In the Third World.* New York: Holmes & Meier
        Publishers, 1981. 375pp. Bibliography. $12.50
.114   Companion volume: *Crisis: In the World Economy.* 1980. 366pp. Bibliogra-
        phy. $12.50
        Though his numerous works on the "development of underdevelopment" in
        the Third World are usually heavy going for those new to this subject, Andre
        Gunder Frank assures us in his preface to *Crisis: In the Third World* that it is his
        intention in this book "to employ an analysis and to write in a language that any
        interested reader can understand." By and large he does just that.
        Crisis begins with a look at seven Third World nations that Frank describes
        as "semiperipheral economies." These are: Brazil, Mexico, Argentina, India,
        Iran, Israel, and South Africa. The next two chapters analyze the situation of
        export-dependent economies in the Third World. This is followed by Frank's
        examination of features that are more or less common to all Third World
        countries, such as debt, exploitation, political and economic repression, and so
        forth.
        Frank concludes this work with some questions about socialism and national-
        ism in a single world system.

1.115   Girling, John S. *America and the Third World: Revolution and Intervention.* Boston: Routledge & Kegan Paul, 1980. 276pp. $25

Girling, a foreign policy specialist at the Australian National University, characterizes America's relationship with the Third World as one of "patronage." The United States—the new imperial patron—provides protection, a share in wealth, and a sense of participation in the common endeavor. In return, the clients—Third World elites—provide "loyal" services, economic facilities, and the wherewithal (jointly or individually) to maintain security.

Professor Girling advances three propositions: that the overriding interest of American policy-makers is in the stability of the global system of relationships; that this interest coincides with those of most Third World elites; and that the global system normally operates peacefully, although continually subject to internal and external challenges. When challenges become critical, Girling says, the imperial patron is liable to move from involvement to intervention, "for crises are the test of the system."

1.116   Harrington, Michael. *The Vast Majority: A Journey to the World's Poor.* New York: Simon & Schuster, 1977. 280pp. $9.95

Using a mix of economic theory and personal reports on his journeys to the Third World, Michael Harrington describes how the Western capitalist powers—led by the United States—have exploited and "underdeveloped" the peoples of the Third World economically, culturally, socially, and politically.

1.117   Horowitz, David. *Empire and Revolution: A Radical Interpretation of Contemporary History.* New York: Random House, 1970. $1.95

Horowitz situates this study of U.S. foreign policy in the context of the ideological struggle between the capitalist and socialist worlds that dates back to the Bolshevik revolution in 1917. He is critical of many aspects of Stalinist Russia's foreign and domestic policies and he cites political exploitation by western capitalist nations as the source of much of the poverty in the Third World.

1.118   Horowitz is also the author of *The Free World Colossus* (New York: Hill & Wang, Inc., 1971. 465pp. $6.95).

1.119   Hudson, Michael. *Global Fracture: The New International Economic Order.* New York: Harper & Row, 1977. 296pp. $12.50

Economist Michael Hudson describes the New International Economic Order as a movement by Europe and by Third World countries to become both independent of the U.S. economic orbit and more closely integrated economically and politically with one another. The title of this book embodies Hudson's thesis that the world is moving away from liberal One-Worldism and entering an era of regional economic blocs, each with its own currency and trading system.

1.120   Equally challenging is Hudson's *Super Imperialism: The Economic Strategy of American Empire* (New York: Holt, Rinehart, & Winston, 1972. 304pp. $9.95).

1.121   Inter-Religious Task Force for Social Analysis. *Must We Choose Sides?* Vol. 1: 1979. 128pp. $5.95. *Which Side Are We On?* Vol. 2: 1980. 200pp. $6.95. The two-volume set is available for $12.00 from the IRTFSA, 464 19 St., Oakland, CA 94612.

These two study/action guides for social change were prepared by the Inter-Religious Task Force for Social Analysis and published by the Episcopal Church

Publishing Co. Though they are not directly related to U.S. involvement in the Third World these two collections of readings have proven to be effective tools in the hands of Christians who are concerned about their role in national and international affairs in the 1980s.

Volume 1 explores the role of working people in the U.S. economic system and investigates the harsh realities of everyday life in this country. Who owns America? Who pays the price? Group exercises probe individual experience and insight, apply tools of social analysis, and spur theological reflection.

Volume 2 deepens the reader's understanding of the present crisis—inflation, unemployment, the danger of war—and moves beyond the historical criticisms of capitalism to explore other alternatives. *Which Side Are We On?* raises provocative questions for Christian activists: Can we reclaim our radical heritage? How do we confront political and religious ideology? This volume offers seven in-depth sessions for group study and action.

.122   Jalée, Pierre. *The Pillage of the Third World.* New York: Monthly Review, 1968. 115pp. $2.95.

.123   *The Third World in World Economy.* New York: Monthly Review, 1969. 207pp. $3.95

Though Jalée's statistical data are now dated, the structure of his analysis of relations between capitalist nations and the Third World remains as valid as it was when these two books were first written in French in the late 1960s. Both works seek to illustrate the workings of neo-colonialism: colonialism operating entirely through economic relations instead of, as before, through economic relations accompanied by political domination.

Jalée's writings are an excellent introduction to the dynamics of international investment, trade, and aid.

.124   Johansen, Robert C. *The National Interest and the Human Interest: An Analysis of U.S. Foreign Policy.* Princeton, N.J.: Princeton University Press, 1980. 517pp. $6.95

The impact of U.S. foreign policy is the focus of this book. Issues studied are strategic arms limitation, human rights in Chile, economic well-being in India, and environmental protection of the oceans. Consideration is given to the development of an alternative U.S. foreign policy.

.125   Kolko, Gabriel. *The Roots of American Foreign Policy: An Analysis of Power and Purpose.* Boston: Beacon Press, 1969. 166pp. $3.95

In *The Roots of American Foreign Policy* historian Gabriel Kolko investigates "the respectables," the self-styled liberal realists and businesspeople (in and out of government) who are the architects of American foreign policy. Kolko also outlines the nature of American power and interest in the modern world and provides an assessment of who gains and who loses as a result of the policies Washington pursues.

.126   Kolko, Joyce. *America and the Crisis of World Capitalism.* Boston: Beacon Press, 1976. 202pp. $4.95

Kolko's analysis focuses our attention on the identity and workings of "the ruling class" in capitalist societies. For it is this class, Kolko contends, and not the military, politicians, or "mandarins," who set the directions for U.S. foreign policy.

"There is nothing mystical, or even ideological, about the decisions of the ruling class," says the author, "nor its disagreements. Their aim is not even to expand the 'Empire' of American power per se. Their aim is, and must be, to expand their own corporate interests."

Joyce Kolko brings this analytical framework to a challenging—yet readable—examination of two decades of U.S. involvement in the world economy, of multinational corporations, and of the Soviet Bloc, China, and the "capitalist crisis."

1.127   McCuen, Gary E., and Bender, David L. *American Foreign Policy: Opposing Viewpoints.* St. Paul, Minn.: Greenhaven Press, 1972. 108pp. $4.60

This is Volume 6 in Greenhaven's Opposing Viewpoints Series. The Series is designed to provoke and stimulate classroom discussion around domestic and international current affairs. Though the issues treated in *American Foreign Policy* are dated—America's China policy, for instance—these debates between liberals and conservatives can still be used to analyze some of the underlying tendencies in Washington's foreign policy.

1.128   McGinnis, James B. *Bread & Justice: Toward a New International Economic Order.* New York: Paulist Press, 1979. 358pp. $4.95

Bread & Justice was written, says the author, for three groups of people: those concerned about world hunger; those concerned about justice; those looking for a way to understand, evaluate, and act on global economic issues, particularly the New International Economic Order. McGinnis, a founding member of the Institute for Peace and Justice, provides the three groups with a clearly written and carefully argued textbook on a variety of issues related to global issues.

1.129   Magdoff, Harry. *Imperialism: From the Colonial Age to the Present.* New York: Monthly Review, 1978. 279pp. $5

This volume contains a series of essays aimed at illuminating from a Marxist point of view the theory, history, and roots of imperialism—from the period of Western Europe's global expansionism during the Industrial Revolution to the era of multinational corporations.

The core essay, "European Expansion Since 1763," is reproduced from volume 4 of the fifteenth edition of the *Encyclopaedia Britannica* (1974).

As in his earlier work, *The Age of Imperialism: The Economics of U.S. Foreign Policy* (Monthly Review, 1969), Magdoff treats challenging and troubling issues with clarity and with a great deal of sensitivity.

1.130   Mische, Gerald, and Mische, Patricia. *Toward a Human World Order.* New York: Paulist Press, 1977. 399pp. $3.95. (Bulk rates available.)

The authors consider the transformation they see taking place in this historical period toward world community. They examine the present nation-state system, explore alternatives, and suggest strategies for a multi-issue movement toward achieving those alternatives.

.131   Payer, Cheryl. *The Debt Trap: The International Monetary Fund and the Third World.* New York: Monthly Review, 1975. 256pp. $5.95

The author labels the International Monetary Fund "the most powerful supranational government in the world today" and she accuses the IMF of using its huge resources to interfere in the internal affairs of borrowing nations and of promoting policies favorable to the rich countries at the expense of less developed countries.

.132   Singham, A.W., ed. *The Non-Aligned Movement in World Politics.* Westport, Conn.: Lawrence Hill & Co., 1977. 273pp. $7.95

This work consists of twenty papers that were presented to the Conference on Non-Alignment held at Howard University (April 8–10, 1976). The conference was designed to inform the people of the United States—particularly Afro-Americans—of the global interests and activities of non-aligned peoples and of their positions on such issues as hunger, energy problems, national liberation movements, territorial integrity, technological development, and international conflicts and peace strategies.

Also included in the book are a number of significant articles on the non-aligned movement that have appeared since the Howard conference, as well as the Political and Economic Declarations of the Fifth Summit Conference of Non-Aligned Nations in Sri Lanka (August 1976).

1.133   Sklar, Holly, ed. *Trilateralism: The Trilateral Commission and Elite Planning for World Management.* Boston: South End Press, 1980. 604pp. $9

Trilateralism is a collection of readable essays on the highly influential Trilateral Commission and its relation to national and international events, power, propaganda and policy-making from World War II into the 1980s. A special feature of the book is a forty-page Who's Who of Commission members that includes government figures and top corporate executives from the United States, France, West Germany, Japan and other industrialized nations.

1.134   Steel, Ronald. *Pax Americana.* Rev. ed. New York: Viking Press, 1970. 368pp. $2.95

However deep and sincerely felt the utopian idealism of many Americans might be toward other nations, Steel contends that those who feel the direct effects of American power are the best ones to sit in judgment on U.S. foreign policy. "As the most powerful nation on earth," he says, "—the richest, the most deeply involved, and in some ways the most ideologically committed—the United States has intervened massively in the affairs of other nations." *Pax Americana* takes a critical look at these interventions from the point of view of those on the receiving end of U.S. power.

1.135   Thompson, Carol L.; Anderberg, Mary M.; and Antell, Joan B., eds. *The Current History Encyclopedia of Developing Nations.* New York: McGraw-Hill Book Co., 1982. 295pp. Cloth $45

This attractive book by the editors of *Current History* magazine is divided into six major sections: Africa South of the Sahara; North Africa and the Middle

East; South Asia; East Asia, Southeast Asia, and the Pacific; Central America and the Caribbean; and South America. Within each major section, individual countries are arranged alphabetically. The descriptions of each country are concise and thorough.

Though the relationship of these Third World countries to the United States is not at all the focus of the *Encyclopedia*, the valuable content and usable format of the book make it worth knowing about.

1.136   Unger, Linda, and Schultz, Kathleen, eds. *Seeds of a People's Church: Challenge and Promise from the Underside of History.* Detroit: Christians for Socialism, 1981. 63pp. $5.25 (postage included). (Payment must accompany order. Bulk rates available.) Available from Seeds of a People's Church.

These presentations from the Neil C. McMath Lectureship of the Episcopal Diocese of Michigan feature fifteen authors addressing four major themes: (1) The challenge and promise from the underside of history; (2) Solidarity with Southern Africa and Central America; (3) Working in God's creation: afflictions and challenges for today's workers; and (4) Building the people's church in North America: documents of Christian witness.

1.137   White, Margaret, and Quigley, Robert N., eds. *How the Other Third Lives.* Maryknoll, N.Y.: Orbis Books, 1977. 437pp. $4.95

Asian, African, and Latin American poets and writers are represented in this anthology of poems, songs, prayers, stories, and essays. Love and hope in the midst of oppression and injustice is the overall theme of the selections. The book furnishes a unique insight into culture as well as into crucial issues facing Third World peoples today.

1.138   Williams, William Appleman. *Empire as a Way of Life: An Essay on the Causes and Character of America's Present Predicament Along with a Few Thoughts About an Alternative.* New York: Oxford University Press, 1980. 226pp. $14.95

Distinguished historian William Appleman Williams writes a book that is—in his own words—an attempt to help the American people "understand and accept our past as an imperial people who must now 'order' ourselves rather than policing and saving the world."

Periodicals

Two valuable indexes that are unique sources of information related to periodicals:

1.139   The first is the *Alternative Press Index* (API), published quarterly by the *Alternative Press Center,* Box 7229, Baltimore, MD 21218. This library reference work is the only complete guide to over 150 alternative and radical newspapers, magazines, and journals. Articles are indexed by subject in a format similar to the *Reader's Guide to Periodical Literature.* Major public and university libraries should be encouraged to purchase the *API.* It is unique in providing access to a significant body of analysis and commentary on national and international affairs.

The *Center* began publishing the *API* in 1969 and still makes back issues available. Volume 14 (1982) sells for $90; prices vary for other back issues.

The *Alternative Press Center* also publishes a free list of 250 alternative periodicals.

1.140   The second index, called *The Left Index,* began publication in spring 1982 and comes out quarterly. It intends to "extend the spectrum of indexed scholarly and professional journals to include viewpoints from the left." Each issue contains an author list, a subject index, a book review index, a journal index and a section listing new serial publications of the left.

The Left Index is available from 511 Lincoln St., Santa Cruz, CA 95060. A year's subscription is $50; back issues are $15 each.

The *Data Center* has current and back issues of the periodicals listed below, as well as many other Third World-related publications. These latter include periodicals that originate outside the United States, as well as those published in the country; they are representative of a variety of political points of view: business, labor, government, community, progressive political parties and organizations, neo-conservatives and so forth. The *Center*'s Search Service can help you gain access to this unique library collection.

1.141   *Alternative Media,* c/o Alternative Press Syndicate, Box 1347, Ansonia Station, New York, NY 10023. Quarterly magazine. $7.50/year.

Articles, ads, and notices concerning alternative press and media coverage around the world.

1.142   *Coalition Close-Up,* c/o Coalition for a New Foreign and Military Policy, 120 Maryland Ave., NE, Washington, DC 20002. A 12-page monthly magazine. With $10 annual membership.

This monthly publication features readable articles on the issues that concern Coalition members: military spending, the protection of human rights, the promotion of arms control and disarmament, support for majority rule and authentic self-determination in southern Africa, and more.

1.143   *Dollars & Sense,* 38 Union Sq., Rm. 14, Somerville, MA 02143. A 20-page monthly magazine. $9/year individual; $18/year institutional.

Written by a group of professional economists and journalists, this attractive and highly readable magazine is committed to making the U.S. economy understandable to everyone, not just to economists. The domestic and international impact of the U.S. economy is examined in clearly written articles, in charts and graphs, and in monthly features that include "The Economy in Numbers," "Capitol Contacts," "MisFORTUNE," and "Bits & Pieces."

1.144   *engage/social action,* 100 Maryland Ave., NE, Washington, DC 20002. Monthly magazine. $6/year.

e/sa is published by the Board of Church and Society of the United Methodist Church. In addition to articles on a variety of social concern issues, this magazine includes a pullout section (*e/sa forum*) that explores one particular issue in depth, and regular columns on UN affairs and happenings in Washington.

1.145   *Foreign Policy*, Box 984, Farmingdale, NY 11737. Quarterly magazine. $15/year.

This quarterly is noted for its liberal analyses of U.S. foreign affairs. It bills itself as the journal to read, analyze and refer to in government committee rooms, corporate headquarters, embassies, and the homes and offices of concerned citizens and policy makers around the world.

1.146   *Greenpeace Examiner*, Box 6677, Portland, OR 97228. Quarterly magazine. Contribution.

News of international events and actions around issues of environment, ecology, nuclear energy and the like.

1.147   *The Guardian*, 33 W. 17 St., New York, NY 10011. Weekly tabloid newspaper. $23/year. Inquire about special introductory six-month rates.

For over thirty years *The Guardian*, the largest of America's independent leftwing weekly newspapers, has been reporting on and analyzing political and economic issues from a radical point of view. *The Guardian* tries to be "long on facts" and "short on (radical) rhetoric."

1.148   *Intercontinental Press* (combined with **Inprecor**), 410 West St., New York, NY 10014. Weekly magazine. $35/year.

This weekly is devoted entirely to international affairs, with analyses from the point of view of Trotskyists primarily from the United States and Britain.

1.149   *In These Times*, 1509 N. Milwaukee Ave., Chicago, IL 60622. A weekly tabloid newspaper (42 issues/year). $23.50/year individual; $35/year institutional.

This "independent socialist newspaper" is published by the Washington-based Institute for Policy Studies. *ITT* offers readable coverage of the political and economic impact of U.S. foreign policy, as well as analyses of the U.S. domestic scene.

1.150   *Maryknoll*, Maryknoll, NY 10545. Monthly magazine. $1/year.

Published by the Catholic Foreign Mission Society of America (Maryknoll), this colorful magazine describes the work of Maryknoll missionaries throughout the Third World and—increasingly—includes as well short, analytical articles on issues such as disarmament, world hunger, native peoples, political repression, and multinational corporations.

1.151   *Monthly Review*, 62 W. 14 St., New York, NY 10011. Monthly magazine (11 issues/year). $15/year individual; apply for other rates.

This highly respected "independent socialist magazine" is one of your best sources for critical analyses of U.S. economic and political issues and of international affairs in general. The editors, Paul Sweezy and Harry Magdoff, have a gift for translating complex issues into brief, coherent, and readable essays. They see to it that others who write for the magazine strive for the same brevity and clarity.

1.152   *Mother Jones*, 1886 Haymarket Sq., Marion, OH 43305 (business office). 10 issues/year. $16/year.

Mother Jones approaches political and economic issues with highly developed skills of critical investigation. This award-winning magazine has produced blockbusting exposés of numerous issues, from the Ford Pinto to the dumping of hazardous products in Third World countries by U.S. corporations.

1.153   *The Nation*, 72 Fifth Ave., New York, NY 10011. Subscription service: Box 1953, Marion, OH 43305. Weekly magazine (47 issues/year). $30/year.

Little more has to be said about the fine commentary and liberal analyses that this magazine offers its readers than that *The Nation* is now in its 234th volume.

1.154   *New America*, 275 Seventh Ave., New York, NY 10001. 11 issues/year. $8/year.

New America is a tabloid newspaper that analyzes national and international affairs from the perspective of the Social Democrats, U.S.A., and Young Social Democrats.

1.155   *New World Review*, 156 Fifth Ave., Suite 308, New York, NY 10010. Bimonthly. $5/year.

The Review examines international issues such as disarmament, Afghanistan, and Indochina from the point of view of the Communist Party, USA.

1.156   *Newsfront International*, c/o Peoples Translation Service, 4228 Telegraph Ave., Oakland, CA 94609. Monthly magazine. $22/year individual; $45/year libraries and institutions.

Newsfront International specializes in providing translations of key feature articles from magazines and newspapers around the world. The magazine's coverage of European affairs is exceptionally good, but its treatment of Third World-related issues such as multinational corporations, native peoples, mineral exploitation and so forth is also noteworthy.

1.157   *The Progressive*, 409 E. Main St., Madison, WI 53703. Monthly magazine. $20/year.

Founded in 1901, this magazine offers a "progressive" slant on issues of nuclear energy, chemical warfare, military spending, and U.S. foreign policy in general. Monthly departments include reviews of books, theatre and films, and reports and commentaries by contributing editors.

1.158   *Race & Class: A Journal for Black and Third World Liberation*, c/o Institute for Policy Studies, 1901 Que St., NW, Washington, DC 20009. Quarterly magazine. $12/year individual; $15/year institutional.

Race & Class, the quarterly journal of the Institute for Race Relations and the IPS-related Transnational Institute, is unique in that its editorial focus on both race and class brings a fresh perspective to the treatment of Third World themes. At the same time this focus challenges readers to give racial and class perspectives the attention they deserve.

1.159   *Radical America*, 38 Union Sq., Somerville, MA 02143. Bimonthly magazine. $12/year.

Radical America is an independent socialist-feminist journal with feature-length articles on the history of and current developments in the working class, the role of women and Third World people, shop-floor and community organizing, the history and politics of radicalism and feminism, and socialist theory and popular culture.

1.160   *Socialist Review*, c/o the Center for Social Research and Education, 4228 Telegraph Ave., Oakland, CA 94609. Bimonthly magazine. $18/year individual; $36/year institutional.

For over ten years *Socialist Review* has been a forum for thoughtful and well-reasoned discussion of political economy and cultural issues from a socialist perspective. Recent issues have dealt with plant shutdowns, El Salvador and the Central American war, and developments in Zimbabwe.

1.161 *Sojourners*, 1309 L St., NW, Washington, DC 20005. 11 issues/year. $12/year.

Sojourners features articles on various aspects of justice and peace from an evangelical Christian perspective. This attractive monthly magazine also includes reviews, announcements, columns, editorial opinion, and a unique Sojourners Book Service.

1.162 *The Witness*, Box 359, Ambler, PA 19002. Monthly magazine. $9/year.

This ecumenical journal of social concern draws its inspiration from the witness of early Christians for an earthly kingdom of justice, peace and freedom for all people. Standing on the shoulders of an earlier version of *The Witness* that dates back to the end of World War I, today's *Witness* examines contemporary issues of church and society such as hunger, nuclear energy, the plight of the cities, and the criminal justice system.

AUDIOVISUAL RESOURCES

Distributors

Some major universities have audiovisual extension services that provide annotated guides, arrange for previews, and also rent films at a discount. Among these are:

1.163 Indiana University Audio-Visual Center
1.164 University of California Extension Media Center
1.165 University of Michigan Audio Visual Center
1.166 University of Minnesota Audio Visual Library Service
1.167 University of Washington Audio-Visual Services

Guides and Catalogs

1.168 *Audio-Visual Resources for Social Change.* Cambridge, Mass.: AFSC. 8 tabloid pages. Free

Audio-Visual Resources is an excellent guide for a number of reasons: it's an annotated list of over one hundred of the best audiovisuals on social change currently available; resources are classified under sixty-two headings and cross-referenced; the catalog is kept up-to-date with the inclusion of periodic supplements; and—best of all—each of the audiovisuals listed in the catalog is available directly from the New England Regional Office of AFSC. Call to discuss rental procedures with AFSC's film librarian: 617-497-5273.

1.169   *Film Programmer's Guide to 16mm Rentals.* Kathleen Weaver, ed. 3d ed. Albany, Calif.: Reel Research, 1980. 320pp. $20

The *Film Programmer's Guide* is a practical reference designed to provide convenient access to 16mm non-theatrical rentals. The entire range of cinematic production is represented (1893–1979): Hollywood and independent releases, American and international classics, experimental and avant-garde works, social and political documentaries, films on arts and artists, international animations, Hollywood cartoons, silent and sound productions, both features and shorts. Educational films fall outside the scope of this directory, but the guide provides cross-references to services that handle such films.

For each film the editor provides the names of producers and directors; date of release; length; distributor; rental and sale prices; and—in some cases—a very short description.

1.170   *A Filmography of the Third World.* Helen W. Cyr, ed. Metuchen, N.J.: Scarecrow Press, 1976. 327pp. $14.50. Out of print.

This annotated collection of Third World-related films is an extremely useful guide—one that should have stayed in print far longer than it did.

1.171   *Films of a Changing World: A Critical International Guide.* Jean Marie Ackermann, ed. 2 vols. Washington, D.C.: Society for International Development, 1972–77. Vol. 1: 105pp. $4; Vol. 2: 73pp. $4

These books are actually compilations of film reviews written by Ms. Ackermann and published from 1963 to 1977 in the *International Development Review.* Though dated and often biased toward development in purely economic terms the information given in *Films of a Changing World* still serves as a useful introduction to films on agricultural development, social change, and international cooperation.

1.172   *Films of the United Nations Family: 16mm Film Catalog 1980–81.* New York: United Nations, 1979. 119pp. in English; 124pp. in French. $5

This catalog describes—in English and French—some 600 16mm films produced and distributed by organizations of the United Nations such as the Food and Agriculture Organization, the International Labour Organisation and the United Nations Development Programme.

Many UN films can be borrowed free or rented inexpensively.

1.173   *Films on International Affairs.* New York: Third World Newsreel, 1980. 12pp. Free

This brochure lists films available from Third World Newsreel on international issues.

1.174   *General Board of Global Ministries Catalog.* Cincinnati: United Methodist Church, Service Center, Annual. 38pp. Free except postage

The "Media and Methods" section of this catalog contains annotated listings of films, filmstrips, slides, audiovisual kits, and other resources.

1.175   *Global Education Catalog.* Culver City, Calif.: Social Studies School Service, Annual. 48pp. Free

This catalog from the Social Studies School Service is a particularly useful guide to sound filmstrips and videocassettes for use in educational programs.

1.176 *In Focus: A Guide to Using Films.* Linda Blackaby, Dan Georjakas, and Barbara Margolis. New York: Cine Information, 1980. 206pp. $8.95

While *In Focus* doesn't list films, it is worth mentioning for two reasons: (1) the book is an excellent handbook of information on planning film programs and offers a wealth of resource material on distributors, filmographies, periodicals, and funding sources; and (2) it includes a form that you can fill out in order to join a Film Users' Network. The Network is a free informational service that will bring you notices of new film releases in subject areas of interest to you.

1.177 *Media Resources 1980–1982.* Berkeley, Calif.: University of California Extension Media Center, 1980. 214pp. Free

This directory consists of alphabetical listings of hundreds of films and videotapes on a variety of topics. Each item is fully annotated and includes the necessary information for rental or purchase. The directory is well indexed and cross-referenced.

1.178 *Reel Change: A Guide to Social Issue Films.* Patricia Peyton, ed. New York and San Francisco: The Film Fund, 1979. 140pp. $6.95

One of the best guides available on social change films, *Reel Change* annotates and classifies over 500 dramatic features, documentaries, shorts, animation, videotape, and slideshows in several subject categories: Global Concerns; International—Asia, Africa and the Middle East, Latin America; Political Movements—International; Work and Labor Movements.

This guide also contains a directory of film distributors and a very valuable resource section with information on film guides, magazines and periodicals.

1.179 *Resource Catalog.* New York: Presbyterian Distribution Service, United Presbyterian Church.

This catalog lists Mission Films available through Distribution Centers of the United Presbyterian Church throughout the country. Films borrowed are subject to a service charge of $8.50 per film, plus the costs of postage from and to the Centers.

1.180 *Resources.* Chicago: 8th Day Center for Justice, 1981. 15pp. Free

Resources describes eighteen audiovisuals that are available for rental from the Center.

1.181 *The War/Peace Film Guide.* John Dowling. Rev. ed. Chicago: World Without War Publications, 1980. 188pp. $5. Available from the World Without War Council nearest you.

This *Guide* is more than just a carefully annotated selection of films on themes of war and peace. Like its predecessor version edited by Lucy Dougall in 1973, Dowling's 1980 edition is intended to provide the means necessary to view the films listed in an educational setting. To this end *The War/Peace Film Guide* offers pages of program development aids and background readings and resources. Especially useful are the study guides, study units, and curriculum resources that are keyed to specific films.

The War/Peace Film Guide classifies films in categories such as the following: area studies; arms race; children's films; the impact of war; nonviolence; nuclear war; revolution; world community and world development.

Audiovisuals

.182   *Development Without Tears.* 1979 28 min color film. Available in Arabic, English, French, and Spanish. United Nations. Free

This Vision Habitat/United Nations film looks at several countries with widely different social systems (China, India, Cuba, and Jamaica among them) and at their efforts to meet the needs of their own rural peoples. Filmed interviews with development specialists from Africa, Asia, and Latin America stress the importance of political action in overcoming the enormous obstacles to economic progress in Third World countries.

.183   *Economics and the Global Society.* 20 min color filmstrip with records. AFSC (N.Y.). Rental $5

This set of three filmstrips documents the growing interdependence among nations and raises questions about the values we bring to international relations: how should we use technology and natural resources? what will be our economic priorities?

.184   *The Economics Game.* 1977 12 min color film. Available in Arabic, Dutch, English, French, and Spanish. United Nations. Free

The complex concepts of the new international economic order are presented in the form of a game, acted out by the Richard Morse Mime Theatre group and set to an original electronic music score. The players are shown sitting around a table and are dealt cards according to the extent in real life that they possess natural and human resources and technological capabilities. *The Economics Game* demonstrates the need for developing countries to be directly involved in changing the "rules of the game."

.185   *An Essay on Poverty.* 1977 24 min color film. United Nations. Free

This "essay" was produced for the UN by the World Bank. It explores the implications—for both the developed and the developing countries—of the enormous problems of poverty in today's world. Rural development, the migration to urban areas, the role of women in developing societies, and the maldistribution of income, wealth, and opportunities are all discussed in terms of their impact on the basic needs of the very poor.

The film concludes with questions the World Bank raises about the duties and responsibilities of both the rich and the poor countries in the face of such massive poverty.

.186   *Five Billion People.* 1979–80 13-part series, each color film running 27 minutes. Directed by Nicole Duchene and Claude Lortie. Unifilm. Apply for rates.

This series of educational films brings a critical and historical perspective to the many complex economic concepts and issues that animate our contemporary world. Each of the thirteen films explores the social and political implications of the particular economic issues analyzed, showing how economic decisions determine the quality of the society in which we live.

The films are:

1. *Money*: a wide-ranging introduction to this key economic concept.

2. *Financial Institutions*: an examination of the rules that govern the operation of all contemporary financial institutions.

3. *The Gear*: an analysis of the three basic sectors of economic activity—the extraction of raw materials, the transformation of raw materials, and the service industries.

4. *Unfair Exchange*: an investigation of the economic relationship between "developed" and "underdeveloped" countries.

5. *The Conspiracy, or How the Transnationals Do It*: an explanation of the ways in which the transnationals operate and of the implications of their international control.

6. *The Nature of Work*: a study of the nature of work, as seen from a historical perspective and as we know it in today's society.

7. *Temporary Admission*: a critical look at the contemporary situation of immigrant laborers.

8. *Colonialism and Neo-Colonialism*: an analysis of the neo-colonial relationship between the former colonial powers and today's Third World nations, taking the African region as a case study.

9. *Underdevelopment*: a demystification of one of the most controversial concepts in contemporary political literature, the notion of underdevelopment.

10. *International Aid*: a critical examination of the many misconceptions surrounding international or "development" aid.

11. *Any Way/Any Price*: an exploration of the whys and wherefores of our consumer economy, including such aspects as mass production, the credit system, advertising, and the social implications of an economy built on consumerism.

12. *Information*: an investigation of the communications industry and of the social and political implications of the control of the industry by a handful of giant corporations.

13. *Economic Growth*: an analysis of the concept of economic growth, challenging the conventional wisdom that the constant proliferation of an already considerable flow of goods and services is a desirable goal.

1.187　　*The History Book.* 1972 157 min (each episode in the nine-part series averages 15-20 minutes) color film. Directed by Jannik Hastrup and Li Vilstrup. Produced by the Danish Government Film Office, Document Associates. Rental $45 each; $275 for the complete series. Also available for purchase in video cassette format.

This engaging series of nine animated films presents the history of Western civilization from a grassroots perspective, showing history as it has been lived and experienced by the "common people."

Designed for use on the secondary school level, *The History Book* outlines the main forces and processes of history, including feudalism, the development of trade routes, the Industrial Revolution and the rise of capitalism, the colonization of America and Africa, the growth of slavery, the conflicts between major industrial countries leading to world wars, and the socialist revolutions and national liberation struggles of our own day.

The nine modules in the series are:

1. *A Flickering Light in the Darkness* (18 min): feudalism and the rise of the merchant class.

2. *At Dawn, Overcoming All Difficulties* (17 min): the beginnings of ocean trade and the conquest of native populations in South America.

3. *A Bright Future...For Some* (15 min): the appearance of the first nation-states and the consolidation of power by the merchant class.

4. *Bloody Schemes* (18 min): start of the slave trade and the opening up of the Caribbean and North American regions.

5. *Triumphant Symphony* (15 min): the Industrial Revolution and mass migrations to the cities.

6. *Makeshift Solutions* (18 min): the colonization of the African continent as a way of relieving worker unrest in Europe.

7. *The Coming of Darkness* (18 min): two world wars and the rise of socialism in the Soviet Union and China.

8. *The Night is Sinister* (18 min): emergence from colonialism into neo-colonialism.

9. *A New Dawn* (20 min): the struggle of one African nation, Guinea-Bissau, to achieve meaningful independence from both colonialism and neo-colonialism.

.188   **The Journey of Fabio Pacchioni.** 1966 27 min color film. Available in English and Spanish. United Nations. Free

An Italian theatre director, Fabio Pacchioni, is sent by UNESCO to establish a national theatre company in Ecuador. Believing that the theatre plays an important role in improving the quality of life, Pacchioni finds and trains his actors and brings their efforts to bear on the problems of poverty and isolation surrounding them. Though filmed and set in Ecuador this film is a beautiful illustration of the awakening of a consciousness of oppression in peoples wherever they may be.

.189   **New England and the Global Economy.** 1979 20 min color slideshow with script. AFSC (Cambridge). Rental $15

This AFSC slideshow illustrates how our lives are linked to those of people in the Third World. It explores the social and economic trends that are rapidly changing the quality of life in New England, e.g., the loss of industry and jobs and the demise of the family farm, and it explains related trends in much of the Third World. The slideshow closes with recommendations about how each of us can become involved in bringing peace to our troubled planet.

.190   **New International Economic Order.** 1978 20 min color slideshow with script. AFSC (Cambridge). Rental $15

This slideshow takes a look at the structures of global injustice that lead to poverty, unemployment, over-population, hunger, crime, and the destruction of the environment. At the root of these problems—the show contends—is not limited resources, but the maldistribution and abuse of resources. *New International Economic Order* then examines the plans being put forth by the United Nations and the developing countries as a solution to these international problems.

.191   **People: A Matter of Balance.** 1979 28 min color film. Available in Arabic, English, French, and Spanish. United Nations. Free

Based on filming done by Roberto Rossellini shortly before his death, this Vision Habitat film describes the global inequalities between rich and poor countries in terms of distortion and imbalance, pointing out that science teaches us that no system can survive without achieving equilibrium—a balanced relationship between parts. With major sequences filmed in the Amazon and Africa, *People* illustrates how development in one area is too often gained at the cost of underdevelopment in another.

1.192   *Sharing Global Resources: Toward a New Economic Order.* 1977 35 min color slideshow with cassette tape. AFSC (Cambridge). Rental $15

A factual, non-rhetorical action tool to stimulate thinking and discussion about the complicated issues of the world economic order, the distribution of the world's resources, and the problems involved in the development of political and economic systems capable of meeting the crying needs of Third World peoples. *Sharing Global Resources* illustrates what "development" by multinational corporations has meant for the poor countries.

1.193   *Toward a Human World Order.* 1982 4 color filmstrips with cassettes, study guides, and illustrated reading scripts. Gerald and Patricia Mische. Produced by Franciscan Communications Center. Available from Global Education Associates. Sale $121 (includes a copy of the book *Toward a Human World Order*).

Authors Gerald and Patricia Mische have condensed the social analysis and historical perspective presented in their book, *Toward a Human World Order*, into four filmstrips. The filmstrip titles are: (1) The Whole Earth Community: A Crisis of Growth; (2) The National Security Straitjacket; (3) World Order Alternatives; and (4) Strategies for World Order.

1.194   *Who Invited Us?* 1971 59 min b&w film. Produced by Alan Levin for National Educational Television. Available through the film services of both Indiana University and the University of California (Berkeley). Rental $60

This hard-hitting NET documentary traces U.S. military interventions from the takeover of the Philippines at the end of the last century to the war in Vietnam. Motives are examined, including the economic needs of American corporations. The role of the CIA in Chile and other areas of the Third World is also scrutinized.

OTHER RESOURCES

Directories

195   Alternative Press Syndicate. *Advertising & Membership Directory: Alternative Press Syndicate 1982-3.* 22pp. $5 plus postage.

Listings for nearly 200 alternative publications from around the world include address, editorial description, circulation, and subscription and advertising data for each entry.

196   Fenton, Thomas P., ed. *Education for Justice: A Resource Manual.* Maryknoll, N.Y.: Orbis Books, 1975. 464pp. $7.95.

This sourcebook contains an introduction to the various approaches to education for justice; a set of background readings; twenty-one field-tested experiential educational exercises; guidelines for formulating a course of studies; and an extensive, annotated listing of additional resources.

197   *Global Perspectives in Education: Organization Resource Directory* and *Global Perspectives in Education: Consultant Resource Directory.* Both directories are available from Global Perspectives in Education.

198   Graff, Sandra. *Global Education Resource Guide.* East Orange, N.J.: Global Education Associates, 1981. 70pp. $4. Bulk rates available.

A useful tool for educators, this guide contains an annotated listing of books, audiovisual materials, teaching aids, and other action resources on global issues.

199   Jane Addams Peace Association. *Education for a Global Society: A Resource Manual for Secondary Education Teachers.* Philadelphia, Pa.: Women's International League for Peace and Freedom. 53pp. Available only in microfiche from ERIC Document Reproduction Service for $1.

Designed for secondary school teachers, this guide catalogs over four hundred books, articles, and other resource materials related to global education. Materials are organized into four major sections: peace, economic equity, social justice, and ecological balance.

Education for a Global Society also includes lists of forty related resource manuals and bibliographies, sixty-seven periodicals that provide information on education for global interdependence, and over one hundred agencies involved in concerns of peace and justice.

200   Kennedy, James R., Jr., et al. *Guide to Reference Sources on Africa, Asia, Latin America and the Caribbean, Middle East and North Africa, and Russia and East Europe: Selected and Annotated.* Williamsport, Pa.: Bro-Dart Inc., 1972. 90pp. $8.95

This bibliography was prepared under the auspices of the National Council of Associations for International Studies of the New York State Education Department with the needs of college students and college librarians in mind. Entries include encyclopedias, handbooks, yearbooks, important books and articles, and specialized studies. Much of the material is arranged under disciplines generally taught in the liberal arts curriculum.

1.201   Project Upward Bound, Northwestern University. *The Bibliographic Index of U.S. Resources on Third World Movements: 1950-Present.* 1982 in progress.

The Research Team of Northwestern University's Project Upward Bound is compiling this list of resource materials on selected Third World leaders and political movements. It is intended for educators involved with junior high and high school students.

1.202   Task Force on Alternatives in Print, Social Responsibilities Round Table, American Library Association. *Alternatives in Print: An International Catalog of Books, Pamphlets, Periodicals and Audiovisual Materials.* 6th ed. New York: Neal-Schuman Publishers, 1980. 668pp. Title, Subject, Author, and Geographical Indices.

This comprehensive guide covers organizations that are alternative in nature—whether they be political, cultural, or literary. Information given includes the name and address of the organization and (unannotated) citations—with author, title, price—of books, periodicals, and audiovisuals published by the organization. *Alternatives in Print* encompasses both U.S. and international organizations.

1.203   U.S. Department of Education. *International Education Resources: Cumulative Second Edition, 1956-77.* Washington, D.C.: U.S. Government Printing Office, 1980. 245pp. $7.95

This directory presents a summary of research projects and reports funded by the former Office of Education, the National Institute of Education, and the Fund for the Improvement of Postsecondary Education. Materials are available either from the originating agency or—in "paper copy" or microfiche—from the Educational Research Information Center in Arlington, Virginia.

Areas covered include: Teaching and Learning About Other Countries (on the preschool level, the elementary through higher education levels, and the teacher training level), Crosscultural and Crossnational Aspects of Education, and Bibliographies and Directories of International Education Resources.

A complete description and full ordering information accompany each item. The directory also contains an index by country and region.

1.204   World Without War Council (Berkeley). *Americans & World Affairs: A Directory of Organizations & Institutions in Northern California.* 1981. 210pp. $5

Americans & World Affairs contains an alphabetical listing of organizations active in Northern California in world affairs. These range from the Center for World Business to the Friends of the Earth, and from Amnesty International to the California Council for International Trade. Eighty-five of these organizations are featured in two-page Organizational Profiles (with data given on their national offices).

The guide closes with a cross-referenced index and various appendices.

Curriculum Guides and Materials

205   Epstein, Irving, and Garvey, Helen. *World Education in the Classroom: A Video-Tape and Leader's Handbook for In-service Programs.* Program I: Making a Commitment; Program II: Charting a Course. Leader's Handbook $7; video-tape rental (with permission to copy) $3. Available from the World Education Center.

Program I attempts to help educators come to an agreement on what world education will mean in their school or school district. It is designed to assist groups in identifying a curricular focus and specifying program objectives.

Program II invites participants to examine a range of approaches to world education.

These in-service workshops can be used by an entire school faculty, departments within a school, or by groups of teachers who want to combine their talents and efforts.

206   *Friendship Global Outline Map.* New York: Friendship Press, n.d. 95 cents

This 35x24½-inch outline map of the world is unique—and accurate— in not placing the American continents at the center. Thus, it is a useful educational tool for Third World studies at all levels.

207   Kaiser, Ward L., ed. *People and Systems.* New York: Friendship Press/ IDOC/North America, 1975. $6.95

This unique educational resource is a series of four booklets that illustrate how four countries cope with five universal issues: education, health care, religion, work, and the role and status of women. By looking at the way in which these very different societies approach similar problems the series hopes to provide fresh perspectives and potential solutions for our problems.

Booklets may be purchased separately, though they are more effectively used as a set.

China: People-Questions. 32pp. $1.75
Cuba: People-Questions. 32pp. $1.75
Tanzania: People-Questions. 32pp. $1.75
United States: People-Questions. 16pp. $1.25
Leader's Guide on People and Systems. 12pp. $1

208   National Association of Independent Schools. *Internationalize Your School: A Handbook.* 1977. 37pp. Available only in microfiche from ERIC Document Reproduction Service for $1.

Directed to administrators, teachers, and students, this handbook aims to facilitate the internationalization of curricula on the elementary and secondary school levels. The philosophy and methodology of global studies is discussed and educational frameworks are provided for five subject areas: the historical dimension of global studies; planetary environment; futuristics; conflict resolution; and global population and resources.

The handbook concludes with a directory of forty-three organizations that sponsor programs and publish curriculum materials with a global focus.

1.209 Overly, Norman V., and Kimpston, Richard D., eds. *Global Studies: Problems and Promises for Elementary Teachers.* 1976. 82pp. $4.50. Available only in microfiche from ERIC Document Reproduction Service for $1.

Intended for use by classroom teachers and supervisors, this guide identifies rationale, content, and materials for teaching about world problems on the elementary school level.

The four chapters in this publication are entitled: (1) A Perspective on Global Studies; (2) An Approach to Global Studies: Balancing Problems and Promises; (3) Who's In Charge—How to Proceed; (4) Resources for Teachers. This final chapter includes background materials on the food crisis, resource shortages, environmental pollution, income disparity and poverty, and war, conflict, and nuclear proliferation.

1.210 Spurgin, John H., and Smith, Gary R. *Global Dimensions in the New Social Studies.* Boulder, Colo: Social Science Education Consortium, 1973. 160pp. $4.75. Pub. No. 165.

The aim of this survey is to provide a handy, practical tool for teachers and curriculum supervisors to select new materials—with a global dimension—that are appropriate for integration into the existing curriculum. Fourteen projects are analyzed and indexed by subject, director, source, publisher, and grade level; twenty-two simulation games and eight global education projects and organizations are annotated.

The authors' introduction and a concluding bibliography present a survey of global/international education on the secondary school level from the early 1960s to the date of publication.

1.211 Switzer, Kenneth, and Mulloy, Paul T. *Global Issues: Activities and Resources for the High School Teacher.* Denver: University of Denver, Center for Teaching International Relations, 1979. $7.95

This introduction to teaching about contemporary global concerns in the high school social studies classroom contains background material and lesson plans for seven units, as well as thirty-nine reproducible student handouts.

1.212 Urso, Ida. *Teacher's Resource Manual on Worldmindedness: An Annotated Bibliography of Curriculum Materials Kindergarten through Grade Twelve.* Occasional Paper No. 8. Los Angeles: Curriculum Inquiry Center, University of California, 1981. 132pp.

The compiler of this compendium of information chose to list materials, for the most part, not commercially produced, thus making more accessible publications within the "network," as she puts it. Resources in these categories are covered in the manual: "Farther Reaches of Human Nature"; Global Education and Futuristics; Interdependence and Global Problems; Peace; and General and Miscellaneous. A set of appendices lists: Bibliographies/Directories/Guides; Periodicals; Resource Centers; Opportunities for Active Student Participation/Action-Learning Careers; Addresses of Publishers and Distributors; and Evaluation.

Simulation Games

213   Belch, Jean. *Contemporary Games*. Detroit: Gale Research Co., 1973–74. Vol. 1: 560pp. Vol. 2: 408pp.

As with many other library reference works published by Gale these two volumes are exhaustive annotated listings of simulation games and the literature surrounding them.

Volume 1 contains over 900 listings (current up to 1972) with: brief annotations; bibliographical and cross references; a guide to seventy-four subject areas; age and grade level indicators; and an index of developers/producers of simulations.

Volume 2 is a bibliography with over two thousand entries divided into seven categories: General Information on Educational Gaming; Games in the Classroom; Business Games and Management Simulations; Conflict Resolution; Land Use and Resource Allocation; Research Employing or Evaluating Games; Directories; Bibliographies, and Lists. This volume includes items from 1957 through 1973.

214   Lamy, Steven L., et al. *Teaching Global Awareness with Simulations and Games*. Denver: University of Denver, Center for Teaching International Relations, 1981. $14.95

Designed to be used with grades 6 through 12, this handbook contains activities on World Trade; Constitutional Convention; and Creating World Maps.

215   Stadsklev, Ron. *Handbook of Simulation Gaming in Social Education*. **Part 2: Directory for Non Computer Material**. 2d ed. University, Ala.: University of Alabama, Institute of Higher Education Research and Services, 1979. 380pp. $18. Various indices.

This handbook is the most comprehensive guide available to simulation games. Though much of the gaming material roams far wide of our concern with the United States and the Third World, Stadsklev's work is still worth knowing about and having access to for your educational programming.

The handbook contains narrative descriptions of all materials and a unique 28-page cross reference matrix that gives the name of the game, the subject area, grade level, cost, and availability. Other features are: a source index, a directory of action centers, annotated listings of current research, a free referral service, and an update service.

Accompanying this volume is a *Handbook of Simulation Gaming in Social Education. Part 1: Textbook*, also by Ron Stadsklev. 167pp. $6

216   Zuckerman, David W., and Horn, Robert E. *The Guide to Simulations/Games for Education and Training*. With a "Basic Reference Shelf on Simulation and Gaming" by Paul A. Twelker and Kent Layden. 2d ed. Lexington, Mass.: Information Resources, 1973. 501pp. $15

This enormous guide contains complete information on 613 games and simulations in areas such as ecology, economics, geography, international relations, social studies, and sociology. Other areas not germane to our focus in this directory include business finance, general science, language skills, and the like.

The following categories are used in the description of each game:
- playing data (age level; number of players; playing time; preparation time)
- materials (components; special equipment)
- comments
- summary description (roles; objectives; decisions; purposes)
- cost
- producer (name and address).

The Guide to Simulations/Games also contains articles about simulations/games, including a "basic reference shelf on simulation and gaming," and various indices.

Listed below are ten simulation games that deal with the dynamics of the use/abuse of power, the resolution of international conflicts, economic development, oppression, social and revolutionary change. They are included in this Third World chapter because they are general in nature and not specific to any one country or region.

Because of the length of this list only the essential data are given for each simulation. Most of the simulations are inexpensive and could easily be purchased for review. Full descriptive information is available from each of the publishers.

1.217   *The ABZ Games.* Defiance, Ohio: Defiance College, Dept. of Social Systems, 1977. $1. Level: secondary school and above. Players: 20 or more. Time: extended.

1.218   *Access.* Del Mar, Calif.: Simile II, 1978. $5. Level: secondary school and above. Players: 8 or more. Time: 2–3 hours.

1.219   *Afaslapol.* Rev. ed. Indiana, Pa.: Indiana University of Pennsylvania, Education Consortium, 1975. $4. Level: senior high and above. Players: 10–30. Time: 5–12 hours.

1.220   *Catalyzer.* Cincinnati, Ohio: Friendship Press, 1973. $1.95. Level: junior high and above. Players: 16–28. Time: 2–4 hours.

1.221   *Class Struggle.* New York: Class Struggle, 1978. $9.95. Level: junior high and above. Players: 2–6. Time:1–3 hours.

1.222   *Crisis.* Del Mar, Calif.: Simile II, 1966. $30. Level: junior high and above. Players: 35. Time: 2–6 hours.

1.223   *Island.* Cincinnati, Ohio: Friendship Press, 1974. $10. Level: junior high and above. Players:13–24. Time: 3–6 hours.

1.224   *Powderhorn.* Del Mar, Calif.: Simile II, 1971. $15. Level: upper primary and junior high. Players: 18–35. Time: 2–3 hours.

1.225   *The Power Game.* Detroit, Mich.: Pact, Community Services Department, Wayne County Community College, 1973. $1. Level: junior high and above. Players: 12 or more. Time: 2–3 hours.

226   *Revolutionary Society.* Indiana, Pa.: Indiana University of Pennsylvania, Education Consortium, 1975. $4. (Contained in the same booklet with *Afaslapol*—see above.) Level: senior high and above. Players: 7–35. Time: 4–6 hours.

227   *Starpower.* Del Mar, Calif.: Simile II, 1969. $30. Level: junior high and above. Players: 24–45. Time: 3 or more hours.

Chapter 2

Africa

KEY RESOURCES

Organizations

The **American Committee on Africa** on the East Coast and the **Africa Resource Center** on the West Coast are the two organizations that will serve as your best overall sources for information. Both centers distribute literature, maintain a speaker's bureau, and keep current with who's doing what on African issues.

Local chapters of both the **American Friends Service Committee** and **Clergy and Laity Concerned** could be contacted for news of regional interest in and actions related to Africa. If you're concerned about banks in your area and their involvement in loans to South Africa, contact the **Campaign to Oppose Bank Loans to South Africa** for the name of a local affiliate.

The **Washington Office on Africa** brings a foreign policy and legislative focus to African issues, while the **Interfaith Center on Corporate Responsibility** has long concerned itself with the churches and corporate responsibility in southern Africa.

Printed Resources

Kevin Danaher's annotated bibliography, *South Africa and the United States,* will give you a feel for the breadth of approaches to this issue and for the wealth of resources at your disposal. Seidman's study, *South Africa and U.S. Multinational Corporations,* is a readable analysis of the political and economic impact of U.S. corporate investments in South Africa— and, by extension, in other areas of the Third World. In *How Europe Underdeveloped Africa,* Walter Rodney describes the ways in which the development of Europe and the underdevelopment of Africa were and are linked.

For up-to-date news of Africa in a digestible and attractive format there is no better source than the weekly, *Africa News.*

The best single source for literature on Africa—southern Africa especially—is the **American Committee on Africa**'s "Southern Africa Literature List." The 100-item list covers the full range of printed resource materials from books to one-page fact sheets.

Two excellent introductory resources are: the **Africa Fund**'s *Southern Africa Information Packet* and the **American Friends Service Committee**'s *Southern Africa Must Be Free: Resources for Education and Action.*

Audiovisual Resources

The **Southern Africa Media Center (California Newsreel)** and the **Africa Fund** jointly produced "Investing in Apartheid," a handbook containing questionnaires, simulation games, checklists, a discussion guide, background readings, and a resource guide, as well as the films *Generations of Resistance, Last Grave at Dimbaza, Free Namibia!* and *Six Days in Soweto* (described below).

The **Africa Fund** publishes a "Southern Africa Film List" on a periodic basis. This list, along with the film catalog from the **Southern Africa Media Center**, should be consulted for a fuller listing and description of audiovisuals on Africa and related issues.

Last Grave at Dimbaza and *Generations of Resistance* are significant introductory films to apartheid and resistance to the white minority regime in South Africa. *A Luta Continua* and *O Povo Organizado* deal with the liberation of Mozambique from the Portuguese.

All of the slideshows listed below are exceptional resources in that they are more current than commercial films and they are more focused on aspects of U.S. involvement in southern Africa. As with most resources on Africa, however, these deal predominantly with southern Africa, not with the United States and the continent as a whole.

ORGANIZATIONS

2.1 **Africa Research and Publications Project**, Box 1892, Trenton, NJ 08608.
FOCUS: Africa • international. Human rights • foreign trade and aid • political economy • national liberation struggles • corporate responsibility.
ACTIVITIES: Popular education • research and writing • intern programs • library services • documentation and information • policy-oriented research and writing • workshops and seminars.
RESOURCES: Speakers • clearinghouse for African movement literature • publications • study-action guides • consultant services • research services • library • reports.
PERIODICALS: **2.2** *Forward*. Quarterly. $8/year. **2.3** *Direction*. Quarterly. $8/year.

2.4 **Africa Resource Center**, 464 19 St., Oakland, CA 94612. Tel: 415-763-8011; 415-763-9998.
FOCUS: Africa • southern Africa. Human rights • political repression • militarism • nuclear arms and energy • foreign trade and aid • political economy • international awareness • corporate responsibility • social justice • national liberation struggles.
ACTIVITIES: Popular education • constituency education • political action • legislative action • research and writing • congressional testimony • solidarity work • intern programs • library services • networking • media • overseas project support • documentation and information • justice and peace ministries • workshops and seminars • investment alternatives.
RESOURCES: Library • literature • speakers • research services • audiovisuals • publications • study-action guides • consultant services • reports.
PERIODICALS: **2.5** Membership *Newsletter*. Occasional. $5/year.
SPECIAL PROJECTS: Labor Project: developing materials for use by trade unionists. Divestment of pension funds. Fostering relations between trade unions in South Africa and the United States.

2.6 **African Bibliographic Center**, 1346 Connecticut Ave., NW, Washington, DC 20036. Tel: 202-223-1392.
FOCUS: Africa. Political economy • national liberation struggles • current affairs in Africa.
ACTIVITIES: Research and writing • intern programs • foreign service • networking • media • documentation and information • writing.
RESOURCES: Research services • library • reports • news service.
SPECIAL PROJECTS: HABARI, a telephone information and news service on African affairs. Call 202-659-2529 for free report.

2.7 **American Committee on Africa** and **The Africa Fund**, 198 Broadway, New York, NY 10038. Tel: 212-962-1210.
FOCUS: Africa and southern Africa. U.S. policy vis-à-vis Africa • corporate responsibility • national liberation struggles.
ACTIVITIES: Popular education • constituency education • political action •

legislative action • research and writing • congressional testimony • solidarity work • intern programs • documentation and information • policy-oriented research and writing.

RESOURCES: Publications • research services • speakers • literature.

PERIODICALS: **2.8** *ACOA Action News.* 2 issues/year. With $15 annual membership. **2.9** *The Africa Fund's Perspectives* series. 4–6 issues/year. **2.10** *ACOA Action Mailings.*

.11 **American Friends Service Committee**, Southern Africa Program, 1501 Cherry St., Philadelphia, PA 19102. Tel: 215-241-7169.

RELIGIOUS AFFILIATION: Religious Society of Friends (Quakers).

FOCUS: Southern Africa. Social justice • human rights • political repression • national liberation struggles.

ACTIVITIES: Networking (through regional offices) • popular education • support work.

RESOURCES: Distribution of audiovisuals and literature • speakers • reports • publications.

.12 **Amnesty International**, South Africa Coordination Group, 9007 Garland Ave., Silver Spring, MD 20901.

FOCUS: South Africa. Human rights.

ACTIVITIES: Popular education and action • networking (through regional offices) • documentation.

RESOURCES: Speakers • literature • publications • reports.

.13 **Campaign to Oppose Bank Loans to South Africa**, 1901 Que St., NW, Washington, DC 20009. Tel: 202-234-9382.

FOCUS: South Africa • Namibia. Human rights • foreign trade and aid • political economy • corporate responsibility.

ACTIVITIES: Popular education • constituency education • legislative action • testimony at city and state hearings • networking • documentation and information • policy-oriented research and writing • workshops and seminars.

RESOURCES: Speakers • literature • study-action guides • research services.

PERIODICALS: **2.14** *COBSLA News.* 4–5 issues/year. Contribution, $10/year requested.

SPECIAL PROJECTS: National Day of Action on the Banks.

.15 **Clergy and Laity Concerned**, 198 Broadway, Rm. 302, New York, NY 10038. Tel: 212-964-6730.

FOCUS: South Africa. Human rights • political repression • international awareness • corporate responsibility.

ACTIVITIES: Popular education and action • networking (through regional chapters) • workshops.

RESOURCES: Distribution of literature • speakers.

PERIODICALS: **2.16** *CALC Report.* $15/year. Apply for other rates.

.17 **Episcopal Churchmen for South Africa**, 853 Broadway, Rm. 1005, New York, NY 10003. Tel: 212-477-0066.

FOCUS: South Africa • Namibia. Human rights • political repression • corporate responsibility • national liberation struggles • international awareness • Christian ministry.

ACTIVITIES: Church constituency education and action • networking • lobbying • congressional testimony • support work.

PERIODICALS: **2.18** *For a Free Southern Africa.* Donation requested.

2.19   Interfaith Center on Corporate Responsibility, 475 Riverside Dr., Rm. 566, New York, NY 10115. Tel: 212-870-2200.

FOCUS: South Africa. Human rights • corporate responsibility.

ACTIVITIES: Constituency education and action • stockholder actions • research • documentation.

RESOURCES: Research services • consultant services • audiovisuals • publications.

PERIODICALS: **2.20** *Corporate Examiner* (includes *CIC Brief*). Monthly. $25/year.

2.21   International Defense and Aid Fund for Southern Africa, Box 17, Cambridge, MA 02138. Tel: 617-495-4940.

FOCUS: International • southern Africa. Human rights • political repression • international awareness • national liberation struggles.

ACTIVITIES: Solidarity work • foreign service (relief) • popular education.

RESOURCES: Speakers • audiovisuals • publications • bookstore.

PERIODICALS: **2.22** *Focus.* Bimonthly. $10/year.

SPECIAL PROJECTS: The Women's Committee has speakers and publications pertinent to women in southern Africa, and it networks among women in the United States for the support and assistance of black women in southern Africa.

2.23   National Council of Churches, African Office, 475 Riverside Dr., Rm. 612, New York, NY 10115. Tel: 212-870-2645.

FOCUS: Africa. Human rights • political repression • Christian ministry.

ACTIVITIES: Church constituency education.

RESOURCES: Audiovisuals • publications.

2.24 $top Banking on Apartheid, 464 19 St., Oakland, CA 94612. Tel: 415-763-8011; 415-763-9998.

FOCUS: Africa • southern Africa. Human rights • nuclear arms and energy • transnational corporations • corporate responsibility • foreign trade and aid • political economy.

ACTIVITIES: Popular education • intern programs • press service • networking • documentation and information • special programs on religion and labor links.

2.25   TransAfrica, 545 Eighth St., SE, Suite 200, Washington, DC 20003. Tel: 202-547-2550.

FOCUS: Africa • Caribbean. Human rights • political repression • foreign trade and aid • U.S. foreign policy • national liberation struggles • economic development • refugees and immigrants.

ACTIVITIES: Constituency education • political action • legislative action • research and writing • congressional testimony • networking • media • policy-oriented research and writing • conferences • letter-writing campaigns • foreign policy lobby for black Americans.

RESOURCES: Speakers • publications • consultant services • reports.

PERIODICALS: **2.26** *TransAfrica News Report.* Quarterly. With $5 annual membership. **2.27** *Issue Briefs.* Monthly. **2.28** *TransAfrica Forum.* Quarterly. 80-page journal. $15/year for both the *Briefs* and the *Forum*.

.29 United Nations Centre Against Apartheid, UN Secretariat, Rm. 2775, New York, NY 10017.

FOCUS: South Africa. Human rights • political repression.

ACTIVITIES: Popular education • research • documentation.

RESOURCES: Publications • reports.

PERIODICALS: **2.30** *Notes and Documents.* Inquire for rates.

.31 U.S. Catholic Conference, Africa Desk, Office of International Justice and Peace, 1312 Massachusetts Ave., NW, Washington, DC 20005. Tel: 202-659-6812.

FOCUS: Africa. Human rights • political repression.

ACTIVITIES: Church constituency education • research • documentation.

RESOURCES: Publications.

.32 Washington Office on Africa, 110 Maryland Ave., NE, Washington, DC 20002. Tel: 202-546-7961.

FOCUS: Africa. Human rights • political repression • nuclear arms and energy • foreign trade and aid • national liberation struggles • U.S. foreign policy toward southern Africa.

ACTIVITIES: Popular education • constituency education • political action • legislative action • research and writing • congressional testimony • solidarity work • intern programs.

RESOURCES: Speakers • distributor of literature • publications • study-action guides.

PERIODICALS: **2.33** *Washington Notes on Africa.* Quarterly. $1/year.

PRINTED RESOURCES

Books

2.34   American Friends Service Committee, in cooperation with the African Studies Program, Indiana University. *South Africa: Challenge and Hope*. Philadelphia: AFSC, 1982. $4.95

This AFSC publication offers an analysis of the situation in South Africa along with proposals for action based on nonviolent philosophies and strategies.

2.35   Carter, Gwendolen M., and O'Meara, Patrick, eds. *Southern Africa: The Continuing Crisis*. Bloomington, Ind.: Indiana University Press, 1979. 404pp. Bibliography, maps, tables. $7.95

After an introductory chapter on international rivalries in the southern Africa region, this book devotes a chapter each to the nine nations of southern Africa: Zimbabwe, Mozambique, South Africa, Namibia, Angola, Zambia, Botswana, Lesotho, and Swaziland. Two items make this book particularly useful for readers new to the issues: (1) a 50-page chapter on U.S. policy toward South Africa from the Truman administration through former President Carter's, and (2) a compilation of source materials on southern Africa that includes basic reference works, periodicals, newspapers, and titles for further reading.

2.36   Corporate Data Exchange. *Bank Loans to South Africa, 1972–1978*. New York: UN Centre Against Apartheid, May 1979. 114pp. Inquire about current price from Corporate Data Exchange and Africa Resource Center.

Bank Loans to South Africa documents for the first time the extent of loans to South Africa from foreign commercial banks.

2.37   Danaher, Kevin. *South Africa and the United States: An Annotated Bibliography*. Washington, D.C.: Institute for Policy Studies, 1979. 26pp.

Danaher provides paragraph-length reviews of over 200 books, articles, and pamphlets on U.S. political and economic involvement in Africa—southern Africa in particular. Each item is numbered and classified in a comprehensive index under headings such as Corporate Involvement, Liberation Movements, Nuclear, and U.S. Government Policy. *South Africa and the United States* closes with a two-page annotated list of organizations, periodicals, and official representatives of African liberation movements.

2.38   El-Khawas, Mohamed A., and Cohen, Barry, eds. *The Kissinger Study of Southern Africa: The National Security Study Memorandum 39 (Secret)*. Westport, Conn.: Lawrence Hill, 1976. 189pp. Tables. $3.95

NSSM 39 outlines the foreign policy stance of the Nixon administration toward southern Africa. The 1969 study predicts that "the whites are here to stay" and recommends that Washington forge closer ties with the white minority regimes in southern Africa.

39   Foreign Policy Study Foundation. *South Africa: Time Running Out*. Berkeley
and Los Angeles: University of California Press, 1981. 517pp. $8.95

The Study Commission of U.S. Policy Toward Southern Africa, formed in
1979, produced this work in an effort to answer questions about America's de-
pendence on South Africa's strategic minerals, apartheid, and the significance of
south Africa in the balance of power. Basically, the work speaks to the question
of U.S. interests in South Africa and what policies and objectives need to be
pursued in order to safeguard them.

40   Friedman, Julian R. *Basic Facts on the Republic of South Africa and the Policy
of Apartheid*. New York: United Nations Centre Against Apartheid, 1977. 88pp.
Tables. $6

Descriptions of apartheid and its effects on the people of South Africa. Covers
education, political system, Bantustans, economy, foreign investment, military,
and other issues.

41   Gutkind, Peter, and Waterman, Peter, eds. *African Social Studies: A Radical
Reader*. New York: Monthly Review, 1977. 481pp. Bibliography. $6.95

This collection is more theoretical and Marxist-oriented than other titles in this
bibliography. As such it makes heavy reading for those new to the subject. Never-
theless, the *Reader* is an excellent resource for a number of reasons: it is a unique
collection of the writings of radical scholars and activists—many of them
Africans—including Samir Amin, Amilcar Cabral, and Issa Shivji; it covers
Africa north of the Sahara in greater depth than other books listed here; and it
contains a very useful bibliographical guide to works on Africa in English and
French.

42   Hecathorn, Miloanne; Johnson, Karen; and Ragent, Samuel, eds. *Our Town
Out of South Africa: A Key to Gaining Community Control of Public Funds*.
Oakland, Calif.: Africa Resources Center, 1982. 125pp. $10

Voters in Berkeley, California, have passed the first law requiring a major
American city to withdraw its public monies from banks doing business with
South Africa. This manual provides readers with examples of campaign literature, flyers, press releases, alternative investment ideas and other materials helpful in duplicating Berkeley's success in towns across America.

43   Hope, Marjorie, and Young, James. *The South African Churches in a Revolutionary Situation*. Maryknoll, N.Y.: Orbis Books, 1981. 268pp. $9.95

On one level this book is a historical and critical examination of the role of
Christian churches in South Africa—churches that "have not lived up to the
challenge of practicing the essential message of the gospel." On another level the
authors have written a readable and moving personal account of "the lives and
hopes of individuals immersed in the struggle" in South Africa.

44   Litvak, Lawrence; DeGrasse, Robert; and McTigue, Kathleen. *South Africa:
Foreign Investment and Apartheid*. Washington, D.C.: Institute for Policy
Studies, 1978. 100pp. Appendices. $4.95

This informed and readable study of foreign investment in South Africa challenges the assertion that U.S. involvement in that nation benefits black South Africans by liberalizing apartheid. The authors contend that American investments in any form constitute support for the oppressive regime in power. Total economic and political disengagement is the only appropriate course, in the minds of the authors.

2.45   Morel, E. D. *The Black Man's Burden: The White Man in Africa from the Fifteenth Century to World War I*. New York: Monthly Review, 1969. First published in Great Britain in 1920. 241pp. $4.50

Monthly Review's republication of this classic by one of this century's foremost authorities on Africa makes available to the general reader a compact and authoritative history of the white man's invasion of black Africa. Morel reviews the history of each area of Africa describing the ways by which Africans were exterminated, enslaved, and exploited in the 500 years before World War I.

2.46   Myers III, Desaix, with Kenneth Propp, David Hauck and David M. Liff. *U.S. Business in South Africa: The Economic, Political, and Moral Issues*. Bloomington, Ind.: Indiana University Press, 1980. 375pp. $22.50

This book is a useful reference for those engaged in corporate responsibility campaigns with a focus on U.S. investments in and bank loans to South Africa. It offers a history of apartheid and of foreign business involvement in South Africa with an eye toward the issues raised by the influence of each on the other. Appendices in the book contain the investment policies of colleges and universities in the United States, along with a record of sales of stocks by U.S. academic institutions in protest against U.S. investments in South Africa.

2.47   NARMIC. *Automating Apartheid: U.S. Computer Exports to South Africa and the Arms Embargo*. Philadelphia: NARMIC, 1981. 107pp. $3.50. Bulk rates available.

This booklet by AFSC's National Action/Research on the Military Industrial Complex presents an in-depth look at how the export of U.S. computers, electronic, and communications equipment aids repression in South Africa. Tables list not only the names of U.S. computer and electronics companies doing business with and in South Africa, but also particular installations for and sales to the South African government and State-owned corporations. Other related resources are listed at the end of this small but substantial work.

2.48   Nkrumah, Kwame. *Neo-Colonialism: The Last Stage of Imperialism*. New York: International Publishers, 1965. 280pp. Bibliography, charts, tables. $3.25

This classic study by the former president of Ghana is both an introduction to the dynamics of neo-colonialism (economic bondage without political ties) and a clearly presented history of foreign political and economic activity in Africa. Dr. Nkrumah lays bare the skeletal system of international finance and ownership "by which the world monopoly groups assure their exploitation of African labor and resources."

2.49   Rodney, Walter. *How Europe Underdeveloped Africa*. Washington, D.C.: Howard University Press, 1974. 288pp. $4.95

Walter Rodney's analysis of the ways in which the development of Europe depended on the underdevelopment of colonial territories in Africa is now a classic. Rodney's historical approach and radical analysis is an eye-opener for those who know the African continent only through high school textbooks.

.50   Schmidt, Elizabeth. *Decoding Corporate Camouflage: U.S. Business Support for Apartheid*. Washington, D.C.: Institute for Policy Studies, 1980. 127pp. $4.95

A thorough study of the economic roots of apartheid, the Sullivan Principles, and the strategic role of the signatories of the Principles in the motor vehicle, computer, military, and energy sectors of South Africa's economy.

.51   Seidman, Ann, and Makgetla, Neva S. *Outposts of Monopoly Capitalism: Southern Africa in the Changing Global Economy*. Westport, Conn.: Lawrence Hill, 1980. 370pp. $8.95

Outposts is a sequel to the Seidman work listed below. It seeks to place the theoretical issues raised in the earlier work in a global context by investigating the impact of multinational corporations from the United Kingdom, the Federal Republic of Germany, France, and Japan, as well as from the United States. Chapters are devoted to transnational agribusiness, the industrial core, the oil majors, and transnational finance capital.

.52   Seidman, Ann, and Seidman, Neva. *South Africa and U.S. Multinational Corporations*. Westport, Conn.: Lawrence Hill, 1978. 251pp. Tables, charts, maps. $4.95

The authors describe the interrelationships between foreign corporations and South Africa's ruling white minority regime, specifically the vital role played by multinational corporations in strategic sectors of the South African economy.

.53   Smith, Stuart. *U.S. Neocolonialism in Africa*. New York, N.Y.: International Publishers, 1974. 270pp. $2.95

Though dated and somewhat rhetorical, *U.S. Neocolonialism in Africa* is still a significant analysis of the full range of U.S. involvement in all of the areas of the African continent. "Smith" (actually political analyst Stuart J. Seborer) gives us some appreciation of the historical development and the deep roots of present-day U.S. policies.

.54   Turner, Richard. *The Eye of the Needle: Toward Participatory Democracy in South Africa*. Maryknoll, N.Y.: Orbis Books, 1978. 197pp. $5.95

Richard Turner, a South African political scientist, was banned in 1973 and assassinated in 1978. In this book he attacks apartheid as a prop and product of capitalist development. He examines capitalism in South Africa in the light of both Christian morality and Marxist analytic categories. The book was reissued as a memorial to the author.

.55   Western Massachusetts Association of Concerned African Scholars, eds. *U.S. Military Involvement in Southern Africa*. Boston: South End Press, 1978. 262pp. Bibliography. $5

This book discusses the policies and practices of the U.S. government and U.S.-based transnational corporations within the overall Western strategy of economic and military support for white minority rule in southern Africa. Articles in the book treat such issues as the Rapid Deployment Force that the U.S. military is basing in the Indian Ocean, the transfer of U.S. nuclear technology to South Africa, and the role of the CIA in covert operations in southern Africa.

See also:
6.37, 7.27, 7.31, 7.32, 7.37, 7.39, 10.31, 10.35, 10.45, 10.46

Periodicals

2.56   *Africa News*, Box 3851, Durham, NC 27702. Weekly 12-page newsletter. $25/ year.

Offers the most up-to-date and complete coverage of African affairs, with attention paid to U.S. involvement in the political economy of Africa.

2.57   *Africa Today*, c/o Graduate School of International Studies, University of Denver, Denver, CO 80208. Quarterly magazine. $10/year.

This highly respected periodical has covered Africa for over a quarter of a century. *Africa Today* has included the writings of Julius Nyerere, Kwame Nkrumah, Amilcar Cabral, Alan Paton, and Martin Luther King, Jr.

2.58   *Focus*, c/o International Defense and Aid Fund for Southern Africa, Box 17, Cambridge, MA 02738. Bimonthly. $10/year. Back issues available.

Focus provides comprehensive coverage of the issue of political repression in South Africa and Namibia. Topics include political trials, bannings, detentions, treatment of political prisoners, and military and security measures.

2.59   *The Guardian*, 33 W. 17 St., New York, NY 10011. Weekly newspaper. $23/ year.

The Guardian has exceptionally good coverage of African affairs from an independent radical perspective.

2.60   *MERIP Reports*, c/o Middle East Research and Information Project, 1470 Irving St., NW, Washington, DC 20010. Monthly magazine. $14/year.

This publication offers progressive analyses of developments in North Africa, particularly the Horn of Africa, Egypt, and Syria.

2.61   *Southern Africa*, 198 Broadway, New York, NY 10038. Monthly magazine. $10/year individual; $18/year institutional.

News, interviews, reviews, and lists of resource materials.

Pamphlets and Articles

2.62   *Action Guide on Southern Africa*. American Friends Service Committee (Philadelphia), rev. ed., 1977. 59pp. $1

Includes a list of local, regional, and national organizations active around southern Africa issues. Publications, films, educational tools, and other useful sources of information are suggested.

63   *Angola: The American-South African Connection.* Mohamed A. El-Khawas.
African Bibliographic Center, 1978. 15pp. $2.75

El-Khawas documents U.S. and South African attempts to prevent the Popular
Movement for the Liberation of Angola (MPLA) from coming to power in
Angola and to destabilize the governing MPLA regime.

.64   *Apartheid in Practice.* Leslie Rubin. Office of Public Information, United Nations, 1971. 70pp. $1.25

Some 300 statements set out in simple form the very complex apartheid laws of
South Africa. The statements are arranged by topic: Home, Work, Education,
Marriage, Ownership of Land.

.65   *The Banks Say—On South Africa.* Beate Klein. American Committee on
Africa and the Interfaith Center on Corporate Responsibility, 1978. 13pp. $1

Includes a short introduction followed by statements of several U.S. banks and
a few European banks on their loan policies to South Africa.

.66   *Black South Africa Explodes.* Transnational Institute, Institute for Policy
Studies, 1977. 63pp. $2

Chronicles the struggle in South Africa beginning with the June 16, 1976, student rebellion in Soweto. Includes bibliography and appendix listing arms and
suppliers.

.67   *Breaking the Links: The South African Economy and the U.S.* Southern
Africa, September 1979. 50 cents each for orders of 10 or more copies (orders
under 10 not accepted).

A reprint of a 20-page supplement to *Southern Africa* magazine.

.68   *Casting New Molds: First Steps toward Worker Control in a Mozambique
Steel Factory.* Peter Sketchley and Frances Moore Lappé. Institute for Food and
Development Policy, 1981. 60pp. Illustrations and resources. $2.95

Casting New Molds is a personal account of the day-to-day experiences of
Mozambican workers at CIFEL, a steel foundry and rolling mill, as they struggle
to continue desperately needed production after virtually all the Portuguese technical and managerial personnel had fled the country.

.69   *The Church and Southern Africa.* National Council of Churches, African Office, 1977. 80pp.

A report of a consultation convened by the National Council of Churches of
Christ in the United States and the United States Catholic Conference, March
7–11, 1977. Includes sections on Angola, Mozambique, Zimbabwe, Namibia,
and South Africa, and two pages of resources.

.70   *A Continent Besieged: Foreign Military Activities in Africa Since 1975.* Daniel
Volman. Institute for Policy Studies, 1980. 32pp. $2

A study of the growing military involvement of the United States and the Soviet
Union (and their allies) in Africa. The study challenges the usual exclusive focus
on Soviet and Cuban activities and suggests that the continuing escalation of
French and American involvement threatens to engulf the continent in armed
chaos and to bring the two superpowers into direct confrontation. The booklet

contains extensive data on African arms trade, the strength of African military forces, and the role of foreign military personnel.

2.71   *The Fight for Freedom in South Africa: And What it Means for Workers in the United States*. Boston Organizing Committee, 1980. 44pp. Bibliography, maps, graphics, photos. $2.50, postage included. Inquire for bulk rates.

A well-written analysis of the link between the struggle for political and economic democracy in the United States and support for the liberation of South Africa.

2.72   *Focus: Africa*. Fr. Rollins E. Lambert. U.S. Catholic Conference, Africa Desk, 1976. 8pp. Free

This series of four articles was written by the USCC's adviser for African Affairs for the National Catholic News Service. The articles examine life in South Africa, racial discrimination, Namibia, and Rhodesia.

2.73   *Investors in Apartheid: U.S. Firms with Subsidiaries in South Africa*. NARMIC, 1978. 6pp. 35 cents each plus postage. Bulk rates available.

This list is based on data compiled by the U.S. Department of Commerce and published in *Resource Development in South Africa and U.S. Policy* (U.S. House of Representatives, Committee on International Relations, hearings, 1976), and augmented by the names of a number of firms (obtained through the Freedom of Information Act) that listed South African subsidiaries in applying to the U.S. State Department for registration as munitions manufacturers and exporters.

2.74   *Militarism and Disarmament Reports: Africa*. Institute for Policy Studies, dates vary. Apply for rates.

A packet of current articles from the Militarism and Disarmament Project at IPS. The focus of one recent Africa packet was on arms sales to South Africa.

2.75   *Namibia in the 1980's*. Catholic Institute for International Relations and the British Council of Churches (London). 1981. 84pp. $2.25. Available from Oxfam-America.

Namibia in the 1980's presents an excellent background to the drive for independence in Namibia. The booklet examines the history of South Africa's role in the country, the attempts at diplomatic settlements, and the rise of SWAPO (the South West African People's Organization) and other political movements within Namibia.

2.76   *Nuclear Leaflet*. $top Banking on Apartheid, 1980. 2pp. $3/100.
Summary of U.S.-South Africa nuclear links.

2.77   *Nuclear South Africa: Background and Prospects*. John Lamperti. Reprinted by NARMIC, 1979. 16pp. Bibliography. 25 cents, plus postage. Bulk rates available.

2.78   *One Step—in the Wrong Direction: The Sullivan Principles as a Strategy for Opposing Apartheid*. Elizabeth Schmidt. *For a Free Southern Africa*, May 1982. 9pp.

Elizabeth Schmidt, a longtime student of Africa and apartheid, was instrumental in recent efforts to require the limiting of investments by Connecticut state officials in South Africa to businesses that have become signatories of the Sullivan Principles. The latter, drawn up in 1977, serves as a code of conduct that

American businesses are requested to observe in their dealings with black employ-ees in South Africa. *One Step* is a reprint of Ms. Schmidt's testimony before the Connecticut governor's task force in February 1982.

2.79 *Race Against Race: South Africa's "Multinational" Sport Fraud*. Joan Brick-hill. International Defense and Aid Fund for Southern Africa, 1976. 77pp. $1.60

This illustrated pamphlet examines the origins of "multinational" sports in South Africa and the white minority government's various attempts to cloak its policies of racial discrimination.

2.80 *Sahel Packet of Information*. Oxfam-America. 1981. $3.50

A packet of six articles on the Sahel region of West Africa. Nomads of the area are quoted talking about their way of life; development experts examine the ef-fects of colonialism and unsuccessful development projects in the region. The packet includes a bibliography and a poster.

2.81 *South Africa Information Packet*. The Africa Fund, 1979. $2

Articles on U.S. government and corporate policy, women workers, and the South African military.

2.82 *Southern Africa: A Select Guide to U.S. Organizational Interests*. Carolyn J. Goshen and Philip Musser. African Bibliographic Center, unpublished.

This reference work is an annotated list of over 300 church, business, and other organizations concerned with or operating in southern Africa. Well-indexed and cross-referenced.

2.83 *Southern Africa Literature List*. The Africa Fund, updated regularly. Free

A list of current literature consisting of about 100 items; covers southern Africa (general), South Africa, Zimbabwe, Namibia, Mozambique, Angola, and Guinea-Bissau.

2.84 *Southern Africa Must Be Free: Resources for Education and Action*. American Friends Service Committee (Philadelphia), 1977. 34pp. 50 cents. Bulk rates available.

Outlines major issues affecting southern Africa; describes U.S. policy, the case against investment; includes descriptions of actions and organizations of Afri-cans against governments and imperialism; lists U.S. organizations working on issues, offers short lists of resources, including books, slideshows, films, periodi-cals.

2.85 *The United States and South Africa*. Thomas P. Fenton. A series of four arti-cles from the *Maryknoll* magazine (Spring 1980). 25pp. Available from the author at 464 19 St., Oakland, CA 94612. $2.50 for the set.

This popularly written series describes South Africa's apartheid system, ex-plores the paradox of Washington's relations with the ruling white regime, and critically examines the role that U.S. banks and corporations play in maintaining the status quo.

2.86 *The United States and the Arms Embargo Against South Africa: Evidence, Denial, and Refutation*. Sean Gervasi. *Southern Africa* pamphlet #2. 1978. 49pp. Available from the Braudel Center, State University of New York, Binghamton, NY 13901.

A description of how the United Nations arms embargo against South Africa has been circumvented by U.S. and other corporations. The pamphlet contains congressional testimony by Gervasi, along with a paper on U.S. arms transfers that he presented to the United Nations in May 1978.

2.87 *United States Trade with South Africa and the Role of United States Banks*. Craig Howard. United Nations Centre Against Apartheid. *Notes and Documents*, July 1979. 11pp. Free

This analysis was prepared for the Interfaith Center on Corporate Responsibility and reprinted in the UN Centre Against Apartheid's publication *Notes and Documents*.

2.88 *U.S. Data Processing Corporations Are Supplying South Africa with the Brains of Its Military and Police Services*. *Multinational Monitor*, April 1982. 4pp. 50 cents. Available from NARMIC.

See also:
10.70, 10.80, 10.83

AUDIOVISUAL RESOURCES

Guides and Catalogs

2.89 *Africa Film Library*. Icarus Films. Free

This periodic flyer from Icarus Films is an annotated listing of films and videotapes from or about Africa and the African peoples. All are available from Icarus.

2.90 *Africa from Real to Reel: An African Filmography*. Steven Ohrn and Rebecca Riley, eds. Waltham, Mass.: African Studies Association, Brandeis University, 1976. 144pp.

A very detailed and comprehensive list of over one thousand films on Africa.

2.91   *Black and Afro-American Studies*. Audio Visual Library Service. Minneapolis: Audio Visual Library Service, University of Minnesota, n.d. 12pp.

An annotated list of films available on various topics pertinent to Africa: apartheid, African history, African arts, social and economic conditions, civil rights, and others. Included are rental fees and an order blank.

2.92   *Films on Africa: An Educator's Guide to 16mm Films Available in the Midwest*. Madison, Wisc.: African Studies Program, University of Wisconsin, 1974. 74pp. $1

Description of almost 700 films on Africa that are available to educators in the midwestern United States. The guide also includes recommended age levels of usage.

2.93   *South African Politics: A Film Guide*. Rebecca Riley and Steven Ohrn, eds. Bloomington, Ind.: African Studies Program, Indiana University.

A description of thirty-six films on South Africa with suggestions for use in educational programs.

2.94   *Southern Africa Film List*. New York: Africa Fund, 1979. Free

Annotated list of films on several of the countries of southern Africa (South Africa, Namibia, Angola, Mozambique, Zimbabwe) along with a list of film distributors by state. List indicates which films are available from which distributors.

2.95   *Southern Africa Media Center Film Catalog*. San Francisco: Southern Africa Media Center/California Newsreel.

The Media Center carries on a very active program of film distribution and makes an effort to enhance the showing of films on Africa by designing educational materials to accompany its films.

2.96   *Investing in Apartheid Activation Kit* is a detailed study guide available for $3 (free when renting any film) from the Southern Africa Media Center. It outlines a series of learning activities designed to improve the effectiveness of film use. It focuses particularly on the issue of American investments in South Africa, and will help any group concerned about this potential instrument for influencing government and corporate policy toward South Africa. It was jointly produced by the Southern Africa Media Center and the Africa Fund.

Audiovisuals

2.97   *Abaphuciwe/The Dispossessed*. 1981 40 min color film. Southern Africa Media Center/California Newsreel. Rental $60. Sale $600

"Abaphuciwe" is a Zulu word meaning "those who have had everything taken from them by force." This film exposes the fact that millions of black people in South Africa are being uprooted from their plots of land and herded into the bantustans as part of apartheid's extensive system of labor control. The film exposes apartheid as a strategy designed to maintain economic and political control in white hands indefinitely, and shows how this strategy is failing. The film challenges those who think that South Africa has reformed its apartheid structure.

2.98   *Banking on South Africa.* 1977 20 min 140 color slides (or filmstrip) with cassette tape. Southern Africa Media Center/California Newsreel. Also available from some local AFSC offices. Apply for rates.

Exposes the role played by U.S. banks in supporting the apartheid system. Suggests practical follow-up activity.

2.99   *Crossroads.* 1980 50 min color film. Southern Africa Media Center/California Newsreel. Rental $70. Sale $685

Crossroads is a squatters' town set up on the edge of Capetown by black families in defiance of apartheid's system of contract labor, which separates working men from their families. The film, showing how the struggle of daily life can become an act of rebellion, is effective for introducing audiences unfamiliar with South Africa to the social drama unfolding there today.

2.100   *The Discarded People.* 1982 28 min color film. Produced by Granada TV. Southern Africa Media Center/California Newsreel. Rental $50. Sale $450

A shocking examination of South Africa's "reserves," barren areas assigned to black South Africans by the white minority government. Details the suffering caused by this policy of the apartheid regime.

2.101   *Free Namibia!* 1978 27 min color film. Produced and distributed by the United Nations. Free. Available also from Southern Africa Media Center/California Newsreel ($40).

This film details the torment and the struggle of Namibia under South African rule. It captures the rituals and myths of the affluent white settler society as well as the strength of SWAPO's (South West African People's Organization) resistance.

2.102   *Generations of Resistance.* 1979 52 min color film. Peter Davis and the UN Centre Against Apartheid. Available from Southern Africa Media Center/California Newsreel. Rental $70

Story of the rise of black nationalism in South Africa. Uses rare archival footage and testimony from those who led and participated in the events depicted.

2.103   *Last Grave at Dimbaza.* 1975 55 min color film. Nana Mahomo. Available from some AFSC local offices, Southern Africa Media Center, and Unifilm. Apply for rates.

Powerful indictment of the day-to-day impact of apartheid in South Africa and how Western business interests support it. The film was shot illegally by a team of whites and blacks in the bantustans and smuggled out of the country to Europe where it was edited. It is an unmatched analysis of the system of apartheid, though it fails to mention the rising liberation movement in South Africa. It is recommended that a knowledgeable speaker on this subject accompany the film.

2.104   *People's War in Zimbabwe: Defeating the U.S. Mercenary Strategy.* 1979 40 min color slides with cassette. South Africa Anti-Mercenary Coalition. Apply for rates.

History of colonial oppression in Zimbabwe. Explains U.S. stake in the region, emphasizing covert support for the Rhodesian war machine; documents workings of the CIA/U.S. Army mercenary recruiting network and exposes the links between the mercenary machine and U.S. domestic policy forces and right-wing organizations that terrorize and control black and Third World communities in the United States.

.105   *Six Days in Soweto.* 1978 55 min color film. Anthony Thomas. Southern Africa Media Center/California Newsreel. Rental $75

Causes and aftermath of Soweto rebellion of June 1976 in South Africa. Re-creates the six days with reports from those who took part in the uprisings.

.106   *South Africa and U.S. Global Corporations.* 1976 15 min slides. AFSC (Cambridge). Rental $15

A detailed presentation of the presence and power of U.S. businesses in South Africa.

.107   *South Africa Belongs to Us.* 1980 55 min color film. Chris Austin, Peter Chappell, and Ruth Weiss. Produced by Gerhardt Schmidt. Available from Southern Africa Media Center/California Newsreel. Rental $80

This film describes how apartheid affects the lives of six South African women: a housewife in the bantustans, a black public service nurse in Johannesburg, a black factory worker who lives in a hostel, a black maid, the wife of a political prisoner, and a leader of the Indian community.

.108   *South Africa: Freedom Rising.* 1976 140 color slides with cassette 20 min. Dayton Community Media Workshop. Available from many local AFSC offices. Rental $15

Comprehensive view of the history of and daily life under apartheid. Appropriate for a wide variety of audiences. Includes an examination of the role of U.S.corporations in the apartheid system.

.109   *South Africa—The Nuclear File.* 1979 58 min color film. Peter Davis. Available from Villon Films. Apply for rental rates. Sale $100

Thorough report on how the United States has contributed to South Africa's nuclear development. Includes footage of South Africa's actual nuclear facilities at Pelindaba and interviews with Donald Sole, a nuclear expert and now South Africa's ambassador in Washington. Evidence of nuclear weapons testing by South Africa is examined.

2.110   *Soweto and the Uprising of 1976 in South Africa.* 40 min 155 slides with cassette. International Defense and Aid Fund for Southern Africa. $35 donation per showing.

A record of the events that shook South Africa in June of 1976 and of the strength of the people's resistance to racial oppression. A peaceful protest by school children became a national uprising against the apartheid system.

2.111   *There Is No Crisis.* 1976 30 min color film. Thames TV. Available from Southern Africa Media Center. Rental $35

Documentary of the 1976 Soweto uprisings and other protests against racial oppression. Includes interviews with community and student leaders.

See also:
1.187, 7.76, 10.97, 10.103, 10.105, 10.106

OTHER RESOURCES

Curriculum Guides and Materials

2.112   *Africa South of the Sahara: A Resource Guide for Secondary School Teachers.*
Interim Report. Barry K. Beyer, ed. Pittsburgh, Pa.: Carnegie-Mellon University, 1968. 217pp. $11.37. Available from ERIC Document Reproduction Serv-
ice.

Intended to help educators develop a program of study about Africa south of
the Sahara for the secondary level, this guide includes the laying out of objectives
and concepts for a study of Africa, guidelines for instruction, a survey of the
literature on teaching about the region, a summary of the attitudes held by American secondary school students toward Africa, an extensive annotated bibliography listing materials and audiovisual aids on curriculum development on regions
as well as specific countries of Africa, and a bibliography of recommended basic
instructional materials on the region. A 52-page update of the guide, entitled *New
Instructional Materials on Africa South of the Sahara (1969–1970)*, was
published in 1970.

2.113   *African Studies Information Resources Directory.* The Archives–Libraries
Committee of the African Studies Association is compiling a guide to African
Studies libraries, map collections, collections of aural and visual documentation,
computerized data sets, and related information resources and information services dealing with Africa south of the Sahara and African Studies. The directory
was scheduled to be published in 1982. Write: Jean Gosebrink, Project Director,
3533A Wyoming, St. Louis, MO 63118 for details.

2.114   *For Anyone Interested in Africa.* Helen Garvey, SNJM, ed. Berkeley, Calif.:
World Education Center, 1979.

This 8-page special issue of *Peace Notes* (November 1979) describes South
Africa's political parties, non-white political organizations, and U.S. govern-
ment policy vis-à-vis South Africa. Guidelines are offered for teaching about
South Africa and educational goals and strategies are suggested.

2.115   *Resources for Teaching about Africa.* Madison, Wis.: African Studies Program, University of Wisconsin, February 1981. 7pp. One copy free

The African Studies Program is an excellent source of curriculum materials
and ideas—as is evident in this 7-page descriptive listing of their resources.

2.116   *Teacher's Resource Handbook for African Studies: An Annotated Bibliography of Curriculum Materials, Preschool through Grade Twelve.* Occasional Paper No. 16. John N. Hawkins and Jon Maksik. Los Angeles: African Studies
Center, University of California, 1976. 68pp. $1.50

The editors provide annotated listings of books and audiovisuals organized
under geographical headings (General Africa; Western; Eastern/Central; and
South) and according to the age levels of the students. The materials cover a range
of interests from culture to political economy.

Simulation Games

117   *Kama*. Lebanon, Ohio: Simulation and Gaming Association, 1974. $3.95. Level: mid-primary and above. Players: 30 or more. Time: one day.

    Modeled on political developments in Uganda, *Kama* introduces participants to the complexities of decision-making in a "typical" developing African country.

See also:
1.200, 1.207, 7.78, 7.82, 10.124, 10.126

Chapter 3

Asia and the Pacific

KEY RESOURCES

Organizations

Most of the organizations in this chapter are country-specific. We'll leave it to you to select among these the ones that best meet your interests and information needs.

Of those organizations that relate to the Asia region as a whole or to at least a fairly wide geographical territory these are especially noteworthy: the **Church Committee on Human Rights in Asia, Pacific Concerns Resource Center (PCRC), Pacific Studies Center (PSC)**, and the **Southeast Asia Resource Center (SRC)**.

Each of these four groups brings particular strengths to the study of U.S. involvement in the Asia region.

• The **Church Committee** enlists the active participation of church-related people in its efforts to improve the human rights situation, especially in South Korea and the Philippines.

• **CALC**'s interests include Indochina, East Timor, the Philippines, and Taiwan. Regional CALC chapters provide opportunities for study and action at the local level.

• The **PCRC** covers the Pacific and Oceania region and is especially well-informed about nuclear issues in Hawaii and throughout Asia.

• **PSC**'s strengths lie in its abundant and well-ordered files, particularly on the military and the electronics industry, and in the research skills of Center staff.

• **SRC** has a long-established and well-deserved reputation for accurate and readable analyses of U.S. political and military activity in Indochina, Indonesia, and the Philippines.

Printed Resources

Books written and edited by Mark Selden offer an overview of a number of facets of U.S. relations with Asia from a progressive—though non-rhetorical—point of view.

The works of Frank Baldwin, Noam Chomsky and Edward Herman, Thomas Lobe, and William Shawcross present readable analyses of U.S. relations with particular Asian countries.

The *Bulletin of Concerned Asian Scholars*, *Pacific Research*, and the *Southeast Asia Chronicle* are three leading periodicals with an Asian regional focus. All three tend to treat one significant theme per issue.

Back issues of these three magazines are very useful inexpensive resources for educational programs and for personal study. The Washington-based **Center for International Policy** publishes well-respected articles in its *Current Issues* and *Indochina* series.

Audiovisual Resources

Of the many audiovisuals described in this section the films and slideshows produced and/or distributed by the **American Friends Service Committee** can be recommended without any reservation. AFSC-sponsored audiovisuals are always a skillful blend of uncompromising political analysis and of mature awareness of the sensitivities of American audiences.

Other Resources

Two leading organizations with credible and field-tested curriculum materials on U.S. relations with Asia are the **Indochina Curriculum Group** and Stanford University's **SPICE/China Program**.

ORGANIZATIONS

3.1 American Friends Service Committee, Korea Program, 1501 Cherry St., Philadelphia, PA 19102. Tel: 215-241-7149.

RELIGIOUS AFFILIATION: Religious Society of Friends (Quakers).

FOCUS: Korea. Human rights • political repression.

ACTIVITIES: Networking (through regional offices) • popular education • documentation.

RESOURCES: Films and audiovisuals • speakers • publications • reports.

PERIODICALS: **3.2** *Korea Report*. Monthly. $10/year.

3.3 Asia Monitor Resource Center, 2 Man Wan Rd., 17-C, Kowloon, Hongkong. Tel: 3-7135271.

FOCUS: International • Asia. Investment • trade • aid • militarism • political economy • international awareness • corporate responsibility.

ACTIVITIES: Research and writing • public interest research and information center • documentation.

RESOURCES: Publications • reports • news clippings • library • research services.

PERIODICALS: **3.4** *Asia Monitor*. Quarterly. $22/year individual. $34/year institutional.

SPECIAL PROJECTS: Chemical Hazards in Asia. U.S. Military in Asia.

3.5 Asia Society, 725 Park Ave., New York, NY 10021. Tel: 212-288-6400.

FOCUS: Asia and Pacific. Broad understanding of Asian countries.

ACTIVITIES: Popular education • constituency education • research and writing for own publications • intern programs • library services • media relations program • networking • media • workshops and seminars • performing arts program • educational aids for high school teachers.

RESOURCES: Speakers • audiovisuals • literature • publications • bookstore • study guides • curriculum guides • consultant services • library.

PERIODICALS: **3.6** *Asia*. Bimonthly magazine. $16/year. **3.7** *Focus on Asian Studies*. 3 issues/year. $5/year.

3.8 The Center for Teaching About China, U.S.-China People's Friendship Association, Box 15, 110 Maryland Ave., NE, Washington, DC 20002. Tel: 202-544-7010.

FOCUS: China. International awareness.

ACTIVITIES: Constituency education • networking • workshops.

RESOURCES: Audiovisuals • literature • curriculum guides • consultant services.

3.9 Church Coalition for Human Rights in the Philippines, 110 Maryland Ave., NE, Rm. 103, Washington, DC 20002. Tel: 202-543-1094.

FOCUS: Philippines. Social justice • human rights • political repression.

ACTIVITIES: Networking (through regional offices) • church constituency education and action • lobbying • congressional testimony.

RESOURCES: Reports • speakers • audiovisuals.

3.10   **Church Committee on Human Rights in Asia,** 1821 W. Cullerton, Chicago, IL 60608. Tel: 312-226-0675.

FOCUS: Asia • Taiwan • South Korea • Philippines. Human rights • political repression • militarism • disarmament • foreign trade and aid • political economy • international awareness • national liberation struggles • corporate responsibility.

ACTIVITIES: Popular education • solidarity work • constituency education • legislative action • intern programs • library services • overseas project support • documentation • workshops and seminars.

RESOURCES: Speakers • audiovisuals • literature • study-action guides • consultant services • reports.

PERIODICALS: **3.11** *Asian Rights Advocate.* Monthly. $5/year.

3.12   **Committee for a New Korea Policy,** 221 Central Ave., Albany, NY 12206. Tel: 518-434-4037.

FOCUS: Korea. Human rights • political repression • militarism • disarmament • foreign trade and aid.

ACTIVITIES: Popular education • legislative action • networking • documentation and information • policy-oriented research and writing • workshops and seminars.

RESOURCES: Speakers • publications • consultant services • audiovisuals.

3.13   **East Timor Human Rights Committee,** Box 363, Clinton Station, Syracuse, NY 13201. Tel: 315-479-5020.

FOCUS: Indonesia • East Timor. Human rights • political repression • militarism • international awareness • national liberation struggles.

ACTIVITIES: Research • popular education • research and writing • networking • media • documentation and information • workshops and seminars.

RESOURCES: Speakers • audiovisuals • literature • publications.

PERIODICALS: **3.14** *East Timor Update* and *Action Alerts.* Quarterly. $5/year. Back issues available. **3.15** *Media Coverage on East Timor.* Occasional. 50 cents. **3.16** *Congressional Activity on East Timor.* Occasional. 50 cents.

3.17   **Friends of the Filipino People,** Box 2125, Durham, NC 27702.

FOCUS: Philippines. Human rights • political repression • militarism • nuclear arms and energy • political economy • national liberation struggles • social justice.

ACTIVITIES: Popular education • research and writing • solidarity work • networking (through regional offices).

RESOURCES: Literature • speakers • audiovisuals • reports. Resource list available.

PERIODICALS: **3.18** *FFP Bulletin.* Bimonthly newsletter. **3.19** *Action Alerts.* Occasional. Both with $10 annual membership.

3.20   **General Union of Afghan Students Abroad (GUAFS),** Box 17622, Los Angeles, CA 90017.

FOCUS: Afghanistan. Human rights • political repression • foreign trade and aid • political economy • international awareness.

ACTIVITIES: Popular education • solidarity work • networking.

RESOURCES: Publications • reports.

PERIODICALS: **3.21** *Independent Afghanistan*. Quarterly. Contribution.

3.22 Indochina Curriculum Group, 11 Garden St., Cambridge, MA 02138. Tel: 617-354-6583.

FOCUS: Asia. Southeast Asia. Militarism • political economy • international awareness • national liberation struggles.

ACTIVITIES: Popular education • curriculum development.

RESOURCES: Audiovisuals • speakers • literature • publications • curriculum guides.

3.23 International Committee for Human Rights in Taiwan, Box 5205, Seattle, WA 98105. Tel: 206-365-8242.

FOCUS: Taiwan. Human rights • political repression.

ACTIVITIES: Political action • legislative action • congressional testimony • press service • networking • documentation and information.

RESOURCES: Publications.

PERIODICALS: **3.24** *Taiwan Communiqué*. Quarterly. $10/year.

3.25 KDP (Union of Democratic Filipinos), Box 2759, Oakland, CA 94602.

FOCUS: Philippines. Human rights • political repression • militarism • foreign trade and aid • national liberation struggles.

ACTIVITIES: Popular education • legislative action • research and writing • solidarity work • documentation.

RESOURCES: Publications • consultant services.

PERIODICALS: **3.26** *Ang Katipunan*. Monthly. $7.50/year.

3.27 Micronesia Support Committee, 1212 University Ave., Honolulu, HI 96826. Tel: 808-942-0437.

FOCUS: Asia and the Pacific. Human rights • militarism • nuclear arms and energy.

ACTIVITIES: Popular education • political action • research and writing • congressional testimony • workshops and seminars.

RESOURCES: Speakers • audiovisuals • publications • reports.

PERIODICALS: **3.28** *Micronesia Bulletin*. Quarterly. $5/year individual; $10/year institutional.

3.29 Midwest China Study Resource Center, Schools Outreach Program, 2375 Como Ave. W, Saint Paul, MN 55108. Tel: 612-641-3238.

FOCUS: China. International awareness.

ACTIVITIES: Popular education • workshops.

RESOURCES: Speakers • audiovisuals • literature • curriculum guides.

PERIODICALS: **3.30** *China Update*. Quarterly. $3/year.

3.31 North American Coalition for Human Rights in Korea, 110 Maryland Ave., NE, Washington, DC 20002. Tel: 202-546-4304.

FOCUS: Korea. Human rights • political repression • militarism • labor.

ACTIVITIES: Networking • religious constituency education and action • lobbying.

RESOURCES: Speakers • reports • consultant services.

PERIODICALS: **3.32** *Korea/Update* and *Korea/Action*. Bimonthly. $5/year.

3.33   Pacific and Asian American Center for Theology and Strategies (PACTS), 1798
Scenic Ave., Berkeley, CA 94709. Tel: 415-848-0173.
FOCUS: Asia and the Pacific • U.S.-Pacific and Asian American communities.
Human rights • political repression • national liberation struggles • social jus-
tice.
ACTIVITIES: Church constituency education • solidarity work • intern pro-
grams • library services • networking • documentation and information • justice
and peace ministries • workshops and seminars.
RESOURCES: Publications • curriculum guides • library • reports.
PERIODICALS: **3.34** *PACTS Occasional Bulletin.* Quarterly. $10/year.
SPECIAL PROJECTS: Establishing a national ecumenical network of Pacific
and Asian American women in ministry; cosponsoring a national ecumenical
convention of Pacific and Asian Americans. Implementing an orientation/de-
briefing for Asian American mission interns to Asia. Initiating a refugee/
immigration program of education and advocacy.

3.35   Pacific Concerns Resource Center, Box 27692, Honolulu, HI 96827. Tel: 808-
538-3522.
FOCUS: Asia • Pacific. Militarism • human rights • disarmament • nuclear
power • foreign trade and aid • international awareness.
ACTIVITIES: Popular education and action • solidarity work • documentation •
library services • networking.
RESOURCES: Audiovisuals • literature • research services • library.
PERIODICALS: **3.36** *Pacific Concerns Resource Center Bulletin.* Every 6
weeks. $6/year.

3.37   Pacific Studies Center, 222B View St., Mountain View, CA 94041. Tel: 415-969-
1545.
FOCUS: Asia • Pacific. Political economy • militarism • foreign trade and aid •
electronics.
ACTIVITIES: Research and writing • library services • networking • documenta-
tion and information • policy-oriented research and writing.
RESOURCES: Speakers • publications • research services • library • reports.
PERIODICALS: **3.38** *Pacific Research.* Quarterly. $10/2 years. **3.39** *Global
Electronics Information Newsletter.* Monthly. $5/year.

3.40   Pakistan Committee for Democracy and Justice, Box 776, Peter Stuyvesant Sta-
tion, New York, NY 10009. Tel: 212-927-4240.
FOCUS: Pakistan. Human rights • political repression • militarism • foreign
trade and aid • international awareness.
ACTIVITIES: Popular education • solidarity work • documentation and infor-
mation • workshops and seminars.
RESOURCES: Publications • reports.
PERIODICALS: **3.41** *Justice.* Monthly. Contribution.

3.42   Philippine Education and Support Committee (PESCOM), Box 4365, Berkeley,
CA 94704. Tel: 415-848-2242.
FOCUS: Philippines. Human rights • political repression • nuclear arms and
energy • foreign trade and aid • national liberation struggles • social justice.

ACTIVITIES: Popular education • constituency education • political action • legislative action • research and writing • solidarity work • overseas project support • documentation and information.

RESOURCES: Speakers • audiovisuals • literature.

SPECIAL PROJECTS: Committee on hunger in the Philippines: research and education on the extent of malnutrition in the Philippines, and its connection to the overall socioeconomic conditions and institutions in the country.

3.43 **Philippine Solidarity Network**, Box 84, Oakland, CA 94668. Tel: 415-839-7066.

FOCUS: Philippines. Human rights • militarism • political repression • foreign aid • political economy • national liberation struggles.

ACTIVITIES: Workshops • popular education and action • networking (through regional offices) • research and writing • policy oriented studies • lobbying • political education and action.

RESOURCES: Audiovisuals • speakers • publications.

3.44 **Philippines Research Center**, Box 101, Mansfield Depot, CT 06251.

FOCUS: Philippines. Human rights • political repression • militarism • nuclear arms and energy • foreign trade and aid • national liberation struggles.

ACTIVITIES: Popular education • research and writing • solidarity work • documentation and information.

RESOURCES: Speakers • literature • publications. Publications list available.

3.45 **Southeast Asia Resource Center**, Box 4000D, Berkeley, CA 94704. Tel: 415-548-2546.

FOCUS: Southeast Asia • Asia and the Pacific. Human rights • political repression • militarism • foreign trade and aid • political economy • national liberation struggles.

ACTIVITIES: Popular education • research and writing • library services • press service • networking • media • documentation and information.

RESOURCES: Speakers • literature • publications • consultant services • research services • library.

PERIODICALS: **3.46** *Southeast Asia Chronicle*. Bimonthly. $12/year individual; $25/year institutional.

3.47 **Southeast Asia Resource Center-East**, 198 Broadway, Rm. 302, New York, NY 10038. Tel: 212-964-6730.

FOCUS: Southeast Asia. Human rights • foreign trade and aid • political economy • national liberation struggles • international awareness.

ACTIVITIES: Popular education • research and writing • networking • documentation and information.

RESOURCES: Speakers • audiovisuals • publications • reports.

3.48 **Stanford Program on International and Cross-Cultural Education, SPICE/China Project**, Rm. 221, Lou Henry Hoover Bldg., Stanford University, Stanford, CA 94305. Tel: 415-497-1114.

FOCUS: Asia and the Pacific • China. International awareness.

ACTIVITIES: Popular education • library services • networking • workshops and seminars • outreach center • teacher in-service training.

RESOURCES: Speakers • audiovisuals • literature • publications • curriculum guides • consultant services • library.

.49   TAPOL, c/o Dept. of Anthropology, Montclair State College, Upper Montclair, NJ 07043. Tel: 201-893-4133.
FOCUS: Indonesia. Human rights • political repression.
ACTIVITIES: Popular education • documentation • research • support work.
RESOURCES: Speakers • reports • consultant services.
PERIODICALS: **3.50** *TAPOL Newsletter* (Box 609, Montclair, NJ 07042), $5/ year.

.51   Thai Information Center, Box 8995, Los Angeles, CA 90008.
FOCUS: Thailand. Human rights • political repression • militarism • disarmament • national liberation struggles • social justice • women • political economy • transnational corporations.
ACTIVITIES: Documentation and information • solidarity work • press service • networking.
RESOURCES: Publications • audiovisuals.
PERIODICALS: **3.52** *TIC News*. Monthly newsletter. $12/year individual; $24/ year institutional.

.53   Union of Democratic Thais, Box 17808, Los Angeles, CA 90017.
FOCUS: Thailand. Human rights • militarism • political repression.
ACTIVITIES: Networking • documentation • support work.
RESOURCES: Publications • reports • speakers.
PERIODICALS: **3.54** *Thailand Update*. Bimonthly newsletter. $10/year individual; $20/year institutional.

.55   US-China People's Friendship Association, National Office, 110 Maryland Ave., NE, Washington, DC 20002. Tel: 202-544-7010.
FOCUS: China. International awareness.
ACTIVITIES: Travel arrangements • popular education • workshops.
RESOURCES: Speakers • audiovisuals and literature • curriculum guides • publications.
PERIODICALS: **3.56** *US-China Review*. Bimonthly magazine. $6/year.

PRINTED RESOURCES

Books

3.57   Asia Monitor Resource Center. *The U.S. Military's Game Plan for Asia*.
        Hongkong: Asia Monitor Resource Center, 1981. 101pp. $6.50, plus postage.
        This press profile contains clippings selected from newspapers and magazines
        from Asia, Europe, and the United States. Articles in the profile examine several
        issues: America's growing ties with China, the debate over Japan's remilitariza-
        tion, arms sales to Pakistan, proposed U.S. military bases in the Palauan archi-
        pelago, and stepped-up naval activity in the South China Sea, among others.
3.58   Baldwin, Frank, ed. *Without Parallel: The American-Korean Relationship
        Since 1945*. New York: Pantheon Books, 1974. 376pp. $3.95. Available from
        North American Coalition for Human Rights in Korea.
        A comprehensive collection of articles from a range of political views dealing
        with the U.S. role in Korea.
3.59   Bello, Walden; Kinley, David; and Elinson, Elaine. *Development Debacle*. San
        Francisco: Institute for Food and Development Policy and Philippine Solidarity
        Network, 1982. 280pp. $6.95
        Development Debacle attempts to demonstrate how the World Bank's control
        over the economy of the Philippines is leading to economic and social disaster for
        the poor majority of the country.
3.60   Bello, Walden, and Rivera, Severina. *The Logistics of Repression and Other
        Essays*. Washington, D.C.: Friends of the Filipino People, 1977. 158pp. $4.50.
        Available from Southeast Asia Resource Center.
        This book concerns itself with U.S. aid and involvement in the Philippines,
        particularly since 1972, the year that martial law was imposed in that country.
3.61   Bryan, C.D.B. *Friendly Fire*. New York: Bantam Books, 1976. 437pp. $2.75.
        Available from Social Studies School Service.
        This is the true story of the Mullen family from Iowa, who were radicalized by
        their son's death by "friendly fire" in Vietnam in 1970. The U.S. government's
        inability to provide an explanation for the death of their son led the family to
        involvement in antiwar activities and brought an end to their unquestioning pa-
        triotism.
3.62   Caldwell, Malcolm, ed. *Ten Years' Military Terror in Indonesia*. Nottingham,
        England: Spokesman Books, 1975. 295pp. $5. Available from Modern Times
        Bookstore.
        A comprehensive collection of essays on modern Indonesia covering the role of
        the military, political parties, the United States, political repression, and a wide
        range of other topics.
3.63   Chomsky, Noam, and Herman, Edward S. *The Political Economy of Human
        Rights*. 2 vols. Vol.2: *After the Cataclysm: Postwar Indochina and the Recon-
        struction of Imperial Ideology*. Boston: South End Press, 1979. 392pp. $6.50
        This book focuses on postwar Indochina and examines the history and lessons

of the Vietnam War. It dispels some of the propaganda surrounding the war and its aftermath, and promotes understanding of the causes of many current problems facing the people of Indochina. It documents and analyzes the role of the media in the process. See 7.31 for Vol. 1.

.64   Claver, Bishop Francisco F., S.J. *The Stones Will Cry Out*. Maryknoll, N.Y.: Orbis Books, 1979. 196pp. $7.95

A collection of pastoral letters and statements by Bishop Claver, a member of the Philippine Catholic hierarchy. Many of the letters were written to the bishop's people after martial law closed the diocesan radio station and newspaper. They show the strength of his beliefs and his courage in the face of oppression.

.65   Committee of Concerned Asian Scholars. *The Indochina Story*. New York: Bantam Books, 1970. 347pp. Out of print.

This book, compiled in the wake of the U.S. invasion of Cambodia, is an attempt to furnish a "comprehensive and comprehensible" picture of American involvement in Indochina to the American people. Its first three sections pose answers to the questions most often raised about U.S. involvement in Indochina. The book includes a chronology of events in Vietnam, Laos, Cambodia, and Thailand.

.66   Drinnon, Richard. *Facing West: The Metaphysics of Indian-Hating and Empire-Building*. Minneapolis: University of Minnesota Press, 1980. 571pp. Cloth $20

Facing West is a major investigation into the link between American racism and Westward expansion. The last two lengthy chapters deal with U.S. involvement in the Philippines and in Vietnam.   •

.67   Filippinengroep. *Makibaka! Join Us in Struggle*. Netherlands: Filippinengroep, 1980. $5. Available from Philippines Research Center.

Originally published in Dutch, this English translation of *Makibaka* presents a history of and documentation surrounding events of seven years of martial law in the Philippines. Particular attention is given to the resistance.

.68   Friedman, Edward, and Selden, Mark. *America's Asia: Dissenting Essays on Asian-American Relations*. New York: Random House, Vintage Books, 1971. 458pp. $2.45

America's Asia explores the dynamic and destructive interaction between American perceptions and American power in the making and unmaking of contemporary Asia. The contributors to this volume of essays focus on both Asia and America, believing that if we could change our relationship to Asia we would be open to learning much from Asian peoples that could help us create a more decent and just society in the United States.

.69   Isaacs, Harold R. *Scratches on Our Minds: American Views of China and India*. Reprint with a new preface by the author. White Plains, N.Y.: M.E. Sharpe, 1980. Originally published in 1958. 416pp. $7.95

This classic study examines the pictures in our heads—the scratches on our minds—about China and India as they turned up in interviews with Americans of the generation that matured during the earlier decades of this century. The interviews show to readers today how far back our impressions of these two enormously complex societies go and how they have been shaped at various stages by the history through which they have passed.

3.70 Klare, Michael. *War Without End*. New York: Random House, Vintage Books, 1972. 464pp. $2.95

This perceptive study of U.S. participation in the Vietnam War—in particular the United States' development of strategies and techniques for counter-insurgency—contributes to a broader understanding and questioning of American foreign policy. It studies the past, but raises questions for the future.

3.71 Lobe, Thomas. *United States Security Policy and Aid to the Thailand Police*. University of Denver Monograph Series in World Affairs XIV:2. Denver, Colo.: University of Denver, Colorado Seminary, 1977. 161pp. $3.50. Available from Southeast Asia Resource Center.

This is a carefully documented history of U.S. military and police aid to Thailand over a 25-year period by a political scientist who has also researched such U.S. aid to Chile, Bolivia, and Paraguay. Lobe supplies a historical background of U.S. attempts at "social control" in the Third World from the days of John F. Kennedy; he then focuses on U.S. police aid, the CIA, and the Office of Public Safety, as these all related to Thailand.

3.72 Micronesia Support Committee and Pacific Concerns Resource Center. *From Trusteeship to . . . ? Micronesia and Its Future*. Honolulu: MSC and PCRC, 1982. 68pp. $4.50 surface; $5.50 airmail.

Two groups whose concern is the Pacific islands collaborated on this booklet, a description of Micronesia under the U.S.-administered United Nations Trusteeship since 1947. The booklet is both a chronology and an analysis of events, and deals particularly with military questions, nuclear weapons, and nuclear waste. Questions for discussion and a bibliography for further reading complete this unique resource.

3.73 Porter, Gareth, ed. *Vietnam: The Definitive Documentation of Human Decisions*. Stanfordville, N.Y.: Earl M. Coleman Enterprises, 1979. Vol. 1: 724pp. Vol. 2: 675pp. $60

Porter's two library reference volumes furnish the most complete documentation available about key decisions and policies of the U.S. government during the Vietnam war. Volume 1 covers the period from 1941 to 1955; Volume 2, 1955 to 1975. Porter's work is obviously not something that an individual will purchase, but these two volumes are worth knowing about and having access to through a university or public library.

3.74 Selden, Mark, ed. *Remaking Asia: Essays on the American Uses of Power in Asia*. New York: Pantheon, 1974. 381pp. Out of print.

In *Remaking Asia* Mark Seldon brings together informed and critical views of the presence and power of the United States in Asia.

3.75 Selden, Mark, and McCormack, Gavin, eds. *Korea, North and South: The Deepening Crisis*. New York: Monthly Review, 1980. 237pp. $5.50

The editors have presented a well-integrated collection of critical essays on the myths of the Cold War, the division of Korea following World War II, and on U.S. military and political policies in Korea since that time.

.76   Shalom, Stephen Rosskamm. *The United States and the Philippines: A Study of Neocolonialism*. Philadelphia: Institute for the Study of Human Issues, 1981. 302pp. Bibliography, maps. Cloth $19.50

This carefully documented study examines the impact of U.S. policy on the Philippines from the closing days of World War II to the present. Shalom illustrates the many ways in which the Philippines has served as the testing ground for the economic, political,and military instruments of American intervention elsewhere in the Third World.

.77   Shawcross, William. *Sideshow: Kissinger, Nixon and the Destruction of Cambodia*. New York: Simon & Schuster, 1979. 467pp. Cloth $13.95

Sideshow is a full-scale investigation into America's secret war against Cambodia. The author uses his own experience as a journalist in Southeast Asia, along with interviews and thousands of pages of classified U.S. government documents to write an eye-opening account of this shameful facet of U.S. involvement in Indochina.

.78   Stone, I.F. *The Hidden History of the Korean War*. New York: Monthly Review, 1969. 368pp. $5.95

Noted columnist I.F. Stone's pathbreaking history of the Korean War was suppressed when it was first written in the early 1950s. The U.S. government and the American public were not receptive in those days of Senator Joseph McCarthy to Stone's piercing questions and on-sight observations about the origins and conduct of the Korean War. Though Stone remains—even in our own more liberal times—a voice crying in the wilderness, his critical account is now a matter of public record.

.79   Whitehead, Raymond L., and Whitehead, Rhea M. *China: Search for Community*. New York: Friendship Press, 1978. $2.75

The authors offer a provocative description and analysis of the affirmation of human values and search for community, which they see at the root of changes in China. Their observations challenge North Americans to examine our own values and society and to overcome our fears and prejudices in looking at China today.

See also:
7.31, 7.32, 7.36, 10.27, 10.32, 10.34, 10.36, 10.38, 10.41

Periodicals

.80   *Ang Katipunan*, Box 2759, Oakland, CA 94602. Monthly newspaper. $7.50/year.

The national newspaper of the Union of Democratic Filipinos (KDP), *Ang Katipunan* reports on the Philippines for the U.S. Filipino community. The paper deals particularly with the current Philippines situation relative to U.S. presence and interests there.

.81   *Asia*, The Asia Society, Box 1398-A, Fort Lee, NJ 07024. Bimonthly magazine. $16/year.

This magazine aims to deepen American understanding of Asia. Its articles take a broad approach to Asian countries and cover their history, culture, and contemporary economic and political affairs.

3.82   *Asia Monitor*, 2 Man Wan Rd., 17-C, Kowloon, Hongkong. Quarterly. $22/ year individual; $34/year institutional. Back issues available.

A news digest of U.S. and other economic, political, and military relations with the developing nations of Asia. *Asia Monitor* covers the news as it appears in national newspapers and regional magazines, such as *The Asian Wall Street Journal*, the *Far Eastern Economic Review*, and *Asian Finance*.

3.83   *The Asia Record*, 580 College Ave., Suite 6, Palo Alto, CA 94306. Monthly newspaper. $12/year.

A monthly newspaper that carries wire service reports and articles about East and Southeast Asia.

3.84   *Bulletin of Concerned Asian Scholars*, Box R, Berthoud, CO 80513. Quarterly journal. $20/year. Back issues available.

A quarterly journal with articles on Asia and on U.S. involvement in Asia written by progressive academics.

3.85   *China Notes*, NCC/DOM, China Program, 475 Riverside Dr., Rm. 616, New York, NY 10115. Quarterly newsletter. $6/year.

This quarterly publication of the National Council of Churches presents issues of "Christian concern relating to China." Each issue consists of a major article, updates by church leaders, and reviews of books and other resources.

3.86   *China Update*, Midwest China Study Resource Center, Schools Outreach Program, 2375 Como Ave., W., Saint Paul, MN 55108. Quarterly. $3/year.

The main purpose of *China Update* is to make available lesson plans in a variety of subjects, such as, geography, law, family, education, human rights, lifestyle, economics, agriculture. It also carries a listing of recent resources.

3.87   *Focus on Asian Studies*, The Asia Society, Box 1308-M, Fort Lee, NJ 07024. 3 issues/year. $5/year.

This is a magazine designed primarily for educators. It includes articles on Asia from both a historical and a current standpoint, model curriculum studies and multimedia teaching sources, graphics for classroom use, and a calendar of major cultural events across the country.

3.88   *Indochina Issues*, Center for International Policy, Indochina Project, 120 Maryland Ave., NE, Washington, DC 20002. Monthly. $7.50/year. Back issues available.

This 8-page publication carries a major article each month pertinent to a better understanding of the countries of Indochina and to their relations with the United States.

3.89   *Korea Report*, AFSC, Asia Desk, 1501 Cherry St., Philadelphia, PA 19102.

Concise activist-oriented information about both North and South Korea, with a special focus on the role of the United States in the country.

3.90   *The Korean Review*, Box 32, Knickerbocker Station, New York, NY 10002. Bimonthly journal. $10/year.

The Korean Review presents documents and analyses on South Korea and U.S. involvement in the country.

91　　*Monthly Review of Korean Affairs*, Friends of the Korean People, Box 3657, Arlington, VA 22203. Monthly. $10/year.

A scholarly analysis of South Korean human rights and politics.

92　　*Pacific Research*, Pacific Studies Center, 222B View St., Mountain View, CA 94041. Quarterly magazine. $10/2 years. Back issues available.

This journal contains investigative articles on such issues as Mattel operations in Asia and the electronics industry in Asia. It also includes notices of other books and resources.

93　　*Southeast Asia Chronicle*, Southeast Asia Resource Center, Box 4000 D, Berkeley, CA 94704. Bimonthly magazine. $10/year. Back issues available.

Each issue of the *Chronicle* deals with a particular topic. The magazine offers excellent articles on recent events and background situations in the countries of Southeast Asia.

94　　*Thailand Update*, Union of Democratic Thais, Box 17808, Los Angeles, CA 90017. Bimonthly newsletter. $10/year individual; $20/year institutional.

The *Update* carries current news of the situation in Thailand as well as more lengthy analytical articles on U.S.-Thailand relations.

95　　*US-China Review*, US-China People's Friendship Association, 110 Maryland Ave., NE, Washington, DC 20002. Bimonthly magazine. $6/year.

This magazine is devoted to US-China relations. It covers changes occurring in China and attempts to serve as a link between people throughout the world who share an interest in China and its efforts to build a new society.

Pamphlets and Articles

96　　*Aid to the Philippines: Who Benefits?* Jim Morrell. Center for International Policy, *International Policy Report* 5:2 (October 1979). 16pp. $1

The author visited aid projects in five provinces of the Philippines, interviewed local residents and senior aid officials, and reviewed aid documents. This is his report.

97　　*Anti-Superport Brochure.* Micronesia Support Committee with the Save Palau Organization, 1977. 12pp. $1. Palauan, Japanese, and English. Photographs and graphics.

This brochure was designed to assist in an education campaign in Palau to stop a proposed joint Japan-U.S.-Iran superport venture. The proposed $20 billion investment included oil tanks, petrochemical plants, a nuclear power plant, and other heavy industry, all to be constructed on the fragile reefs and volcanic islands of Palau.

98　　*Arming Indonesia.* Lenny Siegel. *Pacific Research*, 1976. 10pp. 25 cents. Also available from Southeast Asia Resource Center.

History of U.S. military aid and arms supplies to Indonesia.

99　　*Asian Labor: The American Connection. Pacific Research* 6:5 (1975). $1.35

The article explores U.S. labor policy in Asia and the political ramifications of this policy. It includes sections on Turkey, Korea, Indonesia, and the Philippines.

3.100	*Cambodia: How It Happened, What You Can Do*. Indochina Program, AFSC (Philadelphia), 1980. 4pp. Contribution.

This article is an overview of the situation in Cambodia written by members of an AFSC delegation to that country in 1980.

3.101	*The Challenge of the Philippines*. Jim Morell. Center for International Policy, *Current Issues*, March 1980. 7pp. 75 cents

This is the testimony of Jim Morrell on February 7, 1980 before the Subcommittee on International Organizations and the Subcommittee on Asia and Pacific Affairs of the Committee on Foreign Affairs, U.S. House of Representatives. It covers human rights conditions in the Philippines, the State Department report, the results of U.S. policy on human rights in the Philippines, and a proposal for a different policy.

3.102	*Changing Role of S.E. Asian Women*. *Pacific Research* 9:5–6 (July–October 1978) and *Southeast Asia Chronicle* 66 (January–February 1979). 27pp. Charts, graphics, notes. $2.50

The impact of multinational corporate investment: working conditions, union organizing, and the effect of urbanization on family structure. Why international business prefers women workers.

3.103	*Credibility Gap*. AFSC (Philadelphia), 1972. 128pp. 50 cents. Bulk rates available.

A booklet containing excerpts from the *Pentagon Papers* and official public statements showing the wide gap between what the public was being told and the realities of U.S. policy in Southeast Asia. A useful tool for anyone teaching the history of the period.

3.104	*Diego Garcia*. *Pacific Research* 8:3 (1977). 12pp. $1.35

This is a consideration of the tactical importance to the United States of Diego Garcia. It is presented as an answer to the problem of where to put a permanent base in the face of unstable governments and increasing nationalism in most areas of the Third World. The article considers U.S. military requirements in the Indian Ocean, and outlines the development of the island (harbor, airstrips and so on) toward that purpose.

3.105	*East Timor: Beyond Hunger*. *Southeast Asia Chronicle* 74, August 1980. $2.50

An update on East Timor's five-year struggle for independence, the international press blockade, and the politics of relief efforts.

3.106	*East Timor: The Hidden War*. 4th ed. Richard W. Franke. East Timor Defense Committee, December 1976. 79pp. $1. Available from Southeast Asia Resource Center.

A concise study of the little known war in the former Portuguese colony of East Timor. Covers background history, analysis of the role of East Timor's liberation movement, the Indonesian invasion, and the role of the United States.

3.107	*East Timor/West Papua Packet*. Pacific Concerns Resource Center, October 1981. Donation.

This packet includes introductory articles to the situations in East Timor and West Papua as well as suggested solidarity actions.

08   *Ebeye, Marshall Islands: A Public Health Hazard.* Dr. Greg Dever. Micronesia Support Committee, August 1978. 30pp. $3. Apply for bulk rates.

This is a report on the health and social problems of the more than 8,000 Marshallese living on 78-acre Ebeye Island, Kwajalein Atoll.

09   *Elite Democracy or Authoritarian Rule?* Walden Bello and Elaine Elinson. Philippine Solidarity Network and the Coalition Against the Marcos Dictatorship, 1981. 18pp. $2. Also available from Southeast Asia Resource Center.

This booklet examines U.S. domination in the Philippines and in the Third World from the Kennedy years to the Reagan era.

10   *500 Mile Island: The Philippine Nuclear Deal.* Walden Bello, Peter Hayes, and Lyuba Zarsky. *Pacific Research* 10:1, 1979. 44pp. $2

This special issue of *Pacific Research* includes sections on the part the U.S. Export-Import Bank plays in the sale of reactors to Third World countries and the risks involved, the meaning of rural electrification in the Philippines, uranium mining in the United States, and radioactive waste dumping in the Pacific. It uses the Philippines as a case study, pointing out that conditions there are similar to those throughout the Third World and that opposition to nuclear power not only challenges the particular technology but threatens the international order which imposes it.

11   *Human Rights and the U.S. Foreign Assistance Program in Thailand.* Center for International Policy. 50 cents. Available also from the Southeast Asia Resource Center.

Descriptions of the human rights situation and of the relationship to this situation of U.S. economic and military aid to the countries of Southeast Asia.

12   *Human Rights in South Korea.* Pharis Harvey. *Current Issues*, March 1980. 7pp. 75 cents

This is the testimony of Pharis Harvey, executive director of the North American Coalition for Human Rights in Korea, on February 4, 1980, before the subcommittee on International Organizations and Asian and Pacific Affairs of the House Committee on Foreign Affairs. It covers the present situation in Korea—the use of torture and the restrictions on freedom of press and religion—the U.S. State Department's human rights reports, and suggestions as to what could be done regarding South Korea.

13   *The Kampuchea Debate.* Southeast Asia Chronicle 79, August 1981. $2.50

Contrasting views that have shaped the *Chronicle*'s coverage of Kampuchea. Includes a bibliography of the published debate and background documents.

14   *Key Contact.* North American Coalition for Human Rights in Korea. 12–20pp. $25/year

A biweekly packet of clippings on Korea taken from major newspapers and periodicals as well as documents from Korea. Recommended for anyone who wants to keep abreast of issues and events in Korea.

15   *Korea: Questions and Answers.* Pharis Harvey. *International Policy Report*, September 1981. 10pp. $1.50

This article begins from the questions put to Pharis Harvey in his appearance before a special hearing on Korea called by the Subcommittee on Asian and Pacific Affairs, Committee on Foreign Affairs, U.S. House of Representatives, on March 30, 1981. The questions and Mr. Harvey's answers relate to human rights and U.S. foreign assistance to South Korea.

3.116   *Korea Reports*. AFSC (Philadelphia), Korea Program. 15pp. 15 cents per report or 55 cents for annual subscription.

Periodic reports on the situation in Korea, including pieces on human rights, workers' struggles, the U.S. military, corporate activities, and resource materials.

3.117   *Laos Recovers from America's War*. Southeast Asia Chronicle 61, March–April 1978. $1.25

Church activists reported in detail from Vientiane on Laos' tremendous economic and political problems.

3.118   *Marshall Islands: A Chronology, 1944–1981*. Micronesia Support Committee, July 1978; revised August 1981. 40pp. Photographs and maps. $3

This pamphlet presents documentation on the U.S. nuclear testing program in the Marshall Islands and the consequent health problems for the people. It also includes information on the Kwajalein Missile Range, and the U.S. administration of Micronesia since 1947.

3.119   *Memorandum on U.S. Military Assistance to the Philippines*. Delia Miller. Institute for Policy Studies, 1979. 10pp. 50 cents

This memorandum was prepared as part of the IPS Militarism and Disarmament Project in October 1979. It is a thorough report that includes a look at the internal situation in the Philippines—economic, military, and human rights—as well as U.S. involvement by way of bases and monetary and weapons support. Includes tables on Philippine defense expenditures, U.S. military, and police gear exports to the Philippines.

3.120   *Micronesia Fact Sheet*. Micronesia Support Committee, January 1981. 2pp. Free

Brief history of Micronesia along with its current situation and relationship to the United States (military plans, nuclear waste dumping). Includes map.

3.121   *Militarism and Disarmament Report: Asia*. Institute for Policy Studies. 24pp.

The IPS packet of reprints concerning Asia includes a 19-page report prepared by Flora E. Montealegre, *Background Information on Indonesia: the Invasion of East Timor and U.S. Military Assistance* (1982).

3.122   *Military Coup in Thailand: Class Struggle and U.S. Imperialism*. Peter F. Bell. December 1976. 29pp. $1.50. Available from Southeast Asia Resource Center.

This article analyzes the motives, manner, and impact of the U.S. presence in Thailand.

3.123   *Myth and Ideology in U.S. Foreign Policy: East Timor and El Salvador*. Noam Chomsky. East Timor Human Rights Committee, 1982. 28pp. 60 cents. English and Spanish.

Chomsky analyzes the systematic construction of myths in the ideology of U.S. foreign policy by the U.S. government and the news media. The booklet uses the cases of East Timor and El Salvador as examples.

124   *Neither Food Nor Peace: U.S. Food Policy in Bangladesh.* Bill Christeson. *Pacific Research* 10:4, 1979. 20pp. $2

The author lived in Bangladesh and in the Philippines. This article poses the question of food aid or food self-sufficiency, and contends that U.S. food surpluses are "often handled as weapons to keep Third World countries dependent on the United States." The author sees Bangladesh as a tragic example of this policy.

125   *A New Look at America's Refugee Policy.* Astri Suhrke. *Indochina Issues* 10, September 1980. 7pp. $1

The author of this article spent time in Southeast Asia studying the refugee question. He also served as a consultant for the Library of Congress on U.S. refugee policy. The article includes tables of statistics.

126   *On the Withdrawal of U.S. Bases from the Philippines.* Friends of the Filipino People, 1979. 30pp. 50 cents. Also available from the Campaign to Remove U.S. Bases from the Philippines.

Testimony by Charito Planas, Prof. George McT. Kahin, Rear Admiral Gene R. LaRocque, USN(Ret.), and Francis T. Underhill, Jr., presented before the Subcommittee on Foreign Operations, House Appropriations Committee, April 6, 1979, Representative Clarence D. Long, Chairman.

127   *Pakistan: A People Suppressed.* Pakistan Committee for Democracy and Justice, September 1981. 51pp. $5

The Committee's "report on constitutional, judicial and human rights violations under army rule" surveys the situation in the country since Prime Minister Bhutto's overthrow in July 1977, paying particular attention to human rights violations.

128   *The Philippines in the 80s: From Normalization to Polarization.* Southeast *Asia Chronicle* 83, April 1982. 28pp. $2.50

An issue of the *Chronicle* analyzing recent developments in the Philippines, including the resistance, the Marcos regime, and the economy.

129   *The Political Economy of the Pacific Rim.* Timothy Shorrock. 1980. 35pp. Out of print; available in photocopy form from the Korea Support Committee.

This is an analysis of the relationship between the Pacific Northwest and East Asia. It describes the historical background of the United States in Asia and takes a critical look at the economic link between the Pacific Northwest and its major trading partners, Korea and Japan.

130   *South Korean Human Rights: The Roots of American Responsibilities.* Gregory Henderson. January 1980. 7pp. 50 cents. Available from North American Coalition for Human Rights in Korea.

Based on a presentation by the author at the Columbia University Seminar on Korea.

131   *The Struggle of South Korean Workers and the Urban/Industrial Mission.* Richard Poethig. ICUIS, 1979. 15pp. 25 cents

This is a compilation of abstracts of documents and articles outlining the struggles of factory workers and the churches' efforts to support them.

3.132 ***Thailand Plays the Great Power Game***. *Southeast Asia Chronicle* 69, January–February 1980. $1.25

This article explores Thailand's strategic position following the Vietnam-China war and what this means for both the Thai government and the Thai guerrilla movement. It includes a history of southern Thai resistance and a report from a jungle base camp.

3.133 ***Thailand under Military Rule***. *Southeast Asia Chronicle* 60, January–February 1978. $1.25

A close look at the Thai junta's programs, plus interviews with the students who fled the junta's violence. Explores Thailand's place in U.S. strategy.

3.134 ***A Time to Heal: The Effects of War on Vietnam, Laos, Cambodia and America***. Indochina Resource Center, 1976. 32pp. 50 cents. Available from Southeast Asia Resource Center.

This includes concise and comprehensive statistics together with photos and poetry.

3.135 ***United Front in the Philippines***. *Southeast Asia Chronicle* 62, May–June 1978. $1.25

Dr. Joel Rocamora examines the united resistance to martial law and the way in which the front achieved its unity. The issue includes the first publication of the National Democratic Front's 10-Point Program.

3.136 ***The United States and the Military Coup in Thailand***. Dr. E. Thadeus Flood. Indochina Resource Center, 1976. 8pp. 75 cents. Available from Southeast Asia Resource Center.

A documented study of the role of the CIA and the Defense Department in the Thai counterinsurgency apparatus and in the factional infighting within the Thai military.

3.137 ***U.S. Policy and Presence in East Asia: An Insider's View***. José Diokno. Friends of the Filipino People, 1980. 25 cents. Also available from Philippines Research Center.

Former Senator Diokno, once a political prisoner and long an opponent of the Marcos regime in the Philippines, writes here on a topic he and his co-workers have studied in depth: the relationship, historical and current, of the United States to Asia.

3.138 ***U.S. Policy and the Crisis in Indochina***. Coalition for a New Foreign and Military Policy, 1979. 8pp. 20 cents. Bulk rates available.

Details U.S. policy in Indochina since 1975. Outlines the development of the conflict between Vietnam, Cambodia, and China, and shows how U.S. policy has intensified the regional conflict.

3.139 ***Vietnam-China War***. *Southeast Asia Chronicle* 68, December 1979. 28pp. $1.25

Outlines the diplomatic moves that led to the conflict, the role of the United States, and ASEAN's reaction. An analysis of Vietnam's Chinese minority and the flight of the "boat people."

140   *Vietnam Is Still With Us. Southeast Asia Chronicle* 85, August 1982. 28pp. $2.50

The *Chronicle* considers in this issue the realities of the legacy of Vietnam: the agony of veterans, the struggle of the Vietnamese to rebuild their land, the manipulation of the hopes of the MIA families, the role of the United States in the world. An important effort in the ongoing process of understanding the meaning of Vietnam to the people of the United States.

141   *Vietnam-Kampuchea War. Southeast Asia Chronicle* 64, September–October 1978. 28pp. $1.25

A complete historical study together with an analysis of the role the major powers play in the conflict.

142   *Vietnam: What Kind of Peace?* Indochina Resource Center, 1973. 97pp. 75 cents. Available from Southeast Asia Resource Center.

Text and analysis of 1973 Paris Agreement, with military and diplomatic background. Essential tool for teaching history of the war.

143   *Vietnam's Embargoed Economy: In the U.S. Interest?* Michael Morrow. *Indochina Issues* 3, August 1979. 12pp. $1

This report on Vietnam's attempts to reconstruct touches upon international aid and finance, the importance of agriculture in the country, Vietnam's industry and energy problems, oil, and a consideration of America's trade embargo. Included are a chronology of major grants and loans to Vietnam since the war, and a chart of the country's foreign trade from 1974 to 1978.

144   *Vietnam's Struggle for Independence: America's Longest War.* Rachelle Marshall. Women's International League for Peace and Freedom, 1975. 34pp. $1. Also available from Southeast Asia Resource Center.

An overview of the Vietnam War with suggested questions for students.

145   *What's Behind the Education Act of 1982? A Primer on How Philippine Education Is Made to Serve U.S. Imperialist Needs.* Nationalist Resource Center, Philippines, August 1982. 42pp. $3. Available from Southeast Asia Resource Center.

The Education Act of 1982 has been the target of vigorous student and educators' protests in the Philippines since its drafting in 1980. It has been passed, however, and will soon be signed into law by President Marcos. This booklet was written "to help deepen popular awareness of the real issues behind the Education Act." It provides background to the act, outlines what the effects of the act will be, and shows how closely it relates to an export-based developmental strategy, to worker exploitation, and to the "global assembly line."

146   *Why Are They So Angry at America?* Parker Rossman. *The Christian Century*, August 26-September 2, 1981. 2pp. Available from Church Committee on Human Rights in Asia.

A view of U.S. foreign policy by Filipino students.

147   *The World Bank. Southeast Asian Chronicle* 81, December 1981. 28pp. $2.50

This issue of the *Chronicle* deals with the question of how much the World

Bank serves U.S. interests in Asia. It considers World Bank funded projects in the Philippines, Indonesia, and Thailand.

3.148   *Why We Back Korea's Chun*. Maud and David Easter. *Christianity and Crisis*, February 1981. 7pp. 90 cents. Available from North American Coalition for Human Rights in Korea.

A description of U.S. political, military, and economic interest in Korea.

3.149   *"Yellow Rain": Unanswered Questions*. J. Fred Swartzendruber. *Indochina Issues* 23, January 1982. 7pp. $1

This article, written by a representative of the Mennonite Central Committee who was in Laos from 1979 to 1981, chronicles the State Department reports concerning the possible use by the Soviet Union of a chemical agent in Laos. The author examines the actual physical evidence collected by the State Department, and poses questions surrounding this evidence. He calls for agreement that adequate and scientific study be done before conclusions be drawn.

See also:
7.49, 7.53, 7.57, 7.63, 9.59, 9.63, 10.57, 10.59, 10.71

AUDIOVISUAL RESOURCES

Guides and Catalogs

3.150   *Asia through Film: An Annotated Guide to Films on Asia in the University of Michigan Audio-Visual Education Center*. JoAnn Hymes, ed. Ann Arbor, Mich.: Project on Asia Studies in Education (PASE), 1976. 64pp. $3.50

This guide covers Japan, China, South Asia and Southeast Asia. The annotations describe and evaluate the films. All the films listed are available for rental through the University of Michigan Audio-Visual Education Center. Distributors' addresses are also given.

3.151   *China: A Multimedia Guide*. Mary Robinson Sive. New York: Neal-Schuman, 1982. 245pp. $16.50. See 3.190.

Audiovisuals

152   *The Automated Battlefield*. 1971 40 min color slides or filmstrip with cassette.
NARMIC. AFSC (Cambridge). Rental $15
    This resource was perhaps the most widely used educational aid during the
Vietnam War. It describes the electronic air war waged by the United States and
its effects on the people of Vietnam and Laos.

153   *Backseat Generals*. 1972 25 min color film. Granada Television. AFSC (Cambridge). Rental $20
    This film shows how the CIA financed armies in Laos and exposes the U.S.
secret air war there.

154   *Cambodia: Year One*. 1980 60 min color film. John Pilger. AFSC (Cambridge). Rental $25
    This film made for British TV contrasts the horror of the Kampuchea left by
Pol Pot with the positive determination of the Cambodian people to rebuild their
country. The film offers a balanced appraisal of Vietnam's role and aims in Kampuchea.

155   *Cambodia: Year Zero*. 1979 60 min color film. AFSC (Cambridge). Rental $25
    This film deals with the history of Cambodia from 1975 to 1979. The brutality
of the Pol Pot regime is portrayed realistically and is placed within the context of
the political history of the time. The need for international aid and the politics
underlying the food aid controversy are emphasized.

156   *Chained Hands in Prayer*. 1977 30 min slides with cassette. AFSC (Cambridge). Rental $15
    This slideshow is based on Korean political prisoner Kim Chi Ha's poems.

157   *China Mission*. 2 reels 58 min film. National Film Board of Canada. Rental $60
    This is the story of Chester Ronning, son of Lutheran missionaries in China
and once Canadian ambassador to China. The film, written by his daughter,
Audrey Topping, covers events in China from the Boxer Rebellion to the founding of the People's Republic.

158   *Christians and the Struggle for Human Rights in Korea*. 1979 30 min slides with
script and cassette. Church Committee on Human Rights in Asia. Rental $10
    Gives background on martial law and the Korean Christian response to human
rights violations.

159   *Collision Course*. 1979 40 min color film. British Broadcasting Company.
AFSC (Cambridge). Rental $20
    This BBC analysis of human rights violations by the U.S.-supported Philippine
government includes interviews with political dissidents, religious leaders, and
government officials. It shows the connection between human rights violations
and economic conditions, and is a good case study of political repression under a
U.S.-supported dictatorship.

160   *East Timor*. 1981 36 color slides with script. East Timor Human Rights Committee. Rental $10. Sale $30
    This slideshow briefly but powerfully presents background on East Timor's

struggle for independence. Particular attention is paid to the U.S.-backed invasion of the country by Indonesia and to the genocide that followed.

3.161　*Hearts and Minds*. 1975 90 min color film. Peter Davis/Bert Schneider. Available from AFSC (Cambridge), University of California Extension Media Center, and Paramount Pictures. Inquire for rates.

This documentary film uses historical documents and interviews to probe the American military and political consciousness that led to U.S. involvement in Vietnam. It is probably the best film available to give an accurate picture of the roots and impact of the war and to balance distortions in other popular media presentations of the period.

3.162　*How Yukong Moved the Mountains*. 1977 12 parts 12 hours color film. Joris Ivens/Marcelline Loridan. Cinema Arts Association. Rental $35–$125

This series of twelve films by an outstanding documentary filmmaker covers nearly every aspect of people's lives in modern China. Topics range from women to an army camp, from factories to an experimental pharmacy.

3.163　*In the Year of the Pig*. 1969 101 min b&w film. Emile de Antonio. New Yorker Films. Rental $125

This classic documentary, made at the height of U.S. involvement in Vietnam, is useful as a straightforward history of the period as well as a lesson on the formulation of U.S. foreign policy. The director lets history be told by its participants; thus, Ho Chi Minh, Lyndon Johnson, David Halberstam, Richard Nixon, Madame Ngo Dinh Nhu, Dean Rusk and others are heard directly rather than any single narrator.

3.164　*Korea: Time for a Change*. 1981 25 min color slideshow or filmstrip with cassette. Maud and David Easter. AFSC (Cambridge). Rental $15. Sale $50, slideshow; $40, filmstrip

This audiovisual examines daily life in North and South Korea and studies the impact of U.S. foreign and military policy on the divided country.

3.165　*Looking for China: American Images* (Part 1); *Looking for America: Chinese Images* (Part 2). 1980 50 slides with cassette, 16-18 min each part. China Council, The Asia Society. Sale $10 each part.

This slideshow presents Chinese and American images of each other based on newspaper cartoons, magazines, movies and other sources. It is appropriate for the high school level.

3.166　*Marshall Islands: America's Radioactive "Trust."* 1980 25 min slideshow with script. 120 slides. Micronesia Support Committee. Sale $65

This slideshow focuses on the history and facts of the United States nuclear testing program in the Marshall Islands as well as the effects of this program—both immediate and long-range—on the health and lifestyle of the people.

3.167　*Military Demarcation Zone*. 35 min b&w film. Korea Film Import Co. Available from California Newsreel. Rental $40

This film presents a complete history of the causes of the Korean War and the division of the country into north and south. It uses U.S. government documents to describe U.S. policy in the country.

.168　　*More Than a Million Years*. 1976 28 min b&w film. Amnesty International. Unifilm. Rental $25

This film is a documentary report on the more than 100,000 political prisoners incarcerated since the 1965 CIA-supported coup in Indonesia. It includes an analysis of the support of the United States and other Western powers for the repressive Suharto regime.

.169　　*The New Opium Route*. 1973 54 min color film. Catherine and Marianne Lamour. Icarus Films. Rental $80

This film presents a picture of a little known society: that of the Bashtus, a people who live in an undeveloped region of the Khyber Pass on the border between Afghanistan and Pakistan. The film follows a shipment of opium from the mountains to the coast to European processors, and finally to the American market.

.170　　*Nuclear Power and Martial Law*. 25 min slideshow with script. Mike Bedford. Friends of the Filipino People. Rental $15. Sale $40

Emphasizes the safety hazards involved at the construction site of the nuclear reactor Westinghouse is building in Bataan. Includes maps of the earthquake zone and nearby volcano. Addresses the problems of corporate dumping of nuclear technology in the Third World, the collusion of the Marcos regime with Westinghouse, and the growing opposition in the Philippines to the plant.

.171　　*Perception/Misperception: China/U.S.A.* 4 color filmstrips, 4 cassettes. 1 silent filmstrip, 1 audio cassette, 8 role cards, 30 student booklets, teacher's guide. Social Studies School Service. Sale $175

This is a mini-course on China-United States relations. The four sound filmstrips cover stereotyping, cultural differences, China-U.S. relations since the nineteenth century, and examples of the perceptions and misperceptions each culture has about the other. The silent filmstrip contains experiments in perception. One audio cassette contains case studies of culture shock. The 8 cards are a role-play game that involves participants in planning a model community. Student booklets contain readings and activities.

.172　　*Phantom India*. 1970 7 parts 52 min color film. Louis Malle. New Yorker Films. Rental $125 per episode, $600 for entire film if shown over a two-week period.

This seven part, six and one-half hour documentary attempts to portray the totality of India. Its episodes cover the movie industry, a dancing school, a birth control clinic, a red light district, tribes with unusual customs, esoteric cults, and exotic places.

.173　　*Philippines: Islands in Struggle*. 1981 30 min slideshow. Philippine Solidarity Network (South Bay). Rental $15

This slideshow traces the history of U.S.-Philippine relations, the economic conditions in the Philippines, and the resistance movement there.

.174　　*The Politics of Torture*. 1978 50 min color film. California Newsreel/ABC Close-Up. Rental $70. Sale $650

This film exposes evidence of brutal repression by the Philippine government and other U.S. allies and raises questions about U.S. government and private support for such regimes. It documents examples of repression in Iran and Chile as well as the Philippines.

3.175   *Report from Kwangju.* 1980 30 min color film. AFSC (Cambridge). Rental $20
This film presents never before released footage of the worker-student take-over of the city of Kwangju, South Korea. It shows the violent crushing of the uprising by South Korean army units. The important role the United States plays in South Korea makes an understanding of this democratic uprising crucial.

3.176   *Rough Road to Recovery.* 1980 23 min slideshow with script. AFSC (Cambridge). Rental $15
This slideshow is based on an AFSC tour of Cambodia in early 1980. It presents updated information on food aid to the country, attempts at reconstruction, and the political situation there.

3.177   *Southeast Asia Since Vietnam: Territorial Turmoil.* 1980 color filmstrip with record or cassette, spirit duplicating master, guide. New York Times. Available from Social Studies School Service. Rental $27
This filmstrip describes the turmoil in Southeast Asia following the withdrawal of U.S. forces from Vietnam. It shows the Boat People, the expelled Chinese of Vietnam, the conditions in Cambodia under Pol Pot, the Sino-Soviet struggle for influence, and the refugee camps in Thailand. It raises the question of U.S. responsibility in Southeast Asia. The teacher's guide contains discussion questions and a map of Southeast Asia on a spirit duplicating master.

3.178   *Tenants in Our Own Land.* 1979 slideshow. Mennonite Missionaries. Rental $60
An examination of Castle & Cooke's Dolefil and Standard Philippine Fruit (bananas and pineapples) operations in the southern Philippines. Told through four characters: Gerardo Sicat, Minister of Economic Development; Mrs. Sales, a small banana grower; O.J. Keichkof, president of Castle & Cooke; and Mario, a pineapple worker.

3.179   *There Was An Evening, There Was A Morning.* 1975 60 min color film. AFSC (Cambridge). Rental $20
This film about the liberation of Vietnam was made by a group of Vietnamese Catholic clergy and laypeople. There are two half hour reels. The first is a documentary and may be used by itself. The second consists of interviews around the role of religious institutions in pre- and post-war Vietnam.

3.180   *This Bloody, Plundering Business.* 1975 30 min color film. Peter Davis. Unifilm ($35); Villon Films ($50)
This satire on American foreign policy traces the history of American intervention in the Philippines. It contains rare archival footage and makes effective use of ragtime as a musical background.

3.181   *Timor: Island of Fear, Island of Hope.* 1976 28 min color film. East Timor Human Rights Committee. Rental $25, plus shipping
This is one of the few films available about the invasion of East Timor by U.S.-backed Indonesian forces. It was made around the time of the Indonesian

invasion and does not therefore cover the conditions that followed the invasion. Slides and a cassette accompany the film and serve as an update.

3.182   *Tongpan*. 60 min b&w film. AFSC (Cambridge). Rental $50

Tongpan is based on the experiences of a peasant in northeastern Thailand. The film grew out of a Quaker-sponsored seminar held in 1975 for the purpose of discussing the impact of the proposed Mekong River Pa-Mong Dam. This was a district where Tongpan lived, and he was a participant in that seminar.

3.183   *The United States in Vietnam: How Did It Happen?* 1975 20 min filmstrip with script and cassette. Indochina Curriculum Group. Also available from the Institute for Peace and Justice and from the American Friends Service Committee. Inquire for rates.

This filmstrip is a very good short history of Vietnam from the 1800s. It outlines the step-by-step involvement of the United States in Vietnamese affairs.

3.184   *Vietnam: An American Journey*. 1979 90 min color film. Bob Richter. AFSC (Cambridge). Inquire for rates.

This was the first film on Vietnam made by an American after the war. The filmmaker traveled the entire length of Highway 1 in Vietnam—from Hanoi to Ho Chi Minh City. He presents a forthright picture of Vietnam in the period immediately following the war and argues for American reparations and international aid for Vietnam.

3.185   *War in Vietnam: Photo Aids* (Series 12). Ten 11 by 14-inch photo aids printed with captions on heavy glossy stock. Social Studies School Service. Sale $7.50

These photographs of events in wartorn Vietnam include pictures of a downed U.S. helicopter, Americans transporting their dead, troops in the jungle, a Vietcong prisoner, and President Johnson decorating a soldier.

3.186   *Where Will We Hang the Lightbulbs?* 1979 15 min slideshow with cassette. Mennonite Missionaries. Available from AFSC (Cambridge). Rental $15

This slideshow presents the story of the Tiboli struggle against an Asian Development Bank-funded dam which would drive them from their ancestral home. Some authentic Tiboli music, quotations from the Tiboli petition to President Marcos, and a discussion of who benefits from capital intensive high level technological development.

3.187   *Who Owns the Sky?* 1978 23 min slideshow with cassette. AFSC (Cambridge). Rental $15

This slideshow uses the example of the Kawasaki Steel Corporation of Japan to show how large corporations from developed countries can take advantage of Third World countries. Kawasaki, required by Japanese citizens to clean up its polluting operations in Japan, chose instead to move its most polluting processes to the Philippines. The presentation points out the economic function of authoritarian governments in Southeast Asia.

See also:
1.194, 7.73, 8.117, 10.110

OTHER RESOURCES

Curriculum Guides and Materials

3.188   *Asia: Teaching About/Learning From*. Seymour Fersh. New York: Teachers College Press, Columbia University, 1978. 180pp. $4.95

This work provides teachers in various disciplines with a rationale and resources for teaching about Asian civilizations. It examines some basic questions: what should be taught, for what results, in what ways and using what kinds of materials. It also provides information useful for teaching about Asia from K-12, including maps, charts, language examples, statistics, and a guide to additional sources and resources. It includes excerpts from the writings of leading Asian studies scholars and educators.

3.189   *Bay Area China Resource Guide*. SPICE/China Program, March 1979. 58pp. $3.50

This is a guide to the resources on China and Chinese culture in the Bay Area. It includes the arts, books and bookstores, crafts, fieldtrips, films, libraries, museums, organizations, periodicals, resource and curriculum materials.

3.190   *China: A Multimedia Guide*. Mary Robinson Sive. New York: Neal-Schuman, 1982. 245pp. $16.50

Mary Robinson Sive, editor of *Media Monitor*, a periodical guide to learning resources, author of *Selecting Instructional Media*, and of "Media Notes" column in *Curriculum Review*, has compiled in *China: A Multimedia Guide* an outstanding source book for anyone involved in teaching or learning about the People's Republic.

The book covers materials produced since 1976 for elementary grades, middle school, junior high, and senior high school. The annotated entries (over 600 of them) are arranged according to grade levels and emphasize materials that break down stereotypical thinking and show a respect for cultural differences. They include maps and atlases, professional resources (books, ERIC documents, and organizations serving as continuing sources of information). A directory of suppliers of the materials is a helpful appendix; author and name, title, institution, and subject indexes complete the work.

3.191   *China in the Classroom: Resources from the Center for Teaching About China*. Washington, D.C.: Center for Teaching About China, 1980. 16pp.

This catalog of resources lists a broad variety of materials for use at the elementary and secondary levels available from the Center for Teaching About China.

3.192   *Southeast Asia*. James I. Clark. Culver City, Ca.: Social Studies School Service, 1978. 95pp. $6.60. Teacher's Guide: $1.80

One of the textbooks in the Peoples and Cultures Series, *Southeast Asia* is written for grades 9–12. It covers early religious and cultural influences, European involvement, the winning of independence (including the Vietnam War), and life today in Burma, Thailand, Vietnam, Java, and major Asian cities.

.193   *Teacher's Resource Handbook for Asian Studies*. John Hawkins. Available
only in microfiche from ERIC Document Reproduction Service for $1.

This is part of the Teacher's Resource Handbook series developed by the Curriculum Inquiry Center at UCLA to help teachers locate useful materials for multicultural educational programs. It is organized by grade level (K-12). Most of the listings are annotated.

3.194   *Teaching the Vietnam War*. William L. Griffen and John Marciana. Montclair, N.J.: Allanheld, Osmun & Co., 1979. 183pp. $6.50

This book is a critical examination of the treatment given the Vietnam War in 28 textbooks. It deals especially with the interpretation given of American motives and the actual facts of American participation before and after initial military actions involving Americans. It points out errors in the texts in actual historical facts, and shows that the texts only play back government-establishment statements of policy, motive, and events. The last part of the book presents an alternative history of the Vietnam War, drawn from material compiled in *The Pentagon Papers* and other nonprejudiced sources.

3.195   *Understanding Indochina Packet*. New York: United Church Press. $19.95

This packet includes the book *Indochina Is People* (Southeast Asia Resource Center), the filmstrip *Tell Them We Are People* (AFSC), and wall maps of Asia and of the peoples of mainland Southeast Asia. It is a good resource for teaching about the land and peoples of Indochina.

3.196   *Understanding U.S.-China Relations: Issues and Resources*. *Intercom* 68, 1972. 72pp. $1.75

This is one of the issues of a quarterly publication put out by Global Perspectives in Education. It includes three lesson plans, an annotated bibliography of books and audiovisual materials on China, and a listing of available curriculum guides and organizational resources on China.

3.197   *The Vietnam Era: A Guide to Teaching Resources*. Cambridge, Mass.: Indochina Curriculum Group, 1978. 105pp. $5. Also available from AFSC (Philadelphia).

The Vietnam Era, compiled by a collective of Boston-area high school teachers and writers, seeks to provide viewpoints other than those included in standard textbooks along with suggestions on a sensitive approach to issues which may well imply preconceptions. It includes annotated resources, teaching suggestions, and an extensive listing of publishers and distributors. A revised edition is planned for 1982.

Simulation Games

3.198   *Dangerous Parallel*. Glenview, Ill.: Scott Foresman & Co., 1969. $72. Level: secondary school and above. Players: 18–36. Time: 6–9 hours.

This very polished simulation—complete with filmstrip and record—deals with international conflicts in general, but the similarities to the Korean War are very evident. *Dangerous Parallel* provides participants with an experience of international decision making and, it is hoped, with an understanding of the complexities involved in shaping foreign policy.

As with all simulations care should be taken to see that participants appreciate the need for detailed study and analysis of actual historical events, lest the simulation be taken to be a replay of history. Furthermore, it's suggested that a final portion of the debriefing be set aside for a critical analysis of the simulation itself. What biases did the game's creators weave into the structure of the simulation? How accurate a picture did the simulation (or its accompanying documentary materials) give of the forces involved in foreign policy decision making?

3.199   *Mission: A Simulation of American Foreign Policy in Vietnam*. Culver City, Calif.: Social Studies School Service. 35 student guides, teacher's guide $16. Players: 25–35. Time: 3 weeks.

Participants in this simulation game represent members of different factions. They research and then argue the viewpoints of "hawks," "doves," and moderates. They assume various identities: senators, college professors and students, military leaders, the president of the United States, the president's press secretary. Other elements include draft protests, prestige factors, and a presidential election.

See also:
1.200, 1.207, 7.78, 7.82

Chapter 4

Latin America and Caribbean

KEY RESOURCES

Organizations

Of the groups in this chapter that approach the Latin American region as a whole the two we'd give our highest recommendation to are the **North American Congress on Latin America (NACLA)** and the **Washington Office on Latin America (WOLA)**. The latter is more church- and Washington-oriented while NACLA brings years of research and progressive political experience to the task of understanding America's role in Latin America. Contact with both organizations would give you a broadened understanding of how to analyze U.S.–Latin America relations and of what the possibilities are for effective action.

EPICA, the **Ecumenical Program for Inter-American Communication and Action**, is highly recommended for those with a particular focus on Central America and the Caribbean.

Printed Resources

Penny Lernoux's *Cry of the People* is far and away the best popular book to read on U.S. involvement in Latin America. We can't think of any other book that would be as good for personal reading or for group study. It is up-to-date, personal, gripping, and uncompromising in stating its case against U.S. private and public interference in Latin American affairs.

EPICA's primers on Nicaragua, Jamaica, Puerto Rico, Grenada, and Honduras are attractive and well-documented presentations on countries in the Caribbean and Central America region.

WOLA's *Latin America Update* and its occasional reports and papers are good periodic sources of information on Latin America. Penny Lernoux's columns in

The Nation make that publication well worth keeping an eye on. *NACLA Report on the Americas* offers consistently hard-hitting and well-researched analyses of political and economic issues in the Americas.

This section features a number of back issues of *NACLA Report on the Americas*. These, along with the studies produced by the **Institute for Policy Studies**, are all excellent resources for private study and for educational programs.

Audiovisual Resources

Many of the audiovisuals is this chapter deal with specific countries in the region—Chile, Cuba, Nicaragua, El Salvador. We have tried to select the most worthwhile and up-to-date country–specific audiovisuals. We consider all of those in this section to be worth your consideration.

From a regional point of view, **AFSC's** *Central America: Roots of the Crisis* and the **NCC's** *Problem of Power* are recommended.

Other Resources

Three groups are important sources for directories and bibliographies: the **Connexions Collective**, the **Latin America Working Group**, and **NACLA**.

Of prime importance in curriculum guides is the special double issue of the *Bulletin* of the **Council of Interracial Books for Children** called *Central America: What U.S. Educators Need to Know.*

Project R.E.A.L. of the **Stanford/Berkeley Latin America Studies Center**, and the **Latin America Studies Program** of the University of Texas at Austin are good ongoing sources for educational materials.

ORGANIZATIONS

4.1   **American Friends Service Committee**, Latin America Program, 1501 Cherry St., Philadelphia, PA 19102. Tel: 215-241-7159.

RELIGIOUS AFFILIATION: Religious Society of Friends (Quakers).

FOCUS: Latin America and Caribbean. Human rights • political repression • militarism • national liberation struggles • corporate responsibility • social justice • women.

ACTIVITIES: Popular education • research and writing • congressional testimony • solidarity work • intern programs • foreign service • networking • documentation and information • justice and peace ministries • workshops and seminars.

RESOURCES: Speakers • audiovisuals • literature • list of resources available.

4.2 Bay Area Ecumenical Committee on Chile, 942 Market St., Suite 709, San Francisco, CA 94102. Tel: 415-433-6055.

FOCUS: Chile. Human rights • political repression • foreign trade and aid • international awareness • national liberation struggles • corporate responsibility • social justice.

ACTIVITIES: Popular education • constituency education • political action • legislative action • solidarity work • foreign service (development, missionary) • networking • overseas project support • documentation and information • justice and peace ministries • workshops and seminars.

RESOURCES: Speakers • publications • study–action guides • curriculum guides.

PERIODICALS: **4.3** *Hope in Chile*. Bimonthly. $5/year.

4.4 Brazil Labor Information and Resource Center, Box 221, Brooklyn, NY 11217. Tel: 212-473-6098.

FOCUS: Brazil. Human rights • transnational corporations • international awareness • social justice • labor.

ACTIVITIES: Popular education • research and writing • solidarity work • networking (international union to union especially) • media • documentation and information • organizing meetings and tours.

RESOURCES: Audiovisuals • publications.

4.5 Committee in Solidarity with the People of El Salvador (CISPES), Box 12056, Washington, DC 20005. Tel: 202-887-5019.

FOCUS: El Salvador. Human rights • political repression • militarism • foreign trade and aid • international awareness • political economy • national liberation struggles.

ACTIVITIES: Popular education • research and writing • legislative action • solidarity work • networking (through local chapters) • documentation and information • workshops and seminars.

RESOURCES: Speakers • publications • reports • curriculum guides • study–action guides • consultant services.

PERIODICALS: **4.6** *El Salvador Alert*. $10/year.

4.7 Community Action on Latin America (CALA), 731 State St., Madison, WI 53703. Tel: 608-251-3241.

FOCUS: Latin America. Human rights • political repression • militarism • disarmament • nuclear arms and energy • foreign trade and aid • political economy • socialism • international awareness • national liberation struggles • corporate responsibility • social justice • rights of indigenous peoples.

ACTIVITIES: Popular education • political action • legislative action • research and writing • solidarity work • library services • networking • media • overseas project support •• documentation and information • policy-oriented research and writing • workshops and seminars • documentary film making • publishing.

RESOURCES: Speakers • audiovisuals • literature • publications • curriculum guides • consultant services • library.

PERIODICALS: **4.8** *CALA Newsletter*. Quarterly. $3/year.

SPECIAL PROJECTS: Wisconsin–Nicaragua Educational Exchange Program.

4.9 **Council on Hemispheric Affairs**, 1900 L St., NW, Suite 201, Washington, DC 20036. Tel: 202-775-0216. 30 Fifth Ave., New York, NY 10011. Tel: 212-673-5470.

FOCUS: Latin America, especially U.S. foreign policy toward Latin America. Human rights • political repression • nuclear arms and energy • foreign trade and aid • corporate responsibility • social justice.

ACTIVITIES: Research and writing • congressional testimony • intern programs • library services • press service • media • documentation and information • policy-oriented research and writing • press conferences • sponsors conferences.

RESOURCES: Speakers • distributor of literature • publications • research services • library.

PERIODICALS: **4.10** *Washington Report on the Hemisphere*. 25 issues/year; $25–$45/year, depending upon nature of subscriber. Classroom subscriptions available; apply for rates. **4.11** *Research Memoranda*. Occasional.

4.12 **Ecumenical Program for Inter-American Communication and Action (EPICA)**, 1470 Irving St., NW, Washington, DC 20010. Tel: 202-332-0292.

FOCUS: Caribbean and Central America. Human rights • political repression • political economy • international awareness • national liberation struggles • social justice.

ACTIVITIES: Popular education • constituency education • political action • solidarity work • networking • documentation and information • justice and peace ministries • workshops and seminars.

RESOURCES: Speakers • publications • reports.

4.13 **Friends for Jamaica**, 1 E. 125 St., New York, NY 10035.

FOCUS: Jamaica and Caribbean. Human rights • political repression • militarism • foreign trade and aid • political economy • national liberation struggles • trade union activity • economic problems.

ACTIVITIES: Research and writing • solidarity work • documentation and information • collections for destitute Jamaicans.

RESOURCES: Literature for distribution • publications.

PERIODICALS: **4.14** *Friends for Jamaica Newsletter*. Monthly. $6/year.

4.15 **Guatemala News and Information Bureau (GNIB)**, Box 4126, Berkeley, CA 94704. Tel: 415-835-0810.

FOCUS: Guatemala. Human rights • political repression • national liberation struggles • social justice • non-intervention.

ACTIVITIES: Popular education • political action • legislative action • research and writing • solidarity work • intern programs • media • documentation and information.

RESOURCES: Speakers • audiovisuals • literature • publications • library.

PERIODICALS: **4.16** *Guatemala!* Spanish and English. Bimonthly newsletter. $7/year individual; $10/year institutional.

.17   Inter-Religious Task Force on El Salvador and Central America, 475 Riverside Dr., Rm. 633, New York, NY 10115. Tel: 212-870-3383.

RELIGIOUS AFFILIATION: Ecumenical.

FOCUS: El Salvador and Central America. Human rights • political repression • militarism • international awareness / national liberation struggles • corporate responsibility • social justice • witness of Christian community.

ACTIVITIES: Constituency education • political action • legislative action • solidarity work • networking • media • documentation and information • justice and peace ministries • workshops and seminars.

RESOURCES: Speakers • audiovisuals • literature • publications • study–action guides • consultant services • reports.

PERIODICALS: **4.18** *El Salvador and Central America News and Alert.* Monthly. $15/year.

.19   Latin America Bureau, U.S. Catholic Conference, 1312 Massachusetts Ave., NW, Washington, DC 20005. Tel: 202-659-6812.

FOCUS: Latin America. Human rights • political repression • international awareness • Latin American church • social justice.

ACTIVITIES: Constituency education • research and writing • justice and peace ministries.

RESOURCES: Literature distribution • consultant services.

.20   Mexico-U.S. Border Program of the American Friends Service Committee, 1501 Cherry St., Philadelphia, PA 19102. Tel: 215-241-7132.

RELIGIOUS AFFILIATION: Religious Society of Friends (Quakers).

FOCUS: International and domestic. Mexico. Transnational corporations • international awareness • corporate responsibility • social justice • women • community-based economic development • workers' rights • immigration.

ACTIVITIES: Popular education • constituency education • legislative action • congressional testimony • intern programs • press service • networking • media • overseas project support • documentation and information • policy-oriented research and writing • defense of workers' rights • community organizing.

RESOURCES: Speakers • audiovisuals • publications.

PERIODICALS: **4.21** *Mexico-U.S. Border Program Newsletter.* Occasional. Free.

.22   National Network in Solidarity with the Nicaraguan People, 980 F St., NW, Suite 720, Washington, DC 20004. Tel: 202-223-2328; 202-628-9598.

FOCUS: Nicaragua and Central America. Human rights • foreign trade and aid • political economy • international awareness • social justice • U.S. covert actions • revolutionary reconstruction • church and revolution.

ACTIVITIES: Popular education • constituency education • political action • legislative action • research and writing • solidarity work • intern programs • networking (through local committees) • media • overseas project support • documentation and information • workshops and seminars • tours to and from Nicaragua.

RESOURCES: Speakers • audiovisuals • literature • publications • bookstore • study–action guides • curriculum guides • library • reports.

PERIODICALS: **4.23** *Nicaragua*. Bimonthly newsletter. $5/year. **4.24** *Fact Sheets*. Occasional.

SPECIAL PROJECTS: People-to-People Tours to Nicaragua. Tours to the United States for Nicaraguan government, church, or organization leaders.

4.25 **National Network in Solidarity with the People of Guatemala (NISGUA)**, 930 F St., NW, Suite 720, Washington, DC 20004. Tel: 202-483-0050.

FOCUS: Guatemala. Human rights • political repression • militarism • foreign trade and aid • transnational corporations.

ACTIVITIES: Popular education • political action • solidarity work • networking • documentation and information • workshops and seminars.

RESOURCES: Speakers • audiovisuals • publications.

PERIODICALS: **4.26** *Network News*. Monthly. With membership.

4.27 **New York Circus/Latin America Information Service (LAIS)**, Box 37, Times Square Station, New York, NY 10108. Tel: 212-663-8112.

RELIGIOUS AFFILIATION: Ecumenical.

FOCUS: International. Latin America. Human rights • political repression • militarism • foreign trade and aid • theology of liberation • political economy • socialism • international awareness • corporate responsibility • social justice • Latin American and domestic issues affecting the churches.

ACTIVITIES: Popular education • research and writing • solidarity work • intern programs • library services • networking • immigration issues • workshops and seminars.

RESOURCES: Speakers • literature • audiovisuals • publications • study–action guides • library • reports • Bible studies.

PERIODICALS: **4.28** *Lucha/Struggle*. Bimonthly. $10/year individual; $20 institutional.

SPECIAL PROJECTS: Immigrants' Rights Project: paralegal training, educational materials, networking between community, union and church. Nicaragua Project: education and seminars addressing the role of Christians in Nicaragua and the role of women. Chilean Health Care Project: support of a missionary developing preventive health care project in Santiago, Chile.

4.29 **Nicaragua Interfaith Committee for Action (NICA)**, 942 Market St., Rm. 709, San Francisco, CA 94102. Tel: 415-433-6057.

RELIGIOUS AFFILIATION: Agency of the Northern California Ecumenical Council.

FOCUS: Nicaragua and Central America. Human rights • U.S. military intervention in Central America • cutbacks in U.S. aid • Nicaraguan model of political and economic development • international awareness • national liberation struggles • social justice.

ACTIVITIES: Popular education through the churches • political action • legislative action • research and writing • solidarity work • foreign service (development) • networking • media • overseas project support • documentation and information • justice and peace ministries • workshops and seminars.

RESOURCES: Speakers • audiovisuals • literature • publications • study–action guides • consultant services • research services • graphics exhibit.

PERIODICALS: **4.30** *Nicaragua Update.* Bimonthly newsletter. $7/year.

SPECIAL PROJECTS: Tours to and from Nicaragua for church personnel.

.31   North American Congress on Latin America (NACLA), 151 W. 19 St., 9th Floor, New York, NY 10011. Tel: 212-989-8890.

FOCUS: Latin America. Foreign trade and aid • transnational corporations • political economy • international awareness • social justice • women.

ACTIVITIES: Popular education • research and writing • library services • policy-oriented research and writing.

RESOURCES: Speakers • publications • consultant services • library • research services.

PERIODICALS: **4.32** *NACLA Report on the Americas* (formerly *Latin America and Empire Report*). Bimonthly. $13/year.

.33   Peru Solidarity Committee, Box 3580, Grand Central Station, New York, NY 10017. Tel: 212-964-6730.

FOCUS: Latin America, especially Peru. Human rights • political repression • foreign trade and aid • political economy • international awareness • basic needs.

ACTIVITIES: Popular education • research and writing • congressional testimony • solidarity work • intern programs • networking • media • documentation and information.

RESOURCES: Speakers • audiovisuals • literature • publications • background information on Peru • educational packets for human rights action groups.

PERIODICALS: **4.34** *Peru Update.* 10 issues/year. Contribution. $5/year suggested minimum.

.35   Puerto Rico Solidarity Committee, Box 319, Cooper Station, New York, NY 10003. Tel: 212-741-3131.

FOCUS: Puerto Rico • Vieques.

RESOURCES: Chapters in major cities.

PERIODICALS: **4.36** *Puerto Rico Libre!* Bimonthly newsletter. $5/year individual; $15/year institutional.

.37   Washington Office on Latin America (WOLA), 110 Maryland Ave., NE, Washington, DC 20002. Tel: 202-544-8045.

FOCUS: Latin America and Caribbean. Human rights • political repression • militarism • political economy • social justice.

ACTIVITIES: Popular education • political action • research and writing • congressional testimony • intern programs • press service • networking • media • conferences.

RESOURCES: Speakers • literature • publications • consultant services • reports.

PERIODICALS: **4.38** *Latin America Update.*Bimonthly newsletter. $10/year.
4.39 *Special Country Reports.* 2–4 issues/year. **4.40** *Occasional Papers.* 2–4 issues/year.

PRINTED RESOURCES

Books

4.41   Arias, Esther, and Arias, Mortimer. *The Cry of My People*. New York: Friendship Press, 1980. 146pp. $2.95

In an effort to help us see the world as Latin Americans view it the authors immerse us in "a living experience in intercultural dialogue." From this experience we come to appreciate, for instance, how the Monroe Doctrine looks to those south of the Rio Grande. In addition we study—with the eyes of Latin Americans—the impact of U.S. investments in the region; terrorist regimes and their abuse of human rights; the women's movement; the plight of Latin America's hungry masses; and the role of the churches in the region's changing societies.

4.42   Armstrong, Robert, and Shenk, Janet. *El Salvador: The Face of Revolution*. Boston: South End Press, 1982. 300pp. $7.50

A consideration of the spirit and reality of El Salvador's revolution, this book examines current notions of a war between extreme left and right in the light of the role of the Catholic Church, political parties, El Salvador's grassroots organizations, the U.S. military, and private investment.

4.43   Arnson, Cynthia. *El Salvador: A Revolution Confronts the United States*. Washington, D.C.: Institute for Policy Studies, 1982. 118pp. $5.95

Arnson traces the evolution of the conflict in El Salvador and provides a background for understanding it as well as the ongoing U.S. response. She draws upon a wide range of historical sources and interviews with key persons in both countries. Included are statistical appendixes, bibliography, and organizational references.

4.44   Baird, Peter, and McCaughan, Ed. *Beyond the Border: Mexico and the United States Today*. New York: NACLA, 1979. 205pp. $5.95

A study of the ways in which Mexico and the United States have grown even more interconnected over the past decade, linked by a common economic crisis and by attacks on working people in both countries. *Beyond the Border* examines runaway shops, transnational banks, Indian resistance to early capitalist development in the Mexican countryside, agribusiness, and more.

4.45   Burbach, Roger, and Flynn, Patricia. *Agribusiness in the Americas*. New York: Monthly Review/NACLA, 1980. 314pp. $6.50

An in-depth look at agribusiness in the United States and Latin America by two former staff members of the North American Congress on Latin America (NACLA). This study identifies the control mechanisms that transnational agribusiness firms exercise in the world food economy. An appendix lists the Latin American subsidiaries of sixty major U.S. agribusiness corporations.

.46   Comblin, José. *The Church and the National Security State*. Maryknoll, N.Y.:
Orbis Books, 1979. 256pp. Bibliography. $8.95

Belgian theologian José Comblin offers a coherent analysis of the ideology,
aims, and strategy of the national security state and the problems it poses for the
Latin American church. As his study shows, authoritarian regimes have cleverly
adopted clerical language to pose as guardians of Christian values, principles,
and traditions while progressively depriving their citizens of basic human rights.
Comblin's examination of the confrontation between church and state suggests
new pastoral strategies for the church in Latin America.

.47   Data Center. *Reagan and El Salvador: The Roots of War*. Rev. ed. Oakland,
Calif.: Data Center, 1981. 103pp. $6.50

One hundred pages of carefully selected clippings from newspapers and periodicals that offer the background necessary for an understanding of the Reagan
administration's military involvement in El Salvador and Central America. The
publications represented in this Data Center Press Profile range in political viewpoint from left to right.

.48   DeBrouker, José. *The Violence of a Peacemaker*. Maryknoll, N.Y.: Orbis
Books, 1970. 167pp. Cloth $6.95

Through the life of Brazil's Archbishop Helder Camara, DeBrouker introduces us to the "institutionalized violence" that is the everyday lot of so many in
Latin America and to the cruel choices that confront concerned Christians and
others in that region.

.49   Dinges, John, and Landau, Saul. *Assassination on Embassy Row*. New York:
Pantheon, 1980. 384pp. Cloth $14.95. Also available from the Institute for Pol-
icy Studies.

A powerful study of the assassination of Orlando Letelier and Ronnie Karpen
Moffitt in Washington, D.C. in 1976. The connections between the assassins and
the Chilean and U.S. governments are devastatingly documented.

.50   EPICA Task Force. *Grenada: The Peaceful Revolution*. Washington, DC:
EPICA, 1982. 132pp. $5 (postage included). Bulk rates available.

On March 13, 1979 the popularly based New Jewel Movement overthrew the
corrupt dictatorship of Eric Gairy and formed the People's Revolutionary Government of Grenada. This most recent of EPICA's attractive and readable
primers explains how Grenada's "peaceful revolution"—the first in the English-
speaking Caribbean—has become a model for creative change in the region on
behalf of the poor and working class peoples of the Caribbean.

.51   EPICA Task Force. *Jamaica: Caribbean Challenge*. Washington, DC:
EPICA, 1979. 119pp. $4.50 (postage included). Bibliography. Bulk rates availa-
ble.

This EPICA primer seeks to show the many ways in which the United States, its
economic and foreign policies, and the actions of North American transnational
corporations have affected Jamaica's history and present realities. Topics covered include: foreign investment, the People's National Party, women in Jamaica, and the International Monetary Fund.

4.52   EPICA Task Force. *Nicaragua: A People's Revolution*. Washington, DC: EPICA, 1980. 103pp. $5.00 (postage included). Bibliography. Also available from the National Network in Solidarity with the Nicaraguan People.

EPICA's *Nicaragua* primer offers a North American audience valuable insights into the true nature of the historical struggle between the Somoza dynasty and the majority of the Nicaraguan people—a majority that cuts across all class and economic lines. The Task Force states their desire to see the North American people "come to grips with the exploitative role of those (U.S.) economic interests . . . which, from beginning to end, supported the Somozas and financed the National Guard."

4.53   EPICA Task Force. *Panama: Sovereignty for a Land Divided*. Washington, D.C.: EPICA, 1977. 128pp. $3.75 (postage included). Bibliography.

Published before the signing of the two Panama Canal treaties in 1977, this collection of articles presents the case of the Panamanian people for total recovery of and total sovereignty over the Panama Canal and the so-called Canal Zone. For Americans who are unaware of the long history of U.S. military, economic, and political activity in Panama this EPICA primer will serve as a useful educational tool.

4.54   EPICA Task Force. *Puerto Rico: A People Challenging Colonialism*. Washington, D.C.: EPICA, 1976. 108pp. $3.25 (postage included). Bibliography.

The focus of this primer on Puerto Rico's history, colonial structures, sociological realities, and current political trends is on the U.S. impact on Puerto Rican society and the political alternatives available to the Puerto Rican people today.

4.55   Fagen, Richard R. *The Nicaraguan Revolution: A Personal Report*. Washington, D.C.: Institute for Policy Studies, 1981. 60pp. $4

A primer on the state of Nicaraguan politics and economics today focusing on six areas: armed struggle; internationalization of the conflict; national unity; democratic visions; death, destruction, and debts; and political bankruptcy. Appendixes list the basic documents necessary for a study of contemporary Nicaraguan affairs.

4.56   Galeano, Eduardo. *Open Veins of Latin America: Five Centuries of the Pillage of a Continent*. New York: Monthly Review, 1973. Reprint with an afterword by the author, 1979. 320pp. $6.95

A superb summary of five centuries of foreign exploitation of Latin America. Basic reading for any student of Latin America. Galeano's work has been hailed as "a masterpiece of historical, economic, political, and social writing."

4.57   Goff, James, and Goff, Margaret. *In Every Person Who Hopes*. . . . New York: Friendship Press, 1980. 120pp. $3.75

Two experienced and involved missionaries introduce us to Latin America (the economics, politics, and religions of the region) and to Latin Americans (the songs, the despair, the protest, and the hope of the people).

4.58   Gutierrez, Carlos Maria. *The Dominican Republic: Rebellion and Repression*. New York: Monthly Review, 1973. 176pp. $2.95

A well-researched account of the control that Washington exerts over the Dominican Republic.

.59   Lange, Martin, and Iblacker, Reinhold, eds. *Witnesses of Hope: The Persecution of Christians in Latin America*. Maryknoll, N.Y.: Orbis Books, 1981. 176pp. $6.95

In his Foreword to this volume Jesuit Father Karl Rahner characterizes *Witnesses of Hope* as a "Latin American martyrology." The word reminds Roman Catholics of dusty collections of *Lives of the Saints*. Yet the persecution of Christians is very much a present-day phenomenon. Witnesses chronicle this persecution of countless numbers of Christians and others who struggle for justice in today's Latin America.

.60   Latin America Task Force. *The U.S. in Colombia*. Detroit: Latin America Task Force, 1981. 57pp. $3

This packet of newspaper and magazine clippings was compiled by the Archdiocese of Detroit's Latin America Task Force. The articles deal with violations of human rights, organized resistance in Colombia, worsening economic conditions, and U.S. governmental and corporate involvement in Colombia.

.61   Lernoux, Penny. *Cry of the People: The Struggle for Human Rights in Latin America: The Catholic Church in Conflict with U.S. Policy*. First paperback edition, with a new preface by the author. New York: Penguin Books, 1982. 535pp. $6.95. Also available from Institute for Policy Studies.

Prize-winning journalist Penny Lernoux gives us a volume that is must reading for anyone concerned with understanding the turmoil in present-day Latin America. Her long experience in the region enables her to write with authority, while her obvious commitment to the human rights of Latin America's poor and oppressed fires her prose with a passion that is as understandable as it is disturbing. *Cry of the People* is an exceptionally good introduction to the changes that have taken place in the once conservative Roman Catholic Church in Latin America and to the patterns of U.S. intervention in the region.

.62   MacEoin, Gary. *Revolution Next Door: Latin America in the 1970s*. New York: Holt, Rinehart & Winston, 1971. 243pp. $2.95

The subtitle of MacEoin's book might suggest that *Revolution Next Door* is hardly a book to be recommending for the 1980s. But the strength of MacEoin's work lies not in up-to-the-minute statistical data, but in the author's ability to translate complex economic and political realities into readable and lucid prose. As an introduction to the development of underdevelopment in Latin America, to the church, the armed forces, and to "La Cia," *Revolution Next Door* stands the test of time.

.63   Pearce, Jenny. *Under the Eagle: U.S. Intervention in Central America and the Caribbean*. Boston: South End Press, 1982. 270pp. $7.50

Under the Eagle surveys U.S. actions in Latin America since 1823, unearthing the hidden history of U.S. domination there and tracing the underdevelopment of the region. After 1962, the author focuses on trends since the Cuban Missile Crisis and recent events in El Salvador and Guatemala.

.64   Petras, James. *Critical Perspectives on Imperialism and Social Class in the Third World*. New York: Monthly Review, 1980. $7.50

Essays on class analysis and dependency theory. Petras offers us a well-researched analysis of agribusiness, nationalism, Chile under Allende, the Venezuelan development model, and future prospects for Puerto Rico.

4.65   Rarihokwats, ed. *Guatemala! The Horror and the Hope.* 4 vols. York, Pa.: Four Arrows, 1982. 288pp. $6

This powerful set of four paperback booklets documents the tragic history of Guatemala—from the *conquistadores*, through the U.S. intervention in the early 1950s, and up to the links between the coup in 1982 and the Reagan White House. It's not easy reading—as the editors candidly acknowledge—but an understanding of this history is essential for an adequate comprehension of present-day events in Central America.

4.66   Rius. *Cuba for Beginners: An Illustrated Guide for Americans (and their Government).* New York: Pathfinder, 1970. 153pp. $2.95

Pre-revolutionary Cuba, the events surrounding the revolution, and Cuba today—all presented in comic book style by Mexico's famed cartoonist, Rius.

4.67   Schlesinger, Stephen, and Kinzer, Stephen. *Bitter Fruit: The Untold Story of the American Coup in Guatemala.* Garden City, N.Y.: Doubleday, 1982. 320pp. Bibliography. $8.95

Bitter Fruit tells the story of Operation Success, in which the CIA, the U.S. State Department, and the Executive Branch conspired on behalf of the United Fruit Company to overthrow the government of Guatemala in the early 1950s. Based on scores of CIA and State Department documents obtained under the Freedom of Information Act *Bitter Fruit* tells a chilling tale that is necessary for a proper understanding of the role of U.S. government and private concerns in Central America today.

See also:
1.112, 7.30, 7.31, 7.32, 7.33, 7.34, 7.35, 9.26, 10.24, 10.33, 10.37, 10.39, 10.43

Periodicals

For additional country-specific newsletters and magazines please see each of the organizations listed above.

4.68   **Custom Microfilm Service** has an extensive collection of newspapers and periodicals on Latin America available on microfilm. Write or phone them for a brochure and more information. See index, p. 251

4.69   *CALA Newsletter*, c/o Community Action in Latin America, 731 State St., Madison, WI 53703. Bimonthly. $3/year.

Each issue consists of a feature-length article on subjects such as imperialism and health care in Latin America. Particular attention is paid to critical analyses of U.S. involvement in Latin America.

4.70   *Caribbean Perspective*, c/o Caribbean People's Alliance, Box 2194, Brooklyn, NY 11202. Quarterly magazine. $10/year.

This magazine attempts to give an "accurate perspective on the Caribbean and the world.'' Each issue contains three or four major articles, often concerning Caribbean affairs that have a U.S. connection, and sections on Media, History, Praxis, Cinema, and Recent Publications and Reviews.

71   *Colombia Report*, c/o Program in Comparative Culture, School of Social Sciences, University of California, Irvine, CA 92717. 3 issues/year. $6/year individual; $15/year library. Apply for other rates.

News and analysis of political, economic, and social developments in Colombia and Latin America. Focus on popular struggles, the left and its political activities, and on foreign intervention in Latin America.

72   *CubaTimes*, c/o Cuba Resource Center, 11 John St., Rm. 506, New York, NY 10038. Quarterly magazine. $8/year individual; $16/year institutional.

In-depth feature articles and news about all aspects of life in Cuba and about Havana's foreign policy and relations with the United States. *CubaTimes* is a successor to *Cuba Review*, which the CRC published for ten years.

73   *El Salvador Bulletin*, c/o U.S.–El Salvador Research and Information Center, Box 4797, Berkeley, CA 94704. Monthly. $10/year individual; $16/year institutional.

The *Bulletin* contains summaries of news and analyses of issues relating to El Salvador and Central America and to U.S. involvement in the region.

74   *Facts & Opinion*, c/o Chile Resource Center and Clearing House, 2940 16 St., Suite 7, San Francisco, CA 94103. Bimonthly newsletter. Contribution.

Seventeen pages of news and analyses of Chile–U.S. relations, human rights in Chile, economic issues, and the Chilean labor movement.

75   *ISLA: Information Services on Latin America*, 464 19 St., Oakland, CA 94612. Monthly. Apply for rates.

An attractively arranged monthly compilation of carefully chosen news articles and editorials covering sociopolitical, diplomatic, and economic news on Latin America from the *New York Times, Christian Science Monitor, Manchester Guardian/Le Monde,* the *Financial Times of London,* and five other major newspapers. *ISLA* is available as a Full Service (450–500 articles per month) or a Country/Bloc Service (60–100 articles per month). The Country Service—on Central America, for instance—is available for $12/month.

76   *LADOC*, Apartado 5594, Lima, 100, Peru. Bimonthly documentary service. $16/year.

This 12-year old, 54-page bimonthly publication consists of up-to-date statements, reports, and magazine articles from and about Latin America as reflected by the Catholic Church.

77   *Latin America Update*, c/o Washington Office on Latin America, 110 Maryland Ave., NE, Washington, DC 20002. Bimonthly news report, $10/year. Back issues available.

WOLA's *Latin America Update* is a good way to keep abreast of Latin American current affairs. Issues are sometimes devoted to a single topic, such as Argentina Today (September 1981), but more often conditions and news in more than one Latin American country are covered in some detail. Each issue also has a section entitled ''Newsbriefs.''

4.78   *Latin American Perspectives*, c/o C.M.S., Box 792, Riverside, CA 92502. Quarterly magazine. $14/year individual; apply for other rates.

A highly respected theoretical journal featuring discussions and debates about dependency theory, imperialism, rural underdevelopment, women, and capitalism in Latin America.

4.79   *NACLA Report on the Americas*, 151 W. 19 St., 9th Floor, New York, NY 10011. Bimonthly magazine. $15/year. Back issues available.

Now in its sixteenth year this magazine is one of the best progressive sources of information in the United States on the political economy of the Americas. Each issue contains two or three feature articles on one theme and an Update section with news from around the region.

4.80   *The Nation*, 72 Fifth Ave., New York, NY 10011. Subscription Service: Box 1953, Marion, Ohio 43302. Weekly. $30/year.

One of America's oldest and most respected liberal journals. *The Nation* has its own Latin America correspondent, Penny Lernoux. Its coverage of Latin American affairs is exceptionally good.

4.81   *Nicaraguan Perspectives*. c/o Nicaragua Information Center, Box 1004, Berkeley, CA 94704. Quarterly magazine. $10/year. Back issues available.

This magazine, launched in mid-1981, is an independent journal that seeks to scrutinize and publicize foreign policy decisions taken in Washington that affect Nicaragua and other Central American nations. More generally, *Perspectives* monitors economic, political, and cultural events in Nicaragua.

Pamphlets and Articles

4.82   *Aiding Nicaragua*. Michael T. Clark. *Current Issues*, February 1980. 6pp. 75 cents.

In this issue of the CIP's *Current Issues* magazine Michael Clark analyzes the motives of proponents and opponents of U.S. economic assistance to Nicaragua. Opponents, he finds, want to withhold aid as "the one remaining bargaining chip we have left," while proponents seek to take sides in Nicaragua's internal conflict using aid "to bolster the private sector and the forces fighting for an open democratic society." Neither approach, Clark concludes, "is attuned to the real situation in Nicaragua," and neither will appropriately serve American interests.

4.83   *Argentina: A People's Struggle*. Latin American Task Force of the Third World Coalition (TWC), a nationwide program of the American Friends Service Committee, 1978. 28pp. 75 cents.

This second in a series of pamphlets produced by the Latin American Task Force is an attempt to disseminate what the TWC feels is little known information about Latin America. By doing so the Coalition seeks to provide an alternative "to the body of misinformation often published by the U.S. State Department, the U.S. mass media, and the propaganda operations of many Latin American regimes." *Argentina: A People's Struggle* offers a brief, readable history of the country and its people, focusing particularly on the Argentine military and popular resistance. The final chapter analyzes Argentina, Latin America, and U.S. imperialism.

84 *Background Information on El Salvador and U.S. Military Assistance to Central America.* Cynthia Arnson. Institute for Policy Studies' Militarism and Disarmament Project, March 1982. 11pp. 50 cents, plus postage.

This IPS background paper analyzes the political situation in El Salvador, especially the relations between civilian and military forces in the country, and describes all aspects of U.S. military assistance to the country.

85 *Brazil.* Latin America Documentation (LADOC). 64pp. $1. Available from the Latin America Bureau of the U.S. Catholic Conference.

One of LADOC's "Keyhole Series," this booklet is an anthology of material that appeared in earlier issues of LADOC.

86 *Brazil.* Janet Shenk, coordinator. *NACLA Report on the Americas* 13, no. 3, May–June 1979. 48pp. $2.50

The first two articles in this issue of *NACLA Report on the Americas* explore the forces in Brazil advocating liberalization (following the installation of a new president in March 1979) and those struggling for liberation. A third article deals with the effects of the government's policies on the Brazilian Amazon, its Indian tribes, peasant migrants, and natural resources.

87 *Brazil: Labor Unions on Trial.* Brazil Labor Information and Resource Center, 1982. 16pp. $1. Bulk rates available.

A pamphlet containing essential background on Brazil's growing labor movement. It also explores the corporate involvement of U.S. business and its impact on labor.

88 *Brazil: Riches, Repression, and the U.S. Role.* Latin America Task Force, n.d. 42pp. $1 plus postage.

The LATF's "study journal" on the history, political economy, and current situation of Brazil includes poetry, an analysis of the role of multinational corporations, resource listings, articles on the church in Brazil, a description of Brazil–U.S. relations, and a teaching unit on Brazil.

89 *Caribbean Conflict: Jamaica and the U.S.* Sherry Keith and Robert Girling. *NACLA Report on the Americas* 12, no. 3, May–June 1978. 48pp. $2.50

Caribbean Conflict provides: background for understanding Michael Manley's left-leaning government in Jamaica; a survey of the development of the island's bauxite industry under the control of North American aluminum companies and the part this played in shaping Jamaica's economy, class structure and social conditions; the Manley government's efforts to assert control over the bauxite industry; documentation on the U.S.-backed destabilization campaign against the government and its impact.

90 *Central America 1980: Guatemala, El Salvador, Nicaragua.* Unitarian Universalist Service Committee, 1980. 29pp.

This short report contains the findings of an investigative mission to the Central American region by UUSC staff members in 1980.

4.91 *Central America Resource Packet*. Institute for Policy Studies, 1982. $4.50 plus postage.

The *Resource Packet* includes *Updates* prepared by IPS since March 1980 as well as selected articles and op-eds. It provides accurate, thorough information on U.S. military assistance to countries in the region and on key political events and U.S. policies.

4.92 *Chile*. Chile Democratico, 1981. 40pp. Inquire for price.

This folder of reprints and newspaper clippings includes a statement by Senator Edward M. Kennedy against military assistance to Chile, a chronology of events linking South Africa and the Pinochet regime, a report by the International Commission of Jurists on Chile's new constitution and human rights, and two press statements on Chile by Amnesty International.

4.93 *Chile: Economic "Freedom" and Political Repression*. Orlando Letelier. Institute for Policy Studies, 1976. 17pp. 50 cents.

In this essay, published in the year he was assassinated in Washington, D.C., by agents of the Chilean secret police, Orlando Letelier describes the relationship between an economic development model that benefits only the wealthy few and the political terror that has reigned in Chile since the overthrow of the Allende government in 1973.

4.94 *Chile: The Repression Continues*. Thomas E. Quigley. Reprint from *Christianity & Crisis*, August 18, 1975. 10 cents. Available from the U.S. Catholic Conference.

Describes the courageous action of the Chilean churches in the face of severe repression and suggests concrete assistance that can be offered by concerned people outside of Chile.

4.95 *Christianity and Liberation*. Christian Action Center, n.d. 22pp. $1

This booklet consists of translations of two articles from Isquierda Christiana: "The Integration of Religious Faith and Political Conflict: A Pastoral Testimony by the Archbishop of San Salvador" by Luis Alberto Gomez de Souza and "Sorrows and Hopes on the Occasion of the Assassination of the Martyred Archbishop" by Jose Alvarez Icaza. The Center's purpose in publishing these translations is to demonstrate that the conflict in El Salvador is a struggle, not between "leftist and rightest terrorists," but between the Salvadorean people and an army that is equipped and supported by the U.S. military.

4.96 *Colombia: Growth Without Equity*. Mary Speck. *International Policy Report*, February 1981. 12pp. $1.50

"Aid to the needy" in Third World countries has always been promoted as a means of defusing social unrest. By targeting impoverished communities through integrated rural and urban development programs, the United States and the international agencies it supports have tried to compensate Third World peasants and workers for the inequities of rapid economic growth. But—as the author of this report demonstrates—targeted aid programs, no matter how carefully designed, will have little effect unless the government administering them is at least as dedicated to equity as it is to growth.

97 *Controversial Reagan Campaign Links with Guatemalan Government and Private Sector Leaders*. Allan Nairn. 1981. 13pp. $1. Available from the Council on Hemispheric Affairs. A 6-page reprint of this article appears in the April 1981 (no. 12) issue of *Covert Action Information Bulletin*. See 4.106 below.

 This research memorandum analyzes the numerous links between those close to Ronald Reagan and the government in Guatemala and suggests the directions that Washington's policies toward that country are likely to take.

98 *De-Railing Development: The International Monetary Fund in Jamaica*. Howard Wachtel and Michael Moffitt. Institute for Policy Studies, 1978. 20pp. $1.50

 An IPS issue paper that studies the International Monetary Fund and how it uses its leverage over debtor countries to enforce conservative economic policies, thus perpetuating underdevelopment and hampering the ability of governments—such as Jamaica's—to meet basic human needs.

99 *Dissent Paper on El Salvador and Central America*. U.S. Department of State, November 6, 1980. 31pp. $2 postage included. Available from Overview Latin America.

 A quasi-official U.S. government "dissent paper" that warns against continued U.S. support of El Salvador's ruling junta.

00 *A Documentary History of the U.S. Blockade*. Center for Cuban Studies, 1979. 79pp. $2.50

 This special issue of the Center's monthly publication, *Cuba in Focus*, offers a historical perspective on America's embargo on trade with Cuba.

01 *Documents on U.S. Tolerance of Terrorist Activities within the United States Against Nicaragua*. National Network in Solidarity with the Nicaraguan People, 1981. 20pp. $2

 This collection includes newspaper articles, statements by the Nicaraguan government, and photographs.

02 *El Salvador: A Revolution Brews*. Robert Armstrong and Janet Shenk, coordinators. *NACLA Report on the Americas* 14, no. 4. July–August 1980. 48pp. $2.50

 Part 2 of *El Salvador: Why Revolution?* (see 4.107 below) analyzes events in the country since the coup of October 1979 and describes the popular forces at work in El Salvador.

03 *El Salvador: The Descent into Violence*. Tommie Sue Montgomery. *International Policy Report*, March 1982. 12pp. $1.50

 Dr. Montgomery provides new details in this CIP report on an old phenomenon in Salvadoran politics: *Derechización*, or the drift to the right. She illustrates how the army and right-wing terrorists step up their repression every time reformers gain a foothold in the government and how they drown the reforms in blood.

 The author also outlines the domestic origins of the guerrilla opposition and provides a useful antidote to the extravagant claims of U.S. government officials that the opposition forces in El Salvador are "commanded, controlled, and run externally."

4.104   *El Salvador: The Permanent Tribunal of the Peoples Report*. Vincent Navarro. 1981. 16pp. $2 postage included. Available from Overview Latin America.

This booklet includes the findings and the verdict of a Tribunal held in Mexico City in February 1981. At the Tribunal the military junta of El Salvador was condemned for genocide, torture and other crimes against humanity; the United States was denounced for complicity as a third party to the extermination of the Salvadorean people.

4.105   *El Salvador: The Struggle for Freedom*. *The Guardian*, May 1981. 12pp. 75 cents. Bulk rates available.

This special supplement to the weekly *Guardian* newspaper examines the conflict in El Salvador and Washington's Central American policies from a progressive point of view.

4.106   *El Salvador: U.S. Intervention*. Stewart Klepper. *Covert Action Information Bulletin*, no. 12, April 1981. 10pp. $2.50

A well-documented, highly critical examination of U.S. support for rightwing terrorism in El Salvador. Klepper analyzes the CIA–connected American Institute for Free Labor Development (AIFLD), the U.S. Agency for International Development, the State Department's "White Paper" on El Salvador, and other aspects of U.S. intervention in this Central American country.

4.107   *El Salvador: Why Revolution?* Robert Armstrong and Janet Shenk, coordinators. *NACLA Report on the Americas* 14, no. 2, March–April 1980. 48pp. $2.50

Part 1 of a two-part series (see 4.102 above), *Why Revolution?* traces the roots of the present conflict in El Salvador to the emergence of an agro-export economy in the late 1800s. It analyzes unsuccessful attempts at electoral change and the development and organization of the leftist opposition.

4.108   *From Guatemala: An Epistle to the Believing Communities in the United States*. April 25, 1981. 9pp. Contribution. Available from Agricultural Mission Committee, c/o NCC/DOM.

This statement—commended to the churches by the unanimous action of the Governing Board of the National Council of Churches (USA)— was issued following a visit to Guatemala by a delegation of Protestant and Roman Catholic clergy and religious. The pastoral letter attempts to explain the conflict in Guatemala in terms that church people in America are comfortable with.

4.109   *Guatemala: Repression and Resistance*. National Lawyers Guild, 1979. 33pp. $3.50

This report, prepared together with the La Raza Legal Alliance, describes the human rights situation in Guatemala today.

4.110   *Inside Honduras: Regional Counterinsurgency Base*. Philip E. Wheaton. EPICA, 1982. 60pp. $4. Bulk rates available.

This special report from EPICA takes a brief look at Honduran history, then studies U.S. military control over the country at some length. It concludes with a consideration of parallels between Honduras and Vietnam.

4.111   *Latin America: A Political Guide to Thirty-Three Nations*. Penny Lernoux. *The Nation* 233, no. 5, August 22–29, 1981. 15pp. $1.25

Penny Lernoux, *The Nation*'s Latin America correspondent, offers a very useful survey of Latin America in this 15-page Special Report. She proceeds country by country in three major sections: Mexico and Central America; Caribbean Basin; and South America. The quality of this report combined with the magazine's generous discount for bulk orders makes *Latin America* an ideal choice for classroom use or group study.

2   Look! A New Thing in the Americas: The Church and Revolution in Nicaragua. Peter Hinde. Quixote Center, 1981. 24-page tabloid. $1.25. Bulk rates available.

This vivid eyewitness account of events in Nicaragua at the time of the overthrow of the Somoza dictatorship was written by a Carmelite priest.

3   Lucha! A Special Report on Central America & the Caribbean. Co-produced by the National Network in Solidarity with the Nicaraguan People, the National Network in Solidarity with the People of Guatemala, and the Committee in Solidarity with the People of El Salvador, 1981. 8-page tabloid. 50 cents each; 25 cents each in bulk orders.

Articles in this tabloid include "The Central American Revolution"; "150 Years of U.S. Intervention"; and country/regional reports on El Salvador, Guatemala, Grenada, and the Caribbean. *Lucha!* also features one page of poetry and an excellent sampling of resources on Nicaragua, Guatemala, and El Salvador.

4   Latin America 1980. Janet Shenk and Steven Volk, coordinators. *NACLA Report on the Americas* 14, no. 1, January–February 1980. 48pp. $2.50

This report presents a noted Chilean economist's overview of changing economic trends in Latin America, and two studies on the impact of these trends in Guatemala.

5   Nicaragua: America's Second Chance. Kim Conroy and Max Holland. *International Policy Report* 5, no. 5, December 1979. 8pp. $1.50

This report finds that not only does Nicaragua need and deserve U.S. aid, but also that the United States will promote its own interests as well by supporting the new government.

6   Panama: For Whom the Canal Tolls? Judy Butler, coordinator. *NACLA Report on the Americas* 13, no. 5, September–October 1979. 48pp. $2.50

Two major articles examine the negotiations for the new Canal treaties in 1976 and 1977 from the Panamanian and the U.S. sides. A third article explores the conditions in Panama that brought General Omar Torrijos to power in 1968 and examines the nature of his regime.

7   Peru Packet. Peru Solidarity Committee, 1979. 7 booklets. $2

Peru Solidarity's packet consists of seven attractively designed booklets on subjects such as: a background on Peru, 1979; cost-of-living data; government repression and popular opposition; the church; and U.S. banks and Peru.

8   Puerto Rico: End of Autonomy. Americo Badillo-Veiga, Paul Horowitz, and Ralph Rivera. Karen Judd, guest editor. *NACLA Report on the Americas* 14, no. 2, March–April 1981. 48pp. $2.50

Two articles on the island's economy and the Popular Democratic Party's (PPD) role: the first traces Puerto Rico's postwar economic and political evolution; the second is a case study of transnational corporations in the pharmaceuticals industry seen as part of the PPD's path for economic development.

4.119   *The Sign of Resurrection in El Salvador: A Testimony from Christians Who Accompany the People in Their Struggle.* Latin America Task Force, 1981. 8-panel leaflet. Contribution.

This widely distributed leaflet is a translation of a significant statement by various Protestant and Catholic agencies in El Salvador on the history and present struggles of the people of that country.

4.120   *Symposium on El Salvador and U.S. Policy in the Region.* Faculty Committee for Human Rights in El Salvador, University of California, Berkeley, 1981. 30pp. $4. Available from the Data Center.

A transcript of a symposium held on the U.C. Berkeley campus on Jan. 16, 1981 featuring speakers from a variety of political perspectives.

4.121   *Testimonies from Peasants of El Peten.* Latin America Task Force, 1981. 12pp. 20 cents. Bulk rates available.

Based on actual taped testimonies of Guatemalan peasants who survived torture and attacks by the Guatemalan military in June 1981, this short booklet provides graphic illustrations of right-wing, militaristic repression in Guatemala. The Task Force has distributed over 14,000 copies of this powerful and disturbing document.

4.122   *They Educated the Crows: An Institute Report on the Letelier–Moffitt Murders.* Saul Landau. Institute for Policy Studies, 1978. 44pp. $2.95

An outline of the findings of a two-year investigation of the murder of Orlando Letelier and Ronnie Moffitt. Landau's report describes the reasons for the Pinochet government's desire to assassinate Letelier, as well as the coverup and campaign of disinformation that followed the bombing of Letelier's car in Washington in September 1976.

4.123   *The United States and Latin America Today.* AFSC (Philadelphia), 1976. 56pp. $1

An analysis of the impact of U.S. power—public and private—on Latin American societies.

4.124   *Uruguay After the Plebiscite: Prospects for Democracy.* Proceedings from the June 12, 1981 symposium at American University sponsored by the Washington Office on Latin America (WOLA) and American University Law School's International Law Program, 1981. 45pp. $3. Available from WOLA.

This record of conference proceedings includes a major presentation on "Uruguay in Transition: From Military to Civilian Rule" and four panel presentations with viewpoints on Uruguay in an international context.

4.125   WOLA also published Occasional Paper #1: *Uruguay: The Plebiscite and Beyond* (March 1981. 6pp. $1).

4.126   *U.S. Military Involvement in El Salvador, 1947–1980.* CISPES, 1981. $1.50. Bulk rates available.

Well-researched and documented, this booklet is a record of a quarter century of U.S. intervention in El Salvador.

27   *Vieques: A People for Whom World War II Has Not Ended*. National Ecumenical Movement of Puerto Rico (PRISA), 1978. 12pp. 75 cents. Available from EPICA.

Background and analysis of the struggle in Vieques, Puerto Rico, against U.S. naval occupation.

See also:
6.53, 6.54, 7.45, 7.46, 7.49, 7.50, 7.53, 7.55, 7.56, 7.64, 7.66, 9.44, 9.49, 9.51, 9.65, 9.67, 10.60, 10.63, 10.64, 10.65, 10.67, 10.72, 10.74, 10.82, 10.85, 10.87

AUDIOVISUAL RESOURCES

Guides and Catalogs

28   *Audio-Visual Materials*. AFSC (Philadelphia), Latin America Program. 3pp. Free

AFSC has several films and slideshows for rental and/or sale on Latin America. They are listed in annotated form with full ordering information.

29   *Central America Film Library*. Icarus. 3pp. Free

Latin America films from Icarus are described in this handy brochure. It is updated regularly.

30   *Films on Latin America*. Third World Newsreel. 11pp. Free

A full description of Third World Newsreel's eight films on Latin America.

31   *Latin America*. Audio Visual Library Service, University of Minnesota. 4pp. Free

The University of Minnesota's Library Service makes available an annotated listing of films for rental. The titles are arranged by general topic: politics and economics; social conditions; cultural geography; and native peoples.

Audiovisuals

4.132   *Americas in Transition*. 1982 29 min color film. Narrated by Ed Asner. Produced by Oble Benz. Available from Icarus Films. Rental $50. Sale $495

This short film describes U.S. intervention in Central and Latin American affairs during the twentieth century. It traces the roots of dictatorship, attempts at democracy, communist influences, and the role of the United States.

4.133   *Atencingo*. 1975 58 min color film. Spanish with English subtitles. Directed by Eduardo Maldonado. Third World Newsreel. Rental $75

This unusual film was funded by people in Mexico who approached Eduardo Maldonado and asked him to record their stories of forty years of continuous struggle against foreign landlords, American monopolists, and finally, the Mexican monopolist, Manuel Espinosa Iglesias. The years of struggle were marked by riots, murder, and strikes, which are all documented in the memories of the film's peasant narrators and supplemented by documents and photos.

4.134   *The Battle of Chile*. 1973–1980 Three part b&w film 273 min. Directed by Patricio Guzman. Unifilm. Apply for rates.

Part 1: The Insurrection of the Bourgeoisie

Part 2: The Coup d'Etat

Part 3: The Power of the People.

This three-part documentary is a thorough and moving account of the escalation of rightist violence during the last months of President Salvador Allende's government. *The Battle of Chile* details the political and economic tactics of Chile's rightwing—fueling the black market, the hoarding of goods to create shortages, collaborating with the CIA to support a nationwide truck owners' strike, and other actions that culminated in the 1973 coup d'etat.

Part 3 deals with the all-important Popular Unity period: the creation by workers and peasants of thousands of organisms of "popular power" to establish grassroots social services and securities in defense against the oppressive measures of the landlords and ruling elite.

4.135   *Bay of Pigs*. 1973 103 min b&w film. Unifilm. Apply for rates.

Bay of Pigs is a reenactment of the U.S.-backed attempt by Cuban exiles to recapture Cuba in 1961. Interviews with participants in the invasion are included.

4.136   *The Brick-Makers*. 1972 42 min b&w film. Directed by Marta Rodriguez and Jorge Silva. Unifilm. Apply for rates.

Set in Colombia this film is a devastating report on the living conditions of millions of Latin Americans who live in a "culture of poverty" in shanty-towns surrounding major cities. *The Brick-Makers* offers a detailed look at the daily existence of a family who produces earthen bricks for a living.

4.137   *Campamento!* 1972 29 min color film. Maryknoll World Films. Free

Chile under Socialist President Salvador Allende is the setting for this excellent film. Centering around the housing project Nueva Havana, *Campamento!* recounts the exciting struggle of the Chilean people to take responsibility for their own lives and destiny. Though the spirit so evident in this film was dealt a crushing blow with the CIA-supported coup in 1973, *Campamento!* is still an extremely useful educational film.

38   *Caribbean Crosscurrents*. Color filmstrip with cassette and guide. 79 frames. Friendship Press. Sale $12

    This entertaining filmstrip celebrates the people of the Caribbean—their diversity of language, race, heritage, religion and music, and the resulting wealth of culture. *Crosscurrents* portrays the disunity and lack of growth that have resulted from foreign intervention in the region. This filmstrip comes with separate recordings for adults and children.

39   *Central America: Roots of the Crisis*. August 1981 27 min slideshow with 131 slides, script, instructions, and background materials. AFSC (Philadelphia), Latin America Program. Rental $15 for one week. Sale $50

    This slideshow outlines the history, economics, and politics of Central America, with emphasis on El Salvador, Guatemala, and Nicaragua. *Central America* examines past and present U.S. policy toward the region and considers possibilities for constructive change.

40   *Chile's Watergate*. 1978 52 min color film. British Broadcasting Company. Available from the Institute for Policy Studies. Apply for rates.

    This 1978 BBC documentary is about the assassinations of Orlando Letelier and Ronnie Karpen Moffitt in Washington, D.C. in 1976 and the subsequent investigation by the FBI. Filmed in Chile, *Chile's Watergate* includes interviews with Chilean officials and with the accused Michael Townley.

41   *Cry of the People*. 1972 62 min color film. Unifilm. Apply for rates.

    This film presents an analysis of Bolivia's political and economic history. It features interviews with tin miners and government leaders, describes the effects of land reform, shows a day in the life of a miner, and analyzes U.S. interests in Bolivia.

42   *Don Pedro: La Vida de un Pueblo*. 1975 50 min color film. Produced by Norberto Lopez. Third World Newsreel. Rental $75. Sale $700. Also available in Spanish.

    Life in Puerto Rico as seen through the eyes of Don Pedro and a young boy from a small island village. The boy learns from Don Pedro of the struggles of an Americanized Puerto Rico.

43   *The Edge of Hope*. 1972 24 min color film. Maryknoll World Films. Free

    A lucid examination of oppression in Mexico, Bolivia, Colombia, and Paraguay. *Edge of Hope* documents inequalities between those who work and those who reap the profits in Third World countries.

44   *El Salvador: a Country in Crisis*. 1981 30 min color slideshow with cassette. Overview Latin America. Rental $15. Sale $60. Also available for a fee of $5-per-showing from the Interreligious Task Force on El Salvador and Central America.

    This slideshow has been successfully used as an educational and consciousness-raising tool with groups across the United States, as well as in Canada, Europe, and Latin America itself. *El Salvador* provides excellent background on U.S. intervention in El Salvador, the witness of the church, political repression, and the growth of popular resistance.

4.145   *El Salvador: Another Vietnam*. 1982 50 min color film or video tape. A Catalyst Media Production produced and directed by Glenn Silber and Tete Vasconcellos. Edited by Deborah Shaffer. Available from Icarus Films. Apply for rates.

El Salvador: Another Vietnam, a revised and updated version of the original documentary produced for PBS in January 1981, examines the civil war in El Salvador in the light of the Reagan administration's policies in the Central America region. Archival material in the film offers an overview of U.S. military and economic policy in the region since 1948. More recent footage provides extensive background to the current political crisis, with scenes of military operations by the National Guard and the Army and of guerrilla training camps.

4.146   *El Salvador: The People Will Win/El Pueblo Vencerá!* 1982 80 min color film. Spanish dialogue with English narration and subtitles. Directed by Diego de la Texera. The Film Institute of Revolutionary El Salvador (COMMUSAL). Apply for rates.

This documentary—produced in Salvador—brings El Salvador's revolution home to American audiences with disturbing forcefulness. Reminiscent of television coverage of the war in Vietnam, *El Salvador* is charged with images that are powerful and intimate: a crying widow, a 13-year-old boy crying for the revenge of his murdered father, scenes of peasants and the rich, and the army in action. But, as the subtitle indicates, this film is also a documentary of the faith and hope the people of El Salvador have in the righteousness of their cause.

4.147   *El Salvador: The Seeds of Liberty*. 1981 28 min color film. Produced by Glen Silber and Tete Vasconcellos for Maryknoll World Films. Free. For film purchase contact Catalyst Media.

This documentary film examines the martyrdom of the four North American religious women in El Salvador on December 2, 1980. The conflict in El Salvador between the church, which has sided with the poor, and the economic and military elite that has taken power to itself is explored through interviews with military, government, and church leaders, both in El Salvador and the United States. *Seeds of Liberty* contains scenes from the funeral of Archbishop Romero (assassinated in March 1980), life in a refugee camp, and interviews with the poor as they relate their tragedies and hopes for a dignified life and free society.

4.148   *Fidel*. 1969 95 min color film. Directed by Saul Landau. New Time Films. Rental $100

An in-depth portrait of Fidel Castro and an inside look at the people and process of the Cuban revolution: from the drama of the Bay of Pigs to the comedy of an impromptu baseball game; from a nursery school where Fidel learned children's rhymes to the Sierra Maestra where he learned guerrilla warfare.

4.149   *Forward Together*. 1977 58 min color film. French version available. Directed by Nicole Duchene and Claude Lortie. Unifilm and Latin American Film Project. Rental $150. Sale $750

Forward Together portrays the historical development of Jamaica from its colonial years through its recent attempts, under the government of Michael Manley, to modify its economic, social, and political structures in the direction of democratic socialism.

50   *Free Homeland or Death*. 1978 75 min color film. Spanish with English subtitles. Directed by Antonio Yglesias and Victor Vega. Unifilm. Apply for rates.

Produced during the war against Somoza's National Guard, this documentary provides historical background on the Sandinista resistance and on the decades of foreign intervention in Nicaragua. The film focuses on the military aspects of the resistance forces, including footage of training and a religious service in a secret FSLN camp; it includes interviews with peasants, professionals, and students on why they opted for armed struggle.

51   *From the Ashes*. 1981 60 min color film. Spanish with English subtitles. Directed by Helena Soldberg-Ladd. International Film Project. Apply for rates.

This film portrays the reconstruction of Nicaragua from the point of view of one family. It highlights the literacy campaign, the ongoing political discussions, and the current efforts at destabilization by the Reagan administration. Of particular interest are scenes of the penal system, of the training camps used by militant exiles in Miami, and of the popular mobilization to meet the threats of foreign intervention.

52   *Grave of an Unknown Salvadoran Refugee*. 28 min color filmstrip with cassette, 31-page leader's guide, and script. United Methodist Film Service Center. Sale $15

A U.S. church worker arrives at a refugee camp just across the El Salvador/ Honduras border only eight hours after an unarmed Salvadoran refugee has been shot by Honduran soldiers. This incident is a dramatic illustration of the wider conflict in El Salvador and Central America. *Grave of an Unknown Salvadoran Refugee* shows clearly that it is people—women, men, and children—who are involved in the turmoil in El Salvador. The accompanying guide explains the background of the filmstrip, suggests follow-up questions, and lists additional resources and action ideas.

53   *Guatemala: A People Besieged*. 1978 30 min slideshow with cassette. 160 slides. Accompanying study guide contains instructions, documentation, script, references, bibliography, and action suggestions. AFSC (Philadelphia), Latin America Program. Rental $15 for one week. Sale $40

This AFSC slideshow interprets the strength and beauties of Guatemala as well as the harsher realities of its economic, social, and political situation. Fully documenting the role of the United States in Guatemala, *A People Besieged* covers: general description; experiment in national sovereignty (1944-1954); dictatorship, repression, and the U.S. tie (post-1954); land and power; transnationals and tourism.

54   *Guatemala: Prelude to a Struggle*. Radio documentary. Available in half-hour and one-hour audio cassettes. National Public Radio. Available from the Public Media Foundation. Sale $8 for half-hour cassettes; $12 for one-hour cassettes. Transcript price: $3

Originally aired on National Public Radio, this documentary addresses the issues of political repression in Guatemala and the role of the United States in that country.

4.155   *Haiti: Bitter Cane*. 1982. 60 min color film. Soundtracks in French, English, and Creole. Haiti Films.

This documentary is being filmed primarily inside Haiti, a nation with 90 percent illiteracy, 50 percent infant mortality, a 40-year life expectancy rate, and documented human rights atrocities.

Haiti: Bitter Cane centers on the life of the Haitian peasants—80 percent of the population. Here it seeks to find the roots of the many problems of Haitian society as well as ideas for solutions.

Also included is a look at the sugar plantations of the Dominican Republic, where Haitian migrant canecutters work; the U.S. industries of Port-au-Prince, where workers assemble baseballs, clothes, radios, and toys; the immigrant community of Flatbush in Brooklyn; and the "boatpeople" of Miami. The film provides a rare chance for the Haitian people to speak for themselves.

4.156   *The Hour of the Furnaces*. 1968 260 min b&w film in 3 parts. Spanish with English subtitles. Directed by Fernando Solanas and Octavio Getino. Unifilm. Apply for rates.

Part 1: Neo-Colonialism and Violence

Part 2: An Act for Liberation

Part 3: Violence and Liberation

This forceful film studies the Argentine people and their years of subjugation under colonialism and, more recently, economic domination by foreigners. *Hour of the Furnaces* examines the ten-year reign of Juan Perón and traces the activities of the Peronist labor movement. The film makes a strong case for the inevitable use of revolutionary violence as a means to the liberation of Argentina's poor and oppressed.

4.157   *La Frontera: A Film on the U.S.–Mexican Border*. 1982 30 min color film. Available in English and Spanish. Produced by Victoria Schultz. Hudson River Productions. Rental $50 Sale $450 (print), $400 (videotape). Also available from Project R.E.A.L.

La Frontera is a compelling introduction to border issues, from immigration to labor and trade. The border—a 2,000-mile strip along the U.S.–Mexican frontier—is viewed in the documentary as a unique third country. The film portrays the meeting of two worlds in this third country through the eyes of border residents.

4.158   *Latin America*. 40 min cassette tape. UMC Service Center. Sale $3.50

This tape offers interviews that explore questions of missionary involvement in political economic issues in foreign countries. U.S. military intervention and American cultural domination of Latin America are also addressed.

4.159   *Nicaragua Libre*. 1982 20 min b&w slideshow with cassette. 80 slides. Spanish or English. Photos by Margaret Randall. Sale $65. Available from Jeanne Gallo, S.N.D., 24 Curtis Ave., Somerville, MA 02144.

This slideshow documents the social conditions and the historical events that led up to the war of liberation in Nicaragua. The slides are the work of Margaret Randall, a North American poet and photographer living in Nicaragua.

160 *Nicaragua: Scenes from the Revolution*. 1980 30 min color film. Directed by John Chapman. Unifilm. Rental $60. Sale $450

From the inception of Sandinismo in the 1930s to the general strike called by the Sandinistas in June of 1979 in protest of the Somozan regime and through the first one hundred days of reconstruction after the Sandinista victory, *Scenes from the Revolution* presents a powerful portrait of the forces that shaped the revolution. Chapman's reportage utilizes footage taken under gunfire, as well as historical newsreel footage from the 1920s and 1930s.

161 *Nicaragua: September 1978*. 1978 50 min color film. Spanish dialog with English subtitles. Unifilm. Apply for rates. Also available from the NNSNP ($75).

This firsthand report of the armed conflict between the Sandinistas and Somoza's National Guard won first prize at the Paris film festival in March 1979 and the "Golden Dove" award at the 1978 Leipzig Festival. The film shows the victims of the war and provides historical and economic background to the crisis.

162 *Nicaragua: The Challenge of Revolution*. 1980. Slideshow with cassette. 139 slides, with script and information packet. National Network in Solidarity with the Nicaraguan People. Rental $15

This NNSNP slide/tape show describes the most important developments in the revolutionary process since the triumph of the popular forces on July 19, 1979. *Challenge of the Revolution* covers the history of the struggle against the Somoza dictatorship, U.S. intervention, national reconstruction, agrarian reform, the literacy campaign, and the role of the church.

163 *Panama for the Panamanians*. 1977. 30 min color slideshow with taped narrative. EPICA. Rental $10

This EPICA slideshow offers an economic and political analysis of U.S.-Panama relations. It also provides the historical context for the Panamanian struggle to gain control of the Canal Zone that divides their country.

164 *Panama: The Fifth Frontier*. 1975 78 min b&w film. Unifilm. Apply for rates.

Using archival footage, the film traces the history of the U.S. role in determining the political and economic fate of Panama. The viewpoint of the Panamanians is predominant in the treatment of issues such as the control of the canal.

165 *Paraiso*. 1974 28 min color film. Spanish or English version. Maryknoll World Films. Free

Paraiso is a film about a missioner's fight against injustice and oppression in Nicaragua under the Somoza dictatorship. The film's title is taken from the name of a community that the priest is trying to develop.

166 *The Politics of Torture*. 1978 50 min color film. California Newsreel/ABC Close-Up. Rental $70. Sale $650

This "ABC News Close-Up" exposes evidence of brutal repression by U.S. allies (Chile, the Shah's Iran and the Philippines), and raises questions about U.S. government and financial support to those regimes.

4.167   *A Problem of Power.* 1970 45 min color film. National Council of Churches. Rental $15. Available from the UMC Service Center.

A low-key—yet forceful—examination of the concentration of economic, political, cultural, and military power in the hands of Latin America's ruling elites and of Washington's determination to maintain this status quo.

4.168   *Puerto Rico: Paradise Invaded.* 1977 30 min color film. Unifilm and Latin American Film Project. Rental $75. Sale $400

This award-winning documentary brings to film representative voices that characterize the hopes and aspirations of the Puerto Rican people. Issues treated include: the contemporary relationship between Puerto Rico and the United States; the imposition of short-term economic changes that cause the disintegration of Puerto Rican national identity; life in New York City; and environmental pollution of the island.

4.169   *The Ragged Revolution: The Romance and the Reality of the Mexican Revolution, 1910–1920.* 1980 37 min color and b&w film. Document Associates. Rental $45. Sale $550

Utilizing rare photos and recently discovered footage of the Mexican revolution, *The Ragged Revolution* provides a look at the realities behind the romantic myths of the revolution. This documentary presents the ten-year revolutionary struggle as a "ragged revolution," a brutal civil war between weak and disorganized federal troops and rebel armies led by illiterate peasants and opportunistic bandits who were to become national heroes.

The Ragged Revolution also discusses the U.S. role throughout this period, including the active involvement of the U.S. ambassador in Mexico City and the mobilization and intervention of U.S. troops.

4.170   *Sandino Vive.* 1980 28 min color film. Maryknoll World Films. Free

Made on location within weeks of the overthrow of the Somoza regime in Nicaragua, this film lets the people tell their own story of suffering and express their own hopes for the reconstruction of their war-ravaged country. *Sandino Vive* examines the role of the church in the Nicaraguan revolution.

4.171   *Thank God and the Revolution (Gracias a Dios y la Revolucion).* 1982 55 min color film. Spanish with English subtitles. Icarus. Rental $75. Sale $745 (film), $480 (videotape)

A moving documentary on the church and the Nicaraguan revolution that demonstrates the commitment of Nicaraguan Christians to the struggle against the Somoza regime.

4.172   *Turnabout/Latin America.* United Methodist Church. Filmstrip with cassette and script/guidance booklet. UMC Service Center. Sale $15

This filmstrip looks at several selected countries and portrays the parallel problems facing the majority of Latin America's people who are struggling for education, jobs, and decent living conditions. The title of the filmstrip refers to the stated need for a "turnabout" so that justice may be realized in Latin America.

173　　*The Uprising*. 1981 96 min color film. Spanish with English subtitles. Directed by Peter Lilienthal. Kino International Corp. Apply for rates.

German filmmaker Peter Lilienthal presents an intimate chronicle of the Nicaraguan people's revolution of 1979. *The Uprising*—part documentary and part fiction—is a dramatic narrative written by Lilienthal and Chilean writer Antonio Skarmeta with the participation of Nicaraguan citizens, former guerrilla fighters, and units of the victorious Sandinist Liberation Front.

174　　*Vieques: The Island*. 1979 25 min slideshow with cassette. 80 color slides. Accompanying packet includes: instructions, script and credits; resource/action materials; and an AFSC statement on Puerto Rico. Lisa Wheaton and the Latin America Program staff of AFSC (Philadelphia). Rental $15 for one week.

Vieques presents a close look at the small island of Vieques, just off the eastern coast of Puerto Rico and at the effect the U.S. Navy's presence has had on the land and people since arriving there in the early 1940s. This powerful slideshow explains why the Navy is there and why the people of the island are opposed to its presence.

See also:
1.188, 1.194, 6.88, 7.68, 7.71, 7.75, 7.76, 9.75, 10.93, 10.94, 10.95, 10.96, 10.99, 10.100, 10.101, 10.104, 10.107, 10.109, 10.111

OTHER RESOURCES

Directories of Resources

4.175   Connexions Collective. *Canada–Latin America*. *Connexions* 7, no. 2, May 1982.
44pp.
   This special issue of the Canadian magazine *Connexions* lists some 100 organizations, resources, and publications dealing with active support of popular struggles in Latin America. It furnishes unique access to Latin America materials
available across Canada, describing in some detail the scope of each group's activity and the types of resources they have available.

4.176   *Latin America: Biblical Understandings of Mission to Individuals and Society*.
New York: Friendship Press, 1981.
   This catalog describes books and audiovisual resources that were available for
the Interdenominational Education for Mission Study Year (1980–1981).

4.177   Latin American Working Group. *Books, Books, Books. . . A Basic Bibliography on Latin America*. Toronto: LAWG, 1976. 20pp. $1.50
   This double issue of LAWG's regular publication, *LAWG Letter*, is designed
for those with little knowledge of Latin America. The bibliography is divided into
two parts: Part 1, Narrative Overview of Latin America, an annotated list of
materials; Part 2, Introduction to Individual Countries, a listing of publications
on individual countries.

4.178   NACLA. *NACLA's Bibliography on Latin America*. New York: NACLA,
1973. 48pp. $1 plus postage. Also available from the Data Center.
   Though somewhat dated, *NACLA's Bibliography on Latin America* is still a
useful source of printed resources on the Latin America region. The bibliography, which first appeared in 1973, is an annotated list of news sources, research
publications, and books organized by topic and by country. Topics covered include: church, communism, foreign investment, labor, peasants, theories of capitalism and imperialism, and women.

4.179   National Network in Solidarity with the Nicaraguan People. *Nicaragua Bibliography*. Washington, D.C.: NNSNP, 1981. 5pp. Contribution
   Books and articles arranged by topic. Many of the items listed are available
through NNSNP.

4.180   Wolpin, M.D. *U.S. Intervention in Latin America: A Bibliography*. New
York: American Institute for Marxist Studies, 1971. 56pp. $5. Photocopy availa-
ble from the Data Center. Payment must accompany order.

   The Latin America Studies Center at California State University has a number
of bibliographies available on individual countries and various issues related to
Latin American political economy.

Curriculum Guides and Materials

,181   *Central America: What U.S. Educators Need to Know*. New York: Council on
Interracial Books for Children, 1982. $3.50

This special double issue of the Council's *Bulletin* (Vol. 13, nos. 2/3) is a critical analysis of the content of textbooks and other educational materials on Central America. It covers the following topics:

1. School Books Get Poor Marks: An Analysis of Children's Materials about
Central America. This analysis of children's books on Central America reveals
omissions and stereotypic views that prevent students from understanding current events in that region.

2. Profiles of Central America. This 5-page article presents facts and figures to
aid in an understanding of the region's past and present and to indicate the type of
information missing from almost all student materials.

3. Women in Central America: Survival and Struggle. Women's activities in El
Salvador and Nicaragua point up their separate but integral role in the histories of
two countries.

4. Indian Peoples of Central America: Oppression Continues. A look at the
historical and current realities of the indigenous peoples of Guatemala and Nicaragua.

5. The Black Presence in Central America: Background Information. This
short piece observes that the Black presence in Central America is either ignored
altogether or misinterpreted in U.S. textbooks. Information is given to fill these
gaps.

The double issue concludes with a lesson plan on El Salvador and a 2-page
listing of resources.

This CIBC resource is mentioned not just for the worthwhile materials it contains but also because it points up the need for a sharply critical approach to all
educational materials on Third World–related themes. What the CIBC study illustrates with regard to Central America could be extended as well to Africa,
Asia, the Middle East, and the Third World as a whole.

Other educational resources on Latin America are:

▸.182   *El Salvador: Roots of Conflict*. Rev. ed. 5511 Vicente Way, Oakland, Calif.
94609: Teachers' Committee on Central America, 1982. $8.

An outstanding example of how the principles outlined in the CIBC *Bulletin*
described above can be implemented is to be found in this curriculum guide on El
Salvador developed by the Oakland–based Teachers' Committee on Central
America. The guide is designed for a 10-day program with high school students,
but it's easily adapted for use in other settings.

The curriculum seeks to help students: (1) understand El Salvador's geo-
graphic, political, and socioeconomic conditions; (2) analyze the nature of U.S.
involvement in that country (and the region); and (3) use their new-found knowledge of El Salvador to critically examine the roots of present-day conflicts.

4.183   *Ideals and Reality in Foreign Policy: American Intervention in the Caribbean.*
         Teacher and Student Manuals. Alfred Jamieson. 1969. 84pp. $4.67 plus postage.
         Available from ERIC Document Reproduction Service.
         Sponsored by the Office of Education of the former Dept. of Health, Educa-
         tion, and Welfare, this study takes as case studies U.S. military intervention in the
         Dominican Republic, Haiti, and Nicaragua from 1898 to 1933. Students are
         asked to compare the results of each intervention with the foreign policy goals
         and ideals cited as reasons for the intervention.

4.184   *Journey South: Discovering the Americas.* Mary Hoey. New York: Friendship
         Press, 1980. 20pp. $3.50
         This appealing set of five two-color 11-by-17-inch booklets introduces older
         primary school children to the history of Latin America and to those who shaped
         the destiny of the children of the region's many nations. *Journey South* examines
         myths and stereotypes about the differences and similarities between North and
         Latin American children, as it takes students into the family life and home set-
         tings of their Latin American neighbors.

4.185   *Two Ways to Look South: A Guide to Latin America.* Wilhelm R. Dwight.
         New York: Friendship Press, 1980. 63pp. $2.25
         This manual for group leaders begins by suggesting how to set up and make use
         of a resource center for a sustained and systematic approach to the study of Latin
         America. Wilhelm presents two methods for organizing the study itself: one topi-
         cal, the other geographical. His guide contains a wealth of curriculum sugges-
         tions, supplementary activities, a special children's guidance section, and a sub-
         stantial bibliography.

         The Latin America Studies Departments of major universities are normally a
         good source of curriculum ideas and materials. One center that is especially note-
         worthy is Project R.E.A.L., an outreach program of the Stanford/Berkeley
         Latin America Studies Center.

4.186   **Recursos Educacionales de América Latina (R.E.A.L.)** is one of four cross-
         cultural projects that make up the Stanford Program on International and Cross-
         Cultural Education (SPICE). Project R.E.A.L. aims to (1) promote the use of
         high quality materials about Latin America in precollegiate classrooms, and
         (2) collaborate with teachers and bilingual school districts in the development
         and utilization of multicultural learning materials focusing on Latin America.
         R.E.A.L. offers the following services to pre-collegiate educators:
         • In-service workshops on teaching about Latin America;
         • Development of innovative curriculum materials on Latin America that em-
         phasize cultural awareness, student participation, and social studies skills;
         • Evaluation of existing curricula;
         • School visitations and demonstrations of pilot units.

4.187   The **University of Texas at Austin** is also noted for its Latin America Studies
         program. Curriculum materials developed at Austin include:

188   *Development of Guidelines and Resource Materials on Latin America for Use in Grades 1–12: Final Report.* Clark C. Gill and William B. Conroy. August 1969. 68pp. $3.50

189   *Teaching About Latin America in the Elementary School: An Annotated Guide to Instructional Resources.* Clark C. Gill and William B. Conroy. 1967. 46pp. $2.06 and *Teaching About Latin America in the Secondary School: An Annotated Guide to Instructional Resources.* Clark C. Gill and William B. Conroy. 1967. 77pp. $4.67

These three publications are available at the prices indicated plus postage from ERIC Document Reproduction Service.

Simulation Games

190   *The Coffee Game.* Thomas P. Fenton, in collaboration with Eugene W. Toland and Lawrence F. McCulloch. *Education for Justice* (Maryknoll, N.Y.: Orbis Books, 1975), pp. 297–338. $7.95. Level: secondary school. Players: 18. Time: 90 minutes.

The object of this role-playing simulation is to illustrate the dynamics of international trade and aid as they are operative around the commodity of coffee. Participants in *The Coffee Game* should come to a greater appreciation of the complexity of these dynamics and to an understanding of how an ordinary product such as coffee binds our lives together with the lives of people in other lands.

191   *Destiny.* Lakeside, Calif.: Interact, 1969. $15. Level: secondary school and above. Players: 20–40. Time: 15–25 hours.

Destiny focuses the attention of the participants on relations between Spain and the United States (in relation to Cuba) during the end of 1897 and the early part of 1898. Participants play the roles of journalists, businesspeople, the Cuban junta, Spanish government officials, and imperialist and anti-imperialist pressure groups in the United States.

192   *Imperialism.* New York: Simulation Learning Institute, 1974. $35. Level: upper primary and above. Players: 5 or more. Time: 2–4 hours.

Participants in this simulation set out to resolve differences between the United States and Panama over control of the Panama Canal. In the process they come to appreciate the frustrations of a small developing country such as Panama in its dealings with the United States and other international powers.

See also:
1.200, 1.207, 7.78, 7.82, 10.116, 10.125, 10.130

Chapter 5

Middle East

KEY RESOURCES

Organizations

Most regional offices of the **American Friends Service Committee** have Middle East Programs. The national, New York, and San Francisco offices are notable among them.

Americans For Middle East Understanding is an excellent source of information, especially for educators. AMEU carries study guides, maps, and other materials designed for the classroom.

MERIP is a long-established and respected organization that takes an aggressively critical stand toward U.S. foreign and military policy in the Middle East. MERIP staff members are available for speaking engagements on the East Coast.

Printed Resources

AMEU is your best source for books on the Middle East. The organization's spring and fall catalogs provide annotated listings of books available at generous discounts.

A number of books described below focus on misrepresentations of Middle East political and economic realities in the Western media. These include: Forrest, *The Unholy Land*; Hirst, *The Gun and the Olive Branch*; Polk, *The Elusive Peace*; and Said, *Covering Islam*.

Magazines annotated below all take a critical stand on Mideast affairs. They range from progressive Jewish opinion to staunch support of Palestinian rights.

MERIP Reports is essential reading for those who are looking for a well-documented critical assessment of U.S. public and private power in the region. *The Link* is popular in style and more moderate in approach, though it, too, is critical of distorted presentations of the Arab point of view.

Back issues of *The Link* and *MERIP Reports* are available in single and bulk orders. The Middle East Programs of **AFSC Regional Offices** are often a good source of informative and popularly written leaflets and pamphlets.

Audiovisual Resources

Icarus Films is the primary source for feature and documentary films on the Middle East. In 1981 Icarus organized a Festival of Middle East Films that included program notes, press kits, promotional consultation, names of speakers and other aids for those who want to use Icarus films in an educational setting.

Other Resources

Two key organizations already named—**MERIP** and **AMEU**—are the best sources for educational materials, reading lists, and the like.

ORGANIZATIONS

5.1 **American Friends Service Committee**, Middle East Program, 15 Rutherford Place, New York, NY 10003. Tel: 212-598-0972.

RELIGIOUS AFFILIATION: Religious Society of Friends (Quakers).

FOCUS: Middle East. Human Rights • militarism • foreign trade and aid • international awareness • women.

ACTIVITIES: Popular education • research and writing • documentation and information.

RESOURCES: Speakers • audiovisuals • publications • reports.

PERIODICALS: **5.2** *Middle East Network*. Occasional.

5.3 **American Friends Service Committee**, Middle East Program, 1501 Cherry St., Philadelphia, PA 19102. Tel: 215-241-7000.

RELIGIOUS AFFILIATION: Religious Society of Friends (Quakers).

FOCUS: Middle East. Human rights • militarism • international awareness • women.

ACTIVITIES: Popular education • research and writing • documentation and information.

RESOURCES: Audiovisuals • publications • reports.

5.4   **American Friends Service Committee**, Middle East Program, 2160 Lake St., San Francisco, CA 94121. Tel: 415-752-7766.

RELIGIOUS AFFILIATION: Religious Society of Friends (Quakers).

FOCUS: Middle East. Human rights • militarism • foreign trade and aid • international awareness.

ACTIVITIES: Popular education • research and writing • documentation and information.

RESOURCES: Speakers • audiovisuals • publications • reports.

5.5   **Americans for Middle East Understanding**, (AMEU), 475 Riverside Dr., Rm. 771, New York, NY 10115. Tel: 212-870-2053.

FOCUS: Middle East. Human rights • political repression • militarism • disarmament • nuclear arms and energy • foreign trade and aid • political economy • international awareness • social justice.

ACTIVITIES: Popular education • library services • media • documentation • justice and peace ministries.

RESOURCES: Speakers • audiovisuals • literature • publications • research services • book catalog available.

PERIODICALS: **5.6** *The Link*. Bimonthly. **5.7** *Public Affairs Pamphlet Series*. 3–4 issues/year. Both with $10 annual contribution.

5.8   **Arab Information Center**, 747 Third Ave., 25th Floor, New York, NY 10017. Tel: 212-838-8700.

POLITICAL AFFILIATION: League of Arab States.

FOCUS: Middle East. Human rights • political repression • foreign trade and aid • political economy • international awareness • national liberation struggles • social justice.

ACTIVITIES: Popular education • constituency education • political action • research and writing • library services • press service • networking • documentation and information • policy-oriented research and writing.

RESOURCES: Speakers • audiovisual • literature • publications • consultant services • research services • library • reports.

5.9   **Arab People to American People**, 820 Second Ave., Suite 302, New York, NY 10017. Tel: 212-972-0460.

FOCUS: Middle East. Human rights • militarism • foreign trade and aid • transnational corporations • international awareness • national liberation struggles • social justice.

ACTIVITIES: Popular education • research and writing • solidarity work • networking • documentation and information • policy-oriented research and writing.

RESOURCES: Speakers • publications • reports.

PERIODICALS: **5.10** *Action*. Weekly newspaper. $30/year.

5.11   **Middle East Peace Project**, 339 Lafayette St., New York, NY 10012. Tel: 212-475-4300.

RELIGIOUS AFFILIATION: Jewish; interreligious.

FOCUS: Middle East, especially the Arab-Israeli conflict. Human rights • political repression • militarism • disarmament • nuclear arms • international awareness • national liberation struggles in the Middle East • social justice.

ACTIVITIES: Popular education • constituency education • research and writing • solidarity work • library services • press service • networking • training of peace educators • conducting Middle East "peace tours"/arranging Israeli-Palestinian dialogues.

RESOURCES: Speakers • distributor of literature • publications • study–action guides • curriculum guides • consultant services • research services • library.

PERIODICALS: **5.12** *MEP Information and Resources Packet.* Monthly. $50/year.

SPECIAL PROJECTS: Support for Israeli conscientious objectors. Distribution of a pin showing the flags of Israel and Palestine side by side.

5.13   **Middle East Research and Information Project (MERIP)**, Box 43445, Washington, DC 20010. Tel: 202-667-1188.

FOCUS: Middle East. Political repression • militarism • disarmament • foreign trade and aid • political economy • socialism • national liberation struggles • social justice.

ACTIVITIES: Popular education • research and writing • documentation and information.

RESOURCES: Speakers • distributor of literature • publications • library • reports.

PERIODICALS: **5.14** *MERIP Reports.* 9 issues/year. $15.50/year individual; $26/year institutional.

5.15   **Middle East Resource Center (MERC)**, 1322 18 St., NW, Washington, DC 20036. Tel: 202-659-6846.

FOCUS: Middle East. Human rights • militarism • foreign trade, aid, and policy • transnational corporations • international awareness • political economy.

ACTIVITIES: Popular education • congressional testimony • solidarity work • press service • networking • media • documentation and information • policy-oriented research and writing • workshops and seminars.

RESOURCES: Speakers • publications • consultant services • research services • reports.

PERIODICALS: **5.16** *Palestine/Israel Bulletin.* Co-published with SEARCH for Justice and Equality in Palestine. 10 issues/year. $6/year individual; $15/year institutional.

5.17   **New Jewish Agenda**, 1123 Broadway, Rm. 1217, New York, NY 10010. Tel: 212-620-0828.

FOCUS: International • Middle East. Human rights • militarism • nuclear arms and energy • foreign trade and aid • international awareness • national liberation struggles • social and economic justice • women • racism.

ACTIVITIES: Popular and constituency education • solidarity work • media • networking (through regional chapters and national task forces) • relief work • seminars • documentation and information.

RESOURCES: Speakers • publications • education resources • audiovisuals • training sessions.

PERIODICALS: **5.18** *The Shalom Network Newsletter*. Co-published with the Shalom Network. Bimonthly. $10/year.

5.19   **SEARCH for Justice and Equality in Palestine**, Box 53, Waverly Station, Boston, MA 02158. Tel: 617-899-9665.

FOCUS: Middle East. Human rights • political repression • social justice • peace.

ACTIVITIES: Constituency education • congressional testimony • intern programs • press service • networking • media • documentation and information • workshops and seminars.

RESOURCES: Speakers • literature • publications.

PERIODICALS: **5.20** *Palestine/Israel Bulletin*. Co-published with the Middle East Resource Center. 10 issues/year. $6/year individual; $15/year institutional.

SPECIAL PROJECTS: Work with the United Nations on the International Conference on the Question of Palestine.

5.21   **Shalom Network**, Box 623, Brookline, MA 02146. Tel: 617-965-1495.

FOCUS: Middle East. Human rights • militarism • international awareness • peace in the Middle East.

ACTIVITIES: Popular and constituency education • support for national liberation struggles.

RESOURCES: Speakers • training programs • publications • resource bank.

PERIODICALS: **5.22** *The Shalom Network Newsletter*. Co-published with New Jewish Agenda. Bimonthly. $10/year.

PRINTED RESOURCES

Books

Some of the books listed below are available at a reduced price through **Americans for Middle East Understanding (AMEU)**.

.23   Albert, David H. ed. *Tell the American People: Perspectives on the Iranian Revolution*. Philadelphia: Movement for a New Society, 1980. 160pp. 16pp. of photographs. $3.80. Order from Network Service Collective, Movement for a New Society.

In February 1980, the Committee for an American–Iranian Crisis Resolution sent a delegation of forty-nine Americans to Iran to engage in an "intensive dialogue" with Iranian students holding the hostages at the U.S. Embassy. The delegation represented a broad cross-section of Americans—from farmers to clergy—and included representatives of major racial, religious, and ethnic groups.

Tell the American People addresses itself to several aspects of the Iranian situation—both pre- and post-revolution. It is a forthright—yet sensitive—attempt to share with the American people the truth about U.S. relations with Iran.

.24   American Friends Service Committee. *A Compassionate Peace: A Future for the Middle East*. New York: Hill & Wang, 1982. 226pp. $6.95

This timely report draws on AFSC's long experience in the Middle East as well as on the expertise of the particular members of the Working Party whose joint efforts produced it. Its purpose is to suggest approaches to peace that flow from Quaker faith and values.

A Compassionate Peace discusses the arms race in the Middle East, the politics of oil, the roles of the Soviet Union and the United States, the Iranian revolution, the conflicts in Lebanon, and the Soviet invasion of Afghanistan. The unresolved Israeli–Arab–Palestinian conflict is presented as the core of the matter; the authors make specific recommendations to U.S. policy makers and call for a comprehensive peace between Israel and the Palestinians.

.25   Betts, Robert B. *Christians in the Arab East*. Rev. ed. Atlanta, Ga.: John Knox Press, 1978. 318pp. Bibliography. $12. AMEU price $7.75

A comprehensive study of the Arabic-speaking Christians and the role they have played in the Middle East from the time of the Islamic conquest up to the present. Valuable demographic statistics are included.

.26   Chakmakjian, Hagop. *In Quest of Justice and Peace in the Middle East: The Palestinian Conflict in Biblical Perspective*. New York: Vantage Press, 1980. 157pp. $8.95. AMEU price $6.50

Written for those concerned about, but familiar with, the facts regarding the Palestinian issue, and in particular, the scriptural claims for the Zionist right to the land of Palestine.

5.27   Chomsky, Noam. *Peace in the Middle East: Reflections on Justice and Nationhood*. New York: Random House, Vintage, 1974. 198pp. $2.45

A collection of Chomsky's critical essays dealing with the theoretical aspects of Zionism and with Israel's application of human rights. Chomsky challenges both rigid pro-PLO and pro-Israeli positions. Includes annotated bibliography.

5.28   Dimbleby, Jonathan. *The Palestinians*. New York: Quartet Books, 1979. 265pp. Photographs. $25 AMEU price $17.50

Explores the crisis of a people without a land, demonstrating that the "Palestinian problem" is not an abstract issue but an urgent human tragedy. Photographs are stunning.

5.29   Elfers, Robert A. *A Sojourn in Mosaic*. New York: Friendship Press, Middle East Mosaic Series, 1979. 88pp. $2.95. AMEU price $2

Two young Americans journey through the Middle East, each on a mission to find the other. The narrative reveals much about the culture and religious life of the area, the political scene, the dangers of daily life in war-torn areas. The author introduces a cross section of the population, showing many viewpoints.

5.30   Ennes, James Jr. *Assault on the Liberty*. New York: Random House, 1980. 301pp. $12.95. AMEU price $8.50

The author served as a lieutenant on the USS *Liberty* on its fatal voyage. He was on watch at the bridge during the day of the Israeli attack; his testimony and that of other members of the crew show that the attack was not a mistake and that the subsequent investigation by U.S. authorities was a "whitewash." The attack and subsequent investigation call into question U.S.–Israeli mutual loyalties.

5.31   Feuerwerger, Marvin. *Congress and Israel: Foreign Aid Decision-Making in the House of Representatives, 1969–76*. Westport, Conn.: Greenwood Press, 1979. 235pp. $23.95. AMEU price $18

An insider's look at the Israeli lobby in Washington during the Nixon and Ford administrations. Covers the source of the widespread support for aid to Israel, congressional opposition to assistance to Israel, and the special workings of the House Foreign Affairs Committee.

5.32   Forrest, A. C. *The Unholy Land*. Old Greenwich, Conn.: Devin-Adair Co., 1971. 178pp. $3.95. AMEU price $3.60

The Unholy Land is one author's personal, informed, and uncompromising stand against what he considers to be imbalanced and distorted news coverage of the human tragedy brought about by the Arab-Israeli conflict in the Middle East.

5.33   Gilmour, David. *Dispossessed: The Ordeal of the Palestinians 1917–1980*. London: Sidgwick & Jackson, 1980. 242pp. 12.50 pounds. AMEU price $13.95

Well-documented history of the Palestinians, based in part on revealing quotations from Zionist sources. The author examines the status of the Palestinians in exile, the complex interrelationships of the PLO and the Palestinians vis-à-vis the international community, particularly with the Soviet Union and the Third World.

.34   Halliday, Fred. *Arabia Without Sultans: A Survey of Political Instability in the Arab World*. New York: Random House, Vintage, 1974. 539pp. $6.95

Halliday's intention is to provide a comprehensive analysis of the contemporary Arabian peninsula by presenting and interpreting information that has been dispersed or is inaccessible. He takes his readers beyond the stereotypes of Arab sheikhs and kings and uncovers the world of workers, nomads, and peasants. At the same time he sheds light on the tensions that exist between rulers and ruled and downplays the exaggerated differences between the rulers of the oil states and the major capitalist nations.

.35   Halliday, Fred. *Iran: Dictatorship and Development*. 2nd ed. New York: Penguin Books, 1979. 361pp. Bibliography. $3.95

This book serves as a challenging but readable study of contemporary Iran, especially from the early 1960s. In a 21-page Afterword, Halliday discusses the overthrow of the Shah and its implications for the future of Iran. America's economic and political support for the Shah is critically detailed throughout the book.

.36   Hirst, David. *The Gun and the Olive Branch*. London: Faber & Faber, 1977. 367pp. 6.50 pounds. AMEU price $8.05

Aptly subtitled "The Roots of Violence in the Middle East," the author explodes a number of myths about both Arabs and Zionists. A carefully researched and documented account.

.37   International Press Seminar. *The Arab Image in Western Mass Media*. London: Outline Books, 1980. 280pp. AMEU price $3.75

This is a collection of papers delivered at the 1979 International Press Seminar in London. Contributors include Jack Shaheen, Edward Said, Mohammad Heikal, Claud Morris, Lord Caradon, Hisham Sharabi, and Eric Roleau.

.38   Lilienthal, Alfred. *The Zionist Connection: What Price Peace?* New York: Dodd, Mead & Co., 1978. 872pp. $19.95. AMEU price $12.75

Covers the Arab–Israeli conflict from the time of Herzl to Camp David, treating the subject from various angles. Well-documented and very informative.

.39   Meo, Leila, ed. *U.S. Strategy in the Gulf: Intervention against Liberation*. Belmont, Mass.: Association of Arab-American University Graduates, 1981. 130pp. $6

The contributors to this study, all American scholars, focus on various aspects of U.S. involvement in the Arabian-Persian Gulf over the past 35 years. Chapters include the Mythology of U.S. Intervention; U.S. Military Missions to Iran; U.S. Policy towards the Middle East; and U.S. Military Planning for the Arabian–Persian Gulf and Third World Conflicts.

.40   National Lawyers Guild. *Treatment of Palestinians in Israeli–Occupied West Bank and Gaza*. New York: National Lawyers Guild, 1978. 143pp. $5

Extensive documentation of human rights violations of Palestinian people by Israel.

5.41 Palestine Books Project. *Our Roots Are Still Alive: The Story of the Palestinian People*. San Francisco: People's Press, 1977. 189pp. $6. Also available from Palestine Solidarity Committee.

Focuses on the Arab-Israeli conflict, the role of the U.S. government, and the growth of the Palestinian national liberation movement. Illustrated with many original drawings, maps, and photographs.

5.42 Polk, William R. *The Elusive Peace: The Middle East in the Twentieth Century*. London: Croom Helm, 1981. 184pp. $15.95. AMEU price $11.75

Introductory book on the history of the Middle East; corrects many of the prevailing Western myths.

5.43 Pratt, et al. *Peace, Justice and Reconciliation in the Arab-Israeli Conflict: A Christian Perspective*. New York: Friendship Press, 1979. $2.75

This is a collective statement by seven Canadian groups and individuals urging North American Christians to confront the present in its moral ambiguity and look toward the future. The book includes questions for critical evaluation by Alan Geyer.

5.44 Said, Edward W. *Covering Islam: How the Media and the Experts Determine How We See the Rest of the World*. New York: Pantheon, 1981. 186pp. $3.95

Said's analysis of the U.S. press coverage of the Iranian revolution, the hostage crisis, and other recent events in the Middle East shows that the American press has created a fiction called "Islam" similar to the American picture of "Communism" in the 1950s.

5.45 Said, Edward W. *The Question of Palestine*. New York: Random House, Vintage, 1980. 288pp. $2.95

The author argues that the reason the problem of Palestine remains intractable is because the question of Palestine has not yet begun to be understood.

5.46 Stone, I. F. *Underground to Palestine and Reflections Thirty Years Later*. New York: Pantheon, 1978. 284pp. $3.95. AMEU price $2.95

In 1946 I. F. Stone was the first journalist to accompany survivors of the Holocaust on an illegal voyage to Palestine. He wrote this book as a record of their plight and as a testament to their right to seek a homeland. Thirty years later, he adds two essays, stressing his continuing support for a Palestinian homeland as well.

5.47 Zeadey, Faith, ed. *Camp David: A New Balfour Declaration*. Belmont, Mass.: Association of Arab-American University Graduates, 1979. 90pp. $3.50. Also available from the Palestine Solidarity Committee.

A collection of special papers and documents compiled shortly after the September 1978 Camp David Conference in an effort to show that the conference betrayed Palestinian national rights and failed to advance the cause of peace.

See also:
1.111, 7.32, 10.40, 10.42

Periodicals

48　*Action*, Box 416, Grand Central Station, New York, NY 10017. Weekly newspaper. $30/year.

Presenting news related to the Arab world, this weekly tabloid is "dedicated to better American-Arab understanding." *Action* is a publication of the Arab People to American People group.

49　*Arab Perspectives*, 747 Third Ave., New York, NY 10017. Monthly magazine. $10/year.

Arab Perspectives is a very attractive glossy magazine published by the Arab Information Center. Each issue presents three or four analytical articles (often relative to the United States and its foreign policy in the Arab world); a short story, poem, or cultural piece; American and Arab press reviews with commentary; and book reviews.

50　*Genesis 2*, 233 Bay State Rd., Boston, MA 02215. 8 issues/year. $6/year.

An independent Jewish journal of news, opinion, and the arts, reflecting the newly emerging progressive Jewish movement of the 1980s.

51　*Israel Horizons*, Americans for a Progressive Israel, 150 Fifth Ave., Rm. 1002, New York, NY 10011. Bimonthly. $10/year.

News and comment on the State of Israel and on Jewish affairs throughout the world. The aim of the magazine is to give voice to the activities of the progressive forces in Israel.

52　*Jewish Currents*, 22 E. 17 St., Rm. 601, New York, NY 10003. Monthly magazine. $10/year.

A progressive Jewish monthly that takes a critical stance toward U.S. foreign policy in the Middle East, especially the arms race in that region.

53　*The Link*, Americans for Middle East Understanding, 475 Riverside Dr., Rm. 771, New York, NY 10115. Bimonthly. Free, though a $10/year donation is requested.

AMEU's bimonthly magazine carries one or two popularly written feature articles plus "Book Views" and a listing of books that are available at a discount through AMEU.

54　*MERIP Reports*, Box 1247, New York, NY 10025. 10 issues/year. $12/year.

Begun in 1972 *MERIP Reports* provides an analysis of the political economy of the Middle East and the popular struggles there from a critical and independent socialist perspective. Heavy reading at times, but indispensable for an understanding of events in North Africa and the Middle East.

55　*Middle East Information and Resources Packet*, Middle East Peace Project, 339 Lafayette St., New York, NY 10012. Bimonthly packet. $50/year.

A specialized clipping service presenting important articles arranged according to topic. For example, one packet includes articles on Israeli-Palestinian contacts, a chronology of recent events; articles on Israeli policy and public opinion; Arab and Palestinian policies and opinions; U.S. policy and public opinion; and follow-up on previous articles.

5.56   *The Middle East Journal*, Middle East Institute, 1761 N St., NW, Washington, DC 20036. Quarterly journal. $15/year.

A scholarly journal on contemporary Middle Eastern affairs now in its thirty-sixth year of publication. Each issue contains several articles on current political, economic and social issues, a chronology of quarterly events, state documents, review articles, book reviews, and a bibliography of periodical literature.

5.57   *Middle East Perspective*, 850 Seventh Ave., Suite 703, New York, NY 10019. Monthly newsletter. $20/year.

This newsletter on Eastern Mediterranean and North African affairs attempts to expose inaccuracies, bias, and misinformation in the media, and to present facts on the complex political and current events relating to the Middle East. Each issue contains an editorial and one or two articles by recognized academicians in the field.

5.58   *Palestine!*, Palestine Solidarity Committee, Box 1757, Manhattanville Station, New York, NY 10027. 10 issues/year. $10/year.

This twenty-page monthly is vigorously supportive of Palestinian rights and highly critical of U.S. foreign policy in the Middle East.

5.59   *The Palestine Review*, 1884 Columbia Rd., NW, No. 511, Washington, DC 20009. Monthly. $15/year.

Launched in 1981 the *Review* presents articles on the literary, artistic, cultural, economic, and political aspects of the Palestinian people.

Pamphlets and Articles

5.60   *After the Shah*. Fred Halliday. IPS, 1979. 18pp. $2

Important background information on the National Front, the Tudeh Party, the religious opposition and many other groups whose policies and programs will determine Iran's future.

5.61   *American Jews and the Middle East: Fears, Frustration and Hope*. Allan Solomonow. *The Link* 13, no. 3, July-August 1980, 13pp. Contribution requested.

Some of the material in this article is taken from a more comprehensive study of stereotypes about Palestinians found in typical Jewish educational materials.

5.62   *The Arab Stereotype on Television*. Jack G. Shaheen. *The Link* 13, no. 2, April-May 1980. 14pp. Contribution requested.

This article is the result of research by the author for an upcoming book intended to make television producers and executives more aware of Arab stereotyping and of the media's responsibility to reflect a wide range of positive roles for all people.

5.63   *Arms Buildup in the Middle East*. Gregory Orfaleo. *The Link* 14, no. 4, September-October 1981. 16pp. Contribution requested.

A review of the history of arms sales to and from the Middle East, the introduction of nuclear weapons into that area, and the terms of the U.S. Arms Export Law. The author warns of the implications of the arms race and suggests ways to act for a safer future.

.64   *The Continuing Mideast Palestinian Dilemma. e/sa forum* 79, February 1982.
30pp. 50 cents

A special insert from the magazine *engage/social action*, these articles aim to
help readers better understand the situation and point of view of the Palestinian
people. So as to include concerns from the Israeli viewpoint, excerpts from a
white paper on "The Middle East Today: Questions and Answers for Church
Leaders" are also reprinted in the forum.

.65   *A Cutting Edge toward Israeli-Palestinian Peace.* Middle East Peace Project,
February 1981. $1.50. Available from WILPF.

This is a collection of articles from *The Nation, Le Monde, New Outlook,* and
Peace and Freedom.

.66   *Forging an American Policy for Middle East Peace.* Noam Chomsky. Middle
East Peace Project, 1978. 6pp. $1. Available from War Resisters League.

A reprint of a speech by Chomsky challenging rigid pro-PLO and pro-Israeli
positions on the Middle East.

.67   *The Gulf: Target for Intervention* (Joe Stork) and ***Between Two Revolutions***
(Fred Halliday). *MERIP Reports* 85, February 1980. $2.50

U.S. plans for a rapid deployment force juxtaposed with the social and political
transformation of the Persian Gulf region over the last two decades.

.68   *The Idea of Palestine in the West.* Edward Said. *MERIP Reports* 70, September 1978. $2.50

A good introduction by a Palestinian-American professor of literature.

.69   *Iran Packet.* Women's International League for Peace and Freedom. 1981. $2

This packet contains reprints of articles from various sources; a series of background papers prepared for the United Church of Christ Board of World Ministries; "A Long Overdue Apology to the Iranian People"; and more.

Iran: Two Years After. MERIP Reports 98, July-August 1981. $2.50

In this issue of *MERIP Reports* Eric Rouleau reports on the war with Iraq and
the struggle for state power; Patrick Clawson analyzes the economic crisis in the
country; Fred Halliday dissects U.S. policy and the myth of good intentions.
Eyewitnesses give accounts of approaching civil war.

.70   *Israel's Annexation of the Golan Heights* and *America's Mideast Challenge.*
Rep. Paul N. McCloskey, Jr. AMEU, Public Affairs Series no. 17. Contribution.

Congressman McCloskey takes a critical stance toward the $2.2 billion in for-
eign aid allocated in 1981 for Israel. In a letter to his constituents in California he
pleads for flexibility in U.S. negotiations with the Palestine Liberation Organization and for the creation of an autonomous Palestinian homeland in the West
Bank and Gaza.

71   *Israeli Torture of Palestinian Political Prisoners in Jerusalem and the Ie't
Kank: Three State Department Reports.* Alexandra U. Johnson. AMEU, Public
Affairs Series no. 14, April 1979. 11pp. Contribution.

A reprint of an article from the *Palestine Human Rights Bulletin.*

5.72 *Lebanon Packet*. Women's International League for Peace and Freedom, 1982. $1.50

The WILPF has collected articles from the *Washington Post*, *New York Times*, and *Jerusalem Post International Edition* for this packet on Lebanon.

5.73 *The Middle East: Keystone to Global Stability*. Peace and Freedom, 1980–81. Women's International League for Peace and Freedom. $2. Bulk rates available.

This collection of reprints from the WILPF publication *Peace and Freedom* covers a variety of Middle East issues: U.S. foreign policy and its domestic implications, oil politics, arms exports, and the Israeli–Palestinian conflict.

5.74 *The Middle East: Where Is Peace Now?* AFSC (Philadelphia), 1978. 15pp. 75 cents. Bulk rates available.

This collection of impressions of the Arab–Israeli–Palestinian conflict is taken from columns written by *New York Times* correspondant Anthony Lewis in May and June 1978.

5.75 *National Council of Churches Adopts New Comprehensive Statement on the Middle East*. Allison Rock and Jay Vogelaar. *The Link* 13, no. 5, December 1980, 16pp. Contribution.

The document issued by the National Council of Churches addresses issues such as overseas Christian mission and colonialist attitudes, church ethics vis-à-vis government policies, rights of minorities in Middle Eastern culture, the arms race, discussions with the PLO, statehood for the Palestinians, and the status of Jerusalem. This article furnishes background on the statement, its highlights, and some of the reactions to it.

5.76 *The Palestinians: A People in Crisis*. AFSC (Philadelphia). February 1978, 15pp. 50 cents

This attractive booklet consists of a series of articles on the Palestinians reprinted from early 1978 editions of the *New York Times*. Especially useful is a one-page description of the various organizations and guerrilla groups that represent Palestinian interests throughout the Middle East.

5.77 *The Palestinians and the New Realities in the Middle East*. Dr. Ali Alyami. AFSC (San Francisco), Middle East Peace Education Program. 8pp. 50 cents

"The only way in which a just and lasting peace can be established between the Palestinians and the Israelis is through multilateral recognition of the rights of both peoples to national self-determination," says Dr. Alyami. In this short booklet Dr. Alyami, the director of AFSC's Middle East Peace Project in San Francisco, explains his position and offers background information on the political situation of the more than three million Palestinian people in the Middle East.

5.78 *Questions and Answers: AFSC and the Arab-Israeli-Palestinian Conflict*. AFSC (Philadelphia). 10 cents

Outlines briefly the point of view of the AFSC on the Arab-Israeli-Palestinian conflict. The questions are those raised most often by the public in AFSC's experience. The answers attempt to clarify the issues AFSC considers central to the conflict.

.79   *The Right of Return of the Palestinian People*. United Nations, 1978. 54pp. $3. Available from the Palestine Solidarity Committee.

The right of the refugees from 1948 to return to their homes is documented in a special study of the various UN and other international debates and resolutions concerning the question.

.80   *A Special Report on Israeli-Palestinian Contacts*. AFSC (Philadelphia) and Middle East Peace Project, March 15, 1981. 5pp. $1

This report brings together statements made by representatives of the Palestine Liberation Organization and members of the Israel Council for Israeli-Palestinian Peace in Paris, Tel Aviv, and Beirut during 1980.

.81   *Thinking the Unthinkable: A Sovereign Palestinian State*. Walid Khalidi. AFSC (Philadelphia), 1978. 20pp. 50 cents

A concrete proposal for the possible shape of a sovereign Palestinian state on the West Bank and Gaza Strip, committed to coexisting at peace with the State of Israel.

.82   *The United States and Saudi Arabia*. AFSC (San Francisco), Middle East Peace Education Program. 16pp. 50 cents

The director of AFSC's MEPEP in San Francisco—himself a "Saudi" Arabian—provides us with a brief description of political, economic, and social realities in Saudi Arabia under the rule of the Saudi monarchy. Dr. Alyami analyzes prospects for the overthrow of the House of Saud and discusses the effect that would have on America's considerable interests in the country and the region.

.83   *The Vietnam Syndrome*. Joe Stork and Michael Klare. *MERIP Reports* 90, September 1980. 32pp. $2.50

In this issue of *MERIP Reports*, Joe Stork analyzes President Carter's Middle East doctrine and details U.S. military relations with key states. Michael Klare reports on war games for the 1980s.

See also:
7.49, 8.100, 10.75

AUDIOVISUAL RESOURCES

Guides and Catalogs

5.84   *The Arab World: A Handbook for Teachers*. R. Afifi, Ayad Al-Qazzaz, and
Audrey Shabbas. Albany, Calif.; NAJDA (Women Concerned about the Middle
East), 1978. 128pp. $5. AMEU price $3.50
This handbook includes an appendix of "Free-Loan Audio-Visual Materials"
with addresses of distributors that range from the Arab Information Center to
Standard Oil of California.

5.85   *Films on the Middle East*. Audio Visual Library Service, University of Minnesota. 5pp. Free
The University of Minnesota's Audio Visual Library Service makes available a
brief annotated catalog of films on the Middle East. An order form is included.

5.86   *Middle East Film Library*. Icarus Films. Brochure. Free
Icarus Films regularly puts out this flyer on its Middle East films with complete
details on the films and on how to order them.

Audiovisuals

5.87   *Children of Palestine*. 1979 35 min color film. Directed by Monica Maurer and
Samir Nimer. Icarus. Rental $55/80
Documentary of Israeli bombings in southern Lebanon and their effects on
children in that region. This passionate film, which won a Special Prize at the
1979 Leipzig Film Festival, presents an insider's (Palestinian) perspective on the
civil war in Lebanon.

5.88   *Communists for 1000 Years*. 1973 44 min color film. Produced and directed by
Gordian Troeller and M. Claude Deffarge. Icarus. Rental $75/100
The first and only film in this country on the isolated Carmathian sect in South
Yemen. According to the filmmakers, the egalitarian social structure of the Car-
mathians explains the success of South Yemen. The film is a fascinating study of a
unique social group hardly heard of in this country.

5.89   *Cowboys*. 1971 22 min color film. Produced and directed by Sami Salamani.
Icarus. Rental $25
American cowboys and violent action films provide the visuals; a rock band
provides the sound track. The result is an impressive statement about the United
States and its involvement in the Middle East. The film—a complex mosaic of
documentary footage and clips of U.S. films—provides a rare insight into how
the United States is perceived by the Third World.

5.90   *The Cycle*. 1979 90 min color 35mm film. Directed and produced by Darium
Mehrjui. Icarus. Rental $150
Mehrjui paints a very grim picture of cycles of corruption in Iran under the rule

of the Shah. Using the metaphor of an illegal blood bank where poor, diseased, and handicapped Iranians sell their blood, *The Cycle* graphically portrays a society in which the desperate struggle for mere survival turns people into animals.

.91   *Hope for Life*. 1979 36 min color film. Board of Global Ministries, United Methodist Church. Rental $15

This 16mm documentary shows how concerned Christians, through the Middle East Council of Churches and Church World Service, are helping people to help themselves in Egypt, Lebanon, and the West Bank and Gaza.

.92   *The Key*. 1972 32 min color film. Produced by the Palestine Cinema Unit. Icarus. Apply for rates.

This first indigenous Palestinian film to be distributed in this country gives us the Palestinian version of their own recent history.

.93   *Life Under Occupation: A Slide Show About Palestinians on the West Bank*. 25 min color slideshow. Jewish Committee to End the Israeli Occupation. Apply for rates.

This slideshow grew out of a 1980 trip to Israel and the West Bank by two members of the Jewish Committee to End the Israeli Occupation. The 25-minute presentation includes historical background and a critical analysis of the Israeli occupation. It is designed to spark discussion on the basic questions surrounding the Palestinian-Israeli conflict.

.94   *Many Yet One: The Church and the Churches in the Middle East*. Color filmstrip with cassette. Produced by Friendship Press. Available from the Board of Global Ministries, United Methodist Church. Sale $12

This filmstrip tells the story of the Christian presence in the Middle East, with special attention given to the variety of churches and styles of worship. Emphasis is on the sense of mission expressed by indigenous churches and how this relates to Western churches.

95   *The Palestinian People Do Have Rights*. 1979 48 min color film. Produced by the United Nations. Distributed by the UN (free) and by Icarus ($75/100).

This excellent historical film traces the roots of the current Palestinian-Israeli conflict to the early Jewish settlement in Palestine during the Ottoman rule. The film continues with a survey of Palestine through the time of the British Mandate, the establishment of the State of Israel, and the major wars of 1948, 1956, 1967, and 1973. It concludes with an analysis of the present situation of the Palestinian people.

96   *Palestinian Refugees in Lebanon*. 1975 32 min color film. Directed by Roger Pic. Icarus. Rental $55

By focusing on a single Palestinian family, Roger Pic gives us a graphic introduction to everyday life in Palestinian refugee camps in Lebanon: the bitter fight for survival, the military training, and actual fighting in the south of Lebanon. This film offers the Palestinian side of the story: the work of the PLO in the refugee camps, the health services, schools, the workshops, and the small factories.

5.97 *The Temptation of Power*. 1979 43 min color film. Produced and directed by Gordian Troeller and Marie Claude Deffarge. Icarus. Rental $75/100

This film critically examines the realities behind the myth of Iran (under the Shah) as a progressive Middle Eastern state: the uprooting of the peasantry, the destruction of agriculture, migration to city slums. *Temptation* is a powerful tool for the study of Iran's current crisis and a key to the understanding of this complex society and its leap from semi-feudal monarchy to modern class society.

5.98 *To Live in Freedom*. 1975 54 min color film. California Newsreel. Rental $75

Made by a predominantly Israeli film crew, *To Live in Freedom* exposes Israel as a class society, with the Palestinians and other Arabs at the bottom of the ladder, and the non-European or oriental Jews on the rung just above them. The film offers a brief history of the Zionist movement and of the conditions in Europe that created the drive in the Jewish communities for a "homeland." It contrasts the settlements of the Jews in present-day Israel with the huts and tents that the Palestinians are forced to live in. Zionist discrimination against all Arabs, Palestinian and other, is brought into clear focus as the filmmakers let Arabs describe the conditions on the jobs and discriminatory laws that apply only to Arabs.

5.99 *23rd Cease Fire*. 1976 52 min color film. Produced and directed by Anne Papillaut, Jean Francois Dars, Marc Kravetz, and Marc Mourani. Icarus. Rental $80. Sale $785 (film), $530 (video)

Through the story of one cease fire (in 1976) this film vividly describes life in war-torn Beirut and gives us an insight into the causes of the war. There are long interviews with the rightwing Christian militia, the late Kamal Jumblat, and the striking fisherfolk in Saida whose long strike was the spark that triggered the eruption of hostilities in the late 1970s. The war in Lebanon is shown to be not a religious war, but a struggle between a privileged minority and an impoverished majority.

See also:
7.73, 9.73, 10.112

Neighborhood Celebration Sharea Abdel Hadi Abeid Al Motayri, 9, Kuwait

OTHER RESOURCES

Curriculum Guides and Materials

Americans for Middle East Understanding (AMEU) provides a very useful and inexpensive packet of materials for teachers that includes—among other resources—these two books:

00   *The Arab World: A Handbook for Teachers.* R. Afifi; Ayad Al-Qazzaz; and Audrey Shabbas. Albany, Calif.: NAJDA (Women Concerned About the Middle East), 1978. 128pp. $5. AMEU price $3.50

This book will be of interest not only to teachers but to all who have an interest in the Arab world. The authors intend this handbook to be an antidote to the distortions and stereotyping that they have found in most schools on the Arabs, their culture, history, and society.

01   *The Middle East and South Asia 1980.* Ray Cleveland. Rev. ed. Washington, D.C.: Stryker-Post Publications, The World Today Series, 1980. 106pp. Maps. $3.25. AMEU price $2.95

The author gives a short historical background on the early empires in these areas and follows this with a discussion of each of the countries as they are at present. This excellent study guide contains statistical data, descriptions of the culture, an outline of the economies, and an analysis of future prospects in the region.

Write AMEU for the current price of their teacher's packet.

Other educational resources on the Middle East are:

02   *The Arabs: Perception/Misperception: A Comparative View, Experimental Version.* George G. Otero. Denver: University of Denver, Center for Teaching International Relations, 1975. 78pp. Available for $4.67, plus postage, from ERIC Document Reproduction Service.

This high school-level curriculum guide offers an exciting exploration of stereotypes and racial biases about Arab peoples. Most of the sixteen activities could be adapted to the study of other national or ethnic groups by simply changing the Arab–specific data in these exercises. An appendix includes a bibliography, along with lists of embassies and missions, of major newspapers of the Arab world, of Arab information offices, and of audiovisuals and other resources.

03   *Conflict or Community: A Guide to the Middle East Mosaic.* David H. Bowman. New York: Friendship Press, Middle East Mosaic Series, 1979. 47pp. $2.75. Available from AMEU for $1.85.

A guide for teachers and leaders of children, youth, and adults. The introductory section gives background information on Middle East issues and raises questions relating to justice and peace in that region. Includes activities, games, and a bibliography for different age groups.

5.104   *MERIP Reading Guide. MERIP Reports* 28, May 1974. 11pp.

This special section from the *MERIP Reports*, though dated, is still important and useful. The annotated bibliography is divided into several sections: General Historical, Economic and Political Background; Imperialism and Nationalism; The Early Period; Zionism; Palestine before 1948; Palestine after 1948; Middle East Countries; U.S. Policy, the Oil Industry, and the Military; Periodicals; and Books in Preparation.

5.105   *Middle East Study Materials.* Produced by the WILPF Middle East Committee. Published by the Jane Addams Peace Association. Available from WILPF. $7.50 plus postage

This packet of materials includes a study guide, a manual for study group leaders, a special packet of readings on the Middle East, a dozen articles, booklets, and a large map.

5.106   *Signpost/Middle East.* Anne C. Stephens. New York: Friendship Press, 1979. 20pp. $2.50

This attractive collection of stories, games, maps, crafts, and calligraphy is designed to introduce older primary school children to the daily joys and sorrows of children in Egypt, the Holy Land, Israel, Lebanon, and Turkey.

5.107   *Teacher's Resource Handbook for Near Eastern Studies: An Annotated Bibliography of Curriculum Materials (Preschool through Grade Twelve).* John N. Hawkins and Jon Maksik. Los Angeles: University of California, Gustave E. von Grunebaum Center for Near Eastern Studies, 1976. 102pp. $2.50. Available from the Curriculum Inquiry Center.

The authors provide teachers with over 800 books, audiovisuals, maps, bibliographies, and other resources on North Africa, and the Arab- and non-Arab Middle East. Most of the items are annotated, though the evaluative descriptions are very brief. The handbook is arranged by grade levels, with materials within each section divided by region and listed alphabetically in format categories. The handbook concludes with two model evaluation forms that may assist teachers in their selection of appropriate materials.

Simulation Games

5.108   *Arab-Israeli Conflict: A Decision-Making Game.* Washington, D.C.: American Political Science Association, 1977. $4. Level: secondary school and above. Players: 18 or more. Time: 3–7 hours.

This role-playing simulation engages participants in political and military decision making surrounding Middle East conflicts in general.

5.109   *Global Powderkeg.* Bloomington, Ind.: Mid-America Program for Global Perspectives in Education, Social Studies Development Center, Indiana University, 1975. $3. Level: late primary and above. Players: 16 or more. Time: at least 2 hours.

This simulation is more timely and sophisticated than the foregoing. Participants grow to appreciate the complexities of international decision making as

they serve in the roles of the Palestinian Liberation Organizations and the seven
major nations involved in the Middle East conflict.

110   *Middle East Crisis.* Sun Valley, Calif.: Edu-Game, 1976. $3. Level: mid-
primary and above. Players: 15 or more. Time: 3 hours.

This loosely structured game aims to bring home to participants the difficulties
involved in reaching workable and satisfactory compromises around conflicts in
the Middle East.

111   *Middle East Simulation.* Available from Education Consortium, Indiana University of Pennsylvania. 1974. $4. Level: late primary and above. Players: 30 or
more. Time: at least 2 hours.

The *Middle East Simulation* focuses on Arab-Israeli conflicts in the period
1968-1972. Participants are required to do quite a bit of preparation before actually playing their roles in the simulation. As a result the potential for significant
learnings is that much greater.

Church-related Middle East Programs

Many Protestant denominations have at their national headquarters persons
who are responsible for programs and relationships with the Middle East. They
often have study materials and projects in the pertinent countries.

For information write to the Middle East Office:

112   *American Baptist Churches*, Valley Forge, PA 19481.

113   *American Lutheran Church*, 422 S. Fifth Ave., Minneapolis, MN 55415.

114   *Christian Church (Disciples of Christ)*, Division of Overseas Ministries, Box
1986, Indianapolis, IN 46206.

115   *Church of the Brethren*, 1451 Dundee Ave., Elgin, IL 60120.

116   *Episcopal Church*, 815 Second Ave., New York, NY 10017.

117   *Lutheran Church in America*, 231 Madison Ave., New York, NY 10016.

118   *Mennonite Central Committee*, 21 S. 12 St., Akron, PA 17501.

119   *National Council of Churches of Christ*, Middle East & Europe (DOM), 475
Riverside Dr., Rm. 626, New York, NY 10115.

120   *Presbyterian Church in the U.S.*, 341 Ponce de Leon Ave., Atlanta, GA 30308.

121   *Reformed Church in America*, Secretary for World Ministries, 475 Riverside
Dr., Rm. 1827, New York, NY 10115.

122   *United Church Board for World Ministries*, 475 Riverside Dr., 16th Floor,
New York, NY 10115.

123   *United Methodist Church*, Board of Global Ministries, World Division, 475
Riverside Dr., 15th Floor, New York, NY 10115.

124   *United Presbyterian Church in the USA*, Liaison with Middle East, 475 Riverside Dr., Rm. 1133, New York, NY 10115.

See also:
1.200, 7.82

PART TWO

ISSUES

Food, Hunger, Agribusiness

Human Rights

Militarism, Peace, Disarmament

Transnational Corporations

Women

Chapter 6

Food, Hunger, Agribusiness

KEY RESOURCES

Organizations

World hunger has captured the interest of many, many organizations. *Who's Involved With Hunger: An Organization Guide* suggests the number and breadth of such groups.

Of the ones described in this directory **Bread for the World** and the **Institute for Food and Development Policy** are exceptionally good. Both situate the hunger issue in its proper economic and political context and both produce popularly written educational materials. **BFW** provides opportunities for local initiative through regional chapters and for legislative action. Staff from the **Institute** are often available for speaking engagements around the country.

On the particular question of infant formula abuses **INFACT** is the group with which to be in touch.

Printed Resources

Publications from the **Institute for Food and Development Policy**—*Food First*, in particular—and books by Susan George are uniformly good introductions to the root causes of world hunger. Jack Nelson's *Hunger for Justice* and Suzanne Toton's *World Hunger* both cover much of the same ground as the forementioned books, though these two authors broaden the focus by situating the issues in a scriptural context (Nelson) and in an educational setting (Toton).

Food Monitor is the best regular source for popularly written articles on food-related issues.

Bread for the World's background papers and the **Interfaith Center on Corporate Responsibility**'s *Corporate Examiner Briefs* are excellent resources for personal or group study. They cover a wide range of issues related to food, hunger, and agribusiness; they are inexpensive; and they usually point readers to further resources and to action possibilities. Some of **BFW**'s and **ICCR**'s materials are described in this section. It is worth writing to both organizations, though, for complete and up-to-date lists of their publications.

Audiovisual Resources

Earthwork's catalogs, *Films on Food and Land* and its supplement, are indispensable guides to audiovisuals on these issues.

The three-unit filmstrip from the **Institute for Peace and Justice** and **IFDP**'s *Food First Slideshow/Filmstrip* are highly recommended introductions to the study of food, hunger, and agribusiness.

Other Resources

Science for the People's *Feed, Need, Greed* curriculum guide is a good resource for high school and adult education programs. The **Bread for the World Educational Fund** carries abundant and well-designed educational resources for all levels.

ORGANIZATIONS

6.1 **Agricultural Mission Committee,** c/o NCC/DOM, 475 Riverside Dr., Rm. 624, New York, NY 10115. Tel: 212-870-2553.

RELIGIOUS AFFILIATION: Ecumenical.

FOCUS: Third World general. World hunger • development • appropriate technology • leadership development • land reform • agricultural research and extension.

ACTIVITIES: Networking • constituency education • overseas project support • support of people's organizations at the grassroots • assistance to denominational rural development programs.

RESOURCES: Consultant services • publications.

6.2   **American Friends Service Committee**, World Hunger/Global Development
Project, 15 Rutherford Place, New York, NY 10003. Tel: 212-777-4600.

RELIGIOUS AFFILIATION: Religious Society of Friends (Quakers).

FOCUS: Third World general. Domestic and world hunger • development.

ACTIVITIES: Popular education • training programs for organization and community leaders • policy consultations for the heads of national organizations,
corporations, and voluntary organizations.

RESOURCES: Audiovisuals • resource and program materials • literature.

PERIODICALS: **6.3** *World Hunger Actionletter*. Monthly newsletter. Contribution.

6.4   **Bread for the World**, 802 Rhode Island Ave., NE, Washington, DC 20018. Tel:
202-269-0200.

RELIGIOUS AFFILIATION: Christian ecumenical citizen's movement.

FOCUS: Third World general. Basic causes of world hunger • foreign trade and
aid • appropriate technology • grain reserves • hunger and global security.

ACTIVITIES: Constituency education • legislative action • research and writing •
workshops and seminars.

RESOURCES: Speakers • audiovisuals • literature • publications • study-action
guides • curriculum guides • reports • election kits.

PERIODICALS: **6.5** *BFW Newsletter*. Monthly newsletter. With membership.

6.6   **CROP (Community Hunger Appeal of Church World Service)**, Box 968,
Elkhart, IN 46515. Tel: 219-264-3102.

RELIGIOUS AFFILIATION: Christian ecumenical.

FOCUS: Third World general. World hunger • development.

ACTIVITIES: Constituency education • overseas educational experiences •
workshops and seminars • clothing appeals • overseas project support • CROP
Walks and Fasts.

RESOURCES: Audiovisuals • publications • consultant services.

PERIODICALS: **6.7** *Service News*. Bimonthly. Free.

IMPACT. See **National IMPACT Network**.

6.8   **Infant Formula Action Coalition (INFACT)**, 1701 University Ave., SE, Minneapolis, MN 55414. Tel: 612-331-2333.

FOCUS: Third World general. Infant formula abuse in Third World countries •
corporate responsibility.

ACTIVITIES: Popular education • political action • legislative action • boycotts •
research and writing • documentation and information • media.

RESOURCES: Speakers • literature • consultant services • bibliography on infant
feeding.

PERIODICALS: **6.9** *INFACT Update*. Monthly. With membership.

6.10   **Institute for Food and Development Policy**, 1885 Mission St., San Francisco, CA
94103. Tel: 415-864-8555.

FOCUS: Global. Foreign trade and aid • political economy • corporate responsibility • social justice • food and agriculture.

ACTIVITIES: Popular education • research and writing • documentation and information • policy-oriented research and writing.

RESOURCES: Speakers • audiovisuals • literature • publications • curriculum guides • consultant services.

PERIODICALS: **6.11** *Food First News*. Quarterly newsletter. Free to those on mailing list.

6.12 **National IMPACT Network**, c/o Interreligious Taskforce on U.S. Food Policy, 110 Maryland Ave., NE, Washington, DC 20002. Tel: 202-544-8636.

RELIGIOUS AFFILIATION: Interreligious. National Protestant, Roman Catholic, and Jewish agencies.

FOCUS: Third World general. Food aid • U.S. food policy • international development assistance • agricultural policy • energy crisis.

ACTIVITIES: Constituency education • networking • legislative action • policy-oriented research and writing • political action.

RESOURCES: Speakers • literature • background papers • action bulletins.

PERIODICALS: **6.13** *Hunger*. Periodic background paper. With membership. **6.14** *Prepare*. Background/study papers. 1–2 issues/year. With membership. **6.15** *Action*. 8–12 issues/year. With membership.

6.16 **Oxfam-America**, 115 Broadway, Boston, MA 02116. Tel: 617-482-1211.

FOCUS: Third World general. Hunger • nutrition • appropriate technology • agriculture • poverty.

ACTIVITIES: Study tours • popular education • overseas project support.

RESOURCES: Audiovisuals • literature • study-action guides • speakers.

PERIODICALS: **6.17** *Oxfam-America*. Monthly newsletter. Free.

6.18 **Science for the People**, 897 Main St., Cambridge, MA 02139. Tel: 617-547-0370.

FOCUS: Global. Asia and Pacific. Agribusiness • human rights • political repression • militarism • disarmament • nuclear arms and energy • political economy • socialism • corporate responsibility • social justice.

ACTIVITIES: Popular education • political action • research and writing • solidarity work • networking • media • workshops and seminars.

RESOURCES: Speakers • audiovisuals • literature • publications • curriculum guides.

PERIODICALS: **6.19** *Science for the People*. Bimonthly magazine. $12/year individual; $25/year supporting members.

6.20 **World Hunger Education/Action Together (WHEAT)**, Box 189, Nashville, TN 37202.

FOCUS: Third World general. World food crisis • U.S. food policy • self-help cooperatives • water resources • appropriate agricultural training • personal lifestyles.

ACTIVITIES: Covenant fellowship • constituency education • "enabling events" • legislative action • leadership training • workshops and seminars • community education and action • support advocacy.

RESOURCES: Speakers • literature • consultant services.

6.21 **World Hunger Education Service**, 1317 G St., NW, Washington, DC 20005. Tel: 202-223-2995.

FOCUS: Global. Food and hunger • self-reliant development • militarism • foreign trade and aid • political economy • international awareness • corporate responsibility • social justice.

ACTIVITIES: Popular education • intern programs • library services • networking • documentation and information • workshops and seminars.

RESOURCES: Literature • study-action guides • curriculum guides • consultant services • research services • library.

PERIODICALS: **6.22** *Hunger Notes*. 10 issues/year. $10/year individual; $15/year institutional.

6.23 **World Hunger Year, Inc.**, 350 Broadway, Suite 209, New York, NY 10013. Tel: 212-226-2714.

FOCUS: Third World general. Root causes of hunger • development • foreign trade and aid • corporate responsibility • political economy.

ACTIVITIES: Popular education • political action • legislative action • research and writing • intern programs • media • networking • workshops and seminars.

RESOURCES: Reports.

PERIODICALS: **6.24** *Food Monitor*. Bimonthly magazine. $12.95/year individual; $18/year institutional.

PRINTED RESOURCES

Bibliographies and Catalogs

6.25   *Bibliography on Hunger.* Compiled by Kimberly Bobo, staff associate, Bread for the World. 4pp. For single copy, send self-addressed stamped envelope to Bread for the World. Bulk rates available.

This short, annotated bibliography covers: General Introduction; Theological Reflection; Domestic Hunger; Commodities; Development Assistance; Trade and Investment; and U.S. Land Use.

6.26   *Books About Food and Land from Earthwork.* n.d. 15pp. Available in photo-copy from the Data Center. Payment of $2.50 must accompany order.

This excellent catalog, published by the now-defunct Center for Rural Studies/ Earthwork in San Francisco, covers many topics including: agribusiness and transnationals; appropriate technology in food; farmworkers; action and research groups; and teachers' aids and educational materials.

6.27   *Food and Agriculture Books from Food for Thought.* n.d. 22pp. Donation requested: 25 cents plus postage. Food for Thought Books.

This useful annotated bibliography lists books and other materials that are available directly from Food for Thought Books.

Books

6.28   Burbach, Roger, and Flynn, Patricia. *Agribusiness in the Americas.* New York: Monthly Review Press/NACLA, 1980. 314pp. $6.50

This in-depth look at agribusiness in the United States and Latin America by two former members of the North American Conference on Latin America (NA-CLA) is an excellent introduction to a study of the control mechanisms that transnational agribusiness firms exercise in the world food economy. An appendix lists the Latin American subsidiaries of sixty major U.S. agribusiness corporations.

6.29   Cahill, Dr. Kevin M., ed. *Famine.* Maryknoll, N.Y.: Orbis Books, 1982. 163pp. $8.95

Papers read at a symposium sponsored by the Tropical Disease Center of Lenox Hill Hospital (New York) serve as the basis of this study. Contributors to this volume address issues such as: Famine in History; Whose Right to Food; Feeding China's One Billion; Response to Famine: The Voluntary Sector; and Developing a Coordinated and Coherent U.S. Government Policy.

6.30   de Castro, Josue. *The Geopolitics of Hunger.* New York: Monthly Review, 1973. 524pp. $7.50

This classic study, originally published as *The Geography of Hunger,* was revised and enlarged by the author in 1973. It develops two theses: (1) that hunger is human-made, and (2) that the threat of poverty and starvation causes overpopulation, not the other way around.

6.31   Frundt, Dr. Henry J. *Agribusiness Manual: Background Papers on Corporate Responsibility and Hunger Issues.* New York: Interfaith Center on Corporate Responsibility, 1978. 231pp. Looseleaf, 3-hole punched. $6

This manual is designed for persons concerned about the social responsibility of corporations and the alleviation of hunger at home and abroad. It is meant for use by institutional investors, church study groups, students, food activists, and local organizers. Some thirty articles in the manual cover topics such as corporate control of the world food trade, food production, commodity speculation, agricultural inputs, nutrition of processed foods, a case study of John Deere and Co. and tractor technologies, and resource listings.

6.32   George, Susan. *Feeding the Few: Corporate Control of Food.* Washington, D.C.: Institute for Policy Studies, 1978. 79pp. $4.95

A thorough examination of a world food system that is geared toward profit not people. *Feeding the Few* draws the links between the hungry at home and those abroad, exposing the economic and political forces pushing us toward a unified global food system.

6.33   George, Susan. *How the Other Half Dies.* Montclair, N.J.: Allanheld-Osmun, 1977. 308pp. $6.95. Available from the Institute for Policy Studies.

This powerful study is an excellent source for information on the interlocks among governments, elites, banks, and corporations whose programs perpetuate hunger instead of ending it. George explains why technology and the "Green Revolution" are artificial non-solutions to pressing problems of hunger and malnutrition in the Third World.

6.34   Hessel, Dieter T., ed. *Beyond Survival: Bread and Justice in Christian Perspective.* New York: Friendship Press, 1977. 222pp. $4.25

Beyond Survival recognizes that, in a hungry world, hope is essential and neutrality impossible. This collection of readings helps readers grapple with rationales for doing little and offers fresh reasons for doing more.

6.35   Institute for Food and Development Policy. *Food First Resource Guide: Documentation on the Roots of World Hunger and Rural Poverty.* San Francisco: Institute for Food and Development Policy, 1979. 80pp. Photographs. $3

This supplement to the book *Food First* is a point-by-point outline presenting both the causes of hunger and the approaches to food security. For each point, the *Resource Guide* provides selected documentation from around the world and all the information needed to acquire documentation.

6.36   Jegen, Mary Evelyn, and Wilber, Charles, eds. *Growth with Equity: Strategies for Meeting Human Needs.* New York: Paulist Press, 1979. 252pp. $4.95

The essays in this volume are the fruit of a seminar on "Growth with Equity: Economic Strategies" co-sponsored by the Bread for the World Educational Fund and Notre Dame University. Each major section approaches the issue from a different perspective: theological; basic human needs; agricultural development; employment; international institutions, and the new international order.

6.37   Lappé, Frances Moore, and Beccar-Varela, Adele. *Mozambique and Tanzania: Asking the Big Question.* San Francisco: Institute for Food and Development Policy, Food Security Project, 1980. 128pp. Photographs. $4.75. Bulk rates available.

This IFDP publication takes a look at two young African nations as they struggle to address some of the most critical questions of development: participation in decision-making; accountability of leadership; personal motivation; and shared control over national resources.

6.38   Lappé, Frances Moore, and Collins, Joseph, with Cary Fowler. *Food First.* Rev. ed. New York: Ballantine Books, 1977. 620pp. $2.75. Bulk order discounts available only through Ballantine Books. Single copies available from the Institute for Policy Studies and from the Institute for Food and Development Policy.

This excellent study addresses fifty of the most urgent questions asked about the causes and proposed remedies for world hunger. The authors draw upon a worldwide network of research to offer their response to the fifty questions.

6.39   Lappé, Frances Moore, and Collins, Joseph. *World Hunger: Ten Myths.* 2d. ed. San Francisco: Institute for Food and Development Policy, 1979. 72pp. Photographs. $2.25. Spanish language edition: 72pp. $1.45. Bulk rates available for both editions. Also available from the Institute for Policy Studies.

This synopsis of *Food First* is a useful educational resource for students, teachers, study groups, journalists, and development activists all over the world.

6.40   McGinnis, James B. *Bread and Justice: Toward a New International Order.* New York: Paulist Press, 1979. 358pp. $4.95. Available also from the Institute for Peace and Justice.

Bread and Justice is geared to high school and college students with an action orientation. McGinnis treats the impact of today's economic systems on human lives, focusing on the injustice of world hunger. The teacher's manual (*Bread and Justice Teacher's Manual*) provides in-depth background on world hunger in relation to current economic practices and structures, and offers step-by-step lesson plans as well as suggestions for further research and other activities.

6.41   McGinnis, James B. *Those Who Hunger.* New York: Paulist Press, 1979. 32pp. $1. Also available from the Institute for Peace and Justice.

This parish-oriented version of *Bread and Justice*, is a seven-week program designed for use during Lent. *Those Who Hunger* can serve as a prayer book and an action guide for groups or for individuals. A *Leader's Guide* is also available.

6.42   Mooney, Pat Roy. *Seeds of the Earth: A Private or Public Resource?* Toronto: Canadian Council for International Cooperation, 1980. 120pp. Tables and charts. $8 postage included. Available from the Institute for Food and Development Policy.

Co-published with the International Coalition for Development Action, *Seeds of the Earth* is a ground-breaking study of how thousands of seed varieties are being eliminated from the seed "gene pool" and how multinational corporations are beginning to control the ultimate source of our daily bread.

6.43   Morgan, Dan. *Merchants of Grain*. New York: Penguin, 1980. 515pp. $5.95
This readable study documents the power and profits of the five giant grain
companies at the center of the world's food supply.

6.44   Nelson, Jack A. *Hunger for Justice: The Politics of Food and Faith*. Maryknoll, N.Y.: Orbis Books, 1980. 230pp. $5.95
Hunger for Justice presents a comprehensive overview of the colonial roots of
poverty and underdevelopment in the Third World today and of the ways in
which U.S. economic and military policies reinforce existing inequalities. Nelson
analyzes the role of transnational corporations, the crisis in American values,
overpopulation, and the Green Revolution, as he situates world hunger in a biblical context.

The staff of Clergy and Laity Concerned has prepared a 28-page study guide to
accompany Nelson's work. The guide is available for $1 per copy from either
CALC or Orbis Books.

6.45   Perelman, Michael. *Farming for Profit in a Hungry World: Capital and the
Crisis in Agriculture*. New York: Land-Mark Studies, Universe Books, 1977.
238pp. $7.50. Also available from the Institute for Policy Studies.
Farming for Profit examines the role of transnational corporations, banking
institutions, government policy, and government-directed research relative to
worldwide problems of hunger, dislocation of rural populations, pollution, de-
pletion of fossil fuel reserves, and loss of soil fertility.

6.46   Toton, Suzanne C. *World Hunger: The Responsibility of Christian Education*.
Maryknoll, N.Y.: Orbis Books, 1982. 210pp. Bibliography. $7.95
World Hunger provides educators with an informed and readable overview of
the causes of the food crisis, the roots of poverty in the Third World, the structure
of world trade and its effects on the Third World, multinational corporations,
and many other issues. Professor Toton examines the public and political responsibility of Christians and studies the role and function of education for justice.

Toton's work concludes with two very useful bibliographies and an annotated
listing of religiously affiliated organizations involved with world poverty and
hunger.

6.47   Weir, David, and Schapiro, Mark. *Circle of Poison: Pesticides and People in a
Hungry World*. San Francisco: Institute for Food and Development Policy, 1981.
101pp. $3.95
Weir and Schapiro describe the international marketing of pesticides restricted
or banned for use in the United States. The "circle" is completed when foods,
imported from Third World countries and contaminated with restricted pesticides, find their way back to grocery shelves in the United States.

6.48   Valentine, William, and Lappé, Frances Moore. *What Can We Do?* San Francisco: Institute for Food and Development Policy, 1980. 50pp. $2.45
What Can We Do? offers a series of interviews with more than a dozen food
and agriculture-related activists all over North America. Designed to encourage
those who may be overwhelmed by the scope of the problems of world hunger,

this guide includes an introduction to the analysis and aims that orient the work of the IFDP and a compendium of groups and resources organized by issue.

See also:
1.128, 4.45, 9.30, 9.31

Periodicals

6.49   *Ceres*, Unipub, 650 First Ave., Box 433, Murray Hill Station, New York, NY 10016. Bimonthly magazine. $8/year.
   Ceres is a review of agriculture and development from the United Nations Food and Agriculture Organization (FAO).

6.50   *Food, Agriculture, and Rural Affairs Information Services*, Center for Rural Studies, 2305 Irving Ave. S, Minneapolis, MN 55405. Monthly. $300/year. Single Section Report: $70/year.
   This is a comprehensive library reference source of news, trends, and developments for the entire food chain in the form of reprints of important articles. Sections are: Agriculture, Food Products, and Rural Affairs; Agribusiness and the Food Industry; Food, Nutrition, and Consumer Issues; Natural Resources and the Environment; and International Affairs.

6.51   *Food Monitor*, World Hunger Year, 350 Broadway, Suite 209, New York, NY 10013. Bimonthly magazine. $9.95/year individual; $15/year institutional.
   This informative and attractive magazine covers all aspects of food, hunger, and agribusiness in articles that are as provocative as they are clear and concise. In addition to four or five feature articles each issue contains book reviews, editorials, resources, and other departments.

Pamphlets and Articles

6.52   *Agrarian Reform and Counter-Reform in Chile*. Joseph Collins. Institute for Food and Development Policy, 1979. 24pp. $1. Bulk rates available.
   A first-hand look at Chile's current economic policies and how they affect the rural majority in the country.

6.53   *Agrarian Reform in El Salvador: A Program of Rural Pacification*. Philip Wheaton, Peter Shiras, Alberto Arene. EPICA. Also available from the Inter-Religious Task Force on El Salvador and Central America.
   A hard-hitting exposé of the myths of land reform in El Salvador and a challenging look at U.S. agrarian policies in that country.

6.54   *Agribusiness Targets Latin America*. *NACLA Report on the Americas* 11, no. 1, January–February 1978. 36pp. $2.50. Also available from the Data Center.
   A critical examination of the expansion of U.S. agribusiness in Latin America and how this is transforming the countryside and creating rural poverty and urban slums.

6.55   *An Appeal to the President and the Congress of the United States for a Morally Responsible U.S. Food Policy*. Adopted by the 117th General Assembly of the Presbyterian Church in the United States, 1977. 4pp. Free

This church statement notes the marks of a morally responsible policy and then presents an overview of a U.S. food policy that would increase the world's supply of food, provide more equitable access to available food, and take interim measures to bring food and food assistance to those unable to purchase what they need.

6.56   *The Christian Rural Mission in the 1980s: A Call to Liberation and Development of Peoples*. Agricultural Mission Committee, 1978. 28pp. Free

This document presents a critical analysis of the present context of rural mission, as well as Agricultural Mission's self-understanding of the biblical basis of that mission.

6.57   *A Cry for Bread and Justice: Action/Education Opportunities in Response to World Hunger*. United Methodist Church, Board of Global Ministries, 1975. 11pp. Available for the cost of postage and handling from the UMC Service Center.

This booklet, prepared for the Women's Division by the Education and Cultivation Division of the UMCBGM, is a useful combination of analysis, further resources for study, and encouragement to action. Its message is specifically addressed to United Methodist Women, but it could well be used by others.

6.58   *Del Monte: Bitter Fruits*. *NACLA Report on the Americas* 10, no. 7, September 1976. 31pp. $2.50. Also available from the Data Center.

Historical, economic, and political analysis of Del Monte, the world's largest canner of fruits and vegetables, and a growing agribusiness influence in the Third World.

6.59   *Do Cash Crops Benefit Third World Nations?* Interfaith Center on Corporate Responsibility. *CIC Brief* 6:2, February 1977. 4pp. 60 cents. Bulk rates available.

6.60   *El Salvador Land Reform: Impact Audit*. Laurence R. Simon and James C. Stephens, Jr. Supplement by Martin Diskin. Oxfam-America, 1982. 55pp. $5. Bulk rates available.

A well-documented critique, with maps and appendix, of land reform in El Salvador.

6.61   *Fact Sheet on U.S. Food Concentration*. Institute for Food and Development Policy, 1980. 1p. $1

This is a graphic compilation of the basic facts illustrating the alarming concentration of control in our food system. Gleaned from testimony before a Senate Judiciary subcommittee, it is a primer for any study related to the U.S. food system.

6.62   *Food, Agriculture, and Agribusiness*. *Science for the People* 11, no. 3, May–June 1979. 45pp. $1.15 postage included.

This entire issue of the bimonthly magazine *Science for the People* examines migrant workers, food as a weapon, the Del Monte corporation, and food and agriculture in China.

6.63 *Hunger Series*. Lutheran Church in America (New York), Occasional. 4pp. Free

The LCA's Advocacy Coordinator for World Hunger Concerns publishes and distributes background papers on various food-related issues, such as land use, justice in food marketing, and comparative theologies on hunger and social action.

6.64 *Infant Formula Program: List of Publications*. Interfaith Center on Corporate Responsibility, Fall 1980. 4pp. Free

ICCR has compiled a thorough listing of printed and audiovisual materials on infant formula in general, the Nestlé boycott, public policy, and breast feeding. All the items are available directly from ICCR's Infant Formula Program.

6.65 *Justice in a Hungry World*. engage/social action forum 28, April 1977. 46pp. 10 cents. Bulk rates available.

This *forum* presents a number of analyses, action models, and action suggestions on world hunger.

6.66 *Our Daily Bread*. 3 volumes. *World Hunger: Policy, Background and Action Suggestions* (February 1975); *National Legislation* (September 1975); *The Church's Response to Public Policy* (April 1976). U.S. Catholic Conference, Office of International Justice and Peace. 24pp. 50 cents each.

These three attractive booklets bring together position papers, statements, action suggestions, and policy recommendations from the U.S. Catholic Conference.

6.67 *Reprint Packet #1*. Institute for Food and Development Policy, 1979. 16pp. $1.50

This collection of eight published articles by IFDP staff members includes "Mozambique Nourishing a New Nation," "American Aid Goes to Agribusiness, Not Hungry," "Turning the Desert Green for International Agribusiness," "Puerto Rico: The Hunger Crop," and "On the Bottle from Birth."

6.68 *Response to the Presidential Commission on World Hunger Preliminary Report*. Institute for Food and Development Policy, 1980. 6pp. $1

The *Presidential Commission Report* calls for a tripling of U.S. foreign assistance to help solve the world hunger problem. IFDP's response to the *Report* points out that its prescription is based on a fallacy.

6.69 *Still Hungry After All These Years*. Joseph Collins and Frances Moore Lappé. Institute for Food and Development Policy. Reprint from *Mother Jones*, August 1977. 6pp. 50 cents

This article shows how multinational food firms search for cheap labor and land in underdeveloped countries with which to grow luxury crops for export.

6.70 *The Trilateral Commission Takes on World Hunger: Planning for International Agriculture*. Center for Rural Studies/Earthwork Publications. 1979. 54pp. $2.50. Available from Straight Talk Distributing.

This booklet provides background on the Trilateral Commission and carefully analyzes the political interests of the Commission as well as its perspective on the world hunger crisis.

5.71   *The United States and World Hunger*. Thomas P. Fenton. *Maryknoll,* February-May 1981. 25pp. Available from the author at 464 19 St., Oakland, CA 94612. $2.50 for the set. Payment must accompany order.

This set of four articles from *Maryknoll* magazine examines the root causes of world hunger and critically analyzes the role of the U.S. government and U.S. transnational corporations in creating hunger.

5.72   *U.S. Grain Arsenal*. *NACLA Report on the Americas* 9, no. 7. October 1975. 31pp. $2.50. Available also from the Data Center.

U.S. Grain Arsenal is a pioneer analysis of the use of U.S. grain production as a political weapon by both the government and multinational grain trading companies.

5.73   *World Hunger Fact Sheet*. Office of Interpretation and Promotion, Division of Overseas Ministries, National Council of Churches. Occasional. 4pp. Free

These *Fact Sheets* are intended to be "continuing reports on present conditions and on what the churches are doing."

5.74   *World Hunger: Statement for Peacemakers in Mission*. 1981. 4pp. Free from Peacemakers in Mission.

This brochure explodes several myths about world hunger and the church's role in socio-economic issues. It concludes with suggestions for action and for further reading.

See also:
3.105, 3.124, 9.40, 10.76

AUDIOVISUAL RESOURCES

Directories

6.75   *Films on Food and Land*. San Francisco: Earthwork, 1977. 18pp. $1. Supplement: 1980. 16pp. $1. The organization Earthwork no longer exists, but its catalogs are available from Straight Talk Distributing at the prices indicated.

This excellent directory and its 1980 supplement includes Spanish-language films, suggestions for obtaining and using films as educational tools, a comprehensive index by subject, brief descriptions of about three hundred films, and a list of sources and distributors.

6.76   *World Hunger Audio-Visual Resource Guide*. United Methodist Church, Board of Global Ministries. 50 cents plus postage. Available from the UMC Service Center.

This guide includes films and filmstrips useful in discussions of world hunger.

Audiovisuals

6.77   *Bottle Babies*. 1975 26 min color film. Peter Krieg/Teldik Films. Unifilm. Rental $35. Also available from the Institute for Peace and Justice.

This award-winning documentary, originally entitled *Nestlé Kills Babies*, first brought the dangers of infant formula malnutrition to widespread public attention. *Bottle Babies* shows the tragic and disastrous consequences when corporations, faced with stagnating markets at home, push their expensive artificial formulas in underdeveloped countries.

6.78   *Bread, Justice and Global Interdependence. Bread, Justice and Multinational Corporations. Bread, Justice and Trade*. 1979 3 parts 15 min each color filmstrips with cassette tapes. Institute for Peace and Justice. Rental $11 each. Sale $73 for the set. Also available from the 8th Day Center ($15 each).

These three filmstrips provide audiovisual support for the pivotal ideas in the textbook *Bread and Justice*. Each filmstrip concentrates on a major theme of the world hunger crisis.

The *Global Interdependence* filmstrip presents the concept of "global city" as a way of thinking about human interdependence. It distinguishes between "vertical" interdependence, which permits some groups to dominate others, and "horizontal" interdependence, which encourages a true equality among all people. The "Shakertown Pledge" is highlighted as a way of achieving an interdependent life style.

The filmstrip *Bread, Justice and Multinational Corporations* shows the effects that these corporations have on people, especially the small farmer, the farm worker, and consumers. Suggestions are given on how to challenge large corporations to take their social responsibility more seriously.

Bread, Justice and Trade examines the trade relations between rich and poor nations and shows how these unbalanced relationships perpetuate poverty and hunger among the "have-not" nations. The filmstrip tackles complex economic concepts such as export cropping, the debt spiral, balance of trade deficits, and tariffs and explains how the proposed New International Economic Order would alter today's unjust trade situation.

.79 *A Celebration of Bread.* 14 min color filmstrip with cassette. Board of Global Ministries, United Methodist Church. Sale $10 plus 15% for postage. Available from UMC Service Center.

This short filmstrip is designed to introduce the issue of world hunger in a group worship experience.

.80 *The Cost of Coffee.* 14 min 80 frames color filmstrip. Franciscan Communications Center/TeleKETICS. Sale $36.95

Through the life of Gerardo Roman, this filmstrip deals with the unequal relationship between international coffee corporations and small coffee growers.

.81 *Food First Slideshow/Filmstrip.* Part 1: *Why Hunger?* Part 2: *Toward Food Security.* 1979 15 min each, color, 2 15-minute cassettes with a study guide. Institute for Food and Development Policy. Sale $89, slides; $34, filmstrip. Cassettes and study guide included. Also available for rent from the 8th Day Center and AFSC (Cambridge) for $15 each.

This two-part IFDP audiovisual presents the experience of people throughout the world in their efforts to gain control over their food resources. It suggests actions that can help to remove the obstacles now in the way of achieving food security.

.82 *Formula for Malnutrition.* 16 min color filmstrip with cassette. ICCR. Available from the UMC Service Center. Sale $10. Also available for rent from the 8th Day Center ($15).

Formula for Malnutrition deals with the marketing by multinational corporations of infant formula and artificial milk products in Third World countries, citing problems that arise from mothers' inability to read product labels, from unsafe water, and from the lack of refrigeration. Steps to change this situation are suggested.

.83 *Give Ye Them to Eat—A Modern Miracle.* 1982 color filmstrip with cassette. United Methodist Church, Board of Global Ministries. Sale $5, plus 15% for postage. Available from the UMC Service Center.

Focused primarily on Niger, Africa, this filmstrip depicts the transition from the tragedy of poverty, drought, and famine to a society producing its own food with dignity. The growing role of the church is emphasized.

.84 *Habbanaae: The Animal of Friendship.* 1979 20 min 136 visuals color slideshow or filmstrip with cassette and study guide. Packard Manse Media Project. Sale $63, slideshow; $30, filmstrip. Also available from AFSC (Cambridge) $15.

In the early 1970s the world was shocked by the famine in the Sahel region of Africa. Americans were led to believe that this human tragedy was caused by natural catastrophe and the technological backwardness of Third World people. *The Animal of Friendship* makes it clear that to a great extent this tragedy and others like it result from a particular type of "modern" economic development, and are thus the result of human actions.

6.85   *Hamburger USA.* 1979 28 min color slideshow. AFSC (Cambridge) $15

This slideshow examines each layer of a typical cheeseburger pointing to some of the social and environmental costs therein and illustrating the economic concentration of the food system of this country and the world.

6.86   ***Hunger and Public Policy.*** 113 frames 22 min. ***Hunger: What Are the Issues?*** 112 frames 22 min. ***Hunger: What Can I Do?*** 87 frames 17 min color filmstrips. These filmstrips were produced by Bread for the World. They are available for use through regional offices of BFW for a nominal fee. Sale price is $15 for each from Friendship Press (Cincinnati); Paulist Press; or Word, Inc., Educational Products Division.

Hunger and Public Policy. This BFW filmstrip, based on Arthur Simon's award-winning book, *Bread for the World*, is an excellent introduction to the problem of global hunger and to the Bread for the World organization. Emphasizing the public policy dimensions of hunger, it suggests ways citizens can become personally involved in shaping U.S. government policy on matters that affect hungry people.

Hunger: What Are The Issues? This filmstrip focuses on the importance of creating the "political will" necessary to deal effectively with hunger and poverty. Issues treated include: (1) international food reserves, (2) U.S. food aid and development assistance, (3) international economic issues such as a Common Fund, the mounting debt burden of developing nations, export cropping, trade, and the role of transnational corporations, and (4) hunger in the United States.

Hunger: What Can I Do? Through the story of one individual's commitment to ending hunger and of her growing involvement with Bread for the World, this filmstrip illustrates the practical steps involved in public policy advocacy on hunger issues. It shows how individual Christians and groups, working through BFW's citizen action network, can make a significant difference in the U.S. government's response to hunger.

6.87   ***Hunger in the Global Community.*** 1969 15 min color filmstrip with cassette tape. AFSC (Cambridge) $15

This AFSC audiovisual demonstrates the relationship between high per capita consumption of food in rich nations, talks of population growth in poor nations, and describes the limitations of global production in agriculture. Traditional nationalism is shown to be an inadequate base for management of the emerging interdependence of all on this planet.

6.88   ***Into the Mouths of Babes.*** 1978 30 min color film. Produced by CBS Reports. California Newsreel. Rental $40. Also available from AFSC (Cambridge) ($15); the NCC TV Film Library ($25); 8th Day Center ($15).

This award-winning report is an excellent introduction not only to the infant formula issue but also to the more general impact of transnational corporations in the Dominican Republic.

.89   *When the Almsgiving Stops.* 1980 22 min color slideshow with cassette. AFSC (Cambridge) $15

Taking Bangladesh and its poverty, overpopulation, and hunger as a case study, this audiovisual focuses on the real causes of hunger: the maldistribution of wealth and patterns of land ownership and land use. *When the Almsgiving Stops* helps people appreciate the fact that the distribution of economic and political power is the key issue to address in order to end hunger.

.90   *World Hunger and Our Response.* 22 min color filmstrip. Institute for Peace and Justice. Rental $10

This filmstrip focuses on the need to redistribute power as well as food to hungry nations. It discusses the need to examine U.S. food consumption patterns, the importance of political action, and the need to change institutional practices even more than individual lifestyles.

.91   *A World Hungry.* 1970 5 parts 11 min each color filmstrips with cassette tapes. Produced by Franciscan Communications Center. Available from AFSC (Cambridge) $15

These five filmstrips compassionately examine the roots of world hunger today and offer practical suggestions for change. The first filmstrip in the series analyzes common myths about hunger; the second probes historical to present-day causes of hunger; the third looks at what hungry nations need to do to improve their situation; and the final two filmstrips suggest ways that we can effect changes in our community and personal lifestyles.

See also:
9.74, 9.76, 10.92

Rachel Burger

OTHER RESOURCES

Resource Guides

6.92   *Questions & Answers: Where to Go for Information About Hunger.* A special
resource issue of *Service News* 32, no. 5, September 1979. Published by and
available from CROP, the Community Hunger Appeal of Church World Service.
6pp.

This tabloid resource directory covers films, slideshows, books, periodicals,
organizations, and study guides.

6.93   *Who's Involved With Hunger. An Organization Guide.* Linda Worthington,
ed. 3d. ed. Sponsored by The Presidential Commission on World Hunger.
Washington, D.C.: World Hunger Education Service, 1982. 54pp. $4

This annotated directory of nearly 400 organizations covers: (1) Government
Organizations—United Nations; multilateral agencies; U.S. Congress; Federal
Government agencies. (2) Private Agencies—global focus (information/educa-
tion; policy oriented research; political advocacy); national focus (food programs; food system; local self-reliance; poverty action and research); U.S. regional (by area). Complete information is given for each organization, including
address, telephone, officers, publications, and other resources.

Curriculum Resources

6.94   *Ending Hunger: It's Possible, It's Happening.* Jerold Ciekot and Douglas
Groyn. New York: American Friends Service Committee, 1981. $5.50 postage
included.

Designed for use by local community organizations, this study/action kit begins with the future: development experts project that hunger and absolute poverty can be eliminated by the year 2000. It ends with the present: local groups
acting effectively to make the end of hunger real. *Ending Hunger* includes a simulation game ("The Twenty-First Year"), five case studies of successful development strategies, four background papers, and an action plan and resource
list.

6.95   *Feed, Need, Greed: Food, Resources & Population.* The Food & Nutrition
Group, Boston Science for the People, 1980. 86pp. $5.50

Feed, Need, Greed is a highly recommended alternative curriculum guide designed for use on high school and adult education levels. Eighteen pages of
"teacher's notes" give objectives; timetable; background information; facts and
statistics; activities; and other references for each of the eighteen chapters. Topics
covered include: exploding the population myth; resource limitations; the price
of hunger; nutritional content of everyday foods; breast feeding; community action; and much more.

.96   *A Hungry World.* Bread for the World Educational Fund, 1979. 32pp. $2.25 prepaid.

This six-session series, designed for adult educational programs and for individual study, contains reading and discussion materials, prayer services, action suggestions, and a discussion guide. Major categories are: (1) A Hungry World: an introductory overview of the problem of hunger and an exploration of some of our attitudes towards the hungry; (2) A Hungry World—The Why and How: an exploration of the causes of hunger and the dimensions of public policy; (3) Biblical Perspective on Hunger; a look at the reality of hunger from a biblical perspective; (4) The Churches and the Hungry: an analysis of the role of the churches in the struggle against hunger; (5) Bread for the World: the history and operation of the Bread for the World organization; (6) Christian Living in a Hungry World: an invitation to plan ways of living Christian lives of concern for the hungry and to become actively involved in seeking justice.

.97   *Land and Hunger Study Guide.* New York: Bread for the World Educational Fund, 1982. $2.50. Bulk rates available. Leader's manual $1

This educational exercise gives participants an understanding of the need for land reform in Third World countries and illustrates the ways in which the land reform efforts of some governments actually hurt the poor and landless.

.98   *Teaching About Food and Hunger: 33 Activities.* Environmental Relations Series, Volume 1. George G. Otero and Gary R. Smith. Denver: University of Denver, Center for Teaching International Relations, 1976. 135pp.

This guide consists of thirty-three supplementary teaching activities designed to complement existing curricula related to food. Issues treated include: food production and distribution; nutrition; food shortages, and food habits, as well as global issues of poverty, malnutrition, and disease. Two bibliographies identify twenty organizations with information on food and hunger and thirty-two food resources such as books, kits, and journals.

.99   *When I Was Hungry.* Bread for the World Educational Fund, 1979. 69pp. Teacher's Manual $5. Action Packet $2. Student Packet $3.

This "Hunger Course for High School Students" focuses on hunger and Christian responses to the hungry. In ten chapters students cover the underlying causes of hunger, possible solutions, the biblical and theological reasons for Christian involvement in the hunger issue, and ways that they can also become involved. The course is designed to run for a semester and is best used with juniors and seniors.

Church-related Hunger Programs

100   A central coordinating body for information on the involvement of U.S. churches in hunger is the **Office of Hunger Coordination**, c/o National Council of Churches (USA).

For information on the policies and programs of specific denominations, write:

6.101   **American Baptist Churches**, Dr. Russell E. Brown, American Baptist Churches, Valley Forge, PA 19481.

6.102   **American Lutheran Church**, Rev. Charles Lutz, 422 S. Fifth St., Minneapolis, MN 55415.

6.103   **Christian Church (Disciples of Christ)**, Dr. JoAnne Kagiwada, 222 S. Downey Ave., Box 1986, Indianapolis, IN 46219.

6.104   **Christian Reformed Church**, Ms. Karen De Vos, World Relief Committee, 2850 Kalamazoo Ave., Grand Rapids, MI 49504.

6.105   **Church of the Brethren**, Rev. Wilfred Nolen, 1451 Dundee Ave., Elgin, IL 60120.

6.106   **Eastern Orthodox Churches**, Rev. Paul Schneirla, 8005 Ridge Blvd., Brooklyn, NY 11209.

6.107   **Episcopal Church**, Rev. Charles Cesaretti, 815 Second Ave., New York, NY 10017.

6.108   **Evangelical Covenant Church of America**, Dr. Clifford Bjorklund, Covenant World Relief Committee, 5101 N. Francisco, Chicago, IL 60625.

6.109   **Lutheran Church in America**, 231 Madison Ave., New York, NY 10016 .

6.110   **Lutheran Church**, Missouri Synod, Dr. Melvin Witt, 500 N. Broadway, St. Louis, MO 63102.

6.111   **Mennonite Churches**, Mr. Paul Longacre, Mennonite Central Committee, 21 S. 12 St., Akron, PA 17501.

6.112   **Moravian Church**, Rev. Bernard Michel, Box 1245, Bethlehem, PA 18018.

6.113   **Presbyterian Church in the United States**, Dr. James Cogswell, 341 Ponce de Leon Ave., NE, Atlanta, GA 30308.

6.114   **Reformed Church in America**, Rev. Joseph Muyskens, 18525 Torrence Ave., Lansing, IL 60438.

6.115   **Reorganized Church of Jesus Christ of Latter-Day Saints**, Dr. Parris Watts, Box 1059, Independence, MO 64015.

6.116   **Roman Catholic Church**, Rev. Bryan Hehir, U.S. Catholic Conference, Office of International Justice and Peace, 1312 Massachusetts Ave., NW, Washington, DC 20005.

6.117   **Southern Baptist Churches**, Dr. David Sapp, 460 James Robertson Parkway, Nashville, TN 37219.

6.118   **United Church of Christ**, Rev. Neill Richards, 475 Riverside Dr., 16th Floor, New York, NY 10115.

6.119   **United Methodist Church**, Rev. Frank Smith, 475 Riverside Dr., 14th Floor, New York, NY 10115.

6.120   **United Presbyterian Church in the U.S.A.**, Ms. Ann Beardslee, 475 Riverside Dr., Rm. 1268, New York, NY 10115.

Simulation Games

6.121   *Baldicer.* Atlanta: John Knox Press, 1970. $25. Level: junior high and above. Players: 12–20. Time: 2–4 hours.
          Baldicer puts the responsibility for feeding the world's people on the shoulders

of participants who play the role of Food Coordinators for 150 million people each. The intent of this simulation is to encourage the participants to think about, analyze, and search for solutions to the world hunger crisis.

22   *Hunger on Spaceship Earth.* AFSC (New York). 1975. $2.50 (one part of a complete unit, *World Hunger*). Level: junior high and above. Players: 15–50. Time: 2–3 hours.

The aim of this AFSC exercise is to provide participants with a graphic and personal experience of inequality and to motivate them to analyze both the feelings and the political options of those who suffer from the inequities in today's world. *Hunger on Spaceship Earth* calls for a meal or snacktime setting to illustrate the constraints on equal access to the food that does exist.

See also:
10.117, 10.128

Chapter 7

Human Rights

KEY RESOURCES

Organizations

The North America office of the internationally renowned human rights organization **Amnesty International** is the first place to turn for information on the general human rights situation in any particular Third World country. **Human Rights Internet** functions as a clearinghouse of information on groups all over the world that take human (political and economic) rights as their focus.

The **Human Rights Program** of the **National Council of Churches**, and denominational efforts such as the **International Human Rights Program** of the **Disciples of Christ**, bring a more focused U.S. perspective to the human rights question.

Printed Resources

The annual reports from **Amnesty International** and the **U.S. State Department** are sourcebooks of descriptive data on nearly every country in the world. The **State Department** report is naturally biased in favor of U.S. foreign policy objectives, but the critical information it does contain on Chile, South Korea, and other U.S. "allies" is all the more useful given the source.

The two volumes by Noam Chomsky and Edward Herman are hard-hitting examinations of all facets of U.S. involvement in the violation of human rights in Third World countries.

Articles on human rights will, of course, be found in many of the periodicals described in this directory. One hefty publication that is specifically devoted to human rights is the **Human Rights Internet**'s *HRI Reporter*. This periodical contains a wealth of information on organizations, printed resources, and conferences.

The **Coalition for a New Foreign and Military Policy** publishes a number of attractive, inexpensive, and well-written publications on human rights. Their *Human Rights Action Guide* is especially useful.

The *Human Rights Week Organizers' Guide* is also noteworthy.

Audiovisuals

The ABC News Closeup *The Politics of Torture* is, perhaps, the best visual focal point for group study of the issue of human rights. The 50-minute color film examines U.S. policies in three Third World countries: Iran, the Philippines, and Chile.

Other Resources

Publications from **Human Rights Internet** are essential reference works on human rights issues. The **Meiklejohn Institute**'s directory of organizations and periodicals is also a valuable library tool.

ORGANIZATIONS

.1 **Amnesty International North America**, 304 W. 58 St., New York, NY 10019. Tel: 212-582-4440.

FOCUS: Global. Human rights • release of prisoners of conscience • torture and the death penalty.

ACTIVITIES: Networking • constituency education • research and writing • intern programs • media • information and documentation.

RESOURCES: Reports • speakers • publications list available.

PERIODICALS: **7.2** *Matchbox*. 3 issues/year. Free to contributors. **7.3** *Amnesty Action*. 8 issues/year. With membership of $20, individuals; $30, couples; $12, students and senior citizens. **7.4** *AI Briefing Papers*. Periodic. $2.50 each.

.5 **Campaign for Political Rights**, 201 Massachusetts Ave., NE, Washington, DC 20002. Tel: 202-547-4705.

FOCUS: International. Human rights • political repression • nuclear arms and energy • U.S. secret intervention • CIA covert action.

ACTIVITIES: Popular education • research and writing • intern programs • press service • networking • media • policy-oriented research and writing.

RESOURCES: Speakers • audiovisuals • literature • publications • study-action guides • curriculum guides • research services • reports.

PERIODICALS: **7.6** *Organizing Notes*. 8 times/year. $15.

7.7 **Christian Church (Disciples of Christ)**, International Human Rights Program, 222 S. Downey Ave., Box 1986, Indianapolis, IN 46206. Tel: 317-353-1491.
FOCUS: Global. Human rights.
ACTIVITIES: Constituency education • political action • legislative action • research and writing • networking • documentation.
RESOURCES: Speakers • literature • audiovisuals.
PERIODICALS: **7.8** *Issues and Concerns*. Quarterly newsletter. Free. **7.9** *Action Alert*. Bimonthly newsletter. Free.

7.10 **Clearinghouse on Science and Human Rights**, American Association for the Advancement of Science, 1515 Massachusetts Ave., NW, Washington, DC 20005. Tel: 202-467-5237.
FOCUS: Third World general • global • international. Human rights • scientific responsibility.
ACTIVITIES: Research and writing • workshops.
RESOURCES: Speakers • publications • reports.
PERIODICALS: **7.11** *Clearinghouse Report on Science and Human Rights*. Quarterly. Free.

7.12 **Human Rights Internet**, 1338 G St., SE, Washington, DC 20003. Tel: 202-543-9200.
FOCUS: Global • international. Human rights • political repression • militarism • national liberation struggles • social justice.
ACTIVITIES: Popular education • research and writing • intern programs • library services • networking • documentation • workshops.
RESOURCES: Publications • curriculum guides • library • reports.
PERIODICALS: **7.13** *The Human Rights Internet Reporter*. 5 times/year. $35/year individual; $50/year institutional.

7.14 **Institute for the Study of Human Issues**, 3401 Market St., Rm. 252, Philadelphia, PA 19104. Tel: 215-387-9002.
FOCUS: Human rights • political repression • nuclear arms and energy • foreign trade and aid • political economy • social justice.
ACTIVITIES: Popular education • research and writing • media • documentation and information • workshops and seminars.
RESOURCES: Speakers • audiovisuals • literature • publications • curriculum guides • consultant services • research services • library.

7.15 **International League for Human Rights**, 236 E. 46 St., New York, NY 10017. Tel: 212-972-9554.
FOCUS: International. Human rights.
ACTIVITIES: Popular education • policy-oriented research • support work • documentation • investigative missions • negotiations.
RESOURCES: Publications • reports.
PERIODICALS: **7.16** *International League for Human Rights Bulletin*. Quarterly. With $20 annual membership. **7.17** *International League for Human Rights Review*. Biannual. With membership.

18 Lawyers Committee for International Human Rights, 36 W. 44 St., New York, NY 10036. Tel: 212-921-2160.

> FOCUS: International. Human rights • refugees • political asylum.
> ACTIVITIES: Seminars • documentation • training workshops.
> RESOURCES: Consultant services • library.
> PERIODICALS: **7.19** *Lawyers Committee Bulletin.* Periodic. Contribution.

20 Meiklejohn Civil Liberties Institute, Box 673, Berkeley, CA 94701. Tel: 415-848-0599.

> FOCUS: National and international. Civil liberties • human rights.
> ACTIVITIES: Intern programs • documentation • compilation of source materials.
> RESOURCES: Archives of National Lawyers Guild • library • consultant services.

21 National Council of Churches (USA), Division of Overseas Ministries, Human Rights Program, 475 Riverside Dr., Rm. 634, New York, NY 10115. Tel: 212-870-2424.

> FOCUS: International. Human rights.
> ACTIVITIES: Constituency education • congressional testimony • networking • media • justice and peace ministries • workshops • advocacy on human rights cases.
> RESOURCES: Speakers • publications.
> PERIODICALS: **7.22** *Human Rights Perspectives.* Quarterly. Free.

23 New England Human Rights Network, c/o AFSC, 2161 Massachusetts Ave., Cambridge, MA 02140. Tel: 617-661-6130.

> FOCUS: International • Third World general. Human rights • militarism • political repression • social justice.
> ACTIVITIES: Popular education • networking • film festivals.
> RESOURCES: Consultant services • library • speakers • audiovisuals • literature.
> PERIODICALS: **7.24** *NEHRN Newsletter.* Monthly. $7/year individual; $17/year organizational.
> SPECIAL PROJECTS: **7.25** *New England Human Rights Directory*, 1982–1984.

PRINTED RESOURCES

Books

7.26   Adjali, Mia, ed. *Of Life and Hope: Toward Effective Witness in Human Rights*. New York: Friendship Press, 1979. 90pp. $2.95. Available from the United Methodist Church, Board of Global Ministries.

This book looks at the International Covenants on Human Rights that are now law in many countries. It includes guidance sections with ideas and positive steps for study groups wishing to work for human rights.

7.27   *Amnesty International Report*. London: Amnesty International, annual. 1981: 426pp. $6.95. Available from AI (New York).

This annual publication of Amnesty International surveys the situations of prisoners of conscience in the countries of Africa, the Americas, Asia, Europe, and the Middle East. It includes information on the missions undertaken by Amnesty International during the previous year. It also contains a series of appendixes on Amnesty publications, the organization's statutes, its supporters, and various statistics pertinent to human rights.

7.28   Billings, Peggy. *Paradox and Promise in Human Rights*. New York: Friendship Press, 1979. 126pp. $2.95. Available from the United Methodist Church, Board of Global Ministries.

This book traces the sources of human rights, the events leading to the adoption of the Universal Declaration of Human Rights, and developments of the past three decades. Korea is used as a case study. The author discusses the U.S. and Human Rights Covenants, the changes in the Third World, and the role of Christians as world citizens.

7.29   *The Case of the Disappeared*. New York: International League for Human Rights, 1979. 61pp. $4

The phenomenon of disappearances is defined and analyzed in this testimony of Jerome J. Shestack presented on behalf of the International League for Human Rights before the Subcommittee on International Organizations, House Foreign Affairs Committee on September 20, 1979.

7.30   *Central America 1981: El Salvador, Guatemala, Nicaragua, Honduras, Costa Rica*. Boston: Unitarian Universalist Service Committee, 1981. 60pp. $3

This publication is a report of a UUSC-sponsored fact-finding mission to Central America by three members of Congress, two UUSC executives, and others. The report provides background on the countries in the region and offers observations and recommendations of the mission members. Appendixes include: "Report to the Committee on Foreign Affairs, U.S. House of Representatives" (March 1981) by Rep. Gerry Studds; "Security Assistance and El Salvador: What the Law Says" by Bruce Cameron of Americans for Democratic Action; and suggestions for further reading.

31   Chomsky, Noam, and Herman, Edward S. *The Political Economy of Human Rights*. 2 volumes. Vol. 1: *The Washington Connection and Third World Fascism*. Boston, Mass.: South End Press, 1979. 441pp. $5
This study analyzes the role of the U.S. government, corporations, and media establishments in the affairs of Third World countries. Volume 1 documents the complicity of these U.S. institutions in Latin American, Asian, and African repression and torture. See 3.63 for Vol. 2.

32   *Country Reports on Human Rights Practices for 1981*. Report submitted to the Committee on Foreign Affairs, U.S. House of Representatives and the Committee on Foreign Relations, U.S. Senate, by the Dept. of State. Washington, D.C.: U.S. Government Printing Office, February 1982. 1,142pp. For sale by the Superintendent of Documents, U.S. Government Printing Office.
This annual publication contains reports on human rights practices in the countries of Africa, Central and South America, East Asia and the Pacific, Europe and North America, and the Near East, North Africa, and South Asia. Its information is drawn from U.S. missions abroad, congressional studies, nongovernmental organizations, and human rights bodies of international organizations.

33   Crahan, Margaret E., ed. *Human Rights and Basic Needs in the Americas*. Washington, D.C.: Georgetown University Press, 1982. 343pp. $8.95
This book questions U.S. support for authoritarian governments, maintaining that hemispheric security and the promotion of human rights are, in the long run, complementary, not antithetical.

34   Helfeld, Dr. David M., and Wipfler, Dr. William L. *Mbareté: The Higher Law of Paraguay, Report on the Denial of Human Rights in Paraguay*. New York: Third Commission of Enquiry of the International League for Human Rights, May 1980. 213pp. $7 (English), $8 (Spanish)
Mbareté is a detailed analysis of the institutionalized abuse of civil and political rights in Paraguay based on the findings of three League fact-finding missions. A 1982 update of the original report was prepared by Ligia Bolivar O.: *Mbareté: Two Years Later*.

35   Hennelly, Alfred, S.J., and Langan, John, S.J. *Human Rights in the Americas: the Struggle for Consensus*. Washington, D.C.: Georgetown University Press, 1982. 291pp. $8.95
This collection of essays, written by philosophers and theologians, is intended as an aid for reflection by human rights activists and policy makers. The editors have selected articles to provide an intellectual framework for understanding human rights claims for responding to these claims through policy and law. The book examines the moral and religious roots of American interest in human rights.

36   *Human Rights Conditions in Non-Communist Countries in East Asia*. New York: International League for Human Rights, 1980. 50pp. $2
Gross violations of human rights in Taiwan, Indonesia, South Korea, and the

Philippines are documented in this testimony presented by Harris L. Wofford, Jr. and Maureen R. Berman on behalf of the International League for Human Rights before the Asian and Pacific Affairs Subcommittee on International Organizations, House Foreign Affairs Committee, February 4, 1980.

7.37   Kannyo, Edward. *Human Rights in Africa: Problems and Prospects*. New York: International League for Human Rights, May 1980. 39pp. $4

This report, prepared especially for the International League for Human Rights, examines the increasing concern for human rights in Africa and the steps being taken by the Organization of African Unity (OAU) to create an African regional human rights system. A copy of the OAU Charter is included.

7.38   *Principalities and Powers and People*. New York: Board of Global Ministries, United Methodist Church, 1980. $2.50

This collection of essays on human rights and the international order was written by a group of interns in the Methodist Mission Intern program. It contains their reflections, results of their experiences working in Third World countries.

7.39   Pump, Ron. *A Report on the United Nations Seminar on the Establishment of Regional Commissions on Human Rights with Special Reference to Africa*. New York: International League for Human Rights, October 1979. 86pp. $3

The author of this League report provides a detailed examination of the historical inter-governmental seminar on the establishment of an African regional mechanism on human rights.

7.40   *Report of the Conference on Strategies for Strengthening the Implementation of Human Rights: The Role of National and International NGOs*. New York: International League for Human Rights, October 1979. 41pp. $5

This report on the role of non-governmental organizations in human rights issued from a conference jointly sponsored by the League and the Federation Internationale des Droits de l'Homme. Background papers written in preparation for the conference are included.

See also:
1.110, 4.61, 8.47

Periodicals

7.41   *HRI Reporter*, Human Rights Internet. 1338 G St., SE., Washington, DC 20003. 5 times/year. $35 individual; $50 institutional.

This is a publication of approximately 170 pages per issue containing detailed news of human rights activities, developments, and research around the world. Each issue contains listings of human rights organizations and other resources currently available. There is an annual index and back issues are available in print and microfiche.

7.42   *Human Rights Quarterly*, The Johns Hopkins University Press, Journals Division, Baltimore, MD 21218. Quarterly. $18 individual; $36.50 institutional.

This quarterly journal attempts to bridge the gap between scholarship and policymaking. It is an international forum for scholars from many disciplines—the social sciences, philosophy, and law—to discuss the nature, history, abuse, and future of human rights.

,43   *Organizing Notes*, Campaign for Political Rights, 201 Massachusetts Ave., NE, Washington, DC 20002. 8 issues/year. With contribution of $15 or more.
    This publication reflects the Campaign's concerns to end U.S. intelligence agency abuse at home and abroad; to defend the freedom to speak and organize; and to promote government accountability and access to information about government policies and actions.

Pamphlets and Articles

Amnesty International has numerous, inexpensive "Briefing Papers" and "Reports of AI missions" on the human rights situations in Third World countries. Write for their most recent publications list.

,44   *Achievement of the 1970's: U.S. Human Rights Law and Policy*. Jim Morrell. *International Policy Report*, November 1981. 6pp. $1.50
    This article is an overview of U.S. human rights legislation during the 1970s. It covers military aid legislation, economic aid legislation, and multilateral bank legislation.

,45   *Central America 1982: Report of two fact finding missions sponsored by the Unitarian Universalist Service Committee*. UUSC (Boston), May 1, 1982. 7pp. $1. *Central America 1980: Guatemala, El Salvador, Nicaragua*. 1980. 29pp. $3
    These reports from UUSC fact-finding missions are readable surveys of the current political and economic situation in each of the countries of the region.

,46   *Chile: Economic "Freedom" and Political Repression*. Orlando Letelier. Institute for Policy Studies, Issue Paper, 1976. 17pp. $1
    This is an analysis by a former official of the Allende government showing the relationship between an economic development model that benefits the wealthy few in Chile and the political repression in that country since the overthrow of President Allende's government. Letelier was assassinated in Washington by agents of the Pinochet junta.

,47   *Congressional Hearings*. Available from CALC. 50 cents each
    Each of these documents probes the role of the U.S. government in the abuse of human rights abroad. Countries examined include South Korea, Iran, Thailand, Namibia, Indonesia, East Timor, Uruguay, and Chile.

,48   *Country Profiles*. CALC/NARMIC (American Friends Service Committee), 1979. 4pp. Contribution.
    Each of the country profiles in this series contains information on history, culture, economics, political and human rights conditions. There is a profile for each of these countries: Argentina, Brazil, Indonesia, Iran, Nicaragua, Philippines, South Korea, and Thailand.

7.49   *DINA, SAVAK, KCIA: Our Allies' Secret Agents Have Come to the United States.* CALC, 6pp. 15 cents

This article summarizes the complicity of the United States with these foreign spy agencies. It suggests ways for ordinary citizens to register their disapproval of such activities by their government.

7.50   *Guatemala: Repression and Resistance.* National Lawyers Guild (New York), 1980. 33pp. $3

This is a paper by the joint Guatemala delegation of the National Lawyers Guild and La Raza Legal Alliance.

7.51   *Human Rights: Selected Documents.* U.S. Dept. of State, Bureau of Public Affairs, Office of Public Communication. Publication 8961 General Foreign Policy Series 310 No. 5 (Revised), November 1978. 63pp. Available from the Superintendent of Documents, U.S. Government Printing Office (stock no. 044-000-01713-0) or in photocopy from the United Methodist Office for the United Nations. Apply for prices.

The Carter administration prepared this collection containing the texts of eight documents on human rights. The selection includes: excerpts from the UN Charter; Universal Declaration of Human Rights; International Covenant on Civil and Political Rights; International Covenant on Economic, Social, and Cultural Rights; Convention on the Prevention and Punishment of the Crime of Genocide; and others.

7.52   *Human Rights Action Guide.* Coalition for a New Foreign and Military Policy, updated regularly. 16pp. 25 cents

The Coalition produces this informative *Action Guide* on a periodic basis. The guide contains feature articles, practical suggestions for working on human rights issues, and annotated lists of resources.

7.53   *Human Rights and the U.S. Foreign Assistance Program, Fiscal Year 1980.* Center for International Policy, Annual. $2.50

This document, made available annually, consists of two parts. Part 1 covers Latin America (Chile, Brazil, Nicaragua, Argentina); Part 2, Asia (Philippines, South Korea, Indonesia, Thailand.)

7.54   *Human Rights and Vital Needs.* Peter Weiss. Institute for Policy Studies, Issue Paper, 1977. 5pp. 50 cents

This address, delivered one year after the assassination of Orlando Letelier and Ronni Karpen Moffitt in Washington, D.C., commemorates the two by calling for a progressive, broad definition of human rights. Weiss concludes that the United States must include economic, social, and cultural rights along with political and civil rights in an adequate human rights policy.

7.55   *Human Rights, Economic Aid and Private Banks: The Case of Chile.* Michael Moffitt and Isabel Letelier. Institute for Policy Studies, Issue Paper, 1978. 16pp. $2

This paper documents the tremendous increase in private bank loans to the Chilean military dictatorship after the overthrow of President Allende in 1973. It shows how private banks rescued the Chilean military government at a time when international institutions and governments were reducing their loans because of human rights violations.

.56   *Human Rights in El Salvador.* Unitarian Universalist Service Committee, 1978. 87pp. $3

This UUSC publication reports the findings of an investigatory mission to El Salvador by Rev. Robert F. Drinan, Professor Thomas P. Anderson, and UUSC executive John J. McAward.

.57   *Human Rights in South Korea.* Pharis Harvey. *Current Issues*, March 1980. 7pp. 75 cents

This is the testimony of Pharis Harvey, executive director of the North American Coalition for Human Rights in Korea, before the subcommittee on International Organizations and Asian and Pacific Affairs of the House Committee on Foreign Affairs. It covers torture and other human rights violations in South Korea, the U.S. State Department report, and suggestions for what could be done.

.58   *Human Rights/Human Needs: An Unfinished Agenda.* U.S. Catholic Conference, Office of International Justice and Peace, January 1978. 32pp. 75 cents

The study materials in this pamphlet respond to the question of human rights and the church's involvement in their protection. It uses the Catholic Church's social teaching and the UN Human Rights Covenants as a basis for reflection and an agenda for action.

.59   *Human Rights Today: An Unending Struggle.* Engage/social action forum 73, July–August 1981. No. E2073, 31pp. 50 cents each. Bulk rates available.

This *e/sa forum* contains a number of feature articles on various aspects of human rights written by church executives, a former "political prisoner," and an official of the Carter administration.

.60   *Human Rights Week Organizers' Guide.* Sarah Buss. *International Policy Report*, December 1981. 10pp. $2

This article includes a description of Human Rights Weeks, cites examples of violations and violators of human rights throughout the world, and lists in chart form human rights legislation from 1974 to 1980.

.61   *If You Want Peace.* CALC/U.S. Catholic Conference, 1978. 26pp. 50 cents

This booklet examines human rights violations in five countries. It includes materials for liturgies, case studies, and group reflection/action.

.62   *The Links between Struggles for Human Rights in the United States and the Third World.* U.S. Representative Ron Dellums. 1978. 14pp. 50 cents. Available from the Institute for Policy Studies.

The keynote address at the 1978 Letelier-Moffitt Human Rights Memorial. Stating that human rights violations stem from the system, not the individual, Dellums calls for a coalition of all minorities, Third World people, and progressives to change America and the world.

7.63 *"Made in Taiwan": A Human Rights Investigation*. Becky Cantwell, Don Luce, Leonard Weinglass. Southeast Asia Resource Center—East, 1978. 20pp. $2

The articles in this report had their origin in a two-week trip to Taiwan in mid-July 1978 by Cantwell, Luce, and Weinglass. The articles describe the repressive political atmosphere on the island, the courageous role of Taiwan's Presbyterian Church, and the economic exploitation of women workers in foreign-owned industries.

7.64 *Symposium on El Salvador and U.S. Policy in the Region*. Faculty Committee for Human Rights in El Salvador, University of California, Berkeley, 1981. 30pp. Available in photocopy from the Data Center. Payment of $3.50 must accompany order.

This is a transcript of a symposium held on the U.C. Berkeley campus on January 16, 1981, featuring speakers from a variety of political perspectives.

7.65 *The Universal Declaration of Human Rights*. Ecumenical Service Commission (CESE). 1973. 50 cents. Available from the U.S. Catholic Conference.

An ecumenical edition of the Universal Declaration of Human Rights prepared to celebrate the twenty-fifth anniversary of the Declaration. It endorses the Declaration and calls for action on the unfinished agenda of human rights questions.

7.66 *U.S. Human Rights Policy: Latin America*. Richard E. Feinberg. *International Policy Report* 6, no. 1, October 1980. 12pp. $1.50. Bulk rates available.

It was in Latin America that the Carter administration made its most consistent effort to integrate human rights into its foreign policy. This CIP report by a former U.S. State Department official identifies the successes and failures of Carter's policies, examines the relationship of human rights to national security and economic development, and assesses the organization and practices of the State Department in carrying out human rights policies.

See also:
3.111, 3.112, 3.113, 3.127, 3.130, 3.168, 4.109, 9.44

AUDIOVISUAL RESOURCES

.67   *As We Sow*. 28 min film. United Methodist Film Service. Rental $15
This film on human rights deals with corporate responsibility, torture, racism, Native American land rights, Korea, and handicapped persons.

.68   *Brazil: A Report on Torture*. 1971 60 min color film. Saul Landau and Haskell Wexler. New Time Films. Rental $60
In this film torture victims reenact their torture at the hands of the Brazilian secret police. They link their experience to the economic and political conditions in their own and in many Third World states.

.69   *Human Rights*. 10 min color slideshow with script. 8th Day Center. Rental for non-members $15
This is a presentation of the UN Universal Declaration of Human Rights. It focuses on the civil, political, economic, social, and cultural rights set forth in the Declaration. It is suitable for use as part of a liturgy or prayer service.

.70   *Human Rights Slide Set*. 20 color slides. United Methodist Church Service Center. Rental $6
These slides interpret fundamental economic, social, and civil rights in the United States and abroad.

.71   *Missing Persons*. 1980 26 min b&w film. Spanish and English dialogue with English voice-over. Spanish version available. Icarus. Rental $50. Sale $395. Also available for rent from United Methodist Church Service Center ($25).
This film is a documentary on "disappeared" political prisoners in Chile and on the implications of this situation for the international human rights debate. It considers the role of U.S. policies toward Chile. Presented against the background of the debate in the United Nations and in the U.S. government on the situation of human rights in Chile, three Chilean women describe the arrest of their husbands and children and their efforts to find them.

.72   *The Politics of Torture*. 1978 50 min color film. ABC News Closeup. California Newsreel. Rental $70. Sale $650. Also available from AFSC (Cambridge) ($25) and Third World Newsreel.
Using the examples of Iran, the Philippines, and Chile, this film is an exploration of the U.S. record in fulfilling a highly publicized and emphatic promise to promote human rights. ABC News Closeup journalists Tom Bywaters and William Sherman spent six months investigating and documenting the evidence of repression—including the use of torture—by U.S. allies. Their film raises questions regarding the role of the U.S. government and major financial institutions in supporting such regimes.

.73   *Prisoners of Conscience*. 1978 45 min b&w film. Anand Patwardhan. Icarus. Rental $60. Sale $495
During the State of Emergency imposed on India by Indira Gandhi (June 1975 to March 1977) over 100,000 people were arrested without charge and imprisoned

without trial. *Prisoners of Conscience* examines the situation of political prisoners in India during and prior to the Emergency.

7.74   *Sounds in Struggle: Experiences in Human Rights*. 30 min audio cassette. Available from United Methodist Church Service Center. Sale $3.50

This cassette records the experiences of persons and groups who have actively engaged in the struggle for human rights. An accompanying booklet gives guidance for engaging listeners in discussions of what rights are and how to see them in relationship to each other.

7.75   *To the People of the World*. 1975 21 min color film. Barbara Margolis and the Latin American Film Project. Available from California Newsreel ($30) and Unifilm ($65).

This is a factual report on the human rights situation and conditions of political prisoners in Chile after the coup in 1973. It presents personal accounts of two women who were released from prison as a result of international pressure: Laura Allende, past member of Congress and sister of President Salvador Allende, and Carmen Castillo, a member of the Revolutionary Left Movement. Both women were members of the resistance. The film contains important documentary material on the coup of September 11, 1973.

7.76   *World Human Rights: Policy and Practice*. 1980 color filmstrip, record or cassette, spirit duplicating master, and guide. New York Times. Available from the Social Studies School Service. Rental $27

This multimedia program explores the human rights issue, discussing the work of Amnesty International and assessing the role of the United States in human rights in countries such as Chile, Argentina, and South Africa. Included is a teacher's guide with discussion questions and a student worksheet on a spirit duplicating master.

See also:
3.159, 3.174, 4.166

OTHER RESOURCES

7.77   *Covenants Action Guide*. Washington, D.C.: Coalition for a New Foreign and Military Policy, 1979. 16pp. 20 cents

This booklet is designed to complement the Coalition's nationwide campaign to ratify the UN Human Rights Covenants. It explains the Covenants, the ratification process, and citizen action. It shows the link between the international movement for human rights and the movement in the United States.

7.78   *Human Rights Directory: Latin America, Africa, Asia*. Washington, D.C.: Human Rights Internet, 1980. 244pp. $22.50

This directory lists nearly four hundred organizations in Latin America and the Caribbean, Africa, the Middle East, Asia, and the Pacific concerned with issues of human rights and social justice. It also includes some seventy international groups based in Europe and North America. This book provides information on the objectives, activities, publications, and library holdings of all entries. It includes four indexes: English names, non-English names, acronyms, and subjects. The directory is revised periodically.

.79   *Human Rights Organizations and Periodicals Directory*. David Christiano, ed. 5th ed. Berkeley, Calif.: Meiklejohn Civil Liberties Institute, 1982. 256pp. $11.95

This publication contains nearly 650 entries describing groups and publications dedicated to the advancement and protection of basic human rights. It is composed of three sections: an alphabetical guide, a subject index, and a periodical index. Entries are well annotated.

.80   *International Human Rights Kit*. Robert Woito, ed. 2d ed. Chicago: World Without War Publications, 1981. 200pp. $6

This kit includes the texts of the basic international human rights declarations, covenants, and conventions. It also includes ideas on how to promote human rights, proposals for improving the human rights performance of countries, and resources for action.

.81   *New England Human Rights Directory, 1982–1983*. Cambridge, Mass.: New England Human Rights Network, 1983. 76pp. $4.50

This informative sourcebook reflects a growing human rights movement in New England that is part of a national movement for peace and justice. Listing over 150 organizations working from many perspectives, the *New England Human Rights Directory* provides important contacts for information and mutual support. Descriptions of groups are detailed and up-to-date. The *Directory* includes regional and national resource lists, a categorical index, an essay on UN covenants and declarations on human rights, and information on the New England Human Rights Network.

.82   *North American Human Rights Directory 1980*. Washington, D.C.: Human Rights Internet, 1981. 182pp. $12

This directory lists nearly five hundred groups in the United States and Canada active in international human rights. It also includes governmental and intergovernmental bodies with responsibility or concern in this field. Each entry is well annotated. Alphabetical and geographical listings for organizations are included, as is an index to their serial publications.

.83   *A Research Manual on Human Rights*. Richard Greenfield and Lee Regan, eds. Washington, D.C.: Human Rights Internet, forthcoming 1984.

This manual is intended to facilitate the work of researchers, librarians, and documentalists in the field of international human rights. It will describe relevant references and research tools, data banks, bibliographies, fugitive materials, governmental documentation, and U.S. human rights collections.

.84   *Teacher's Packet on Human Rights*. Washington, D.C.: Coalition for a New Foreign and Military Policy, 1979. $1.25

This packet includes a lesson plan and resource list.

7.85   *Teaching Human Rights*. Washington, D.C.: Human Rights Internet, 1981. 134pp. $20

This book contains twenty-seven syllabi for human rights courses using legal, philosophical, and social science approaches. It includes a human rights bibliography and a directory of human rights bibliographies.

See also:
10.123

Chapter 8

Militarism, Peace, Disarmament

KEY RESOURCES

Organizations

Organizations working on militarism, peace, and disarmament are legion—and with good reason, given the gravity of the issues. Peace education programs of the **American Friends Service Committee** and the nationwide networks of both **Clergy and Laity Concerned** and the **Coalition for a New Foreign and Military Policy** are good places to start. They all offer the chance to become involved locally; they publish excellent educational resources; and they have a wealth of experience in dealing with these issues.

Research studies from the **Council on Economic Priorities** and from the **Militarism and Disarmament Project** of the **Institute for Policy Studies** are noteworthy.

Printed Resources

Any book or publication that Michael Klare is involved with is *must* reading for those who desire to understand the structure, function, and plans of U.S. armed forces in and vis-à-vis the Third World.

The studies by Richard Barnet and Shoup and Minter provide valuable insights into the "men and institutions behind U.S. foreign policy."

For serious students of war and peace-related issues, William Arkin's research guide is indispensable.

Coalition Close-Up and other worthwhile resources are some of the benefits that accompany a membership in the **Coalition for a New Foreign and Military Policy**.

Fellowship magazine is a long-established publication that takes a non-violent editorial stand on military issues. *The Other Side* and *Sojourners* magazines approach issues of militarism, peace, and disarmament from an evangelical Christian perspective.

Literature lists and reprint services are numerous on the issues of militarism, peace, and disarmament. Rather than highlight any two or three publications on these issues we'll simply recommend that you write for the lists described below and then make your own selections from these and from our own annotated lists.

Audiovisual Resources

The War/Peace Film Guide is a useful resource for educators. *War Without Winners* is already a classic film on the dangers of nuclear war. The background materials that the Center for Defense Information has prepared to accompany the film make it a powerful tool in educational programs.

Though dated, the NET documentary *Who Invited Us?*—a moving, critical look at America's foreign and military policy—is still worth viewing.

ORGANIZATIONS

8.1 American Friends Service Committee, Peace Education Program, 1501 Cherry St., Philadelphia, PA 19102 Tel: 215-241-7168.

RELIGIOUS AFFILIATION: Religious Society of Friends (Quakers).

FOCUS: International • Middle East • Southern Africa • Indochina. Peace • equality • simplicity • abolition of war • arms race • nonviolent world order • more equitable sharing of world's resources • support for struggles to realize universal human rights.

ACTIVITIES: Popular education • networking • documentation and information • workshops and seminars.

RESOURCES: Speakers • audiovisuals • literature. **8.2** *Peace Education Resources* literature brochure available.

8.3 American Library Association, Peace Information Exchange Task Force, c/o Elizabeth Morrissett, 1325 W. Quartz, No. 204, Butte, MT 59701.

FOCUS: Global. Peace • militarism • disarmament.

ACTIVITIES: Education of librarians and library users in the area of peace • identification of peace collections and encouragement of their public use • development of a bibliography of materials on peace • formulating a directory of groups that are involved with peace efforts, research, or education • acting as a clearinghouse for materials on peace.

RESOURCES: Resource lists • consultant services.

8.4 Catholic Peace Fellowship, 339 Lafayette St., New York, NY 10012. Tel: 212-673-8990.

RELIGIOUS AFFILIATION: Roman Catholic.

FOCUS: Third World • Asia and Pacific • Latin America. Human rights • militarism • nuclear arms and energy • disarmament • political economy • socialism • social justice.

ACTIVITIES: Popular education • political action • resistance • legislative action • networking • documentation and information • justice and peace ministries • workshops and seminars.

RESOURCES: Speakers • literature distribution • publications • study-action guides • curriculum guides • consultant services.

PERIODICALS: **8.5** *CPF Bulletin*. 3 issues/year; with $10 annual membership.

SPECIAL PROJECTS: The Atlantic Life Community Network.

8.6 Center for Defense Information, 303 Capital Gallery West, 600 Maryland Ave., SW, Washington, DC 20024. Tel: 202-484-9490.

FOCUS: Global. Militarism • nuclear arms • arms sales • military spending • balance of forces and military power.

ACTIVITIES: Popular education • research and writing • congressional testimony • intern programs • library services • media • documentation and information • policy-oriented research and writing • conferences.

RESOURCES: Speakers • literature distribution • publications • study-action guides • research services • library • reports.

PERIODICALS: **8.7** *Defense Monitor*. 10 issues/year. $25/year.

SPECIAL PROJECTS: Conference on Business and Military Spending.

8.8 Center for War/Peace Studies, 218 E. 18 St., New York, NY 10003. Tel: 212-475-0850.

FOCUS: Global • international • Middle East. Militarism • disarmament • nuclear arms and energy • international awareness.

ACTIVITIES: Popular education • research and writing • policy-oriented research and writing • workshops and seminars.

RESOURCES: Publications.

PERIODICALS: **8.9** *Global Report*. Quarterly newsletter. $20/year. Subscription includes copies of the Center's *Special Studies*.

8.10 **Coalition for a New Foreign and Military Policy**, 120 Maryland Ave., NE, Washington, DC 20002. Tel: 202-546-8400.

FOCUS: Third World. Human rights • disarmament • nuclear arms and energy • U.S. military spending.

ACTIVITIES: Popular education • legislative action • intern programs • networking • policy-oriented research and writing.

RESOURCES: Speakers • literature distribution • publications • study-action guides • speakers brochure available.

PERIODICALS: **8.11** *Coalition Close-Up.* Three times/year. Contribution.

8.12 **Consortium on Peace, Research, Education, and Development (COPRED)**, Center for Peaceful Change, Stopher Hall, Kent State University, Kent, OH 44242. Tel: 216-672-3143.

FOCUS: Global. Peace research, education, and action.

ACTIVITIES: Popular education • networking • media • documentation and information • justice and peace ministries • workshops and seminars • conferences.

RESOURCES: Speakers • audiovisuals • literature • publications • curriculum guides • consultant services • reports • resources catalog available.

PERIODICALS: **8.13** *COPRED Peace Chronicle.* Monthly magazine. With membership. **8.14** Co-sponsor of *Peace and Change.* Quarterly. $15/year for non-members.

8.15 **Council on Economic Priorities**, Conversion Information Center, 84 Fifth Ave., New York, NY 10011. Tel: 212-691-8550.

FOCUS: International. Military spending and employment • peaceful conversion • Defense Department contracting and procurement policies and trends • Federal adjustment policies and programs • arms sales • defense dependency.

ACTIVITIES: Research assistance • analysis • documentation and information.

RESOURCES: Reports.

8.16 **Fellowship of Reconciliation**, 523 No. Broadway, Box 271, Nyack, NY 10960. Tel: 914-358-4601.

RELIGIOUS AFFILIATION: Religious pacifist organization.

FOCUS: International. Human rights • disarmament • nuclear arms and energy • pacifism • social justice.

ACTIVITIES: Intern programs • library services • press service • networking • media • workshops and seminars.

RESOURCES: Speakers • audiovisuals • literature • publications • bookstore study-action guides • library.

PERIODICALS: **8.17** *Fellowship*, 10 issues/year. $10/year.

SPECIAL PROJECTS: Nuclear freeze campaign. New Abolitionist Covenant.

8.18 **Institute for Policy Studies**, Militarism and Disarmament Project, 1901 Que St., NW, Washington, DC 20009. Tel: 202-234-9382.

FOCUS: International. Arms sales • U.S. military intervention • militarism • disarmament.

ACTIVITIES: Popular education • policy-oriented research and writing • documentation and information.

RESOURCES: Speakers • publications • reports.

8.19 **Mennonite Central Committee**, Peace Section (International), 21 S. 12 St., Akron, PA 17501. Tel: 717-859-1151.

FOCUS: Third World. Human rights • political repression • militarism • disarmament • nuclear arms and energy.

ACTIVITIES: Constituency education • legislative action • research and writing • congressional testimony • conflict management and conciliation • workshops and seminars.

RESOURCES: Speakers • literature • publications • consultant services • resources catalog available.

8.20 **Mid-Peninsula Conversion Project**, 222B View St., Mountain View, CA 94041. Tel: 415-968-8798.

FOCUS: Militarism • disarmament • nuclear arms and energy.

ACTIVITIES: Popular education • research and writing • congressional testimony • solidarity work • intern programs • library services • workshops and seminars.

RESOURCES: Speakers • literature distribution • publications • consultant services • research services • library • reports.

PERIODICALS: **8.21** *Plowshare Press*. Bimonthly tabloid newspaper. $10/year.

8.22 **Mobilization for Survival**, National Office, 3601 Locust Walk, Philadelphia, PA 19104. Tel: 215-386-4875.

AFFILIATION: Coalition of more than 130 peace, environmental, religious, women's, labor, and community groups.

FOCUS: National and international. Zero nuclear weapons • banning of nuclear power • reversal of the arms race • meeting of human needs • political repression • anti-draft.

ACTIVITIES: Popular education • networking • political action • legislative action.

RESOURCES: Educational publications • organizing materials • lists of speakers • audiovisual guides • research reports.

PERIODICALS: **8.23** *The Mobilizer*. Quarterly. With membership contribution of $5 or more.

SPECIAL PROJECTS: Jobs With Peace Education Week. Reclaim America rallies.

8.24 **NARMIC (National Action/Research on the Military Industrial Complex)**, c/o AFSC, 1501 Cherry St., Philadelphia, PA 19102. Tel: 215-241-7175.

RELIGIOUS AFFILIATION: Society of Friends (Quakers).

FOCUS: Third World • Africa • Latin America. Human rights • political repression • militarism • disarmament • corporate responsibility.

ACTIVITIES: Research and writing • documentation and information • policy-oriented research and writing • production of audiovisuals.

RESOURCES: Audiovisual distribution • literature distribution • publications • study-action guides • research services on Dept. of Defense prime contracts • literature list available.

8.25 **Network to Educate for World Security**, an independent project of the **Institute for World Order**, 777 United Nations Plaza, New York, NY 10017. Tel: 212-490-0010.

FOCUS: Global. Disarmament • peace • alternative security.

ACTIVITIES: Popular education • press service • networking • media • documentation and information.

RESOURCES: Audiovisual distribution • literature distribution • publications.

SPECIAL PROJECTS: Support of UN World Disarmament Campaign.

8.26 **New Manhattan Project**, c/o AFSC, 15 Rutherford Place, New York, NY 10003. Tel: 212-598-0971.

FOCUS: Global. Nuclear freeze • disarmament.

ACTIVITIES: Popular education • legislative action • political action • networking • workshops and seminars.

RESOURCES: Speakers • study-action guides • publications.

PERIODICALS: **8.27** *The New Manhattan Project Newsletter*. Monthly. Contribution.

8.28 **Pax Christi USA**, 3000 N. Mango Ave., Chicago, IL 60634. Tel: 312-637-2555.

RELIGIOUS AFFILIATION: Roman Catholic.

FOCUS: Global. Disarmament • just world order • primacy of conscience • alternatives to violence • nuclear freeze • education for peace.

ACTIVITIES: Networking • annual national assembly • popular education.

RESOURCES: Speakers • publications • consultant services • audiovisual distribution.

PERIODICALS: **8.29** *Pax Christi Newsletter*. Quarterly. With membership.

8.30 **Riverside Church Disarmament Program**, 490 Riverside Dr., New York, NY 10027. Tel: 212-272-5900.

FOCUS: Militarism • disarmament • nuclear arms and energy.

ACTIVITIES: Popular education • constituency education • political action • legislative action • intern programs • workshops and seminars.

RESOURCES: Speakers • audiovisual distribution • literature distribution • publications • study-action guides • curriculum guides • resources brochure available.

PERIODICALS: **8.31** *Disarming Notes*. Monthly. Free.

SPECIAL PROJECTS: Peace Sabbath. Conference on Disarmament (yearly).

8.32 **Syracuse Peace Council**, 924 Burnet Ave., Syracuse, NY 13203. Tel: 315-472-5478.

FOCUS: Third World • Asia and Pacific • Middle East • Latin America. Militarism • disarmament • nuclear arms and energy • political economy • national liberation struggles.

ACTIVITIES: Popular education • solidarity work • library services • networking • media • documentation and information • workshops and seminars • production of posters and calendars • audiovisual production.

RESOURCES: Speakers • audiovisual distribution • literature distribution • publications • bookstore • study-action guides.

PERIODICALS: **8.33** *Peace Newsletter*. Monthly. $8/year individual; $12/year institutional.

SPECIAL PROJECTS: American Myths calendar.

8.34 **War Resisters League**, 339 Lafayette St., New York, NY 10012. Tel: 212-228-0450.

FOCUS: Global • international. Militarism • disarmament • nuclear arms and energy • feminism • nonviolence.

ACTIVITIES: Popular education • political action • research and writing • workshops and seminars • organizing • war tax resistance.

RESOURCES: Speakers • literature distribution • publications • bookstore • study-action guides • consultant services.

PERIODICALS: **8.35** *WRL News*. Bimonthly. With membership.

8.36 **Washington Peace Center**, 2111 Florida Ave., NW, Washington, DC 20008. Tel: 202-234-2000.

FOCUS: Global. Militarism • equitable sharing of world's resources • nonviolence • disarmament • police surveillance • social justice.

ACTIVITIES: Popular education • draft counseling • networking.

RESOURCES: Speakers • literature distribution.

PERIODICALS: **8.37** *Washington Peace Center Newsletter*. Monthly. Contribution.

SPECIAL PROJECTS: Disarmament Program. Youth and Militarism.

8.38 **Women's International League for Peace and Freedom**, 1213 Race St., Philadelphia, PA 19107. Tel: 215-563-7110.

FOCUS: International • Middle East. Human rights • militarism • disarmament • nuclear arms and energy • transnational corporations • self-determination • economic development • nonviolence • military spending • women • United Nations • civil liberties.

ACTIVITIES: Popular education • political action • legislative action • public meetings • education of children and youth • networking • study groups.

RESOURCES: Speakers • distribution of literature • consultant services.

PERIODICALS: **8.39** *Peace and Freedom*. Monthly newsletter. With membership.

8.40 **Women Strike for Peace**, National Office, 145 S. 13 St., Philadelphia, PA 19107. Tel: 215-923-0861.

FOCUS: International. Militarism • disarmament • nuclear weapons and testing.

ACTIVITIES: Popular education • networking • political action.

RESOURCES: Speakers • literature distribution • publications.

8.41 **World Conference on Religion and Peace**, 777 United Nations Plaza, New York, NY 10017. Tel: 212-687-2163.

RELIGIOUS AFFILIATION: Interreligious.

FOCUS: International. Human rights • disarmament • development • social justice.

ACTIVITIES: Constituency education • research and writing • library services • networking • documentation and information • foreign service • workshops and seminars.

RESOURCES: Speakers • distribution of literature • publications • research services • reports • literature list available.

PERIODICALS: **8.42** *Religion for Peace*. 3 issues/year. With $15 annual membership.

8.43 **World Without War Council**, 421 S. Wabash, 2d Floor, Chicago, IL 60605. Tel: 312-663-4250.

RELIGIOUS AFFILIATION: Christian and Jewish.

FOCUS: Global. Human rights • disarmament • economic development • nonviolent change • world community • democracy in Third World countries • international organizations • U.S. and Soviet foreign policy.

ACTIVITIES: Research and writing • intern programs • teacher training • workshops and seminars • regional offices.

RESOURCES: Literature • publications • bookstore • study-action guides • curriculum guides • consultant services • library • resource list available.

PERIODICALS: **8.44** *World Without War Newsletter*. Quarterly. Free.

SPECIAL PROJECTS: American Initiatives Project. World Without War calendar.

PRINTED RESOURCES

Books

.45   Adams, Gordon. *The Iron Triangle: The Politics of Defense Contracting*. New York: Council on Economic Priorities, 1981. 465pp. Bibliography. $20

This fascinating and informative study exposes the ways in which Congress, the Pentagon, and U.S. defense contractors—the "Iron Triangle"—function to boost military spending. Adams describes the institutions, roles, and people within the weapons business and then analyzes politics and power in what he calls the "influence business" in Washington. *The Iron Triangle* concludes with a revealing set of profiles of eight major defense contractors.

.46   Arkin, William M. *Research Guide to Current Military and Strategic Affairs*. Washington, D.C.: Institute for Policy Studies, 1981. 232pp. $7.95

Arkin's *Research Guide* is *the* source to turn to when you need information on military expenditures, the budget process in Congress, personalities in the U.S. armed services, U.S. bases overseas, military issues in Third World countries, and a host of other military and strategic affairs. This indispensable guide clearly describes data sources and tells you how to gain access to them. Periodicals and organizations are listed in two appendices.

.47   Arnson, Cynthia, and Klare, Michael T. *Supplying Repression: U.S. Support for Authoritarian Regimes Abroad*. Washington, D.C.: Institute for Policy Studies, 1981. 100pp. $4.95

This update of a study originally done in 1977 describes the various vehicles through which the U.S. government and U.S. corporations supply weapons to Third World nations. These include arms sales through the Foreign Military Sales Program as well as the provision of equipment, training, and advisory support through the State Department's International Narcotics Control Program. The details of what the authors term the "repression trade" are set in the context of the Carter administration's concern with human rights in Third World countries.

.48   Barnet, Richard J. *Roots of War: The Men and Institutions Behind U.S. Foreign Policy*. New York: Penguin Books, 1973. 350pp. $5.95. Available from the Institute for Policy Studies.

Barnet's thorough investigation of the forces in American life that have kept this country in a succession of wars since World War II addresses questions such as: Why has killing in the national interest become routine? How much does personal ambition affect America's role in the world? What is the part played by business in determining U.S. foreign policy? How important is public opinion?

.49   Davies, J.G. *Christians, Politics and Violent Revolution*. Maryknoll, N.Y.: Orbis Books, 1976. 216pp. Bibliography. $4.95

This informed and clearly reasoned analysis presents a convincing defense of the right of Christians to participate in revolutions, even violent ones.

8.50   DeGrasse, Robert, Jr. with Paul Murphy and William Ragen. *The Costs and Consequences of Reagan's Military Buildup.* A Report to the International Association of Machinists and Aerospace Workers, AFL-CIO and the Coalition for a New Foreign and Military Policy. New York: Council on Economic Priorities, 1982. 54pp. $2.50. Available from CEP, the Coalition, or from the IAM.

While not directly concerned with the Third World this booklet is well worth the interest of anyone involved in a study of U.S. foreign and military policy. For it tackles the question that invariably surfaces when the domestic impact of U.S. policies are examined. "But increased military spending creates jobs, doesn't it?" This CEP study demonstrates that increased military production—whether for domestic use or sale to Third World and other nations—"overloads" the U.S. economy, results in a decline in America's economic competitiveness, destroys jobs, and carries with it social costs that are far too much for us to bear.

8.51   Dougall, Lucy, compiler. *War and Peace in Literature: Prose, Drama and Poetry which Illuminate the Problem of War.* Chicago: World Without War Publications, 1982. 171pp. $5

This annotated list of 354 literary works from the Western tradition focuses on themes of war and peace as they appear in the works of the Greek dramatists, Cervantes, Malory, Camus, Akhmatova, Dylan Thomas, and many others. This reference work aims to deepen our understanding of why war has played such a tragically persistent role in human affairs and to shed some light on the requirements for peace.

8.52   Gervasi, Tom. *Arsenal of Democracy: American Military Power in the 1980s and the Origins of the New Cold War.* New York: Grove Press, 1981. 300pp. $10.95

This oversized, illustrated paperback is an excellent sourcebook for data on American weapons systems, defense contractors, arms sales overseas, and many other aspects of the U.S. military-industrial complex. In his narrative introduction, Gervasi treats the rapid deployment force, America's waning power in the world, the role of the oil conglomerates, tactical nuclear weapons, the war in space, and other vital issues.

8.53   Klare, Michael T. *War Without End: American Planning for the Next Vietnams.* New York: Alfred A. Knopf, 1972. 464pp. Research guide and bibliography.

This book is must reading for an understanding of the plans being made for continued U.S. military intervention overseas. Klare dwells particularly on the "counterinsurgency establishment," the "technological war," and the "mercenary" nature of much of U.S. war planning.

8.54   Klare, Michael T. *Beyond the Vietnam Syndrome: U.S. Interventionism in the 1980s.* Washington, D.C.: Institute for Policy Studies, 1981. 137pp. $4.95

This collection of essays by one of America's most insightful and challenging analysts of U.S. military policy covers a variety of topics, such as the preparations that are seen to be underway for a "second Vietnam," the rapid deployment force, access to scarce minerals, and—what Klare calls— the "Vietnam Syndrome.'' Klare describes how U.S. policymakers are uniting to combat the ''Vietnam Syndrome''—the American public's resistance to U.S. military involvement in future Third World conflicts—and to relegitimate the use of military force as an instrument of Washington's foreign policy.

.55   Lamont, Victor. *Hungry for Peace*. New York: Friendship Press, 1976. 64pp. $2.95

This intriguing book contains two simulation games, cartoons and photos, discussion questions, a case study on the arms race, and a provocative interpretation of the insights of Jesus' actions and teachings. *Hungry for Peace* shows its readers that they can make a difference as far as peace is concerned—in their homes, in race relations, and in international affairs.

.56   Lord, Charlie. *The Rule of the Sword*. Newton, Kan.: Faith and Life Press, 1978. 68pp. $1

This short study is intended to provide a working knowledge about militarism by clarifying issues and developing a background to examine the hard questions of Christian responsibility and stewardship.

.57   Rockman, Jane, ed. *Peace in Search of Makers*. Riverside Church Reverse the Arms Race Convocation. Valley Forge, Pa.: Judson Press, 1979. 160pp. $3. Available from Institute for Policy Studies and from Riverside Church Disarmament Program.

A collection of papers denouncing the proliferation of sophisticated weaponry and the diversion of resources from social services and programs. Contributors include: Robert McAfee Brown, Richard Barnet, Betty Lall, and William Sloane Coffin.

.58   Shannon, Thomas A., ed. *War or Peace? The Search for New Answers*. Maryknoll, N.Y.: Orbis Books, 1980. 256pp. $9.95

Dorothy Day, Gordon Zahn, Paul Deats, Eileen Egan, Bryan Hehir, and Bishop Thomas Gumbleton are among the distinguished and committed Christians who address themselves in this book to the urgent questions of church-state relations, nuclear war, Roman Catholic just-war theory, and pacifism.

.59   Shoup, Laurence, and Minter, William. *Imperial Brain Trust: the Council on Foreign Relations and United States Foreign Policy*. New York: Monthly Review, 1977. 334pp. $6.50

An in-depth analysis of one of the most powerful—and unknown—instruments of U.S. foreign policy: the Council on Foreign Relations. *Imperial Brain Trust* is a hard-hitting exposé of the CFR's structure and its links to and influence on government, the media, the universities, the large foundations, and other foreign policy organizations.

.60   Stanford, Barbara, ed. *Peacemaking: A Guide to Conflict Resolution for Individuals, Groups, and Nations*. New York: Bantam Books, 1976. 500pp. $1.95

This collection of essays ranges over many peace-related issues from the interpersonal to the international. Contributors also represent a wide variety of political opinion: Caesar Chavez discusses the grape boycott, Rollo May analyzes ecstasy and violence, Senator Barry Goldwater makes his case for a ''strong defense,'' and Barnet and Müller write on economic imperialism.

8.61   Woito, Robert. *To End War: A New Approach to International Conflict*. New
York: Pilgrim Press, 1982. 450pp. $12.95

To End War introduces the major ideas of some twenty-one subjects relative to
world affairs. It also provides annotations of over two thousand peace-related
books and lists over five hundred world affairs organizations.

See also:
1.110, 2.47, 2.55, 3.57, 3.70, 4.42, 5.39. See resources on the Korean and Vietnam
Wars throughout chapter 3.

Periodicals

8.62   *Coalition Close-Up*, Coalition for a New Foreign and Military Policy, 120
Maryland Ave., NE, Washington, DC 20002. Quarterly. With $10 annual mem-
bership.

Close-Up contains action-oriented material on issues of disarmament, human
rights, military spending, and the struggle for a non-interventionist U.S. foreign
policy. This 12 to 16 page quarterly is supplemented by *Action Guides*, *Action
Alerts*, and other materials mailed to Coalition members throughout the year.

8.63   *Disarmament Times*, NGO Committee on Disarmament at the United Nations,
777 UN Plaza, Rm. 7B, New York, NY 10017. Bimonthly tabloid newspaper.
$5/year.

A four-page tabloid newspaper devoted exclusively to disarmament-related issues with a particular concern for UN disarmament efforts.

8.64   *Fellowship*, Fellowship of Reconciliation, 523 N. Broadway, Box 271, Nyack,
NY 10960. 10 issues/year. $10/year. Back issues available.

This long-established monthly publication embodies the deep concern and
commitment of those associated with FOR. *Fellowship* offers provocative feature articles, as well as news and reviews.

8.65   *The Guardian*, 33 W. 17 St., New York, NY 10011. 50 issues/year. $23/year.

This ''independent radical newsweekly'' contains exceptionally good
coverage—from a radical and critical perspective—of Washington's political and
military policies in the Third World. Of particular note is a special 28-page issue
of the newspaper (summer 1982) devoted entirely to disarmament. This issue
(Vol. 34, No. 37) contains numerous feature articles along with chronologies and
resource guides. It sells for 75 cents for single copies. Bulk rates are available.

8.66   *National Catholic Reporter*, Box 281, Kansas City, MO 64141. 45 issues/year.
$23/year.

The *NCR*—an independent Catholic newsweekly—covers many Third World-
related issues, among them U.S. military intervention and the human rights
stance (or lack thereof) of American political leaders.

8.67   *The Other Side*, 300 W. Apsley St., Philadelphia, PA 19144. Monthly magazine. $16.75/year.

This appealing magazine comes out of the evangelical Christian tradition. It
confronts head-on issues of war and peace—among many other topics of social

justice. But it does so in a manner that is respectful of its readers and sympathetic to the turmoil that such issues usually give rise to in the hearts of readers.

8.68   *Peacework*, AFSC, 2161 Massachusetts Ave., Cambridge, MA 02140. 11 issues/year. $10/year.

This newsletter carries feature articles with reports on peace-related political actions and broader analyses of issues such as the conflict in the Middle East, the draft, and divestment campaigns. A resource section is a monthly feature of this publication.

8.69   *Sojourners*, 1309 L St., NW, Washington, DC 20005. 11 issues/year. $12/year.

Another magazine coming from the Christian evangelical tradition *Sojourners* weds a deep-rooted scriptural faith and an informed analysis of the urgent social issues of our times in a magazine that is professional, attractive, and challenging. Write to *Sojourners* for information on their nuclear weapons-related New Abolitionist Covenant.

.70   *Win*, 326 Livingston St., Brooklyn, NY 11217. 22 issues/year. $20/year. Back issues available.

"Peace and freedom through nonviolent action" is the aim of the editors of this weekly magazine. *Win*'s feature articles treat the arms race, nuclear weapons, economic democracy, the draft, and the Middle East. Each issue also contains news reports and reviews.

Pamphlets and Articles

Literature lists and reprint services are especially numerous on issues of militarism, peace, and disarmament. Among the more significant are:

.71   *Coalition for a New Foreign and Military Policy Literature List.*

.72   *Defense Monitor* index of back issues on arms trade and aid, military budget, nuclear war, Panama Canal, and more.

.73   *Dissent, Freedom, Revolution, Peace: WRL Reading List.* A 12-page list of recommended readings on these subjects from the War Resisters League.

.74   *A Guide to Peace Resources* (with supplement). Mennonite Central Committee, Peace Section International.

.75   *Information Materials and Documents on Disarmament.* Office of Public Information, United Nations.

.76   *Institute for Policy Studies Catalogue of Publications: Disarmament.*

.77   *NARMIC Literature List.*

.78   *Riverside Church Disarmament Program Resource List.*

.79   *Sojourners Reprint Service.* Articles on Christian peacemaking, biblical politics and economics, and the call to discipleship from *Sojourners.*

.80   *World Conference on Religion and Peace: Literature List.*

.81   *Arming the Third World.* NARMIC. 8pp. 15 cents. Bulk rates available.

A synopsis of U.S. arms sales to Third World countries with repressive governments: Iran (under the Shah), the Philippines, South Korea, Chile, Brazil, etc.

8.82   *Arms Export Policies: Ethical Choices*. U.S. Catholic Conference, Office of International Justice and Peace, October 1978. 32pp. 75 cents

This pamphlet is one of a series of information papers prepared by the USCC "on particularly complex and controversial international peace and justice issues." *Arms Export Policies* examines the trade in arms, the motives and policies of U.S. arms transfers, the ethical aspects of conventional arms proliferation, and the implementation of arms transfer restraints.

8.83   *The Arms Race: Illusion of Security*. U.S. Catholic Conference, Office of International Justice and Peace, November 1978. 24pp. 75 cents. Bulk rates available.

These materials developed for the World Day of Peace (1979) present ethical arguments for arms control and provide liturgy and homily suggestions.

8.84   *Arms Race*. Peacemakers in Mission, 1981. 8pp. Single copies free. Bulk rates available.

This leaflet addresses the arms race in general and the question of nuclear arms in particular.

8.85   *The Blue Book Series*. Riverside Church Disarmament Program, 1981. 17 articles $6.

This set of articles features contributions by Seymour Melman, Alan Wolfe, Barry Commoner, Michael Klare, and the Rev. William Sloane Coffin writing of themes of peace and disarmament.

8.86   *Cold War Reading Packet*. Coalition for a New Foreign and Military Policy, 1980. 26pp. $1.50

This packet of individual reprints contains material from *Inquiry*, *The Progressive*, *Seven Days*, the *Washington Post*, and other publications.

8.87   *The Defense Department's Top 100*. Council on Economic Priorities, 1979. 6pp. $1

Discussion and annotated list of major Dept. of Defense contracts over a five-year period.

8.88   *Defense: Moral and Strategic Arguments*. J. Bryan Hehir. A special issue of *NETWORK Quarterly* 7, no. 2, Spring 1979. 12pp. 50 cents. Out of print.

The director of the Office of International Justice and Peace of the U.S. Catholic Conference analyzes how strategic and moral issues are joined in the debate about U.S. nuclear policy.

8.89   *Disarmament Action Guide*. Coalition for a New Foreign and Military Policy, June 1981. 16pp. 25 cents each. Bulk rates available.

This action guide presents an overview of the dangers and costs of the arms race. Included are suggestions for action and a two-page listing of organizations and resources.

8.90   *Militarism and Disarmament Reports*. Institute for Policy Studies. Apply for dates of recent reports and current prices.

These reports provide background information on strategic countries in the Latin America, Africa/Middle East, and Asia regions, including details on arms deliveries, U.S. military operations, human rights violations, and internal economic and political conditions.

.91   *Militarism and Science.* Special issue of *Science for the People* 13, no. 5, July–August 1981. $1

Topics covered in this special issue include: resurgent militarism in academia; biological weapons and Third World targets; space militarism; and the basic economics of rearming America.

.92   *Nuclear War Prevention Kit.* Center for Defense Information, 1980. 20pp. $1. Bulk rates available.

This booklet, designed to be used with CDI's film *War Without Winners*, presents suggestions for citizen action and lists resources for use around the question of nuclear war.

.93   *The Peace Bishops and the Arms Race: Can Religious Leadership Help in Preventing Nuclear War?* George Weigel. 1982. 54pp. Available from World Without War Publications. $2

This booklet presents four statements by Catholic "Peace Bishops" and the author's attempts to marry their concern to a politics actually capable of aiding progress toward an end to war.

.94   *Peace With Justice. engage/social action forum* 63, July–August 1980. No. E2063. 31pp. 40 cents each. Bulk rates available.

This *engage/social action forum* was produced as a study resource for readers who understand that "for Christians there is a special urgency for peace born out of the gospel of Christ."

.95   *Peacemaking: The Believer's Calling.* Office of the General Assembly of the United Presbyterian Church in the USA, 1980. 45pp. $1.25. Bulk rates available.

This UPCUSA official statement analyzes the "new global reality" and then examines the theological and ethical bases for both peacemaking and policymaking. Appendices contain program suggestions, study guides, a glossary, and a list of organizations with peace concerns.

.96   *A Proper Peace Establishment. engage/social action forum* 70, April 1981. No. E2070. 31pp. 50 cents each. Bulk rates available.

The "proper peace establishment" referred to in the title of this *engage/social action forum* is the proposed U.S. Academy of Peace & Conflict Resolution. The chairperson of the U.S. Commission on Proposals for the academy, Sen. Spark Matsunaga, sets out the rationale for such an institution in the forum's lead article. Other articles discuss conflict resolution, the campaign for the academy, and suggested roles for a U.S. Academy of Peace & Conflict Resolution.

.97   *Resurgent Militarism.* Michael T. Klare and the Bay Area Chapter of the Inter-University Committee. Institute for Policy Studies, 1979. 14pp. $2

An analysis of the origins and consequences of the growing militaristic fervor in the United States. Examines America's changing strategic position since Vietnam and the political and economic forces which underlie the new upsurge in militarism.

98   *Toward World Security: A Program for Disarmament.* Earl C. Ravenal with Richard Barnet, Robert Borosage, Michael Klare, and Marcus Raskin. Institute for Policy Studies, 1978. 32pp. $2

An argument for the United States taking independent steps toward disarmament by not deploying new "counterforce" weapons, pledging no first use of nuclear weapons, and by following a non-interventionist foreign policy.

8.99   *Trafficking in Arms: A Catalogue of 300 U.S. Foreign Military Sales Agreements.* NARMIC, 1980. 48pp. $2. Bulk rates available.

This booklet catalogs "arms for export" in state-by-state and company-by-company listings. The names and addresses of major defense contractors are given along with other resources on U.S. arms trade and related issues.

8.100   *The Vietnam Syndrome. MERIP Reports* 90, September 1980. 32pp. $2.50

This entire issue of *MERIP Reports* analyzes the Carter administration's Middle East doctrine and details Washington's military relations with key states in the region.

8.101   *War and Peace: A Handbook for Peacemaking in Upstate New York.* Syracuse Peace Council, 1981. 27pp. 85 cents. Bulk rates available.

This special issue of the Council's newsletter—though regionally focused on upstate New York—contains a wealth of information and organizing ideas useful for activists all across the country.

8.102   *Weapons for the World: 1982 Update. The Corporate Role in Foreign Arms Transfers.* William Hartung. Council on Economic Priorities, December–January 1981-2. 6pp. 4-page supplement of "Major Proposed Letters of Offer by the U.S. Government for Foreign Military Services and Equipment During FY1980." $1

This issue of CEP's newsletter examines the U.S. contribution to international arms proliferation, particularly in five areas of the world: the Middle East, Latin America, North Africa, Asia, and Europe.

See also:
2.70, 2.74, 3.98, 3.104, 3.119, 3.121, 3.126, 4.126, 5.63, 5.67, 9.66, 10.68, 10.69, 10.86

AUDIOVISUAL RESOURCES

Directories

03 *Mobilization for Survival Audio-Visual Guide 1980–81*. Philadelphia: Mobilization for Survival, 1981. $3

This guide includes a list of films arranged by subject and a distributors list.

04 *The War/Peace Film Guide*. John Dowling, ed. Rev. ed. Chicago: World Without War Council, 1980. 188pp. $5

This film guide is more than just a carefully annotated selection of films on themes of war and peace. Like a predecessor book edited by Lucy Dougall in 1973, Dowling's 1980 edition is intended to provide the means necessary to view the films listed in an educational setting. To this end *The War/Peace Film Guide* offers pages of program development aids and background readings and resources. Especially useful are the study guides, study units, and curriculum resources that are keyed to specific films.

The War/Peace Film Guide classifies films in categories such as the following: area studies; arms race; children's films; the impact of war; nonviolence; nuclear war; revolution; world community; world development.

Audiovisuals

05 *Booom*. 1979 10 min color film. Bretislav Pojar. United Nations. Free

An animated film that takes a humorous look at a very serious subject: the global arms race. Produced by a Czech animator Bretislav Pojar, *Booom* takes a look at the history of aggression and the theory that might makes right. By extension, it carries us into the atomic and missile age postulating various scenarios for planetary self-destruction, both intentional and accidental.

06 *Christians and the Arms Race*. 1980 15 min color slideshow/sound presentation. Available from the Riverside Church Disarmament Program. Rental $10. Sale $50

Christians and the Arms Race identifies basic themes regarding arms proliferation and the Christian faith.

07 *Conscience and War Taxes*. 1978 20 min slideshow with cassette tape. Available from AFSC (Cambridge) $15

This audiovisual presents clearly and factually the moral, legal, and political case of Americans who are conscientiously opposed to having close to one-third of their Federal tax payments spent for military purposes and preparations for war.

08 *Every Heart Beats True*. 1980 20 min color slideshow or filmstrip with script. 140 visuals. Packard Manse Media Project. Rental $15 per week. Sale price for individuals $63, slideshow; $30, filmstrip.

This presentation deals with the peace witness of early Christians, the teachings of Jesus, the just war theory, the nature of military service today, and the response of Christians today. Packard Manse recommends *Every Heart Beats True* for use with high school and college groups and in peace studies programs.

8.109   *Gods of Metal*. 1982 27 min color film. Maryknoll World Films. Rental $25. Sale $325

This 27-minute documentary deals with the nuclear arms race and people of faith who are trying to stop it. The arms race is analyzed from a Christian perspective, showing its economic and social effects on people in the United States and in the Third World—especially the poor. *Gods of Metal* shows what individuals and groups are doing to halt the arms build-up and it offers practical suggestions for action.

8.110   *Guns or Butter?* 30 min color slideshow with cassette. SANE (Washington, D.C.). Rental $5

This slideshow, narrated by Paul Newman, discusses the inflated U.S. military budget and the need for re-ordering national priorities.

8.111   *The Hat: Is This War Necessary?* 1964 18 min color film. Produced by John and Faith Hubley, World Law Fund. McGraw-Hill Films. Rental $25

This animated film—with music and narration by Dizzie Gillespie and Dudley Moore—focuses on two border guards. After one drops his hat on the "other" side of the line, they both discuss the history of war and boundaries, disarmament, and the system that stands between them.

8.112   *The H-Bomb Secret*. 1980 30 min slideshow with taped narration. 160 slides. 15 min 80 slides. Howard Morland. Available from Riverside Church Disarmament Program. Rental $15

A description of how the H-bomb works and the study of the many corporations and communities around the country that make components for it. The slideshow is quite technical. It is based on the research done for a series of articles Morland wrote on the H-bomb for the *Progressive* magazine in 1979, which the U.S. government tried to censor.

8.113   *John, Mary, MIRV and MARV: The Arms Race and the Human Race*. 1978 15 min color slideshow with cassette and discussion guide. 100 visuals. Available for sale from the Packard Manse Media Project for $40 and for a rental fee of $15 from both the 8th Day Center (Chicago) and AFSC (Cambridge).

From the vantage point of the future, the dangers of the nuclear arms race and the possibility of a nuclear holocaust are documented as are the possibilities for successful disarmament.

8.114   *The Language of Faces*. 1960 17 min b&w film. John Korty. Kit Parker Films. Rental $10

Depicting a war in slow motion, this film shows the turning of a million heads, a million yawns at the headlines, a million nods to the mass production of mass destruction.

8.115   *The Race Nobody Wins*. 1981 (rev. ed.) 20 min color slideshow or filmstrip with cassette. SANE (Washington, D.C.) Rental $10 Sale $45 ($35 for educators). SANE provides these materials with every rental or sale: a fully documented copy of the script; a *Teacher's Guide* and an *Action Guide*; an extensive bibliography of recent publications on the topic of the arms race. Also available from AFSC (Cambridge) and the 8th Day Center (Chicago) for a rental fee of $15.

This SANE audiovisual translates the often baffling technological terminology of the arms race into understandable terms, explaining that disarmament and economic conversion are realistic alternatives.

16   *The Selling of the Pentagon.* 1971 54 min b&w film. Peter Davis, CBS. California Newsreel. Rental $50

A look at how and why tax money is being spent on the support of the American military establishment. The film received an Emmy Award, the Peabody Award, and the Saturday Review Award.

17   *This Bloody, Blundering Business.* 1975 30 min b&w film. Directed by Peter Davis. Unifilm. Rental $45

A satire on American foreign policy, this film traces the history of U.S. intervention in the Philippines following the Spanish-American War. It uses a silent movie format with ragtime piano music in combination with dramatically understated narration and excerpts from newsreels of the period to show American attitudes toward Third World peoples and cultures. A blue ribbon winner of the American Film Festival.

18   *War Without Winners.* 1979 27 min color film. Directed by Haskell Wexler. Center for Defense Information. Handbook from CDI also available. Rental $35. Available for rental through AFSC (Cambridge) $20. Available for sale from Films, Inc. for $300 (16mm film) and $210 (3/4 inch VHS or BETA videotape).

This excellent film explores the dangers of nuclear war in today's world. The accompanying CDI handbook examines many of the issues raised in the film: the power of nuclear weapons, expected deaths from nuclear war, how nuclear war could start, the size of U.S. and Soviet nuclear arsenals, and the spread of nuclear weapons.

19   *Who Invited Us?* 1970 59 min b&w film. Directed by Alan M. Levin. National Educational Television. Unifilm. Rental $60

A documentary and historical survey of U.S. military interventions abroad. Other issues explored include the interdependence of U.S. military and economic interests abroad and the role of the CIA in triggering U.S. covert and overt military operations.

20   *Who's In Charge Here?* 1980 15 min color film. AFSC (Cambridge). Rental $20

A look at the impact U.S. military spending exerts on the economy—jobs, taxes, inflation—from a human, personal viewpoint. Defense workers talk about energy, inflation, military spending, and security. *Who's In Charge Here?* calls for a reordering of national priorities away from arms spending that many think contributes nothing to national defense.

21   *You Don't Have to Buy War, Mrs. Smith.* 1971 28 min color film. American Documentary Films. Available for rent from AFSC (Cambridge). $15

Bess Myerson explores the Pentagon-inspired myths about "national security,'' describing the bombs and botulism the military has stored in backyards all over the United States. She names America's most familiar manufacturers of household goods, charging them with being war profiteers as the producers of Pentagon products.

See also:
1.181, 2.104, 3.161, 3.175, 4.135

OTHER RESOURCES

Curriculum Guides and Materials

8.122   *Peace Education Packet.* Prepared by the PEN Network of the Consortium on Peace, Research, Education, and Development. Rev. ed. Kent State, Ohio: CO-PRED, 1981. $10.75 postage included.

This COPRED packet contains materials covering a variety of issues in the field of peace education, a sampling of teaching styles and strategies for various grade levels, along with the names, addresses, and descriptive brochures of the organizations contributing to the packet.

8.123   *Peace Notes.* Helen Garvey, ed. Berkeley, Calif.: World Education Center, c/o World Without War Council. Bimonthly newsletter. 8pp. Donation requested.

This newsletter, published bimonthly during the school year, serves educators with narrative introductions to peace-related subjects such as Northern Ireland, economic underdevelopment, and law and conscience. Relevant resources are mentioned and suggestions for the classroom are offered.

8.124   *Peace and World Order Studies: A Curriculum Guide.* Burns H. Weston, Sherle R. Schwenninger, and Diane E. Shamis, eds. New York: Transnational Academic Program, Institute for World Order, 1978. 476pp. $5.

This comprehensive guidebook offers selected essays on peace and world order education, course outlines, learning packages, and annotated lists of organizations, publications, audiovisual materials, academic peace-related programs.

8.125   *The Riverside Disarmament Reader.* New York: The Riverside Church Disarmament Program, 1981. 476pp. $15

This model syllabus is designed for college and seminary use, as well as for study groups in churches, synagogues, and communities. The *Reader* comes in a handy three-ring binder and contains the course outlines, schedule of readings, discussion questions, and forty-four articles on the arms race.

8.126   *Teacher's Resource Manual on Worldmindedness: An Annotated Bibliography of Curriculum Materials—Kindergarten through Grade Twelve.* Ida Urso. Los Angeles: Curriculum Inquiry Center, Graduate School of Education, UCLA. Occasional paper no. 8. 132pp.

Chapter D (pp. 51 to 70) includes resources on aggression, conflict, disarmament, nonviolence, human rights, social justice, and war.

Simulation Games

27   *Alternation*. Denver, Colo.: Center for Teaching International Relations, University of Denver, 1972. $1. Level: junior high and above. Players: 15 or more. Time: 2–4 hours.

     Alternation sets up a situation of systematic oppression and encourages participants to explore alternatives to the use of force to alter the system.

28   *Bombs or Bread: Consumer Priorities vs. National Security*. Sun Valley, Calif.: Edu-Game, 1978. $3. Level: junior high and above. Players: 21–42. Time: 4–6 hours.

29   *Guns or Butter*. Del Mar, Calif.: Simile II, 1972. $30. Level: junior high and above. Players: 18–28. Time: 6–8 hours.

     These two simulations force participants to make the hard choice between the escalation of military spending and the provision of greater goods and services for the population of a country. While to a great extent *Bombs or Bread* and *Guns or Butter* are domestically oriented the relationship of these choices to the Third World should be obvious to informed participants.

30   *Defense*. Lakeside, Calif.: Interact, 1975. $11. Level: junior high and above. Players: 20–40. Time: 10–15 hours.

     This simulation is similar to *Bombs or Bread* in its domestic orientation. It differs in that its focus is on the congressional budget-making process. Applications to Third World realities have to be introduced into the game.

31   *Nationalism: War or Peace*. Sun Valley, Calif.: Edu-Game, 1973. $3. Level: junior high and above. Players: 15 or more. Time: 5 hours.

32   *War Time*. Sun Valley, Calif.: Edu-Game, 1973. $3. Level: junior high and above. Players: 15 or more. Time: 5 hours.

     The relationship between war and political economy is the focus of these two role-playing simulations. Taking on the role of officials of several fictitious nations, participants contract trade agreements and enter into alliances in furtherance of their own national objectives.

Chapter 9

Transnational Corporations

KEY RESOURCES

Organizations

The **Data Center** has files on over five thousand U.S. and foreign corporations and on hundreds of corporate issues related to transnationals. The Center's Corporate Profile Service provides profiles on individual corporations; its Search Service can prepare customized packets of clippings and other resources on topics such as runaway shops, U.S. investments in Latin America, transnational corporations, and labor.

The **Interfaith Center on Corporate Responsibility** has a well-deserved reputation for responsible and effective action in the area of corporate social responsibility.

Printed Resources

Barnet and Müller have written the textbook on transnational corporations: *Global Reach*. Books by Girvan, Ledogar, and Norris provide some of the case studies of corporate abuse in the Third World.

Multinational Monitor is a consistently powerful resource on transnational corporations. The award-winning monthly, *Mother Jones*, has broken new ground with a number of Third World-related stories involving U.S. corporations, while **ICCR**'s *Corporate Examiner* is must reading for church people and others interested in corporate responsibility.

ICCR's *Corporate Examiner* contains a four-page *Brief* in each issue that examines one corporation or one corporate issue in depth. Write to **ICCR** for a list of its back issues.

Audiovisual Resources

Two notable audiovisuals on transnational corporations are *The Conspiracy: Or How Transnationals Do It* and *Controlling Interest: The World of the Multinational Corporation*. The latter is a particularly effective introduction to the subject.

The **NARMIC** slideshow, *Sharing Global Resources*, and *Guess Who's Coming to Breakfast*, from the **Packard Manse Media Project**, are two very effective and inexpensive audiovisuals on TNCs.

Other Resources

This section of the chapter on transnational corporations lists church agencies that are involved in the corporate responsibility movement and reviews a variety of corporate research guides. These latter will be of use to those who wish to do more in-depth research into the operations of TNCs.

ORGANIZATIONS

.1   **Bank Watch**, Box 7108, Oakland, CA 94601.
FOCUS: Guatemala. Bank of America • human rights • military sales • transnational corporations.
ACTIVITIES: Popular education • political action • letter-writing campaigns.
RESOURCES: Literature • reports • consultant services • speakers.

.2   **Corporate Data Exchange**, 198 Broadway, Rm. 706, New York, NY 10038. Tel: 212-962-2980.
FOCUS: International and national. Transnational corporations • corporate responsibility • stock ownership • organized labor • banking in South Africa • use of pension funds.
ACTIVITIES: Documentation and information • specialized research services • workshops and seminars.
RESOURCES: Publications • consultant services • research services.

.3   **Council on Economic Priorities**, 84 Fifth Ave., New York, NY 10011. Tel: 212-691-8550.
FOCUS: International and national. Transnational corporations • militarism • environment • corporate responsibility.
ACTIVITIES: Constituency education • research and writing • library services • media • workshops and seminars.

RESOURCES: Speakers • publications • consultant services • research services.
PERIODICALS: **9.4** *CEP Newsletter.* 10-12 times/year. With $15 annual membership. **9.5** *CEP Reports.* With *Newsletter* $25.

9.6   Data Center, 464 19 St., Oakland, CA 94612. Tel: 415-835-4692.

FOCUS: International and national. Human rights • transnational corporations • corporate responsibility • political economy • New Right and Moral Majority • plant shutdowns • foreign investment, trade and aid.

ACTIVITIES: Library services • search service • clipping services.

RESOURCES: Publications • bookstore • consultant services • research services • library • corporate profiles.

PERIODICALS: **9.7** *Data Center Newsletter.* Quarterly. With $15 annual membership (individuals); $35 (supporting); $100 or more (sustaining); $125 (organizational).

9.8   Global Electronics Information Project, c/o Pacific Studies Center, 222B View St., Mountain View, CA 94041. Tel: 415-969-1545.

FOCUS: International. Transnational corporations • electronics industry • women workers • chemical hazards.

ACTIVITIES: Popular education • research and writing • networking • library services.

RESOURCES: Research services • library • reports.

PERIODICALS: **9.9** *Global Electronics Information Newsletter.* Monthly. Minimum donation of $5/year.

9.10 Interfaith Center on Corporate Responsibility, 475 Riverside Dr., Rm. 566, New York, NY 10115. Tel: 212-870-2295 and 2293.

RELIGIOUS AFFILIATION: Sponsor-related movement of the National Council of Churches.

FOCUS: Third World general • international • Africa • Latin America. Militarism • disarmament • nuclear arms and energy • community reinvestment • transnational corporations • social justice • women • racism • corporate responsibility • domestic equality.

ACTIVITIES: Popular education • research and writing • congressional testimony • intern programs • shareholder resolutions.

RESOURCES: Speakers • literature • publications • reports.

PERIODICALS: **9.11** *The Corporate Examiner.* Monthly. $25/year.

9.12 Investor Responsibility Research Center, 1319 F St., NW, Suite 900, Washington, DC 20004. Tel: 202-833-3727.

FOCUS: National and international • South Africa • Chile. Infant formula • plant closings • corporate social responsibility and public policy • arms sales • trade • foreign policy • energy • nuclear power • health and safety • military conversion • equal employment opportunity • corporate political action committees • institutional investment • corporate structures.

ACTIVITIES: Research and writing • intern programs • library services • networking • media • documentation and information • policy-oriented research and writing • conferences • preparations for shareholder resolutions.

RESOURCES: Publications • consultant services • research services • library • reports • Proxy Issues Reports • Special Issues Reports • Surveys and Case Studies • annual index of IRRC publications.

PERIODICALS: **9.13** *News for Investors*. Monthly newsletter. $175/year.

SPECIAL PROJECTS: Corporate Governance Service: selective reporting on the changing role of corporations' boards of directors and on other corporate governance questions such as takeover proposals and executive compensation. Guidance for institutional investors in dealing with these issues. South Africa Review Service: periodic review of some fifty U.S. companies in South Africa and an analysis of their manner of operating there.

14　Northern California Interfaith Committee on Corporate Responsibility (NC-ICCR), 3410 19 St., San Francisco, CA 94110. Tel: 415-863-8060.

FOCUS: Global. Human rights • nuclear arms and energy • transnational corporations • military production • environmental issues • corporate responsibility • social justice.

ACTIVITIES: Constituency education • legislative action • networking • filing of shareholder resolutions on corporate responsibility issues for constituency.

RESOURCES: Speakers • publications • data bank on corporate responsibility for investors • resource service agency to membership dealing with specific corporations on specific issues.

PERIODICALS: **9.14** *Of Prophets and Profits*. Quarterly newsletter. $10/year or with $25 annual membership.

15　Transnational Institute, c/o Institute for Policy Studies, 1901 Q St., NW, Washington, DC 20009. Tel: 202-234-9382.

FOCUS: International. Racism • militarism • transnational corporations • political economy.

ACTIVITIES: Research and writing.

RESOURCES: Speakers • publications.

PERIODICALS: **9.16** *Race and Class*. Quarterly. $12/year individual; $15/year institutional.

17　Union for Radical Political Economics, Economics Education Project, 41 Union Sq. W., Rm. 901, New York, NY 10003. Tel: 212-691-5722.

FOCUS: International and national. Political economy • transnational corporations • socialism • foreign investment, trade and aid.

ACTIVITIES: Research and writing • workshops and seminars.

RESOURCES: Speakers • publications • reports.

PERIODICALS: **9.18** *Review of Radical Political Economics*. Quarterly magazine. $20/year or with $35 annual membership.

19　United Nations Centre on Transnational Corporations, United Nations, New York, NY 10017.

FOCUS: International. Political, economic and social effects of transnational corporations.

ACTIVITIES: Information analysis • policy analysis • advisory services.

RESOURCES: Publications • reports.

PERIODICALS: **9.20** *The CTC Reporter*. Quarterly. $3/issue.

PRINTED RESOURCES

Books

9.21   Barnet, Richard J., and Müller, Ronald E. *Global Reach: The Power of the Multinational Corporations*. New York: Simon and Schuster, 1974. 508pp. $4.95. Also available from the Institute for Policy Studies.

One of the most readable, incisive, and comprehensive studies of the twentieth century phenomenon of the transnational corporation. Barnet and Müller describe transnationals as "world managers" and study their impact both in the "underdeveloped world" and in the United States.

9.22   Bruyn, Severyn T.; Faramelli, Norman J.; and Yates, Dennis A. *An Ethical Primer on the Multinational Corporation*. New York: IDOC–North America, 1973. 46pp. Bibliography. Photocopy available from the Data Center. Payment of $5 must accompany order.

This primer describes the phenomenon of the multinational corporation, analyzes its impact from an ethical point of view, and proposes various strategies for action at the factory, national, regional, and world levels. Particular attention is given to appropriate action by religious institutions. A bibliography lists further readings and resources.

9.23   Corporate Data Exchange (CDE). *Banking & Finance: The Hidden Cost*. New York: Corporate Data Exchange, 1980. 60pp. $5

This textbook for the layperson covers nine financial industries including commercial banks, insurance companies, and investment banks. Emphasizing the rapidly growing trend toward greater concentration in the financial community, *Banking & Finance* describes what financial corporations do and how this affects people's jobs and communities.

9.24   Craig, Eleanor. *A Shareowners' Manual: for Church Committees on Social Responsibility in Investments*. New York: Interfaith Center on Corporate Responsibility, December 1977. 175pp. Looseleaf, three-hole punched. $3.50

A complete handbook on church shareholder action reviewing the rationale for the social responsibility of church investors and explaining the technicalities related to owning and voting shares of stock. Appendices contain a research guide, lists of resources, a case study of church activities on one company, and addresses of church groups across the country who are working on corporate responsibility.

9.25   Gilpin, Robert. *U.S. Power and the Multinational Corporation: The Political Economy of Foreign Direct Investment*. New York: Basic Books, 1975. 291pp. Cloth $10.95

Political scientist Robert Gilpin studies the costs and benefits of the multinational corporation from the point of view of the national interest—political and economic, foreign and domestic. His conclusions are that the costs of the multinational corporation for the U.S. economy are beginning to outweigh the benefits and that we should adjust our policy toward them accordingly.

26   Girvan, Norman. *Corporate Imperialism: Conflict and Expropriation: Transnational Corporations and Economic Nationalism in the Third World.* New York: Monthly Review, 1976. 241pp. $5.95

The author, director of the Caribbean Center for Corporate Research in Jamaica, describes in a historical, multi-disciplinary fashion, the ways in which foreign corporations dominate mineral exporting economies such as Chile, Guyana, and Jamaica. The sixth, and final, essay in this collection explores—from a Third World perspective—the issue of compensation for the expropriated property of foreign investors.

27   Green, Mark, and Massie, Jr., Robert, eds. Introduction by Ralph Nader. *The Big Business Reader: Essays on Corporate America.* New York: Pilgrim Press, 1980. 640pp. $4.95

The Big Business Reader brings together an awesome collection of critical analyses of the modern corporation. Big business is looked at from the point of view of consumers and labor; and it is studied in its relationship to health, natural resources, politics, and technology. The chapter on the impact of multinationals has articles on American banks in Chile, U.S. investments in South Africa, the dumping of hazardous products on foreign markets, and the marketing of baby formula in Third World countries.

28   Horowitz, David, ed. *Corporations and the Cold War.* New York: Monthly Review, 1969. 249pp. $3.95

This excellent collection of essays—edited and introduced by David Horowitz—begins with the question: Who makes United States foreign policy? Well-reasoned responses to this question from G. William Domhoff, William Appleman Williams, and others demonstrate that the Cold War foreign policy of the United States has often been shaped in response to the needs of a tiny corporate-based oligarchy and under the close supervision of that oligarchy.

29   Kirby, Donald J., S.J. *Prophesy vs. Profits: An Investment Dilemma for Churches.* Maryknoll, N.Y.: Orbis Books, Probe Series, 1980. 260pp. $13

An analysis of the church's concern for corporate responsibility, this study places the movement within the traditional Judeo-Christian concern for faith and justice, examining its theological and historical roots, and evaluating both theory and practice as it applies to three case studies.

30   Ledogar, Robert J. *Hungry for Profits: U.S. Food and Drug Multinationals in Latin America.* New York: IDOC–North America, 1976. $4.95. Available from ICCR.

A study of the impact of multinational food and drug corporations on consumers in Latin America. Includes an examination of Nestlé's marketing of infant formula, Ralston Purina in Colombia, Gulf & Western in the Dominican Republic, and Coca-Cola in Brazil.

31   Norris, Ruth, ed. *Pills, Pesticides & Profits: The International Trade in Toxic Substances.* Croton-on-Hudson, N.Y.: North River Press, 1982. 167pp. Cloth $10.95. Available from Caroline House Publishers.

This powerful book documents a little known but increasingly critical problem facing the United States and other nations: the export of toxic (and often U.S.-

banned) drugs, pesticides, and other substances to Third World nations. *Pills, Pesticides & Profits* names the exported products and who's exporting them. Contributors A. Karim Ahmed, S. Jacob Scherr, and Robert Richter describe the effects of this trade, why Americans should be concerned, and what's being done nationally and internationally to stop or regulate it.

Included in this book is the transcript of Robert Richter's two-part Public Broadcasting Service Documentary Film, *Pesticides & Pills: For Export Only* (see 9.77).

A student edition and other educational materials related to this book are available from the Council on International and Public Affairs.

9.32 Scheer, Robert. *America After Nixon: The Age of the Multinationals*. New York: McGraw-Hill Book Co., 1974. 326pp. Cloth $7.95

"The American economy," says author Robert Scheer, "is now so hopelessly intertwined with the world economy and so fully under the domination of its largest multinational corporations that any attempt to discuss our outstanding problems (be they inflation, waste, unemployment, or cultural alienation) without primary reference to the role of these corporations, is an act of deception."

America After Nixon is Scheer's case for the prosecution. His thesis is "that the public political process no longer rules this nation, that current political debate does not deal with what is most important, and that the basic decisions about our future are being made for us by several hundred super-large multinational corporations, themselves out of control."

9.33 United Nations. *Transnational Corporations in World Development: A Reexamination*. United Nations, N.Y.: UN Economic and Social Council, 1978. 343pp. $12. Sales No. E.78.II.A.5. E/C.10/38.

This major study, prepared for the UN Commission on Transnational Corporations, situates transnational corporations (TNCs) in their international setting, examines the policies of host and home countries toward TNCs, and sketches some ideas for strengthening the capacity of various "actors" to deal with TNCs. One-half of the book is devoted to analytical and statistical annexes.

See also:
2.36, 2.44, 2.47, 2.50, 2.52, 4.44, 4.45, 4.51, 4.67, 6.31, 6.32, 6.42, 6.43, 6.45, 8.45. 10.28

Periodicals

9.34 *Asia Monitor*, Asia Monitor Resource Center, 2 Man Wan Rd., 17-C, Kowloon, Hongkong. Quarterly. $22/year.

A quarterly digest and index of news of the activities of transnational corporations in the developing nations of Asia as reported in the major English-language newspapers and business journals of the region.

9.35 *The Corporate Examiner*, Interfaith Center for Corporate Responsibility, 475 Riverside Dr., Rm. 566, New York, NY 10115. Monthly. $25/year.

An eight-page newsletter examining policies and practices of major U.S. corporations with regard to labor, environment, consumerism, equal employment, minorities, women, agribusiness, military production, government, and foreign investment. *The Corporate Examiner* carries news of stockholder actions by church groups. Includes notice of new publications.

.36   *The CTC Reporter*, UN Centre on Transnational Corporations, UN Publications, Rm. A3315, United Nations, NY 10017. Quarterly. $3 per issue.

This 56-page magazine is particularly useful for those with a more technical interest in the operations of transnationals. *The Reporter* includes coverage of the work done by each of the UNCTC's three divisions: Information Analysis, Policy Analysis, and Advisory Services, as well as feature articles and a substantial book review section.

.37   *Mother Jones*, 1886 Haymarket Sq., Marion, OH 43305 (business office). 10 issues/year. $16/year.

Mother Jones is known for its hard-hitting investigative reports on corporate abuses.

.38   *Multinational Monitor*, 1346 Connecticut Ave., NW, Rm 411, Washington, DC 20036. 12 issues/year. $15/year.

This informative journal tracks big business activity across the globe, offering a citizen's perspective on corporate power in the international arena.

Pamphlets and Articles

For information on guidelines for social responsibility adopted for use by various Protestant and Catholic church agencies see *Other Resources* below.

.39   *Amazing Grace: The W.R. Grace Corporation*. *NACLA's Latin America & Empire Report* 10, no. 3, March 1976. 32pp. $2.50. Available from NACLA and from the Data Center.

This special issue of NACLA's monthly magazine is an excellent example of critical corporate research at its best. Though it lapses into "radical rhetoric" at times, *Amazing Grace* is a well-researched, informative analysis of Grace's involvement in Latin America and other areas of the Third World.

.40   *The Bottle Baby Lawsuit: the Sisters of the Precious Blood vs. Bristol-Myers*. ICCR. *CIC Brief* 6-4, April 1977. 4pp. 60 cents. Bulk rates available.

Documentation about the legal actions surrounding the involvement of Bristol-Myers in the promotion and sale of infant formula overseas.

.41   *Car Wars*. Marg Hainer and Joanne Koslofsky. *NACLA Report on the Americas* 13, no. 4, July–August 1979. 48pp. $2.50. Available from NACLA and from the Data Center.

Car Wars outlines the historical development of the U.S. automobile industry and studies its growth in Latin America. This special issue of NACLA's bi-monthly magazine analyzes the phenomenon of the "world car" and speculates about the international unity of auto workers.

9.42   *Christian Mission and Multinationals: Friends or Foes? e/sa forum* 82, May 1982. No. 2082. 31pp. 60 cents. Bulk rates available.

This *forum* examines multinationals from ethical and theological points of view and takes a critical look at their operations in the Third World.

9.43   *Church Proxy Resolutions.* Sr. Valerie Heinonen. ICCR, January 1979. 96pp. $2.50.

A compilation of proxy resolutions submitted in the areas of agribusiness, community reinvestment, domestic equality, infant formula, military, transnational corporations, and human development. Includes alphabetical index of corporations and resolution sponsors.

9.44   *Coca-Cola and Human Rights in Guatemala.* Robert Morris. ICCR *CIC Brief,* November 1980. 4pp. 60 cents. Bulk rates available.

This well-researched ICCR. *Brief* describes in detail tragic events that took place in 1980 in Coca-Cola's franchise operation in Guatemala. Morris analyzes the U.S. corporation's response and that of U.S. government officials in the country.

9.45   *Corporate Responsibility: Packet.* United Methodist Church, Board of Global Ministries. $2. Available from the UMC Service Center.

Articles and brochures dealing with the issue of corporate responsibility as it relates to churches and the lives of oppressed peoples.

9.46   *Corporate Social Responsibility Actions, 1979–1981: Report to the Thirteenth General Synod of the United Church of Christ.* 1981. 27pp. $1. Available from the World Issues Office of the United Church Board for World Ministries.

This report by various agencies of the United Church of Christ presents a history and analysis of UCC stockholder actions on Ford and General Motors in South Africa, Bristol-Myers on infant formula, Atlantic Richfield on plant closings, and other issues.

9.47   *Corporate Social Responsibility Challenges, Spring 1982. The Corporate Examiner* 11, no. 1, January 1982. 8pp. 75 cents

This special annual issue of *The Corporate Examiner* lists companies and church agencies involved in shareholder resolutions. The annual review includes a breakdown and discussion of the resolutions under the headings: agribusiness, community reinvestment, domestic equality, energy, infant formula, military, transnational corporations. Annual meeting dates of the companies concerned are listed.

9.48   *The Crisis of the Corporation.* Richard J. Barnet. The Transnational Institute, a program of the Institute for Policy Studies, 1975. 28pp. $1.50. Available from IPS.

This essay analyzes global corporate power and economic transformation, the decline of the corporate myth, and possibilities for the reinvigoration of American democracy.

9.49   *An Evaluation of the Gulf & Western Critique of "Guess Who's Coming to Breakfast."* Dr. Henry J. Frundt. ICCR, October 1978. 35pp. $1

An evaluation of Gulf & Western's criticism of the Packard Manse Media slideshow dealing with the company's operations in the Dominican Republic.

.50 *The Ford Report.* Counter Information Services, London, 1978. 68pp. $2.50. Available from the Institute for Policy Studies.

This "anti-report" by CIS, a London affiliate of the Institute for Policy Studies, is a comprehensive and well-documented study of the Ford Motor Company. The report deals with Ford's activities in South Africa, its role in the Common Market, its plans for the Third World, wages and working conditions, death on the job, profits and production, and Ford's blueprint for the future.

.51 *Gulf & Western in the Dominican Republic: an Evaluation.* Dr. Henry J. Frundt. ICCR, 1979. 110pp. $2.50

An analysis of the reports issued by Gulf & Western Industries in response to church shareholder requests.

.52 *Imperialism in the Silicon Age.* A. Sivanandan. 16pp. $1. Available from the Institute for Policy Studies.

Sivanandan's essay deals with the nature and operations of imperialism in the age of microelectronic technology.

.53 *The Infiltration of the UN System by Multinational Corporations: Excerpts from Internal Files.* 1978. 58pp. Photocopy available from the Data Center. Payment of $5 must accompany order.

This fascinating document consists of excerpts from highly confidential minutes and correspondence of six large Swiss multinationals that describe the ways in which the MNCs sought to infiltrate and frustrate the work of the United Nations Centre on Transnational Corporations.

.54 *Investing Church Funds for Maximum Social Impact.* United Church of Christ, 1970. 61pp. Available in photocopy from the World Issues Office, United Church Board for World Ministries.

This report from the Committee on Financial Investments of the United Church of Christ illustrates the way in which one church set about establishing criteria and making recommendations "toward substantial use of investments of all national Instrumentalities and Conferences (of the UCC) to promote maximum social impact based upon General Synod policies."

.55 *Investment Policies: Does Being a Christian Matter?* n.d. 6-panel brochure. Free. Available from the General Counsel of the Christian Church (Disciples of Christ).

Investment Policies is an abbreviated presentation of a longer, formal statement by the Christian Church entitled *Ethical Guidelines for Investment Policies.* It suggests questions for reflection and highlights factors affecting responsible investments.

.56 *Kennecott Copper Corporation and Mining Development in Wisconsin.* Al Gedicks. Community Action on Latin America (CALA), 1974. 49pp. $1

Though this study of Kennecott focuses particularly on the copper company's involvement in Wisconsin, it also discusses the multinational's operations overseas, e.g., in Chile and Puerto Rico.

9.57   *Multinational Corporations and Global Development*. *Hunger* 24, July 1980.
8pp. 15 cents. Bulk rates available.

This issue of *Hunger* tackles the question: do multinational corporations help
or hinder development? The conclusion the authors come to is that the effects of
multinationals on development are predominantly negative. They explain why
their study and research has led them to make this judgment and they propose
some policy changes that could help in regulating the activities of these corporate
giants.

9.58   *Multinational Corporations' Effects on the Third World: A Statement for
Peacemakers in Mission*. Peacemakers in Mission, 1981. 9-panel brochure. Inquire for price.

This handy brochure describes the activities of various U.S. multinational corporations in the Third World.

9.59   *The Multinationals in Asia*. Pharis J. Harvey. *Christianity & Crisis* 36, no. 4,
March 15, 1976. 6pp. 50 cents for the entire 12-page issue.

A church worker with long years of experience in Northeast Asia describes the
political and economic impact of U.S. multinational corporations in South Korea
and other parts of Asia.

9.60   *The New Gnomes: Multinational Banks in the Third World*. Howard M.
Wachtel. Transnational Institute, 1977. 60pp. Bibliography. Available from the
Institute for Policy Studies.

Who are the multinational banks and where do they come from? How "exposed" are they in the Third World and how responsible are they for the enormous debts of Third World nations? TNI Fellow Howard Wachtel tackles these
and other questions in this clearly presented pamphlet.

9.61   *Rockwell International*. John Markoff, Roger Walke, and John Woodman-
see. With a Foreword by G. William Domhoff. 1975. 68pp. $3.50. Available in
photocopy from the Pacific Northwest Research Center.

This booklet studies the history of Rockwell and its relationship to the production of the B-1 bomber.

9.62   *The Social Accountability of the Corporation*. *ICUIS Occasional Paper* 6, January 1975. 43pp. $2, and *ICUIS Bibliography Series No. 2*, March 1975. 32pp.
$3. Both available directly from ICUIS.

The first ICUIS booklet consists of two papers presented at a consultation on
the social accountability of the corporation at McCormick Theological Seminary
in Chicago in late 1974. The first paper, by Frank Cassell, is entitled: "The Social
Cost of Doing Business." The second, "Multinational Corporations in Less Developed Countries: Impact and Accountability," is by Walter Owensby, a fra-
ternal worker in Bogotá, Colombia.

The accompanying *ICUIS Bibliography* takes as its main focus the question of
corporate accountability. How can multinationals be made accountable for the
power and wealth they hold and for the effects they have on the global economy?
ICUIS performs a double service: first, by producing this excellent bibliography,
and second, by providing access through the ICUIS retrieval service to material
that is often hard to locate.

9.63   *Transnational Corporations in Asia.* Thomas P. Fenton. A series of four articles from the *Maryknoll* magazine (Spring 1982). 25 pp. Available from the author at 464 19 St., Oakland, CA 94612. $2.50 for the set (payment must accompany order).

This popularly written series covers the shutdown of plants in the United States and investments by U.S. transnational corporations in Asia. The impact of plant closings and foreign investments is evaluated as it involves both U.S. and Asian workers.

9.64   *The United Nations and Transnational Corporations.* Roger Naumann. AFSC, February 1978. 8pp. 20 cents

A Quaker International Affairs Report giving background on the work of the Intergovernmental Commission on Transnational Corporations, and the activities of the Centre on Transnational Corporations of the UN.

9.65   *U.S. Bank Loans to Chile.* ICCR, *CIC Brief* 7-12, December 1978. 4pp. 60 cents. Bulk rates available.

This *CIC Brief* is excerpted from an issue paper published by the Institute for Policy Studies, *Human Rights, Economic Aid and Private Banks*, by Isabel Letelier and Michael Moffitt.

9.66   *Weapons for the World Update: The U.S. Corporate Role in International Arms Transfers.* Steven Lydenberg. Council on Economic Priorities, 1977. $3

Weapons for the World profiles the ten U.S. corporations most extensively involved in U.S. arms exports in 1976.

9.67   *Yanqui Dollar: The Contribution of U.S. Private Investment to Underdevelopment in Latin America.* NACLA, 1971. 64pp. $1.50. Available from NACLA and from the Data Center.

Though dated, this solidly researched study stands as a major contribution to a critical understanding of the impact of U.S. investments in Latin America.

See also:
2.65, 2.73, 2.78, 2.87, 2.88, 2.106, 3.110, 6.54, 6.58, 6.62, 6.64, 6.71, 6.72, 8.87, 8.99, 8.102, 10.56, 10.57, 10.58, 10.66, 10.67, 10.73

AUDIOVISUAL RESOURCES

9.68   *Bottle Babies*. 1975 26 min color film. Peter Krieg/Teldik Films. Unifilm.
Rental $35. Also available from the Institute for Peace and Justice.

This is the original award-winning documentary, originally entitled *Nestlé
Kills Babies*, that first brought the dangers of infant formula malnutrition
to widespread public attention. *Bottle Babies* shows the tragic and disastrous consequences for people when corporations, faced with stagnating
markets at home, push their expensive artificial formulas in underdeveloped
countries.

The Institute for Peace and Justice has prepared a packet of action strategies to
accompany this fine film.

9.69   *Bread, Justice and Multinational Corporations*. 1979 3 color filmstrips with
cassette tapes. 15 min each. Institute for Peace and Justice. Rental $11 each. Sale
$73 for the set. Also available for rent from the 8th Day Center ($15 each).

Three Bread and Justice filmstrips accompany James McGinnis' excellent
study of multinational corporations, *Bread & Justice: Toward a New International Economic Order* (see 1.128 and 6.40).

1. *Bread, Justice, and Trade* looks at trade relations between the rich and poor
nations and tells how these unbalanced relationships perpetuate poverty and
hunger in Third World countries.

2. *Bread, Justice, and Multinational Corporations* illustrates what a multinational corporation is and how it is organized. It shows the effects MNCs have on
people, especially the small farmer, the farm worker, and the consumer.

3. *Bread, Justice, and Global Interdependence* approaches the subject of the
ideal "global city" and recommends ways in which students can move toward this
ideal in their own lives.

9.70   *The Churches and the Multinationals*. A television program aired in June 1977
in the CBS "Look Up and Live" series. 28 min color. Available from the World
Issues Office, United Church Board for World Ministries. Apply for rates.

This stimulating program features interviews with church officials and
with representatives of multinational corporations such as Exxon and Control
Data.

9.71   *The Conspiracy: Or How Transnationals Do It*. 1978 26 min color film.
Directed by Nicole Duchene and Claude Lortie. Produced by Les Films Sur Place
Enr., L'Institute Quebecois du Cinema, L'ORTQ. Unifilm. Rental $75.

Decisions made by transnational corporations affect us at every level: the policies of the government, the economy of the country, and the family budget. How
did the transnationals achieve such a range of operations and what are the implications of their international control? *The Conspiracy* is a didactic film that tries
to answer these and other questions as simply as possible, using animation, black
and white prints, and live-action color footage.

9.72   *Controlling Interest: The World of the Multinational Corporation.* 1978 45
         min color film. California Newsreel. Rental $60 Sale $575. Also available from
         the 8th Day Center ($15); AFSC (Cambridge) ($20); and the Institute for Policy
         Studies.
             This award-winning film reveals the connections between such phenomena
         as economic development, runaway shops, world hunger, human rights viola-
         tions, U.S. foreign policy, and the growing power of the multinational corpor-
         ation.
             Translated into eight languages and broadcast in a dozen countries, *Control-
         ling Interest* has become almost universally recognized as indispensable viewing
         for anyone interested in the growing impact of multinational corporations on the
         world economy and global affairs.
             California Newsreel has prepared a discussion guide to accompany the film.

9.73   *Factories for the Third World: Tunisia.* 1979 43 min color film. Gordian Troel-
         ler and Marie Claude Deffarge. Icarus. Rental $75 Sale $650 (16mm); $420
         (video).
             Factories for the Third World analyzes the extent and consequences of the new
         international division of labor that has resulted from increased foreign invest-
         ments in the manufacturing sectors of Third World economies. The film looks at
         the history of economic change and development in Tunisia, the reality of the new
         factory life for the Tunisian people, and some of the responses of the Tunisian
         working class to these developments.
             Factories also examines the history of the labor movement in Tunisia, in par-
         ticular the crackdown and suppression of the unions in 1978 and analyzes the
         elements in the Islamic reaction to the growing influence of Western culture
         and Western economic forces.

9.74   *Formula Factor.* 1977 30 min color film. Produced by the Canadian Broadcast-
         ing Co. California Newsreel. Rental $40
             Formula Factor highlights the efforts of governments, concerned health
         workers, and church organizations to challenge company baby formula market-
         ing practices in the Third World. In the film, Jamaica is portrayed as an example
         of a country struggling to develop appropriate infant care programs and curb
         unnecessary corporate marketing of formula.

9.75   *Guess Who's Coming to Breakfast?* 16 min color slideshow with cassette tape.
         Produced by Packard Manse Media Project. Rental $10. Also available from
         AFSC (Cambridge) and the 8th Day Center ($15).
             Focusing on Gulf & Western in the Dominican Republic, this non-rhetorical
         and low-key slideshow examines the impact of transnational corporations on
         world economic development. It very effectively juxtaposes the misery caused by
         the multinational corporation abroad with its benign image in the United States,
         creating in the show's viewers a sense of shock, concern, and interest in the issues
         raised.

9.76 *Into the Mouths of Babes*. 1978 30 min color film. Bill Moyers, CBS Reports. California Newsreel. Rental $40. Also available from AFSC (Cambridge) ($15); NCC TV Film Library ($25); and the 8th Day Center ($15).

Multinational corporations are selling the image of a well-fed, thriving "Westernized" baby as they market infant formula to mothers of the Third World. This documentary, with Bill Moyers reporting, vividly depicts the situation through extensive documentation and interviews from the Dominican Republic where the promotion of bottle feeding has been directly linked to rising mortality among infants. The experiences of mothers and health workers confirm the far-reaching and deadly implications of this problem.

9.77 *Pesticides and Pills: For Export Only*. 1981 2 color films. 60 min each. Produced by Robert Richter. Robert Richter Productions. Apply for rental rates.

Two one-hour films document the sale by multinationals of prohibited and restricted pesticides and of drugs known to cause cancer, birth deformities, even death. (See 9.31.)

9.78 *Sharing Global Resources: Toward a New Economic Order*. 1977 35 min color slideshow or filmstrip, with tape, documentation, and study/action guide. Spanish language version available. NARMIC, c/o AFSC (Philadelphia). Rental $15. Sale $50 (slideshow); $45 (filmstrip). Also available from the Institute for Peace and Justice and AFSC (Cambridge).

Sharing Global Resources effectively presents the need for a new international economic order and for a new internal economic order within Third World countries.

See also:
2.98, 3.170, 6.77, 6.78, 6.80, 6.82, 6.85, 6.88

OTHER RESOURCES

Corporate Social Responsibility and the Churches

Many Protestant and Catholic member organizations of the **Interfaith Center on Corporate Responsibility** have developed guidelines for social responsibility in investment, as well as other educational materials on corporate responsibility. Write to these organizations for further information:

9.79   **American Baptist Churches in the U.S.A.** Contact: Office of Christian Responsibility in Investments, National Ministries, American Baptist Churches, Valley Forge, PA 19481.

9.80   **Christian Church (Disciples of Christ).** Contact: General Counsel, Christian Church (Disciples of Christ), Box 1986, Indianapolis, IN 46206.

9.81   **Coalition for Responsible Investment,** 20 Washington Sq., New York, NY 10011.

9.82   **Episcopal Church.** Contact: Public Affairs Officer, Executive Council of the Episcopal Church, 815 Second Ave., New York, NY 10017.

9.83   **General Executive Board, Presbyterian Church,** U.S. Contact: Staff Associate for Corporate Witness in Public Affairs, General Executive Board, Presbyterian Church in the U.S., 341 Ponce de Leon Ave., NE, Atlanta, GA 30308.

9.84   **Lutheran Church in America.** Contact: Division for Mission in North America, Lutheran Church in America, 231 Madison Ave., New York, NY 10016.

9.85   **National Catholic Coalition for Responsible Investment,** 1016 N. Ninth St., Milwaukee, WI 53233.

9.86   **Reformed Church in America.** Contact: General Secretary, Reformed Church in America, 475 Riverside Dr., Rm. 1812, New York, NY 10115.

9.87   **United Church of Christ.** Contact: World Issues Office, United Church Board for World Ministries, 475 Riverside Dr., New York, NY 10115.

9.88   **United Methodist Church.** Contact: Council on Finance and Administration, United Methodist Church, 1200 Davis St., Evanston, IL 60201.

9.89   **United Presbyterian Church in the U.S.A.** Contact: Church and Society Program Area, Program Agency, UPCUSA, Rm. 1244K, 475 Riverside Dr., New York, NY 10115.

For a complete list of ICCR members write and request a copy of the Center's latest annual report.

Corporate Research Guides

9.90   AFL-CIO, Food and Beverage Trades Department. *Manual of Corporate Investigation.* Washington, D.C.: AFL-CIO, Food and Beverage Trades Dept., 1978. 57pp. $7.50

This spiral-bound research guide covers a wide variety of resources, including company publications, labor profiles and industrial relations sources, and guides to corporate structure and subsidiaries. It includes, as well, suggestions about how to conduct interviews and an excellent "catalogue of corporate strategies."

9.91   Asia Monitor Resource Center (formerly the Asia/North America Communications Center). *America in Asia: Research Guides on U.S. Economic Activity in Pacific Asia*. 1979. 160pp. $10 plus postage

The aim of this bound set of ten research guides is to provide anyone concerned about U.S. economic power in Asia with a complete listing of primary, in-country sources of information on U.S. investments in, trade with, and loans and aid to these Pacific Asian nations/regions: Hongkong, Indonesia, Japan, South Korea, Malaysia, Philippines, Singapore, Taiwan, and Thailand. In addition, *America in Asia* contains a guide to sources that are regional in origin or regional in focus.

9.92   Corporate Action Project. *Corporate Action Guide*. Washington, D.C.: Corporate Action Project, 1974. 104pp. Out of print.

This guide was designed "to be informative about the nature and dynamics of the corporate system, to be a resource and empowering tool, and to offer some encouragement to those who have become accustomed to frustration and powerlessness." It offers both a narrative introduction to the nature and operations of international corporations and a research and action guide.

9.93   Council on Economic Priorities. *Minding the Corporate Conscience: Public Interest Groups and Corporate Social Accountability*. New York: CEP, 1977. 113pp.

This guide contains over eighty pages of profiles of public interest groups that are concerned with corporate social accountability, as well as lists of other related groups and of additional resources.

9.94   Hernes, Helga. *The Multinational Corporation: A Guide to Information Sources*. Volume 4 in the International Relations Series. Detroit: Gale Research Co., 1976. 190pp. Bibliographies, indexes. Cloth $18

This guide is actually an extended, annotated bibliography on the subject of multinational corporations. Herne's informed and readable survey of the literature covers the multinational corporation (1) as a large organization, (2) and the nation state, and (3) in the international system. Issues treated include corporate strategies and ideologies; the impact on labor; and theories and determinants of direct foreign investment.

The Multinational Corporation concludes with a brief periodicals directory and a recommended library list and with indexes of authors, titles, and subjects.

9.95   North American Congress on Latin America. *NACLA Research Methodology Guide*. New York: NACLA, 1971. 72pp. $2.50. Available also from the Data Center.

In 72 fact-filled pages this guide covers all aspects of corporate power—from the military-industrial complex to the church, from the health industry to the police. Chapter Five on Researching Underdeveloped Countries is divided into fifteen sections, including in-country sources, foreign investment, banking and finance, and radical research organizations, periodicals, and studies.

9.96   Noyes, Dan. *Raising Hell: A Citizen's Guide to the Fine Art of Investigation*.
San Francisco: Mother Jones, 1979. 32pp. Premium with subscription to *Mother
Jones* magazine (see 9.37).

Dan Noyes of the San Francisco-based Investigative Resource Center, con-
denses a wealth of investigative experience and resources into this short booklet.
Raising Hell covers corporations, government, property, public records, and individuals. It also includes a handy "Investigative Checklist" and an "Essential
Investigative Library."

9.97   Rose, Stephen; Hoffman, Joan; Greenhouse, Morton; and Spero, Nat. *How
to Research a Corporation*. New York: Union for Radical Political Economics,
1980. 23pp. $3.50

This booklet includes chapters on searching for data on profits, wages and
benefits, and for basic facts about a corporation.

9.98   Urban Planning Aid. *Open the Books: How to Research a Corporation*. Cambridge, Mass.: Urban Planning Aid, 1974. 100pp. $4.40. Available from the
Midwest Academy, Inc.

Chapter One is specifically focused on researching a multinational corporation: it tells how to discover a company's overseas investments, its ownership, its
subsidiaries, and labor conditions in its overseas operations. *Open the Books*
gives some explanation of the domestic U.S. corporate economy and explains
how to read a company's financial statements.

See also:
10.113

Chapter 10

Women

KEY RESOURCES

Organizations

A good place to begin is with the **Nationwide Women's Program** of the **American Friends Service Committee**. This group is in touch with a variety of other movements and resources throughout the United States. They have particular expertise in the area of women and global corporations.

ISIS, one of the few groups outside the United States listed in this book, is important as an international resource and documentation center. **ISIS** coordinates the International Feminist Network and has probably the richest treasury of resource materials (in fact and on file) of any women's group as well as one of the best communications networks. This network is particularly outstanding in Third World countries.

Certain of the churches have active women's programs: the **Methodist Church** has its Women's Division; the **United Presbyterian Church**, its Third World Women's Coordinating Committee. **Church Women United** is an ecumenical group.

Printed Resources

All of Margaret Randall's books, Stephanie Urdang's *Fighting Two Colonialisms: Women in Guinea-Bissau*, and Gail Omvedt's *We Will Smash This Prison* portray well the double struggle women face. Two books—contrasts in style but not in essence—deal with women and transnational corporations: Linda Lim's study on *Multinational Firms and Manufacturing for Export in Less-Developed Countries* and the **Christian Conference of Asia Women Workers' Concerns Project** book, *Struggling to Survive*.

ISIS Women's International Bulletin and the *AFSC Women's Newsletter* lead the way in periodicals. Both are regularly packed with useful reports and resources.

Getting your name on the mailing lists of the **Women's International League for Peace and Freedom (WILPF)** and the **Women's International Resource Exchange (WIRE)** is the best way to stay abreast of current articles.

NACLA has published several issues of its magazine that are about women and Latin America: a 1975 issue devoted to *Woman's Labor* contains theoretical material that is not outdated; other more recent issues deal with the electronics industry and runaway shops on the Mexican border. Patricia Fernandez Kelly's articles on Mexican women workers and their exploitation on the US-Mexican border are also of interest in this area. *The Changing Role of Asian Women*, a joint issue of the *Southeast Asia Chronicle* and *Pacific Research*, presents a good overview of women and transnational corporations in Asia.

Audiovisual Resources

Two fine resources deal with women and population control. One of these, a film called *The Blood of the Condor*, is somewhat dated but still powerful. It hints at some of the elements that *Pieces of the Population Puzzle* makes explicit. This slideshow covers government policies and agribusiness power, placing the population question in perspective. Women's unique relationship to human rights in Chile is the focus of **AFSC**'s slideshow *Four Women's Stories* and the film *The Dead Are Not Silent*.

National liberation, exploitation by U.S. companies, and women's growth toward active participation in change are all shown in two exceptional films: *Women in Arms* and *My Country Occupied*.

Other Resources

ISIS has a series of bibliographies that are unmatched in quality and comprehensiveness: *Bottle Babies*, *Directory of Women and Health* (co-published with the **Boston Women's Health Book Collective**), and *Women in Development*. The *AFSC Nationwide Women's Program Bibliography* is also a valuable resource.

The **Women's International Resource Exchange Service**'s several resource packets cover topics on women in El Salvador, in Nicaragua, in southern Africa, and in the Third World generally.

AFSC's *Women in a Hungry World* and the **United Methodist**'s *Human Rights of Women* are two other useful packets of materials.

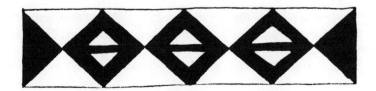

ORGANIZATIONS

10.1   **American Friends Service Committee**, Nationwide Women's Program, 1501
Cherry St., Philadelphia, PA 19102. Tel: 215-241-7160.
RELIGIOUS AFFILIATION: Religious Society of Friends (Quakers).
FOCUS: Third World general • international. Women • transnational corpora-
tions • labor • human rights • refugees • militarism • disarmament • reproductive
rights • lesbian and gay rights • political economy.
ACTIVITIES: Program development and resourcing within AFSC network •
initiatives between AFSC and international feminist movement • popular edu-
cation • networking • documentation and information • political action.
RESOURCES: Speakers • audiovisuals • literature • publications • reports.
PERIODICALS: **10.2** *AFSC Women's Newsletter.* 3 issues/year. $5–$10 donation encouraged. **10.3** *Women and Global Corporations.* 8–12 page insert in
Women's Newsletter.

10.4   **Church Women United**, 475 Riverside Dr., Rm. 812, New York, NY 10115. Tel:
212-870-2347.
RELIGIOUS AFFILIATION: Ecumenical.
FOCUS: International and national. Human rights • militarism • disarmament •
nuclear arms and energy • international awareness • national liberation strug-
gles • corporate responsibility • social justice.
ACTIVITIES: Constituency education • political action • networking • overseas
project support • justice and peace ministries • workshops.
RESOURCES: Speakers • publications.
PERIODICALS: **10.5** *The Church Woman.* Bimonthly. $6/year. **10.6** *lead time.*
Bimonthly. $6/year ($11/year for both).

10.7   **Coalition for Women in International Development**, c/o Overseas Education
Fund, 2101 L St., NW, Suite 916, Washington, DC 20037. Tel: 202-466-3430.
FOCUS: International • Third World general. Women • development • U.S.
foreign policy • UN Decade for Women.
ACTIVITIES: Constituency education • political action • legislative action • con-
gressional testimony • networking • preparations for UN Decade for Women
conferences • policy-oriented research and writing.
RESOURCES: Consultant services • publications • reports.

10.8   **International Center for Research on Women**, 1010 16 St., NW, 3d Floor,
Washington, DC 20036. Tel: 202-293-3154.
FOCUS: International. Economic development • women • social change • em-
ployment.
ACTIVITIES: Applied, policy-relevant research • technical assistance • develop-
ment of strategies for urban and rural women • information dissemination •
popular education.
RESOURCES: Consultant services • reports • resource library • publications.

10.9 **International Defense and Aid Fund for Southern Africa**, The Women's Committee, Box 17, Cambridge, MA 02138. Tel: 617-491-8343.

FOCUS: Southern Africa. Women • labor • apartheid • refugees.

ACTIVITIES: Popular education • networking • solidarity work • documentation and information.

RESOURCES: Speakers • literature • publications • consultant services.

0.10 **International Women's Tribune Centre**, 305 E. 46 St., New York, NY 10017. Tel: 212-421-5633.

FOCUS: International. Women • development • United Nations.

ACTIVITIES: Technical services • information • networking • training.

RESOURCES: Audiovisuals • publications • reports • consultant services • issue papers • training manuals.

PERIODICALS: **10.11** *International Women's Tribune Centre Newsletter.* Quarterly. $5/year. Spanish language edition also available. Free to Third World groups and individuals.

0.12 **ISIS**, Women's International Information and Communication Service, Via dell'Anima 30, Rome, Italy. Tel: 06 • 65 65 842. Case Postale 50 (Cornavin), 1211 Geneva 2, Switzerland. Tel: 022 • 33 67 46.

FOCUS: International. Women • political repression • transnational corporations • national liberation struggles • social justice • militarism • technology.

ACTIVITIES: Documentation and information • networking • research and writing • media.

RESOURCES: Literature • publications • study-action guides • research services.

PERIODICALS: **10.13** *ISIS International Bulletin.* Quarterly. $15/year individual; $25/year institutional.

SPECIAL PROJECTS: International Feminist Network.

0.14 **The United Methodist Church**, Board of Global Ministries, Women's Division, 475 Riverside Dr., 15th Floor, New York, NY 10115. Tel: 212-678-6099.

FOCUS: Third World general. Human rights • women • political repression • militarism • transnational corporations • corporate responsibility • social justice.

ACTIVITIES: Constituency education • political action • foreign service • project support.

RESOURCES: Consultant services.

0.15 **United Presbyterian Church in the U.S.A.** Third World Women's Coordinating Committee, 475 Riverside Dr., Rm. 1164, New York, NY 10115. Tel: 212-870-2885.

FOCUS: Third World general. Human rights • political repression • transnational corporations • political economy • international awareness • national liberation struggles • corporate responsibility • social justice • women.

ACTIVITIES: Constituency education • political action • legislative action • solidarity work • networking • workshops and seminars.

10.16 Women Strike for Peace, 145 S. 13 St., Philadelphia, PA 19107. Tel: 215-923-0861.

FOCUS: International. Militarism • disarmament • nuclear weapons and testing • women.

ACTIVITIES: Popular education • networking • political action.

RESOURCES: Speakers • literature • publications.

10.17 Women's International League for Peace and Freedom, 1213 Race St., Philadelphia, PA 19107. Tel: 215-563-7110.

FOCUS: International. Human rights • militarism • disarmament • nuclear arms and energy • transnational corporations • self-determination • economic development • nonviolence • military spending • women • United Nations • civil liberties.

ACTIVITIES: Popular education • political action • legislative action • public meetings • education of children and youth • networking • study groups.

RESOURCES: Speakers • literature • consultant services.

PERIODICALS: **10.18** *Peace and Freedom*. Monthly newsletter. With membership.

10.19 Women's Institute for Freedom of the Press, 3306 Ross Pl., NW, Washington, DC 20008. Tel: 202-966-7783.

FOCUS: International and national. Human rights • women.

ACTIVITIES: Publishing • networking • media • documentation and information.

RESOURCES: Publications • curriculum guides • reports.

PERIODICALS: **10.20** *Media Report to Women*. Bimonthly. $20/year.

SPECIAL PROJECTS: Development of courses on media and women. Annual conference on planning a national and international communications system for women.

10.21 Women's International Network, 187 Grant St., Lexington, MA 02173. Tel: 617-862-9431.

FOCUS: Third World general • international. Third World women • human rights • women's rights.

ACTIVITIES: Networking • popular education.

RESOURCES: Speakers • literature • study-action guides • research services.

PERIODICALS: **10.22** *WIN News*. Quarterly magazine. $20/year.

10.23 Women's International Resource Exchange Service (WIRE), 2700 Broadway, Rm. 7, New York, NY 10025. Tel: 212-666-4622.

FOCUS: Third World general. Political repression • transnational corporations • political economy • socialism • international awareness • national liberation struggles • corporate responsibility • social justice • women.

ACTIVITIES: Political action • research and writing • solidarity work • networking • documentation and information.

RESOURCES: Literature • publications • annotated catalog of materials available through **WIRE**.

PRINTED RESOURCES

Books

.24   Barrios de Chungara, Domitila, with Moema Viezzar. *Let Me Speak! Testimony of Domitila, a Woman of the Bolivian Mines.* New York: Monthly Review Press, 1979. 235pp. $6.50

Let Me Speak! is the courageous story of a Bolivian woman and the social and economic circumstances that led her to pro-Marxist political action as a leader of a Housewives' Committee dedicated to improving miners' and peasants' conditions. Domitila Barrios de Chungara—herself the wife of a miner—gives a vivid account of her activities and brutal imprisonment. She offers observations on the clergy, military, and upper classes in Bolivia and charges them with abandoning the poor.

.25   Boulding, Elise. *Women in the Twentieth Century World.* New York: Halsted Press, 1977. $15.95

Focusing on women's economic activities, this book explores the differences between women in the industrialized world and in the Third World.

.26   Caplan, Patricia, and Bujra, Janet M., eds. *Women United, Women Divided.* Bloomington, Ind.: Indiana University Press, 1979. 304pp. Cloth $15. Available from Modern Times Bookstore.

Women United, Women Divided is a study of female solidarity in ten contemporary cultures. It includes experiences as varied as those of suburban housewives and of squatters in Nairobi.

.27   CCA-URM. *Struggling to Survive: Women Workers in Asia.* Hongkong: CCA-URM, 1981. 162pp. $1 plus postage.

The Women Workers project of the Christian Conference of Asia–Urban Rural Mission has compiled this series of firsthand stories by Asian women about their day-to-day struggles in the factories of Thailand, Malaysia, Philippines, Sri Lanka, and Hongkong.

.28   Chapkis, Wendy, and Enloe, Cynthia, eds. *Coming Unravelled: Women Textile Workers in the International Political Economy of Textiles.* Amsterdam: Transnational Institute and Washington, D.C.: Institute for Policy Studies, 1983.

An outgrowth of a conference held in Amsterdam in 1982, this book presents the conditions of women who are working in the garment and textile industries in North America, Western Europe, Asia, North Africa, and Latin America. It discusses the ways in which women have been both used and marginalized by the spread of multinational corporations, the changes in technology, and the formulation of government trade policies. Presenting both historical and current views, *Coming Unravelled* describes how women have organized and resisted as workers in the textile industry. It shows the textile and garment industries as directly influencing the work of women in the economic structures of other industries such as microelectronics.

10.29   Etienne, Mona, and Leacock, Eleanor, eds. *Women and Colonization: Anthropological Perspectives*. New York: Praeger, 1980. $9.95

Women and Colonization studies women in twelve pre-industrial cultures, both past and present, illustrating the effects of colonization on the complex relationship between men and women of the colonized land.

10.30   Huston, Perdita. *Third World Women Speak Out*. New York: Praeger, 1979. 153pp. $4.95

Interviewed in fields, markets, clinics, and offices, women in six Third World countries share with the author their personal views and feelings about the impact of rapid change upon their families and themselves, about the problem of earning enough cash to subsist in newly monetized economies, about the constraints of social custom that continue to limit their contributions to family and society, and about their aspirations and opportunities.

10.31   International Defence and Aid Fund for Southern Africa, in cooperation with the UN Centre Against Apartheid. *Women Under Apartheid*. London: Zed Press, 1981. 119pp. $7.50. Distributed in the U.S. by Lawrence Hill. A complete list of IDAF publications on women in southern Africa is available from the Publications Dept., IDAF (London).

Using striking photographs from an exhibition commissioned by the United Nations especially for the World Conference of the UN Decade for Women in 1980, this powerful book illustrates how African women under apartheid are oppressed as black people, as workers, and as women. *Women Under Apartheid* shows, too, the part women have played in the struggle for freedom in South Africa.

10.32   Katoppo, Marianne. *Compassionate and Free: An Asian Women's Theology*. Maryknoll, N.Y.: Orbis Books, 1980. 90pp. $4.95

"By 1987," states Katoppo, "the majority of Christians will live in the Third World." *Compassionate and Free* contains reflections by an Indonesian novelist, journalist, and theologian on what this shift to the Third World means for the Asian churches—and particularly for women in those churches.

10.33   *Latin American Perspectives. Women in Latin America*. Riverside, Calif.: *Latin American Perspectives*, 1979. 164pp. $4.95 plus 50 cents handling.

This compilation of articles from the periodical *Latin American Perspectives* deals with women in specific countries, the part they play in national development, their involvement in the labor movement, and the interaction between sex and class.

10.34   Lim, Linda Yuen-ching. *Multinational Firms and Manufacturing for Export in Less-Developed Countries: The Case of the Electronics Industry in Malaysia and Singapore*. 2 vols. Ann Arbor, Mich.: University of Michigan Press, 1978. 631pp. Available from University of Michigan, Xerox University Microfilms. Cat. no. 7907123. Inquire for price.

This is a study of female-intensive manufacturing for export by multinational firms—many of them U.S. firms—in two Asian nations. Lim covers the effects of this type of employment on women workers and its overall impact on the position of women in developing countries.

0.35   Obbo, Christine. *Town Migration Is Not for Women: African Women's Struggle for Economic Independence*. London: Zed Press, 1980. 240pp. Cloth $18.95. Available in the U.S. from Lawrence Hill.

The author, one of Africa's few women anthropologists, contrasts a woman's viewpoint with the male viewpoint capsulized in the title of the book. The setting is Uganda, but the analysis of the causes and varying styles of women's migration, their occupations, social life and relationships with men in the town, are relevant to much of the rest of Africa as well.

.36   Omvedt, Gail. *We Will Smash This Prison! Indian Women in Struggle*. London: Zed Press, 1980. 192pp. Bibliography, documents, map. $10.50. Available in the U.S. from Lawrence Hill.

This personal account of the development of the women's movement in India in the mid-1970s shows how women of Western India—women from almost every caste and class—injected new issues into the politics of the Indian left. They brought about an expansion beyond issues of landlessness, exploitation, and caste to those of double work, dowry, and patriarchy. The author poses the question of how women of the Third World should be both feminists and socialists and how they are to relate to and help in the building of organized progressive political parties in India.

.37   Randall, Margaret. *Sandino's Daughters: Testimonies of Nicaraguan Women in Struggle*. Vancouver, B.C.: New Star Books, 1981. 220pp. $7.95. Available from Modern Times Bookstore.

Shortly after the end of the revolutionary war in Nicaragua, the author interviewed scores of women who fought and helped win the liberation of Nicaragua from the Somoza regime. *Sandino's Daughters* reveals the women's military and prison experiences, as well as their day-to-day lives throughout the struggle.

.38   Randall, Margaret. *Spirit of the People: The Role of Vietnamese Women in the Revolution*. Vancouver, B.C.: New Star Books, 1975. 95pp. $1.95

This short book recounts the political, social, and personal transformation of the lives of the women who took part in the Vietnamese struggle.

.39   Randall, Margaret. *Women in Cuba: Twenty Years Later*. New York: Smyrna Press, 1981. 167pp. Bibliography, 36 photos. $6.95

Women in Cuba is an appraisal of the gains made by Cuban women throughout the first twenty years of their revolution. Continuing problems are presented, as is a discussion paper on sexism from the Cuban Communist Party.

.40   Saadawi, Nawal El. *The Hidden Face of Eve: Women in the Arab World*. London: Zed Press, 1980. 240pp. $6.95. Distributed in the U.S. by Lawrence Hill.

Nawal El Saadawi offers a rare look into the situation of women today in the Arab world. Opening with a graphic account of female circumcision, *The Hidden Face of Eve* proceeds to a discussion of sexual aggression against female children, prostitution, marriage, divorce, sexual relationships, and other topics pertinent to women in Arab society.

10.41   Siu, Bobby. *Women of China in Struggle 1911-1949*. London: Zed Press, 1980. 240pp. $7.95. Distributed in the U.S. by Lawrence Hill.

Women of China tells the story of the participation of Chinese women in their country's struggles between 1911 and the revolution of 1949. The author contrasts the activities and approaches of the women of the Kuomintang and the women of the Chinese Communist Party. Her account, based on Chinese language sources, is told in readable, but scholarly terms.

10.42   Tawil, Raymonda Hawa. *My Home, My Prison*. New York: Holt, Rinehart & Winston, 1980. 320pp. $12.95

Written while the author was under house arrest, *My Home, My Prison* deals with Palestinian life under Israeli occupation, as well as with the struggle for women's rights.

10.43   Tijerino, Doris, as told to Margaret Randall. *Inside the Nicaraguan Revolution*. Vancouver, B.C.: New Star Books, 1978. 176pp. $5.25

The development of the Nicaraguan revolution is seen through the life story of Sandinist guerrilla Doris Tijerino as told to journalist Margaret Randall. Doris Tijerino's biography provides an excellent introduction to Nicaraguan society, focusing particularly on women, the peasantry, and the revolutionary forces in the country.

10.44   Tinker, Irene, and Bramsen, Michele Bo, eds. *Women and World Development*. Washington, D.C.: Overseas Development Council, 1976. 228pp. $3.50

This volume and its companion bibliography, *Women and World Development: An Annotated Bibliography* (see 10.115), are products of a Seminar on Women in Development sponsored by the American Association for the Advancement of Science. Held in Mexico City just prior to the World Conference of International Women's Year the seminar produced essays by Margaret Mead on the role of women in agriculture, Fatima Mernissi on the exclusion of women from development in the Moslem world, and Mary Elmendorf on the dilemma of peasant women in villages in Yucatan.

10.45   Urdang, Stephanie. *Fighting Two Colonialisms: Women in Guinea-Bissau*. New York: Monthly Review, 1979. 288pp. $7

Paying particular attention to the role of women, Stephanie Urdang analyzes the goals and achievements of the African Party for the Independence of Guinea and Cape Verde (PAIGC), the party that led the Guinean people in their successful war for independence from Portuguese rule.

10.46   World Conference of the United Nations Decade for Women. *Report of the World Conference of the United Nations Decade for Women: Equality, Development, and Peace*. United Nations, N.Y.: World Conference of the UN Decade for Women, 1980. UN publication no. E.80.IV.3 and Corr. $18

Reports from the World Conference held in Copenhagen in July 1980 include: Draft programme of action for the second half of the UN Decade for Women; Special measures of assistance to Palestinian women; The role of women in the struggle for national liberation in Zimbabwe, Namibia, and South Africa; Measures of assistance for women in southern Africa; The effects of apartheid on the status of women in southern Africa; Review and evaluation of progress achieved in the implementation of the World Plan of Action: Employment, Health, Education, and others.

Periodicals

47   *AFSC Women's Newsletter*, AFSC Nationwide Women's Program, 1501 Cherry St., Philadelphia, PA 19102. 3 issues/year. $5–$10 annual donation.
  Each issue contains excellent coverage of women's struggles both in the United States and in the Third World. Resources are listed and reviewed. Includes 8–12 page insert called *Women and Global Corporations*.

48   *The Church Woman*, Church Women United, 475 Riverside Dr., Rm. 812, New York, NY 10115. Bimonthly magazine. $4/year.
  This publication of Church Women United treats a variety of women-related issues, from women and multinationals to women as homemakers.

49   *Connexions*, 4228 Telegraph Ave., Oakland, CA 94609. Quarterly magazine. $10/year.
  This quarterly journal provides translations of articles from the world press "by, for, and about women." Each issue is devoted to a specific theme and contains facts and figures on the context within which women in different regions of the world live, work, and organize; reports on current developments in the international women's movement; cultural notes and interviews; and a resource guide.

50   *ISIS Women's International Bulletin*, Case Postale 50, 1211 Geneva 2, Switzerland. Quarterly magazine. $15/year individual; $25/year institutional.
  This excellent bulletin provides theoretical and practical information and documentation from the women's movement around the world. The *Bulletin* serves as a clearinghouse, listing resources, reports, and notices to help in an exchange of ideas, contacts, experiences, and resources among women and feminist groups.

51   *Media Report to Women*, Women's Institute for Freedom of the Press, 3306 Ross Pl., NW, Washington, DC 20008. Monthly. $20/year.
  In its ninth year of publication, this monthly is the only source of consistent information on women and the media nationally and internationally. It covers ideas and philosophies about what media should do and be, facts about existing media, about changes being made (legal actions, agreements negotiated between media and women's organizations), and notices of resources on the issue. An index to the *Media Report to Women* is also available.

52   *Peace and Freedom*, Women's International League for Peace and Freedom, 1213 Race St., Philadelphia, PA 19107. Bimonthly. $4/year
  This publication is sent to members of WILPF. It discusses the causes of war, sexism and the military, and ways in which women work to end war and create peace. It lists resources and conferences.

10.53 *WIN News* (*Women's International Network News*), 187 Grant St., Lexington, MA 02173. Quarterly magazine. $20/year individual; $25/year institutional.

Launched in 1975, International Women's Year, this magazine of news "by, for, and about women" contains reports from around the world on women and development, women and health, women and human rights, women and media, and other timely issues.

10.54 *Women: A Journal of Liberation*, 3028 Greenmount Ave., Baltimore, MD 21218. 3 issues/year. $10/year individual. Back issues are available.

Women—the oldest national socialist feminist publication— describes itself as having two purposes: "to introduce women to the women's movement, and to further dialogue among women who are working for basic changes in our society."

Pamphlets and Articles

10.55 *Arms and the Woman*. Naomi Marcus. Women's International League for Peace and Freedom, 1981. 35 cents. Bulk rates available.

Arms and the Woman deals with the importance of women's struggles against militarism and the power structure.

10.56 *Cancer: After Three Years of Working in an Electronics Company (Philippines)*. Asian Women Workers Newsletter 1, Fall 1982. 3pp. Available from Women Workers' Concern, c/o CCA-URM (Hongkong), for a donation.

This article tells the story of 22-year-old Elfreda Castellano and how she contracted cancer of the lymph nodes while a worker at the Dynetics semiconductor assembly plant in the Philippines.

10.57 *Changing Role of S.E. Asian Women*. Southeast Asia Chronicle 66 (January-February 1979) and *Pacific Research*, 9:5-6 (July-October 1978). 27pp. Charts, graphics, notes. $2.50. Also available from the Women's International Resource Exchange for $2.50.

This special joint issue of the *Southeast Asia Chronicle* and *Pacific Research* studies the impact of multinational corporate investment on women and family structures in Southeast Asia. It focuses on two foreign-oriented industries—electronics (semiconductor production) and prostitution—as examples of the serious problems Western-style development has created for Third World women.

10.58 *Electronics: The Global Industry*. NACLA Report on the Americas 11, no. 4, April 1977. 25pp. $2.50. Available from NACLA or from the Data Center.

This issue of *NACLA Report on the Americas* centers on electronics "runaways," companies that move their operations abroad to cut labor costs. Most of the foreign workers are young women, paid at the lowest possible rate.

10.59 *Filipino Women in the National Liberation Struggle*. Special issue of the *Philippines Research Newsletter* (No. 21-22) from the Philippines Research Center, 1978. 11pp. 50 cents.

A brief summary of the history of women's participation in today's liberation struggles in the Philippines, this special issue of the Center's newsletter incorporates an earlier paper (1974) from the liberation movement entitled "On the Liberation of the Sexes."

.60 *Francisca Lucero: A Profile of Female Factory Work in Ciudad Juarez.* Maria Patricia Fernandez Kelly. Mexico-U.S. Border Program, AFSC (Philadelphia), 1980. 15pp. Free

An overview of the employment of women in partial assembly plants of multinational corporations on the U.S.-Mexico border.

.61 *Global Corporations: Effects on the Lives and Work of Twelve Women.* AFSC Nationwide Women's Program, 1979. 12pp. $1 including postage.

Quotations from women attending the Conference on Women and Global Corporations: Work, Roles and Resistance in 1979. These personal comments come from a variety of sources: Union Maids, the Arizona Farmworkers, health care workers, the Center for Women Workers (COMO), representatives of the Nestlé boycott, agribusiness workers from the Philippines, and electronics workers from the Santa Clara Valley, to name a few.

.62 *Global Feminist Disarmament Gathering.* AFSC Nationwide Women's Program, June 1982. 22pp. $2 including postage.

A report on workshops held prior to the massive nationwide disarmament demonstrations on June 12, 1982. Workshop topics included: Sexism and Militarism; Disarmament and Development; East/West Feminist Connections; Feminist Opposition to Euro-missiles.

.63 *Hit and Run: Runaway Shops on the Mexican Border. NACLA Report on the Americas* 9, no. 5, July–August 1975. 30pp. $2.50. Available from NACLA or from the Data Center.

A study of the effects of runaway shops on Mexican workers in the garment and electronics industries (where 95 percent of the workers are women), and on U.S. workers.

.64 *Latin American and Caribbean Feminist Meeting. ISIS Women's International Bulletin* 22, March 1982. 29pp. $4

This is the entire report of the First Latin American and Caribbean Feminist Meeting, held in Bogotá, Colombia in July 1981. It includes material taken from tapes of the talks and discussions at the meeting, resolutions and decisions, and an annotated list of participants.

.65 *Latin American Women: One Myth, Many Realities.* Patricia Flynn, Aracelly Santana, Patricia Fernandez Kelly, and Helen Shapiro. *NACLA Report on the Americas* 14, no. 5, September–October 1980. 48pp. Graphics and bibliography. $2.50. Available from NACLA, the Women's International Resource Exchange, and from the Data Center.

Latin American Women offers a conceptual and contextual backdrop against which to understand the oppression of women in Latin America. Articles in the magazine deal with women and work, ideological and legal structures that support the status quo, and the ways in which women's issues are being addressed in Latin America today. A final section deals with changes taking place in Nicaragua.

10.66   *Life on the Global Assembly Line*. Barbara Ehrenreich and Annette Fuentes.
         Ms. Magazine, January 1981. 8pp. 60 cents. Available from NARMIC (60 cents)
         and from AFSC Nationwide Women's Program (3/$2).
             This article details the obstacles facing the two million Third World women
         working in textile and electronics plants.

10.67   *Mexican Border Industrialization: Female Labor Force Participation and Migration*. Maria Patricia Fernandez Kelly. Available from Mexico-U.S. Border
         Program, AFSC (Philadelphia), 1980. 26pp. Free
             A study of the connections between gender, class, family structure and occupational alternatives along the Mexican border.

10.68   *Nuclear Power and Militarization*. ISIS *Women's International Bulletin* 15,
         June 1980. 38pp. $4
             The issues of nuclear power, militarization, and energy are being addressed and
         challenged more and more by women's groups. This issue of the *ISIS Bulletin*
         presents articles and actions by women's groups around the world concerning
         these matters so relevant to health, reproduction, and ecology. Included is an
         annotated section of resources.

10.69   *Peace and War*. Special issue of *Women: A Journal of Liberation* 8, no. 1,
         1981. 64pp. Bibliography. $2.50
             The anti-war movement has stirred controversy among feminists: are women's
         energies being drained from issues that are explicitly feminist? The editors of
         Women respond that militarism must be a feminist issue because increases in the
         U.S. military budget have a staggering effect on women. Articles in this special
         issue cover women in the Nicaraguan revolution; war tax resistance; militarism,
         and the tradition of radical feminism. Also included: poetry, resources, and announcements.

10.70   *Precondition for Victory: The Struggle for the Emancipation of Women in
         Mozambique*. Stephanie Urdang. From *Transition to Socialism in Mozambique*,
         John Saul, ed. (1982), November 1982. $1.65. Women's International Resource
         Exchange.
             Stephanie Urdang's article is an account of the profound changes that have
         taken place in Mozambique since liberation in marriage and family life, in work
         and in political life. She also identifies the major obstacle that still remains: the
         sexual division of labor within the household.

10.71   *Prostitution Tourism*. Asian Women's Association. From *Asian Women's
         Liberation*, June 1980. 13pp. $1.40. Women's International Resource Exchange.
             Japan's tourism-for-prostitution business has spread into Taiwan, Thailand,
         the Philippines, South Korea, Nepal, and Sri Lanka. Moved by the protests of
         their South Korean sisters, the AWA has analyzed this traffic in women as part of
         the North-South problem and as a "business venture" that ultimately benefits
         Japanese capitalists.

10.72   *Puerto Rican Women in the Economic and Social Processes of the Twentieth
         Century*. Marcia Rivera Quintero. 1980. 14pp. Notes. 95 cents. Spanish language
         edition also available: *La mujer puertorriqueña en los procesos económicos y*

sociales del siglo XX. Available from Women's International Resource Exchange Service.

This selection from *The Intellectual Roots of Independence*, (Iris Zavala and Rafael Rodriguez, eds.), presents the situation of women in Puerto Rico in the precapitalist economy of the nineteenth century and their entry, in the twentieth century, into an economy based on new forms of control by the United States. The article profiles the woman as peasant, domestic worker, teacher, and industrial worker (especially in the garment and tobacco industries) and examines the impact of new educational policies and literacy on salaried women.

.73   *Role of Women in Transnational Corporate Expansion*. Jeb Mays. AFSC Nationwide Women's Program. February 1980. 6pp. 50 cents.

This paper was delivered at an international conference on "Women and the Transnationalization of Capital" in Ciudad Juarez, Mexico, in February 1980.

74   *Roles and Contradictions of Chilean Women in the Resistance and in Exile*. Gladys Díaz. 1979. 7pp. $1. Spanish language edition available: *Roles y contradicciones de la mujer militante en la resistencia y en el exilio*. Gladys Díaz. Women's International Resource Exchange.

This report on the International Conference on Exile and Solidarity in Latin America in the 1970s held in Venezuela in October 1979 examines the impact of sexism on relationships between women and men in political struggles in Chile and in organizing in the underground and in exile, highlighting the dynamic between gains made in the political arena and ongoing problems in the realm of male-female relationships. Basing her analysis on her own experiences as a member of a Chilean political party, an ex-prisoner of the Pinochet regime, and a refugee, the author proposes a revolutionary integration of the women's struggle in Chile and the struggle for national liberation.

75   *Socialist Revolution and Women's Rights in Democratic Yemen*. Maxine Molyneux. 1980. 11pp. 90 cents. Women's International Resource Exchange.

An overview of South Yemen's history, geography, and economy, followed by interviews with three senior members of the General Union of Yemeni Women who describe and analyze changes in the position of women since independence from England in 1967. This article is especially important as a portrayal of women in a development process in an Arab country presently attempting to implement a policy of revolutionary socialist development.

76   *Who Really Starves? Women and World Hunger*. Lisa Leghorn and Mary Roodkowsky. Friendship Press Distribution, 1977. 40pp. $1.25

This article probes the facts about women and world hunger (noting women's involvement in worldwide food production) and reports on how systems have discriminated against women.

77   *Women and Appropriate Technology*. International Women's Tribune Centre. *IWTC Newsletter* 7. Rev. ed. April 1979. 32pp. Bibliography. Bulk rates available.

This *IWTC Newsletter* looks particularly at appropriate technology in relation to women's roles in rural communities. It gives concrete examples of technologies for women, and some projects around the world.

10.78   *Women and New Technology. ISIS Women's International Bulletin* 24, September 1982. 40pp. Bibliography. $4

This issue of the *ISIS Bulletin* is divided into three major sections: profile of women in the electronics industry; impact of microelectronics on women workers; and women taking control of new technology. Appendices list feminist groups working on new technology, groups working on multinationals, and selected literature resources. See also the ISIS Documentation Packet: *Women and the New Technology* (10.129).

10.79   *Women and Work. MERIP Reports* 95, March–April 1981. 32pp. $2.20 plus postage.

This special issue of *MERIP Reports* includes an analysis of the impact of labor migration on the sexual division of work and an examination of the condition of working women in an Iranian village and Jordanian factories.

10.80   *Women in Mozambique. Newsfront International*, August 1980. 3pp.

This interview with Anabella Rodrigues of FRELIMO (Mozambique Liberation Front) by Candice Wright of the Liberation Support Movement describes the work of the Organization of Mozambican Women in literacy, employment, and skilled agricultural work. It discusses the country's new family law and suggests the difficulties in eradicating traditions such as polygamy and the dowry.

10.81   *Women in National Liberation Movements. ISIS Women's International Bulletin* 19, July 1981. 35pp. $4

Women confronted by two major issues—national liberation and sexism—speak out in this issue of *ISIS*. Resources from around the world follow the selection of articles.

10.82   *Women in Peru*. Blanca Figueroa and Jeanine Anderson. Reprint from *CHANGE International Reports* (London), September 1981. 16pp. Photographs, notes, charts. $2.25. Available from Women's International Resource Exchange.

This survey of women in contemporary Peru includes sections on health, education, legal protection, employment, and access to services. *Women in Peru* defines Peru's dependent role in the world economy and its impact on women.

10.83   *Women in Southern Africa. ISIS Women's International Bulletin*, Fall 1978. 30pp. $3

This issue of the *ISIS Bulletin* contains articles on African women under apartheid, rural women, SWAPO Women's Campaign, and on women and transnationals. Pertinent resources are also included.

10.84   *Women, Power, and Alternative Futures*. Patricia Mische. *The Whole Earth Papers* 1, nos. 8–9, 1978. 8pp. Part 1: *Women and World Order*. Part 2: *Women and Power*. Available from Global Education Associates for 60 cents each.

The first of these two monographs explores the relationship between women's search for equality and self-realization and the historic drive for national and world security. *Women and World Order* examines the ways in which the arms race and other national security priorities have been a factor in the subordination of women and their needs.

The second monograph, *Women and Power*, studies the nature of power and the ways women have historically related to it. The author asks why, despite over a century of feminist activity, many women do not exercise their power in critical world order issues. Mische calls for the reassertion and reintegration of "feminine" values in future world history and in work for world order alternatives.

85   *Women, Production and Reproduction in Industrial Capitalism: A Comparison of Brazilian and U.S. Factory Workers.* Helen I. Safa. 1979. 31pp. Tables and notes. $1.80. Available from Women's International Resource Exchange.

This article examines a related sample of Brazilian and U.S. women garment workers to determine the relationship between women's access to the labor market and reproductive strategy in the two countries.

86   *Women, SALT, and Arms Control.* Women's International League for Peace and Freedom, 1978. 30pp. $2

This is the report of a December 1978 conference in Washington, D.C., sponsored by the WILPF on the role of women in disarmament. Contents include agenda, speeches, highlights, workshop recommendations, and the closing address by Representative Patricia Schroeder.

87   *Women, the Key to Liberation.* Itziar Lozano Urbieta in *Women in Dialogue*, 1979. 8pp. 70 cents. Available from Women's International Resource Exchange.

The author, a Roman Catholic laywoman, surveys the ways in which Latin American women suffer exploitation: in education, work, and the family (first as daughter, then as wife and mother). *Women, the Key to Liberation* provides an economic analysis of women's status that is addressed to the Latin American church and its idealized view of women and the family. Urbieta exhorts educational institutions and the church to "revise their concepts of the role of women" and support efforts to change a socio-economic system that reinforces the oppression of women.

88   *Women Workers. ISIS Women's International Bulletin* 10, 1978–1979. $2

Articles on women's work situations around the world and a list of pertinent resources and organizations.

AUDIOVISUAL RESOURCES

Guides and Catalogs

10.89   *Catalyst Media Review: An Annotated Bibliography of Audiovisuals on Women and Work*. New York: Catalyst Media. Quarterly magazine with annual index. $12/year

The *Review* provides complete descriptive data, a synopsis, and comments on audiovisuals that treat women in a wide range of work-related situations.

10.90   *Films on Women's Issues*. New York: Third World Newsreel, 1980. 12pp. Free

In addition to descriptions of eight films on women's issues, this catalog offers two pages of film programming ideas and hints on projecting films.

10.91   *Women's Studies/Issues*. Minneapolis: Audio Visual Library Service, University of Minnesota, 1982. 20pp. Free

This annotated list of 16mm films covers various issues, including women in the arts, women's history, filmed portraits of women, and women in other cultures.

Audiovisuals

10.92   *As Strong As the Land*. n.d. 19 min color filmstrip and cassette. AFSC (New York). Rental $5

This AFSC filmstrip presents rural women in different parts of the world, their problems, and their efforts to change their lives. It explores both positive and negative ways in which development programs have affected women.

10.93   *Blood of the Condor*. 1969 85 min b&w film. Jorge Sanjines. Unifilm. Rental $150

Based on actual events that took place in Bolivia in 1968, *Blood of the Condor* is a dramatized and very powerful account of what happened when a U.S.-sponsored population control program sterilized Quechua Indian women without their knowledge or consent.

10.94   *Chile: Four Women's Stories*. 1980 25 min 130 color slides and cassette, script, instructions, background materials, action guide. AFSC (Cambridge). Rental $15

Four women tell in their own words of their lives in Chile before and after the 1973 military coup in this AFSC slideshow. Isolina, a nutritionist, belongs to an organization composed of relatives (mostly women) of disappeared persons; Olga, a 70-year-old retired university professor, helped found the Chile Women's Movement in 1935; Manuella, from the rural south, has belonged to committees for the development of women workers and unemployed workers; Maria Elena, studying to become a teacher, works with young people in the slums of Santiago.

10.95   *The Dead Are Not Silent*. 1978 80 min b&w film. Studio H & S of the German Democratic Republic. Walter Heynowski and Gerhard Scheumann. Available from the Institute for Policy Studies and from New Time Films. Rental $125

The overthrow of the Allende government in Chile and the consequent repression by the Pinochet regime there are told through the stories of two Chilean women, Moy de Toha and Isabel Letelier. Their husbands, both Defense Ministers in the popularly elected government of Salvador Allende, were detained and later murdered.

.96   The Double Day. 1975 56 min color film. Helena Solberg-Ladd. International Women's Film Project/Unifilm. Available for rent from the University of Minnesota Audio Visual Library Service ($26.25) and from Unifilm ($125).

The Double Day is a documentary film focused on women's working conditions in Latin America. Interviews with women who work in agriculture, mining, commerce, domestic services, and manufacturing point up the conflict that exists between the Latin American woman's increasing political awareness and societal traditions.

.97   Fear Woman. 1972 28 min color film. United Nations/McGraw Hill Films. Available from the United Nations (free) and for rent from the University of Minnesota Audio Visual Library Service ($13.40).

This United Nations film examines the social structure of Ghana, showing women's economic power to be about equal to that of men, and indicating equivalent political and social power for women as well. Interviews with three prominent women—a businesswoman, a judge, and a tribal chief—are included. The film provokes thinking on the role of women in emerging nations.

.98   I Have Three Children of My Own. 1979 20 min color slideshow or filmstrip with script. 140 visuals. Packard Manse Media Project. Rental $20. Sale (slideshow) $65, individual; $70, groups; (filmstrip) $35. Also available from Women's International League for Peace and Freedom ($5 plus postage).

A powerful anti-nuclear documentary narrated by Dr. Helen Caldicott of Physicians for Social Responsibility, this audiovisual discusses some of the medical implications of nuclear power.

.99   Lucia. 1969 160 min b&w film. Spanish dialog with English subtitles. Humberto Solas. Cuban Film Institute. Unifilm. Rental $250

A classic film, winner of several awards, which presents a unique view of Cuban history and culture as well as women's struggle for social equality. The film is in three parts: the first, set in 1895 tells of a Lucia during Cuba's war for independence from Spain; the second, in 1933, presents a Lucia who leaves her family to fight for the overthrow of the Cuban dictator Machado; the third, in the 1960s, shows a Lucia learning to read and write during Cuba's literacy campaign and confronting a husband's macho attitudes.

.00   My Country Occupied (Mi Patria Ocupada). 1971 30 min b&w film. Spanish or English. Available from California Newsreel and Third World Newsreel. Rental $40. Sale $250

A film about the life of Oaxaca de Mejia, a Guatemalan woman, who experiences the effects of foreign corporate power, first in the countryside, then in the city. Workers' struggles come to naught with the coming of U.S. armed forces; Oaxaca rejoins the people in her village to take part in the ongoing struggle against oppression.

10.101   *One Way or Another (De Cierta Manera)*. 1978 78 min b&w film. Sara Gomez. Cuban Film Institute. Unifilm. Apply for rates.

This film, directed by a black woman who died before its completion, is built around a relationship between a man and a woman in Cuba after the revolution and their efforts to deal with their changing relationship within their changing society.

10.102   *The Price of Change*. 1982 26 min color film and video with teacher's study guide. Elizabeth Fernea and Marilyn Gaunt. Icarus. Rental $50 (16mm only). Sale (16mm film) $425; (video) $260

For sixty years Egyptian women have been gradually entering all sectors of the public work force. *The Price of Change* examines the consequences of this evolving work pattern in the lives of five women: a factory worker with four children, a rural village leader involved in family planning, a doctor, a social worker, and a member of Parliament who is also speaker for the opposition party.

10.103   *Ramparts of Clay*. 1970 85 min color film. Arabic with English subtitles. Jean-Louis Bertucelli. Cinema 5. Apply for special classroom rental rates.

Set in a small village on the edge of the Sahara, this moving film presents the story of a young woman who comes in conflict with her community over her inability to accept the subservient role ancient tradition has given her. At the same time, the villagers begin to awaken to their own exploitation. The film was banned in Tunisia and Algeria, the very area it so insightfully portrays.

10.104   *Simplemente Jenny*. 1975 33 min color film. Spanish dialog with English subtitles. Helena Solberg-Ladd. Unifilm. Rental $90. Sale $395. Also available from Hudson River Productions.

This film, focusing primarily on three girls in a Bolivian reformatory, explores the images and models presented to Latin American women through the media, the effects these models have had on three young women in particular, and the rejection of these models as expressed by women interviewed in an Argentinian slum.

10.105   *South Africa Belongs to Us: The Struggle of the Black Women of South Africa*. 1980 57 min color film and video. Chris Austin, Peter Chappell, and Ruth Weiss. Icarus. Rental $65. Sale (16mm film) $575; (video) $560

Shot secretly with the help of two black women journalists *South Africa Belongs to Us* presents interviews with four women leaders and portraits of four other South African women. The film depicts the struggle of the black women for human dignity in the face of apartheid—from the fight to keep a roof over their heads, to black consciousness, to the total liberation of their people.

10.106   *A Veiled Revolution*. 1982 26 min color film and video with teacher's study guide. Elizabeth Fernea and Marilyn Gaunt. Icarus. Rental $50 (16mm film only). Sale (16mm) $425; (video) $260

Egypt was the first Arab nation in which women marched in political demonstrations (1919); the first in which women took off the veil (1923); and the first to offer free public secular education to women (1924). Today the granddaughters of those early Arab feminists are returning to traditional Islamic dress. *A Veiled Revolution* probes the reasons for this dramatic shift.

07   *With the Cuban Women*. 1975 48 min color film. Octavio Cortazar. Cuban Film Institute. Unifilm. Rental $125

A documentary on Cuba's "revolution within a revolution," this film explores the changes in the social status of women as well as the changing attitudes of men toward women in post-revolution Cuba. Includes interviews with women and archival footage detailing the old society and the guerrilla struggle on through contemporary Cuban society.

08   *Womanpower: The Hidden Asset*. 1975 17 min color film. United Nations. Rental free. Sale $220

A discussion by high school girls and boys about the changing status of women in Sri Lanka sparked by activity on a women's farm. The purpose of the film is to spur reflection on the fact that women supply a large part of the human power needed for agricultural production in Africa, Asia, and Latin America, and that their very real economic contribution is generally either ignored or simply taken for granted.

09   *Women in Arms (Mujeres en Armas: El Caso de Nicaragua)*. 1981 59 min color film. English or Spanish. Victoria Schultz. Hudson River Productions. Rental $100 Sale $800

A documentary film (winner of the 1981 Special Merit Award at the Athens International Film Festival) examining the role of Nicaraguan women in the struggle before Somoza's fall and in the struggle to reconstruct Nicaraguan society afterward. Oppression, underdevelopment, and machismo are presented as problems to be faced by men and women alike.

10   *Women in Vietnam*. 1973 45 min color slideshow with script. AFSC (Cambridge). Rental $15

This AFSC educational resource traces the degradation of Vietnamese society—of Vietnamese women in particular—under French colonialism and during the American occupation. One section explores the ways in which the Western "male" values of foreign troops in Vietnam led to the dehumanization of the Vietnamese women they encountered.

11   *Women of Nicaragua*. 1980 59 min color film. AFSC (Cambridge). Rental $25

This down-to-earth film on the Nicaraguan revolution and the role of women in the struggle was the first major documentary filmed in Nicaragua after the overthrow of the Somoza dictatorship. *Women of Nicaragua* shatters propagandistic myths about "communist terrorists" and "international communist conspiracies" in Nicaragua and Central America.

12   *Women Under Siege*. 1982 26 min color film or video with teacher's guide. Elizabeth Fernea and Marilyn Gaunt. Icarus. Rental $50 (16mm film only) Sale (16mm film) $425; (video) $260

This film examines the crucial role that women played in a Palestinian refugee community in southern Lebanon. Living under constant harassment and threat of Israeli attack they filled the roles of mothers, teachers, political organizers, farm laborers, and fighters. Rashadiyah, the Lebanese town that serves as the setting for *Women Under Seige*, was bombed and attacked by Israeli forces in June 1982. The Palestinian refugee camp was reduced to ruins.

OTHER RESOURCES

Bibliographies and Directories

10.113 American Friends Service Committee, Nationwide Women's Project. *Women and Global Corporations: Work, Roles, and Resistance*. Philadelphia: AFSC, 1979. 98pp. $4.50

A directory of printed and audiovisual resources, activists, and organizations concerned with women's work and multinational corporations.

10.114 Asian and Pacific Centre for Women and Development/ESCAP. *Women's Resource Book 1979*. New York: IWTC, 1979. 300pp. $6. Available from the International Women's Tribune Center.

This comprehensive resource directory contains several useful sections: the addresses of organizations in Asia and the Pacific concerned with women and development; a list of publications of the Asian and Pacific Centre for Women and Development; descriptions of some women's development projects; the Plan of Action adopted by the United Nations' Economic and Social Commission for Asia and the Pacific for the integration of women in development; and suggestions for obtaining funds and assistance.

10.115 Buvinic, Mayra. *Women and World Development: An Annotated Bibliography*. Washington, D.C.: Overseas Development Council, 1976. 162pp. $2.50

This bibliography was prepared for an international Seminar on Women in Development held in Mexico City in 1975 and sponsored by the Office of International Science of the American Association for the Advancement of Science. Over 400 entries are fully annotated and categorized by subject and by region.

10.116 International Women's Tribune Center. *Caribbean Resource Kit for Women*. New York: IWTC, University of the West Indies, and the Women's Bureau of Jamaica, n.d. 3-ring binder 234pp. $8

This looseleaf collection of resources includes several sections: a description of 230 projects focusing on women and development in the sixteen Caribbean English-speaking areas; a list of financial and technical assistance resources; a bibliography of women in development in the Caribbean; and the United Nations' Regional Plan of Action for the English-speaking Caribbean.

10.117 ISIS. *Bottle Babies: A Guide to the Baby Foods Issue*. Rome, Italy: ISIS, 1976. 48pp. $3

This guide, reprinted since its first publication, deals with the complex issue of the sale of powdered baby milk, the use of feeding bottles, and the imposition of male-oriented Western culture on women and children in the poor regions of the world. It is available in Spanish, French, and German, as well as in English.

10.118 ISIS and the Boston Women's Health Book Collective. *International Women & Health Resource Guide*. Boston and Rome: ISIS and BWHBC, 1980. 177pp. $5. Available in the USA from the Boston Women's Health Book Collective.

This directory is a multilingual resource book containing an annotated list of material available internationally on women's health, reproductive issues, drugs and drug companies, food and eating, aging, and the environment. The guide includes articles, bibliographies, reviews of books, pamphlets, films, slides and videotapes, as well as the names of groups around the world who are involved in health projects.

119   ISIS. *Women in Development: A Resource Guide for Organization and Action*. Geneva: ISIS, 1983. $12

This book is a descriptive and analytical guide to written and audiovisual materials on the issue of women's participation in development, and to projects, groups, and organizations working on the subject in Third World and industrialized countries. It provides an analysis from a feminist perspective of contemporary theories relating women and development. The book points out the indispensable role women have played in all major social and economic processes—in both developing and industrialized countries. A consideration of topics such as multinational corporations, rural development, migration, tourism and prostitution, health, communication, and education indicate that women have been not only "bypassed" by "development," but also systematically oppressed and degraded by the very processes in which they play so central a part.

120   Rihani, May. *Development as if Women Mattered: An Annotated Bibliography with a Third World Focus*. Washington, D.C.: Overseas Development Council, 1970. $3

This volume on Third World women and development gathers together a variety of documents with an action/programming focus and makes accessible a large number of unpublished works that can be obtained through the publications retrieval system of the new TransCentury Foundation in Washington, D.C. The 287 items included in this bibliography are grouped first into subject categories and then into regional subdivisions.

121   Wells-Hargleroad, Bobbi. *Women's Work Is...Resources on Working Women*. Chicago: ICUIS, 1978. 105pp. $4

An annotated bibliography and resource guide on women's work and women workers. Includes information available on the topic in the United States and in developing countries, as well as data on church groups involved in the issue.

122   Women's Institute for Freedom of the Press. *Index/Directory of Women's Media*. Washington, D.C.: Women's Institute for Freedom of the Press, annual. 1982 edition: 114pp. $8

Updated each January, this directory lists over 500 women's groups and individuals relevant to media and the women's liberation movement. It lists periodicals, presses/publishers, news services, film groups, art/graphics, theater, bookstores, and distributors.

Curriculum Guides and Resource Packets

123   *Human Rights of Women: A Resource Packet*. United Methodist Church Service Center. n.d. 12 items and bibliography. $4.95

This packet of twelve articles covers topics such as U.N. declarations, sterilization abuse, effects of apartheid on women, Christians and the ERA, housing, torture, job stress, prisons, physical abuses, brown lung, and alternative futures. It focuses on specific areas where the human rights of women have been uniquely violated and shows that women's condition, as part of a larger oppressed group of persons or nations, makes their situation doubly tragic.

10.124   *Information Kit for Women in Africa.* New York: International Women's Tribune Center, n.d. 3-ring binder $8; Paperback $6
This kit, which provides an introduction to the resources and activities for, by, and about women in development programs in Africa, was prepared by the IWTC and the UN/ECA African Training and Research Centre for Women (Ethiopia).

10.125   *Nicaraguan Women and the Revolution.* New York: Women's International Resource Exchange, 1980. 36pp. Photos and graphics. $2.25. Available also in Spanish: *Las mujeres nicaragüenses y la revolución.*
This packet of resources includes a history of the Luisa Amanda Espinoza Nicaraguan Women's Association; poetry by Gioconda Belli, Olivia Silva, and Claribel Alegria; and articles entitled "Domestic Workers: A Struggle that is Just Beginning" and "Battling Sexism Remains a Key Task."

10.126   *Resistance, War, and Liberation: Women of Southern Africa.* New York: Women's International Resource Exchange, 1982. Approximately 40pp. Interviews, photographs, bibliography. $2.50
This WIRE packet covers women's involvement in the revolutionary struggles of Angola, Mozambique, Namibia, South Africa, and Zimbabwe, discussing women and apartheid, women in the economy, and women's role in military struggles. Articles in the packet provide critical analyses of work to be done to eradicate sexist socio-political roles and values.

10.127   *Voices of Women: Poetry by and about Third World Women.* New York: Women's International Resource Exchange, 1982. 44pp. $2.50
The poems in this WIRE packet, written between 1900 and the present, are the work of both anonymous and recognized poets of Asia, Africa, and the Americas. There are poems by women directly involved in their country's liberation struggle, poems by women of color in the United States, and poems of solidarity by women of many countries. This collection brings to life the politics, the pain, the heroism, and the love of women reaching for freedom around the globe.

10.128   *Women in a Hungry World.* New York: AFSC, World Hunger/Global Development Project, n.d. 60pp. $5.50 prepaid.
Designed for a series of three group meetings, this education/action packet uses a participatory study approach to understanding the role of women in developing nations. It includes background readings on areas of women's lives—economics, population, agriculture, food production—and discusses how development plans exclude women and how U.S. actions affect them.

10.129   *Women and the New Technology.* Rome and Geneva: ISIS, 1982. $6. Available from ISIS (Switzerland).
This third in a series of *ISIS Documentation Packets* is a selection of articles from recent feminist literature from around the world on some of the crucial

issues for women posed by the new technology. The contents include lists of additional material available at ISIS, a selection of groups in various countries dealing with the issue, and suggestions for further reading.

Other packets in this ISIS series are *Women and Peace* and *Older Women*.

130 *Women and War: El Salvador*. New York: Women's International Resource Exchange, 1981. 44pp. Graphics and map. $2.50

This 44-page collection of articles, speeches, poetry, and eyewitness testimonies examines the origins and dynamics of the current conflict in El Salvador, including U.S. involvement, and looks at the daily lives of Salvadoran women—how they are affected by and involved in the struggle.

131 *Women in the Struggle for Liberation*. Cambridge, Mass.: University Christian Movement, 1977. $2.50

This packet, designed by the World Student Christian Federation Women's Project to help students understand the international dimensions of women's struggle, includes several items. Among them: a book (*Women in the Struggle for Liberation*), short stories and excerpted biographies of women from many countries, a study guide, a list and a description of films about Third World women, and a brochure on women in rural development.

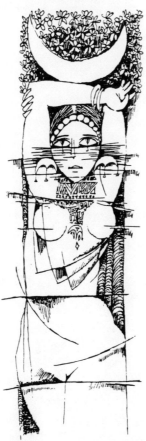

PART THREE

INDEXES

Organizations

Books

Periodicals

Pamphlets and Articles

Audiovisuals

*Audiovisual Bibliographies,
   Catalogs, and Guides*

*Bibliographies, Directories,
   and Curriculum Resources*

Simulation Games

Indexes

Items included in the indexes that follow are the major resources annotated in this directory. Thus, the indexes are *not* comprehensive lists of each and every organization, book, or other resource mentioned in the directory.

Boldface numbers in the *organization* index refer you to a detailed description of the organization in the opening section of one of the chapters.

We have overlapped the indexes of *printed resources* so that a bound book of audiovisual materials will be found in the *books* and *audiovisual bibliographies* sections and a curriculum resource that is in pamphlet form will be listed in both the *pamphlets and articles* and the *curriculum resources* sections.

ORGANIZATIONS

Organizations

—733 Green Bay Rd., Wilmette, IL 60091. Tel: 800-323-4222.
—440 Park Ave. S, New York, NY 10016. Tel: 800-223-6246.
Food for Thought Books, 325 Main St., Amherst, MA 01002. Tel: 413-253-5432. *1.105, 6.27*
Four Arrows, Box 3117, York, PA 17402. Tel: 717-993-6664. *4.65*
Franciscan Communications Center/TeleĸETICS, 1229 S. Santee S, Los Angeles, CA 90015. Tel: 213-746-2916. *1.193, 6.80, 6.91*
Friends Committee on National Legislation, 245 Second St., NE, Washington, DC 20002. Tel: 202-547-6000. **1.44**
Friends for Jamaica, 1 E. 125 St., New York, NY 10035. Tel: 212-831-6561. **4.13**
Friends of Haiti, Box 348, New City, NY 10956. Tel: 914-352-3872. *4.155*
Friends of the Filipino People, Box 2125, Durham, NC 27702. *3.17, 3.126, 3.137, 3.170*
Friends of the Korean People, Box 3657, Arlington, VA 22203. *3.91*
Friendship Press
—Distribution: Box 37844, Cincinnati, OH 45237. Tel: 513-761-2100. *1.206, 1.207, 1.220, 1.223, 3.79, 4.41, 4.57, 4.138, 4.176, 4.184, 4.185, 5.29, 5.43, 5.94, 5.103, 5.106, 6.34, 6.86, 7.26, 7.28, 8.55, 10.76*
—Editorial offices: 475 Riverside Dr., Rm. 772, New York, NY 10115. Tel: 212-870-2586.
Gale Research Co., Book Tower, Detroit, MI 48226. Tel: 313-961-2242. *1.213, 9.95*
General Union of Afghan Students Abroad (GUAFS), Box 17622, Los Angeles, CA 90017. **3.20**
Georgetown University Press, Georgetown University, Washington, DC 20057. Tel: 202-625-4824. *7.33, 7.35*
Global Education Associates, 552 Park Ave., East Orange, NJ 07017. Tel: 201-675-1409. **1.46,** *1.193, 1.198, 10.84*
Global Electronics Information Project, c/o Pacific Studies Center, 222B View St., Mountain View, CA 94041. Tel: 415-969-1545. **9.8**
Global Learning, 40 S. Fullerton Ave., Montclair, NJ 07042. Tel: 201-783-7616. **1.49**
Global Negotiations Information Project, 777 UN Plaza, 11th Floor, New York, NY 10017. Tel: 212-682-3633. **1.50**
Global Perspectives in Education, 218 E. 18 St., New York, NY 10003. Tel: 212-475-0850. **1.52,** *1.197, 3.196*
Greenhaven Press, 577 Shoreview Park Rd., St. Paul, MN 55112. Tel: 612-482-1177. *1.127*
Greenpeace, National Office, 2007 R St., NW, Washington, DC 20009. Tel: 202-462-1177. **1.56**
Grove Press, 196 W. Houston St., New York, NY 10014. Tel: 212-242-4900. *8.52*
Guatemala News and Information Bureau (GNIB), Box 28594, Oakland, CA 94604. Tel: 415-835-0810. **4.15**
Guild Books and Periodicals, 2456 N. Lincoln Ave., Chicago, IL 60614. Tel: 312-525-3667. *1.106*
Haiti Films, Box 348, New City, NY 10956. Tel: 914-352-3872. *4.155*
Halstead Press, 605 Third Ave., New York, NY 10016. Tel: 212-867-9800. *10.25*
Harper & Row. Orders to: Keystone Industrial Park, Scranton, PA 18512. *1.119*
Hill & Wang, 19 Union Sq., New York, NY 10003. Tel: 212-741-6900. *1.118, 5.24*
Holmes & Meier Publishers, IUB Bldg., 30 Irving Pl., New York, NY 10003. Tel: 212-254-4100. *1.113*
Holt, Rinehart & Winston, 383 Madison Ave., New York, NY 10017. Tel: 212-688-9100. *1.120, 4.62, 10.42*
Howard University Press, 2935 Upton St., NW, Washington, DC 20008. *2.49*
Hudson River Productions, 1897 Hamilton Ave., Palo Alto, CA 94301. *4.157, 10.104, 10.109*
Human Rights Internet, 1338 G St., SE, Washington, DC 20003. Tel: 202-543-9200. **7.12,** *7.41, 7.78, 7.82, 7.83, 7.85*
Icarus Films, 200 Park Ave. S, Suite 1319, New York, NY 10003. Tel: 212-674-3375. *2.89, 3.169, 4.129, 4.132, 4.145, 4.171, 5.86, 5.87, 5.88, 5.89, 5.90, 5.92, 5.95, 5.96, 5.97, 5.99, 7.71, 7.73, 9.73, 10.102, 10.105, 10.106, 10.112*
ICUIS. See Institute on the Church in Urban-Industrial Society.
IMPACT. See National IMPACT Network.
Indiana University, Tenth and Morton Streets, Bloomington, IN 47401.
—African Studies Program. *2.34, 2.93*
—Audio-Visual Center. Tel: 812-337-8087. *1.163, 1.194*
—Mid-America Program for Global Perspectives in Education (q.v.)
—University Press. Tel: 812-337-6804. *2.35, 2.46, 10.26*

Indiana University of Pennsylvania, Education Consortium, 101 Keith Hall, Indiana, PA 15701. *1.219, 1.226, 5.111*

Indochina Curriculum Group, 11 Garden St., Cambridge, MA 02138. Tel: 617-354-6583. **3.22,** *3.183, 3.197*

Infant Formula Action Coalition (INFACT), 1701 University Ave., Minneapolis, MN 55414. Tel: 612-331-2333. **6.8**

Information Resources, Box 417, Lexington, MA 02173. *1.216*

Institute for Food and Development Policy, 1885 Mission St., San Francisco, CA 94103. Tel: 415-864-8555. *2.68, 3.59,* **6.10,** *6.35, 6.37, 6.38, 6.39, 6.42, 6.47, 6.48, 6.52, 6.61, 6.67, 6.68, 6.69, 6.81*

Institute for Peace and Justice, 4144 Lindell St., #400, St. Louis, MO 63108. Tel: 314-533-4445. **1.58,** *3.183, 6.40, 6.41, 6.77, 6.78, 6.90, 9.68, 9.69, 9.78*

Institute for Policy Studies, 1901 Que St., NW, Washington, DC 20009. Tel: 202-234-9382. *1.60, 2.37, 2.44, 2.50, 2.66, 2.70, 2.74, 4.43, 4.49, 4.55, 4.61, 4.91, 4.93, 4.98, 4.122, 4.140, 5.60, 6.32, 6.33, 6.38, 6.39, 6.45, 7.46, 7.54, 7.55, 7.62,* **8.18,** *8.46, 8.47, 8.48, 8.54, 8.57, 8.76, 8.90, 8.97, 8.98, 9.21, 9.48, 9.50, 9.52, 9.60, 9.72, 10.28, 10.95*
—Militarism and Disarmament Project. *3.119, 3.121, 4.84*
—Transnational Institute (q.v.)

Institute for the Study of Human Issues (ISHI), 3401 Market St., Rm. 252, Philadelphia, PA 19104. Tel: 215-387-9002. *3.76,* **7.14**

Institute for World Order, 777 UN Plaza, New York, NY 10017. Tel: 212-490-0010 and 1140 Avenue of the Americas, New York, NY 10036. Tel: 212-575-0055. **1.61,** *8.124*

Institute of Higher Education Research and Services. See University of Alabama.

Institute on the Church in Urban-Industrial Society (ICUIS), 5700 S. Woodlawn, Chicago, IL 60637. Tel: 312-643-7111. *3.131, 9.62, 10.121*

Interact, Box 262, Lakeside, CA 92040. *4.191, 8.130*

Intercommunity Center for Justice and Peace, 20 Washington Sq. N, New York, NY 10011. Tel: 212-475-6677. **1.65**

Interfaith Center on Corporate Responsibility, 475 Riverside Dr., Rm. 566, New York, NY 10115. Tel: 212-870-2295. **2.19,** *2.65, 6.31, 6.59, 6.64, 6.82,* **9.10,** *9.24, 9.30, 9.35, 9.40, 9.43, 9.44, 9.49, 9.65*

International Association of Machinists and Aerospace Workers, AFL-CIO, 1300 Connecticut Ave., NW, Rm. 1007, Washington, DC 20036. *8.50*

International Center for Research on Women, 2000 P St., NW, Washington, DC 20036. Tel: 202-293-3154. **10.8**

International Committee for Human Rights in Taiwan, Box 5205, Seattle, WA 98105. Tel: 206-365-8242. **3.23**

International Defense and Aid Fund for Southern Africa, Box 17, Cambridge, MA 02138. Tel: 617-495-4940. (Also 104 Newgate St., London, England EC1A 7AP.) **2.21,** *2.58, 2.79, 2.110*
—The Women's Committee. Tel: 617-491-8343. *2.21,* **10.9**

International Film Project, 3518 35 St., NW, Washington, DC 20017. Tel: 202-966-0260. *4.151*

International League for Human Rights, 236 E. 46 St., New York, NY 10017. Tel: 212-972-9554. **7.15,** *7.29, 7.34, 7.36, 7.37, 7.39, 7.40*

International Publishers, 381 Park Ave. S, Suite 1301, New York, NY 10016. Tel: 212-685-2864. *2.48, 2.53*

International Women's Tribune Center, 305 E. 46 St., New York, NY 10017. Tel: 212-421-5633. **10.10,** *10.77, 10.114, 10.116, 10.124*

Inter-Religious Task Force on El Salvador and Central America, 475 Riverside Dr., Rm. 633, New York, NY 10115. Tel: 212-870-3383. **4.17,** *4.144*

Interreligious Taskforce on U.S. Food Policy. See National IMPACT Network.

Investor Responsibility Research Center, 1319 F St., NW, Suite 900, Washington, DC 20005. Tel: 202-883-3727. **9.12**

ISIS, Via S. Maria dell'Anima 30, Rome, Italy. Tel: 06 / 65 65 842, and Case Postale 50 (Cornavin), 1211 Geneva 2, Switzerland. Tel: 022 / 33 67 46. **10.12,** *10.50, 10.64, 10.68, 10.78, 10.81, 10.83, 10.88, 10.117, 10.118, 10.119, 10.129*

Jesuit Social Ministry, 1717 Massachusetts Ave., NW, Rm. 402, Washington, DC 20036. Tel: 202-462-7008. **1.66**

Jewish Committee to End the Israeli Occupation, Box 43, 2124 Kittredge St., Berkeley, CA 94704. Tel: 415-845-2206, ext. 43. *5.93*

John Knox Press, 341 Ponce de Leon Ave., NE, Rm. 416, Atlanta, GA 30308. Tel: 404-873-1531. *5.25, 6.121*

Johns Hopkins University Press, Baltimore, MD 21218. Tel: 301-338-7832. *7.42*

Judson Press, Valley Forge, PA 19481. Tel: 215-768-2111. *8.57*

KDP (Union of Democratic Filipinos), Box 2759, Oakland, CA 94602. **3.25,** *3.80*

Kino International Corporation, 250 W. 57 St., Suite 314, New York, NY 10019. Tel: 212-586-8720. *4.173*

Kit Parker Films, Carmel Valley, CA 93924. *8.114*

Alfred A. Knopf, 201 E. 50 St., New York, NY 10022. Tel: 212-751-2600. *8.53*

Korea Support Committee, Box 11425, Oakland, CA 94611. *3.129*

Laos, 4920 Piney Branch Road, NW, Washington, DC 20011. Tel: 202-723-8273. **1.68**

Latin America Documentation (LADOC), Apartado 5594, Lima 100, Peru. *4.76, 4.85*

Latin America Studies Program, University of Texas at Austin (q.v.)

Latin America Task Force (LATF), Box 32214, Detroit, MI 48216. *4.60, 4.88, 4.119, 4.121*

Latin America Working Group (LAWG), Box 2207, Station P, Toronto, Ontario, Canada M5S 2T2. *4.177*

Latin American Film Project, Box 315, Franklin Lakes, NJ 07417. Tel: 201-891-8240. *4.168, 7.75*

Lawrence Hill & Co., 520 Riverside Ave., Westport, CT 06880. Tel: 203-226-9392. *1.132, 2.38, 2.51, 2.52, 10.31, 10.35, 10.40, 10.41*

Lawyers Committee for International Human Rights, 236 E. 46 St., New York, NY 10017. Tel: 212-682-8564. **7.18**

Lutheran Church, Missouri Synod, 500 N. Broadway, St. Louis, MO 63102. *6.110*

Lutheran Church in America, 231 Madison Ave., New York, NY 10016. *5.117, 6.63, 6.109, 9.84*

McGraw-Hill Book Co., 1221 Avenue of the Americas, New York, NY 10020. Tel: 212-997-1221. *1.135, 9.32*

McGraw-Hill Films, 110 15 St., Del Mar, CA 92014. Tel: 714-453-5000. *8.111*

Maryknoll Fathers and Brothers, Justice and Peace Office, Maryknoll, NY 10545. Tel: 914-941-7590. **1.69,** *1.150*

Maryknoll Sisters, Desk of Social Concern, Maryknoll, NY 10545. Tel: 914-941-7575. **1.71**

Maryknoll World Films, Maryknoll, NY 10545. Tel: 914-941-7590. *4.137, 4.143, 4.147, 4.165, 4.170, 8.109*

Meiklejohn Civil Liberties Institute, Box 673, Berkeley, CA 94701. Tel: 415-848-0599. **7.20,** *7.79*

Mennonite Churches, Mennonite Central Committee, 21 S. 12 St., Akron, PA 17501. Tel: 717-859-1151. *3.178, 3.186, 5.118, 6.111*

—Peace Section (International). **8.19,** *8.74*

Methodist Federation for Social Action, Shalom House, 76 Clinton Ave., Staten Island, NY 10301. Tel: 212-273-4941. **1.72**

Micronesia Support Committee, 1212 University Ave., Honolulu, HI 96826. Tel: 808-942-0437 and 595-3492. **3.27,** *3.72, 3.97, 3.108, 3.118, 3.120, 3.166*

Mid-America Program for Global Perspectives in Education, Social Studies Development Center, Indiana University, 513 N. Park Ave., Bloomington, IN 47401. Tel: 812-335-0455. **1.74,** *5.109*

Middle East Institute, 1761 N St., NW, Washington, DC 20036. Tel: 202-785-1141. *5.56*

Middle East Project, 339 Lafayette St., New York, NY 10012. Tel: 212-475-4300. **5.11,** *5.55, 5.65, 5.66, 5.80*

Middle East Research and Information Project (MERIP), Box 43445, Washington, DC 20010. Tel: 202-667-1188. *2.60,* **5.13,** *5.58*

Middle East Resource Center (MERC), 1322 18 St., NW, Washington, DC 20036. Tel: 202-659-6846. **5.15**

Mid-Peninsula Conversion Project, 222B View St., Mountain View, CA 94041. Tel: 415-968-8798. **8.20**

Midwest Academy Inc., 600 W. Fullerton Ave., Chicago, IL 60614. *9.98*

Midwest China Study Resource Center, Schools Outreach Program, 2375 Como Ave. W, St. Paul, MN 55108. Tel: 612-641-3238. **3.29,** *3.86*

Mobilization for Survival

    —National Office, 3601 Locust Walk, Philadelphia, PA 19104. Tel: 215-386-4875. **8.22,** *8.103*

    —853 Broadway, Rm. 2109, New York, NY 10003. Tel: 212-533-0008.

Modern Times Bookstore, 968 Valencia St., San Francisco, CA 94110. Tel: 415-828-9246. *1.107, 3.62, 10.37*

Monthly Review Press, 155 W. 23 St., 12th Floor, New York, NY 10011. Tel: 212-691-2555. *1.123, 1.129, 1.131, 2.41, 2.45, 3.75, 3.78, 4.45, 4.56, 4.58, 4.64, 6.28, 6.30, 8.59, 9.26, 9.28, 10.24, 10.45*

Moravian Church, Box 1245, Bethlehem, PA 18018. *6.112*

Movement for a New Society, 4722 Baltimore Ave., Philadephia, PA 19143. Tel: 215-724-1464. **1.76,** *5.23*

NARMIC (National Action/Research on the Military Industrial Complex), c/o AFSC, 1501 Cherry St., Philadelphia, PA 19102. Tel: 215-241-7175. *2.47, 2.73, 2.77, 2.88, 3.152, 7.48,* **8.24,** *8.77, 8.81, 8.99, 9.78, 10.66*

National Catholic Coalition for Responsible Investment, 1016 N. Ninth St., Milwaukee, WI 53233. *9.85*

National Council of Churches (USA), Division of Overseas Ministries, 475 Riverside Dr., New York, NY 10115. Tel: 212-870-2175. *5.75*

—African Office, Rm. 612. Tel: 212-870-2645. **2.23,** *2.69*

—Agricultural Mission Committee, Rm. 624. Tel: 212-870-2553. *4.108*

—China Program, Rm. 616. Tel: 212-870-2371. *3.85*

—Human Rights Program, Rm. 634. Tel: 212-870-2424. **7.21**

—Office of Hunger Coordination, Rm. 828. Tel: 212-870-2331. *6.100*

—Office of Interpretation and Promotion, Rm. 656. Tel: 212-870-2079. *6.73*

—TV Film Library, Rm. 860. Tel: 212-870-2575. *4.167, 6.88, 9.76*

National Federation of Priests' Councils, Ministry for Justice and Peace, 1307 S. Wabash Ave., Chicago, IL 60605. Tel: 312-427-0115. **1.78**

National Film Board of Canada, 1251 Avenue of the Americas, New York, NY 10020. Tel: 212-586-5131. *3.157*

National IMPACT Network, c/o Interreligious Taskforce on U.S. Food Policy, 110 Maryland Ave., NE, Washington, DC 20002. Tel: 202-544-8636. *4.144,* **6.12**

National Lawyers Guild, 853 Broadway, Rm. 1705, New York, NY 10003. *4.109, 5.40, 7.50*

National Network in Solidarity with the Nicaraguan People, 1718 20 St., NW, Washington, DC 20009. Tel: 202-223-2328 and 628-9598. **4.22,** *4.52, 4.101, 4.113, 4.162, 4.179*

National Network in Solidarity with the People of Guatemala, 1718 20 St., NW, Washington, DC 20009. Tel: 202-483-0050. **4.25,** *4.113*

Neal-Schuman Publishers, 23 Cornelia St., New York, NY 10014. Tel: 212-620-5990. *1.202, 3.19, 3.151*

NETWORK, 806 Rhode Island Ave., NW, Washington, DC 20018. Tel: 202-526-4070. **1.80**

Network to Educate for World Security, c/o Institute for World Order, 777 UN Plaza, New York, NY 10017. Tel: 212-490-0010. **8.25**

New Directions Educational Fund, 2000 P St., NW, Suite 515, Washington, DC 20036. Tel: 202-833-3140. **1.83**

New England Human Rights Network, c/o AFSC, 2161 Massachusetts Ave., Cambridge, MA 02140. Tel: 617-661-6130. **7.23,** *7.81*

New Jewish Agenda, 1123 Broadway, Rm. 1217, New York, NY 10010. Tel: 212-620-0828. *5.17*

New Manhattan Project, c/o AFSC, 15 Rutherford Place, New York, NY 10003. Tel: 212-598-0971. **8.26**

New Star Books, 2504 York Ave., Vancouver, 9, British Columbia, Canada. *10.37, 10.38, 10.43*

New Time Films, 1501 Broadway, Suite 1904, New York, NY 10036. Tel: 212-921-7020. *4.148, 7.68, 10.95*

New York CIRCUS, Box 37, Times Square Station, New York, NY 10108. Tel: 212-663-8112. **1.84, 4.27**

New Yorker Films, 16 W. 61 St., New York, NY 10023. Tel: 212-247-6110. *3.163, 3.172*

NGO Committee on Disarmament at the United Nations, 777 UN Plaza, Rm. 7B, New York, NY 10017. *8.63*

Nicaragua Information Center, Box 1004, Berkeley, CA 94704. Tel: 415-549-1387. *4.81*

Nicaragua Interfaith Committee for Action (NICA), 942 Market St., Rm. 709, San Francisco, CA 94102. Tel: 415-433-6057. **4.29**

North American Coalition for Human Rights in Korea, 110 Maryland Ave., NE, Washington, DC 20002. Tel: 202-546-4304. **3.31,** *3.112, 3.114, 3.130, 3.148*

State University of New York, Braudel Center, Binghamton, NY 13901. *2.86*
$top Banking on Apartheid, 464 19 St., Oakland, CA 94612. Tel: 415-763-8011 and 763-9998. **2.24,** *2.76*
Straight Talk Distributing, Box 750, 2351 Bear Valley Rd., Point Reyes Station, CA 94956. *6.70, 6.75*
Syracuse Peace Council, 924 Burnet Ave., Syracuse, NY 13203. Tel: 315-472-5478. **8.32,** *8.101*
TAPOL, c/o Dept. of Anthropology, Montclair State College, Upper Montclair, NJ 07043. Tel: 201-893-4133. **3.49**
Teachers' Committee on Central America, 5511 Vicente Way, Oakland, CA 94609. *4.182*
TeleKETICS. See Franciscan Communications Center.
Thai Information Center, Box 8995, Los Angeles, CA 90008. **3.51**
Third World Newsreel, 160 Fifth Ave., Suite 911, New York, NY 10010. Tel: 212-243-2310. *1.173, 4.130, 4.133, 4.142, 7.72, 10.90, 10.100*
TransAfrica, 545 Eighth St., SE, Suite 200, Washington, DC 20003. Tel: 202-547-2550. **2.25**
Transnational Institute, 1901 Que St., NW, Washington, DC 20009. Tel: 202-239-9382. **9.15,** *9.48, 9.60, 10.28*
Unifilm, 419 Park Ave. S, 19th Floor, New York, NY 10016. Tel: 212-686-9890. *1.186, 2.103, 3.168, 3.180, 4.134, 4.135, 4.136, 4.141, 4.149, 4.150, 4.156, 4.160, 4.161, 4.164, 4.168, 6.77, 7.75, 8.117, 8.119, 9.68, 9.71, 10.93, 10.99, 10.101, 10.104, 10.107*
—International Women's Film Project. *10.96*
Union for Radical Political Economics (URPE), Economics Education Project, 41 Union Sq. W, Rm. 901, New York, NY 10003. Tel: 212-691-5722. **1.96, 9.17,** *9.97*
Union of Democratic Filipinos. See KDP.
Union of Democratic Thais, Box 17808, Los Angeles, CA 90017. **3.53,** *3.94*
Unipub, 650 First Ave., Box 433, Murray Hill Station, New York, NY 10016. *6.49*
Unitarian Universalist Service Committee, 78 Beacon St., Boston, MA 02108. Tel: 617-742-2120. *4.90, 7.30, 7.45, 7.56*
United Church Board for World Ministries, 475 Riverside Dr., New York, NY 10115. Tel: 212-870-2711. **1.99**
—Near East Department. *5.122*
—World Issues Office. *9.46, 9.54, 9.70, 9.87*
United Church of Christ, 475 Riverside Dr., 16th Floor, New York, NY 10115. *6.118, 9.54*
United Church Press, 287 Park Ave., New York, NY 10010. *3.195*
United Methodist Church, Board of Global Ministries, 475 Riverside Dr., New York, NY 10015. Tel: 212-678-6161. **1.101,** *5.91, 5.94, 6.119, 7.38*
—Division of Education and Cultivation, 13th Floor. Tel: 212-678-6135. *6.57*
—Women's Division, 15th Floor. Tel: 212-678-6099. *6.57,* **10.14**
—World Division. *5.123*
United Methodist Church, Council on Finance and Administration, 1200 Davis St., Evanston, IL 60201. *9.88*
United Methodist Church (UMC), Service Center, 782 Reading Rd., Cincinnati, OH 45237. *1.174, 4.158, 4.167, 4.172, 6.57, 6.76, 6.79, 6.82, 6.83, 7.26, 7.28, 7.70, 7.74, 9.45, 10.123*
United Methodist Film Service, 810 12 St. S, Nashville, TN 37203. *4.152, 7.67*
United Methodist Office for the United Nations, 777 UN Plaza, 10th Floor, New York, NY 10017. Tel: 212-682-3633. *7.51*
United Methodist Seminars on National and International Affairs, 777 UN Plaza, 10th Floor, New York, NY 10017. Tel: 212-682-3633 and 100 Maryland Ave., NE, Washington, DC 20002. Tel: 202-488-5611. **1.103**
United Nations, NY 10017. *1.172, 1.182, 1.184, 1.185, 1.188, 1.191, 5.79*
—Centre Against Apartheid, Rm. 2775. **2.29,** *2.36, 2.40, 2.87*
—Centre on Transnational Corporations. Tel: 212-754-8452. **9.19,** *9.37*
—Office of Public Information. *2.64, 5.95, 8.75*
—Publications/Sales. Rm. A-3315. *8.105, 9.33, 10.46, 10.97, 10.108*
—World Conference of the UN Decade for Women. *10.46*
United Presbyterian Church in the USA, 475 Riverside Dr., New York, NY 10115. *6.120*
—Church and Society Program Area. *9.89*
—Liaison with the Middle East, Rm. 1133. *5.124*
—Office of the General Assembly. *8.95*
—Presbyterian Distribution Service. Rm. 935. Tel: 212-870-2774. *1.179*
—Third World Women's Coordinating Committee. **10.15**

University Christian Movement, 11 Garden St., Cambridge, MA 02138. *10.131*
University of Alabama, Institute of Higher Education Research and Services, University, AL
35486. *1.215*
University of California, 2223 Fulton St., Berkeley, CA 94720.
   —Extension Media Center. Tel: 415-642-0460 (to rent a film); 415-642-1340 (for assistance in
selecting films). **1.164,** *1.177, 1.194, 3.161*
   —Faculty Committee for Human Rights in El Salvador. *4.120*
   —University of California Press. Tel: 415-642-4247. *2.39*
University of California, Irvine, CA 92717.
   —Program in Comparative Culture, School of Social Sciences. *4.71*
University of California, 405 Hilgard Ave., Los Angeles, CA 90024.
   —African Studies Center. *2.116*
   —Curriculum Inquiry Center, Graduate School of Education. *1.212, 5.107, 8.126*
University of Chicago Press, 5801 Ellis Ave., Chicago, IL 60637. Tel: 312-753-3344. *3.190*
University of Denver, Denver, CO 80208. *3.71*
   —Center for Teaching International Relations. **1.119,** *1.211, 1.214, 5.102, 6.98, 8.127*
   —Graduate School of International Studies. *2.57*
   —Graduate School of Social Studies.
University of Michigan
   —Audio Visual Center, 416 Fourth St., Ann Arbor, MI 48103. Tel: 303-764-5350. *1.165*
   —Project on Asia Studies in Education (q.v.)
   —University of Michigan Press, Ann Arbor, MI 48106. Tel: 313-764-1817.
   —Xerox University Microfilms, Box 1346, Ann Arbor, MI 48106. Tel: 313-761-4700. *10.34*
University of Minnesota
   —Audio Visual Library Service, 3300 University Ave., SE, Minneapolis, MN 55414. Tel:
612-373-3810. *1.166, 2.91, 4.131, 5.85, 10.91, 10.96, 10.97*
   —University of Minnesota Press, 2037 University Ave., SE, Minneapolis, MN 55455. *3.66*
University of Texas at Austin, Latin America Studies Program, Austin, TX 78712. *4.187*
University of Washington Audio-Visual Services, Seattle, WA 98195. Tel: 206-543-2500. *1.167*
University of Wisconsin, African Studies Program, 1450 Van Hise Hall, 1200 Linden Dr., Madi-
son, WI 53706. *2.92, 2.115*
U.S. Catholic Conference, 1312 Massachusetts Ave., NW, Washington, DC 20005. Tel: 202-
659-6600.
   —Africa Desk. Tel: 202-659-6812. **2.31,** *2.72.*
   —Latin America Bureau. Tel: 202-659-6812. **4.19,** *4.85, 4.94*
   —Office of International Justice and Peace. Tel: 202-659-6812. **1.104,** *6.66, 6.116 , 7.58,
7.61, 7.65, 8.82, 8.83, 8.88*
US-China People's Friendship Association, National Office, 110 Maryland Ave., NE,
Washington, DC 20002. Tel: 202-544-7010. **3.55,** *3.95*
   —The Center for Teaching About China. **3.8,** *3.191*
U.S.-El Salvador Research and Information Center, Box 4797, Berkeley, CA 94704. *4.73*
U.S. Government Printing Office, Superintendent of Documents, Washington, DC 20402.
1.203, 7.32, 7.51
Vantage Press, 516 W. 34 St., New York, NY 10001. Tel: 212-736-1767. *5.26*
Villon Films, Brophy Rd., Hurleyville, NY 12747. Tel: 914-434-5579. *2.109, 3.180*
Viking Press, Orders to: Viking/Penguin, 299 Murray Hill Pkwy., E. Rutherford, NJ 07073.
1.134
Vintage Books/Random House, 201 E. 50 St., New York, NY 10022. *5.27, 5.34, 5.45*
War Resisters League, 339 Lafayette St., New York, NY 10012. Tel: 212-228-0450. *5.66,* **8.34,**
8.73
Washington Office on Africa, 110 Maryland Ave., NE, Washington, DC 20002. Tel: 202-546-
7961. **2.32**
Washington Office on Latin America (WOLA), 110 Maryland Ave., NE, Washington, DC
20002. Tel: 202-544-8045. *4.37, 4.77, 4.124, 4.125*
Washington Peace Center, 2111 Florida Ave., NW, Washington, DC 20008. Tel: 202-234-2000.
8.36
Wayne County Community College, Pact, Community Services Dept., 4612 Woodward Ave.,
Detroit, MI 48201. *1.225*
Westview Press, 5500 Central Ave., Boulder, CO 80301. *1.111*

Women Strike for Peace, National Office, 145 S. 13 St., Philadelphia, PA 19107. Tel: 215-923-0861. **8.40, 10.16**

Women Workers' Concern, c/o Christian Conference of Asia (q.v.).

Women's Institute for Freedom of the Press, 3306 Ross Place, NW, Washington, DC 20008. Tel: 202-965-7783. **10.19,** *10.51, 10.122*

Women's International Information and Communication Service. See ISIS.

Women's International League for Peace and Freedom, 1213 Race St., Philadelphia, PA 19107. Tel: 215-563-7110. *1.199, 3.144, 5.69, 5.72, 5.73, 5.105,* **8.38, 10.17,** *10.52, 10.55, 10.86, 10.98*

Women's International Network, 187 Grant St., Lexington, MA 02173. Tel: 617-862-9431. **10.21,** *10.53*

Women's International Resource Exchange (WIRE) Service, 2700 Broadway, Rm. 7, New York, NY 10025. Tel: 212-666-4622. **10.23,** *10.57, 10.65, 10.70, 10.71, 10.72, 10.74, 10.75, 10.82, 10.85, 10.87, 10.125, 10.126, 10.127, 10.130*

Word, Inc., Educational Products Division, Waco, TX 76710. *6.86*

World Conference of the United Nations Decade for Women: Equality, Development and Peace, Rm. 1061, United Nations, NY 10017. *10.46*

World Conference on Religion and Peace, 777 UN Plaza, New York, NY 10017. Tel: 212-687-2163. **8.41,** *8.80*

World Education Center, 1730 Grove St., Berkeley, CA 94709. Tel: 415-845-1992. *1.205, 2.114*

World Hunger Education/Action Together (WHEAT), Box 189, Nashville, TN 37202. **6.20**

World Hunger Education Service, 1317 G St., NW, Washington, DC 20005. Tel: 202-223-2995. **6.21,** *6.93*

World Hunger Year, Inc., 350 Broadway, Suite 209, New York, NY 10013. Tel: 212-226-2714. **6.23,** *6.51*

World Without War Council
—1730 Grove St., Berkeley, CA 94709. Tel: 415-845-1992. *1.204, 8.123*
—421 S. Wabash, 2d Floor, Chicago, IL 60605. Tel: 312-663-4250. *1.181, 7.80,* **8.43,** *8.51, 8.93, 8.104*

BOOKS

Africa From Real to Reel: An African Filmography, *2.90*

African Social Studies: A Radical Reader, *2.41*

African Studies Information Resources Directory, *2.113*

After the Cataclysm: Postwar Indochina and the Reconstruction of Imperial Ideology. The Political Economy of Human Rights: Volume II, *3.63*

The Age of Imperialism: The Economics of U.S. Foreign Policy, *1.129*

Agribusiness in the Americas, *4.45, 6.28*

Agribusiness Manual: Background Papers on Corporate Responsibility and Hunger Issues, *6.31*

Alternatives in Print: An International Catalog of Books, Pamphlets, Periodicals and Audiovisual Materials, *1.202*

America & the Crisis of World Capitalism, *1.126*

America After Nixon: The Age of the Multinationals, *9.32*

America and the Third World: Revolution and Intervention, *1.115*

America in Asia: Research Guides on U.S. Economic Activity in Pacific Asia, *9.91*

American Foreign Policy: Opposing Viewpoints, *1.127*

Americans and World Affairs: A Directory of Organizations & Institutions in Northern California, *1.204*

America's Asia: Dissenting Essays on Asian-American Relations, *3.68*

Amnesty International Report, *7.27*

The Arab Image in Western Mass Media, *5.37*

The Arab World: A Handbook for Teachers, *5.84, 5.100*

Arabia Without Sultans: A Survey of Political Instability in the Arab World, *5.34*

The Arabs: Perception/Misperception. A Comparative View, Experimental Version, *5.102*

Arsenal of Democracy: American Military Power in the 1980s and the Origins of the New Cold War, *8.52*

Asia: Teaching About/Learning From, *3.188*

Assassination on Embassy Row, *4.49*

PERIODICALS

PAMPHLETS AND ARTICLES

AUDIOVISUALS

AUDIOVISUAL BIBLIOGRAPHIES, CATALOGS, AND GUIDES

BIBLIOGRAPHIES, DIRECTORIES, AND CURRICULUM RESOURCES

A Cry for Bread and Justice: Action/Education Opportunities in Response to World Hunger, *6.57*

Defense Monitor index, *8.72*

Development as if Women Mattered: An Annotated Bibliography with a Third World Focus, *10.120*

Development of Guidelines and Resource Materials on Latin America for Use in Grades 1-12: Final Report, *4.188*

Disarmament Action Guide, *8.89*

Dissent, Freedom, Revolution, Peace: WRL Reading List, *8.73*

Education for a Global Society: A Resource Manual for Secondary Education Teachers, *1.199*

Education for Justice: A Resource Manual, *1.196*

Educational Resources from the International Division (AFSC), *1.6*

El Salvador: Roots of Conflict, *4.182*

Ending Hunger: It's Possible, It's Happening, *6.94*

Feed, Need, Greed: Food, Resources & Population, *6.95*

Food and Agriculture Books from Food for Thought, *6.27*

Food for Thought Books catalog, *1.105*

For Anyone Interested in Africa, *2.114*

Friendship Global Outline Map, *1.206*

Global Dimensions in the New Social Studies, *1.210*

Global Education, *1.109*

Global Education Resource Guide, *1.198*

Global Issues: Activities and Resources for the High School Teacher, *1.211*

Global Perspectives in Education: Consultant Resource Directory, *1.197*

Global Perspectives in Education: Organization Resource Directory, *1.197*

Global Studies: Problems and Promises for Elementary Teachers, *1.209*

A Guide to Peace Resources (with supplement), *8.74*

Guide to Reference Sources on Africa, Asia, Latin America and the Caribbean, Middle East and North Africa, and Russia and East Europe: Selected and Annotated, *1.200*

The Guide to Simulations/Games for Education and Training. With a "Basic Reference Shelf on Simulation and Gaming," *1.216*

Guild Books and Periodicals catalog, *1.106*

Handbook of Simulation Gaming in Social Education. Part I: Textbook; Part II: Directory for Non-Computer Material, *1.215*

How to Research a Corporation, *9.97*

Human Rights Directory: Latin America, Africa, Asia, *7.78*

Human Rights of Women: A Resource Packet, *10.123*

Human Rights Organizations & Periodicals Directory, *7.79*

A Hungry World, *6.96*

Ideals and Reality in Foreign Policy: American Intervention in the Caribbean: Teacher and Student Manuals, *4.183*

Index/Directory of Women's Media, *10.122*

Information Kit for Women in Africa, *10.124*

Information Materials and Documents on Disarmament, *8.75*

Institute for Policy Studies Catalogue of Publications: Disarmament, *8.76*

International Education Resources. Cumulative Second Edition, 1956-77, *1.203*

International Human Rights Kit, *7.80*

International Women & Health Resource Guide, *1.208*

Internationalize Your School: A Handbook, *10.118*

Journey South: Discovering the Americas, *4.184*

Land and Hunger Study Guide, *6.97*

Latin America: Biblical Understanding of Mission to Individuals and Society, *4.176*

Lebanon Packet, *5.72*

Manual of Corporate Investigation, *9.90*

MERIP Reading Guide, *5.104*

The Middle East and South Asia 1980, *5.101*

Middle East Study Materials, *5.105*

Minding the Corporate Conscience: Public Interest Groups and Corporate Social Accountability, *9.93*

SIMULATION GAMES

Abbreviations

AMEU	Americans for Middle East Understanding
AFSC	American Friends Service Committee
CALA	Community Action on Latin America
CALC	Clergy and Laity Concerned
CCA-URM	Christian Conference of Asia—Urban-Rural Mission
CEP	Council on Economic Priorities
CISPES	Committee in Solidarity with the People of El Salvador
C.M.S.	Custom Microfilm Service
COMMUSAL	The Film Institute of Revolutionary El Salvador
COPRED	Consortium on Peace, Research, Education, and Development
DOM	Division of Overseas Ministries
EPICA	Ecumenical Program for Inter-American Communication and Action
IAM	International Association of Machinists and Aerospace Workers
ICCR	Interfaith Center on Corporate Responsibility
ICUIS	Institute on the Church in Urban-Industrial Society
IFDP	Institute for Food and Development Policy
INFACT	Infant Formula Action Coalition
IWTC	International Women's Tribune Centre
LADOC	Latin America Documentation
LATF	Latin America Task Force
LAWG	Latin America Working Group
MERC	Middle East Resource Center
MERIP	Middle East Research and Information Project
NACLA	North American Congress on Latin America
NARMIC	National Action/Research on the Military Industrial Complex
NCC/DOM	National Council of Churches/Division of Overseas Ministries
PACTS	Pacific and Asian American Center for Theology and Strategies
SPICE	Stanford Program on International and Cross-Cultural Education
UCLA	University of California at Los Angeles
UMC	United Methodist Church
WHEAT	World Hunger Education/Action Together
WIRE	Women's International Resource Exchange
WOLA	Washington Office on Latin America
WRL	War Resisters League

(continued from back cover)
Asia and helpful to regional media resource centers. Local churches must all have outreach or mission committees that want to do education about the present global reality, and we know of nothing that compares with this resource." **William J. Nottingham,**
President of the Division of Overseas Ministries, Christian Church

"A must for all educators seeking to give their students a truly global education. There are no shortcuts or easy answers to building a peace based on justice. This directory gives teachers the tools they need to understand issues and share them intelligently and creatively with students of all ages."
Michael J. Fonte, Coordinator, Teacher Education Program,
Immaculate Heart College Center, Los Angeles

"Jam-packed with some 1500 citations of organizations, publications, and A-V materials, this thesaurus of resources is extremely helpful for anyone concerned with Third World justice issues." **Thomas E. Quigley,**
United States Catholic Conference

"The annotated listing of printed resources greatly simplifies the often time-consuming task of locating background readings. The compilation of curriculum guides covering all regions of the Third world and key issues provides teachers with access to excellent but little-publicized materials."
Robert Kessler, History Teacher,
Moraga School District, California

"The publication of the *Third World Resource Directory* is truly heartwarming, for it tells us abundantly that in America not everyone has been silent or silenced and that many are laboring to explain the links between the behavior of the U.S. government and multinationals and the problems that we face in our own countries." **Randolf S. David, Director,**
Third World Studies Center, Manila, Philippines